Henry V

New Interpretations

Henry V

New Interpretations

Edited by
Gwilym Dodd

THE UNIVERSITY *of York*

YORK MEDIEVAL PRESS

First published 2013

A York Medieval Press publication
in association with The Boydell Press
an imprint of Boydell & Brewer Ltd
PO Box 9   Woodbridge   Suffolk IP12 3DF   UK
and of Boydell & Brewer Inc.
668 Mt Hope Avenue   Rochester   NY 14620–2731   USA
website: www.boydellandbrewer.com
and with the
Centre for Medieval Studies, University of York

ISBN 978–1–903153–46–8

A CIP catalogue record for this book is available
from the British Library

The publisher has no responsibility for the continued existence or accuracy
of URLs for external or third-party internet websites referred to in this book,
and does not guarantee that any content on such websites is,
or will remain, accurate or appropriate.

This publication is printed on acid-free paper.

For Christopher Allmand

CONTENTS

PREFACE AND ACKNOWLEDGEMENTS

2013 marks the 600th anniversary of Henry's accession to throne, which took place on 21 March 1413. So began the short reign of a king who has achieved – in scholarship as well as in the popular mind – an unparalleled reputation as the exemplar of successful medieval kingship. In recent years, there has been a great blossoming of interest in the reign of Henry V, and especially in the resounding victory he achieved on the battlefield at Agincourt in 1415. The 600th anniversary of this battle in 2015 is likely to attract far wider interest than the anniversary of his accession, and for good reason: Agincourt is what made Henry's reputation. The battle had a profound impact on the reign: Henry seems to have spent his time either building up to the campaign that would lead to Agincourt, or capitalizing on the advantage which the victory gave him, whether militarily – by opening the way to the conquest of Normandy – or diplomatically, by forcing the French to negotiate from a position of weakness. The enduring image of Henry as the ideal late medieval warrior king is justly deserved. Nevertheless, he still had the kingdom of England to rule and in so doing he faced many and varied domestic challenges. He was also unique amongst late medieval heirs to the English throne in discharging key military and political responsibilities before becoming king, as Prince of Wales, during the reign of his father, Henry IV.

This volume contains a collection of chapters which reflect these larger contexts and considerations. To be sure, the war is never far from the surface in many of the contributions, and in some it is considered directly, but the remit given to the authors was to reflect broadly on different aspects of the life, times and government of Henry, whether as Prince, king, or both. No editorial constraints were placed on the subject matter of the chapters, and contributors were encouraged to choose topics according to their areas of expertise. All of the chapters contained in the volume build on a fine tradition of existing scholarship, and the intellectual debt owed to this work will be evident in the footnotes. Particular mention should be made of Christopher Allmand's magisterial biography *Henry V* (1992), which remains the key reference work for the reign and the unfailing source of accurate detail and sound judgement. The slightly earlier *Henry V: The Practice of Kingship*, edited by Gerald Harriss in 1985, is one of the finest collections of essays ever to be published on a medieval king, and is essential reading for any student of English politics, kingship and government in the fourteenth and fifteenth centuries. It is not the purpose of the chapters in this volume to attempt to supersede this fine body of scholarship, nor indeed to cover all aspects of Henry's life and rule. The aim is to deepen knowledge and understanding and, where possible, to stimulate further research and interest in Henry V and his times.

It remains for me to thank all those who have made this volume possible. First and foremost, thanks are due to the contributors themselves. They originally presented their essays at a colloquium held in the Department of History, at the University of Nottingham, in July 2011. All met the challenge of having their papers ready for pre-circulation ahead of the colloquium, and in the lively and productive discussions during the colloquium itself they showed great intellectual generosity and collegiality. I should also like to thank those who attended but have not contributed to this volume, and Matt Phillips whose assistance with the organization of the event was invaluable. The financial and practical support of the Department of History and the Institute of Medieval Studies at the University of Nottingham helped keep the costs to a manageable level, and the encouragement of Caroline Palmer of Boydell & Brewer, and Professor Peter Biller, of the University of York, at critical stages of the project has been greatly appreciated. I reserve a special vote of thanks to our 'three wise men' – Christopher Allmand, Tony Pollard and Anthony Tuck – who acted as respondents during the colloquium and as reviewers of the chapters in their written up form. I am sure all the contributors will agree when I say that the chapters have benefited enormously from their input; indeed, I feel a particular debt of gratitude for the fact that this is not the first occasion when they have helped in this way. Finally, I should like to pay special tribute to Christopher Allmand, not only for being so generous with his time in the editing stages of the project and for writing the Introduction to the volume – in addition to his duties as respondent and reviewer – but also for the immense contribution his scholarship has made to our understanding of the reign of Henry V. It is to Christopher that this volume is dedicated.

Gwilym Dodd
November 2012

CONTRIBUTORS

Professor Christopher Allmand	University of Liverpool
Professor Anne Curry	University of Southampton
Dr Gwilym Dodd	University of Nottingham
Dr Mark Arvanigian	California State University
Dr Maureen Jurkowski	University College London
Dr Alison K. McHardy	University of Nottingham
Dr Jenny Stratford	Institute of Historical Research, London
Professor Michael Bennett	University of Tasmania
Professor W. Mark Ormrod	University of York
Dr Craig Taylor	University of York
Dr Neil Murphy	Northumbria University

ABBREVIATIONS

Allmand, *Henry V*	C. Allmand, *Henry V* (London, 1992)
BIHR	*Bulletin of the Institute of Historical Research*
BJRL	*Bulletin of the John Rylands Library*
BL	British Library, London
CChR	*Calendar of Charter Rolls*
CCR	*Calendar of Close Rolls*
CFR	*Calendar of Fine Rolls*
CIM	*Calendar of Inquisitions Miscellaneous*
CIPM	*Calendar of Inquisitions Post Mortem*
CPR	*Calendar of Patent Rolls*
Complete Peerage	G. E. Cockayne, *The Complete Peerage*, ed. V. Gibbs et al., 12 vols. (London, 1910–59)
Curry, Agincourt: Sources and Interpretations	A. Curry, *The Battle of Agincourt, 1415: Sources and Interpretations*, ed. A. Curry (Woodbridge, 2000)
Curry, Agincourt: A New History	A. Curry, *Agincourt: A New History* (London, 2005)
EHR	*English Historical Review*
EETS	Early English Text Society
ES	Extra Series
OS	Original Series
Emden, *BRUC*	A. B. Emden, *Biographical Register of the University of Cambridge* (Cambridge, 1963)
Emden, *BRUO*	A. B. Emden, *A Biographical Register of the University of Oxford*, 3 vols. (Oxford, 1957–9)
Foedera	*Foedera, Conventiones et Litterae*, ed. T. Rymer, 20 vols. (London, 1727–35)
GHQ	*Gesta Henrici Quinti. The Deeds of Henry the Fifth*, ed. and trans. F. Taylor and J. S. Roskell (Oxford, 1975)
Harriss, *Cardinal Beaufort*	G. L. Harriss, *Cardinal Beaufort: A Study of Lancastrian Ascendancy and Decline* (Oxford, 1988)
Henry V, ed. Harriss	*Henry V: The Practice of Kingship*, ed. G. L. Harriss (Oxford, 1985)

HP	*The History of Parliament: The House of Commons, 1386–1421*, ed. J. S. Roskell, Linda Clark and Carole Rawcliffe, 4 vols. (Stroud, 1994)
Mortimer, *1415: Henry V's Year of Glory*	I. Mortimer, *1415: Henry V's Year of Glory* (London, 2009)
NGDM	*The New Grove Dictionary of Music and Musicians*, 2nd edn, ed. S. Sadie, 29 vols. (London, 2001)
ODNB	*Oxford Dictionary of National Biography* (Oxford, 2004), online version
POPC	*Proceedings and Ordinances of the Privy Council of England*, ed. H. Nicolas, 7 vols. (London, 1834–7)
PMLA	*Proceedings of the Modern Language Association*
PRO	Public Record Office
PROME	*The Parliament Rolls of Medieval England*, ed. and trans. P. Brand, A. Curry, C. Given-Wilson, R. E. Horrox, G. Martin, W. M. Ormrod and J. R. S. Phillips, 16 vols. (Woodbridge, 2005)
Pugh, *Southampton Plot*	T. B. Pugh, *Henry V and the Southampton Plot of 1415* (Southampton, 1988)
Reign of Henry IV, ed. Dodd and Biggs	*The Reign of Henry IV: Rebellion and Survival 1403–13*, ed. G. Dodd and D. Biggs (York, 2008)
SR	*Statutes of the Realm*, 11 vols. (London, 1810–28)
TNA	The National Archives
TRHS	*Transactions of the Royal Historical Society*
Wylie, *Henry the Fourth*	J. H. Wylie, *History of England under Henry the Fourth*, 4 vols. (London, 1884–98)
Wylie and Waugh, *Henry the Fifth*	J. H. Wylie and W. T. Waugh, *The Reign of Henry the Fifth*, 3 vols. (Cambridge, 1914–29)

INTRODUCTION

Christopher Allmand

Recent years have seen considerable advances made in the study of the reign of Henry V, and, consequently, in our understanding and appreciation of the man himself. If the events of the year 1415, which witnessed the king's first foray into France ending with the victory won at Agincourt, still claim headline status, there is a greater eagerness to view the 'real' Henry rather than a 'creation' of the historical past. Modern historical scholarship demands a more rounded, a more considered, certainly a more complex assessment of him. A better understanding of the king, his times, his policies and his achievements – never an easy task for a single scholar to attempt – can be gained through the shorter contributions offered by individual scholars. The chapters which follow, most of which were originally presented as papers at a small colloquium organized by the editor at the University of Nottingham in July 2011, should be seen as contributions towards a better appreciation of the career and rule of a remarkable king.

Henry's life may be divided into three broadly equal phases: from birth (in 1386) to becoming Prince of Wales (1399); as Prince of Wales (1399–1413); and, finally, as king of England (1413–22). It is important, therefore, that historians should not forget the first two 'thirds' of Henry's life, which made him twenty-six years old when he inherited the throne from his father, Henry IV. Consideration of these early years, their problems and difficulties, as well as their achievements, can tell us much that helps us to understand the personality of the man, the eldest of four sons and two daughters born to Henry, duke of Lancaster, and his wife, Mary Bohun, and some of the problems faced by the kingdom which he would one day come to rule. Leaving aside the matter of historical judgement, our very understanding of the aims, policies (and failures) of Henry V as king rest upon our having the widest possible appreciation of the many factors, personal, political, institutional and economic, which influenced the way that he ruled as king, what he sought to achieve, and how close he came to fulfilling that achievement.

Recent years have witnessed renewed scholarly interest in the reign of Henry IV, whose accession to, or usurpation of, the throne in the late summer of 1399 immediately transformed his eldest son, Henry, into his heir apparent, the king of the future. The relationship between father and son, particularly in the light of the king's uncertain health, has long intrigued and puzzled historians. In the years before 1399, the young Henry appears to have played

1

a role of no consequence in English political life. As Anne Curry shows, he had little money and, consequently, little independence either. Yet the events of 1399 changed his financial position only very slowly. Although the holder of numerous titles, the lands associated with them brought in relatively little, much of which was taken by an impoverished father who interfered directly in the young Prince's affairs. Achieving financial independence was a slow process, made no easier by the need to find the means of resisting and putting down the revolt in Wales which began in 1400, a revolt which had an adverse impact upon areas from which the Prince drew his revenues. Although the economy was recovering by 1407–8, the Prince's financial position remained precarious in the light of the huge responsibilities for which he remained liable. Henry was learning the need for good financial management the hard way.

Besides discussing the financial resources available to 'the young lord Henry', and later to him as Prince of Wales, Curry is first in the field in raising another important matter, continuity of service among those who worked for the first two kings of the house of Lancaster. It is clear that, on taking the throne in 1399, Henry IV continued to employ men who had served his deposed predecessor, Richard II, particularly in low levels of administration, while those serving in the households of both king and Prince were often chosen from among loyal 'family' retainers who thus reaped the rewards of what were sometimes years of service to the house of Lancaster. When Henry V finally became king and, in the process, his 'own man', he too turned to men whose service to his family went back, in some cases, to the 1380s.

The chapter by Gwilym Dodd, which considers the new king's 'establishment' at the start of the reign, takes the matter further, confirming Curry's observation that as 'Lancastrians' had been given the pick of the posts in the youthful Prince's administration, so they were again to be privileged when their master assumed the crown in 1413. An analysis of those chosen to witness charters at the beginning of the new reign shows them to have been men consistently close to the king, while those who had leaned towards his father in the periods of difficulty and tension between father and son a few years earlier were not being consulted. The scale of it made it more a 'reshuffle' than a purge.

Dodd also stresses the prominent position of knights and esquires within the royal household, many of whom had served Henry IV, or had been in the Prince's household before he became king. It is hardly surprising that a man like Henry V should wish to surround himself with men ready to serve him in war, a point emphasized by the number of younger members of the royal household who accompanied the king to France in 1415, leaving the older ones in England to ensure the country's defence in the king's absence. Likewise, analysis of the names of those who received a special royal livery at Henry V's coronation shows the new king to have been anxious to reward certain men for services rendered to both his father and himself since 1400.

Such information is important. Not only did it encourage continuity of personnel working in the service of the crown; it proclaimed that service at court could be used both to reward past loyalty and to encourage the hope of such service in the future, both from those so rewarded and from others.

Soldiers appear to have been particularly favoured by the new king. Men who had served with him in a military capacity in Wales were among those who found favour at court, as were some who, under the leadership of the earl of Arundel, had gone to the help of the duke of Burgundy in 1411, a policy supported by the Prince although opposed by both his father and his brother, Thomas, duke of Clarence. As Dodd points out, few of those who supported Clarence's own expedition to Gascony in the following year (an enterprise not favoured by the Prince of Wales) would be rewarded by the Prince once he had become king, while a number who had served under Arundel would be called to become important officers in Henry V's household. Loyalty, it is clear, was an attribute favoured by the new king.

The theme of continuity of service to the crown is to be found in the chapter offered by Mark Arvanigian. In this case it concerns service in a particular area, the northernmost counties on or close to the border with Scotland, where there was need for both political stability, based on the effective exercise of power and authority, and the achievement of security against threats still emanating from Scotland. Under Henry IV stability in the region had twice suffered, first in 1403, at the time of the Percy rebellion which had ended in the king's victory at Shrewsbury, and again in 1405, the year which had witnessed the execution of Richard Scrope, archbishop of York. These events had created a political vacuum, which the crown needed to fill by reasserting the effectiveness of its authority in the north.

This was achieved, Arvanigian argues, through the conscious employment of, and encouragement given to, leading local supporters of the house of Lancaster to exercise authority in the name of the crown. On the eastern side of the country, royal influence was strongly and effectively exercised by Thomas Langley, a man with a long record of service to the house of Lancaster, appointed in 1406 to the see and lordship of Durham which he would hold for the next thirty years. To the west, Ralph Neville, earl of Westmorland, married to Joan Beaufort, aunt of Henry V, a union which thus made him a son-in-law to the deceased John of Gaunt and brother-in-law to one of the dynasty's most influential supporters, Henry Beaufort, bishop of Winchester and several times chancellor of England, was encouraged to assert and maintain the royal authority in the region. Along with leading members of the gentry community whom they patronized, Langley and Westmorland maintained the rule of law, and saw to the requirements of security in the north. This was the situation inherited by Henry V on his accession in 1413. Since the region remained for a while in a state of relative peace, neither a change of policy nor a change in the personnel involved in applying it was required.

A period of relative calm on the borders, along with the stability restored to Wales after the Glyn Dŵr revolt, enabled the king to concentrate on affairs elsewhere, principally on the war with France. In the north, this 'Lancastrian' group, loyal to the king and to the crown, experienced in the many aspects of local government and administration, permeated and soon came to lead political society in the region. Its success depended on a number of factors. One was the way in which Westmorland, even in his absence, managed, through his 'Lancastrian' links, to influence everyday decisions made by the core group of the royal council which, in effect, was responsible for the governing of the country in the king's absence. Assured of being heard by central government, Westmorland was given a fairly free hand to exercise the royal authority in the north of the country. At the same time, he extended his influence widely through the region, not least through his encouragement of the marriages of some of his twenty-two children (eleven of each gender: he was twice married). One was married to Henry Percy, second earl of Northumberland, as a preliminary to his partial restoration to royal favour; another to a ward, Richard, Lord Scrope; a third to Thomas, Lord Dacre. The families who thus came to live within the Westmorland network were at an advantage.

As some rose in society, others declined. The Scrope of Masham family probably felt itself affected by a decline in its local influence due to the rise of the Neville/Beaufort axis. It was Westmorland who had been responsible for putting down the rebellion of 1405. Another of the future Southampton conspirators, Sir Thomas Grey, was becoming poorer, and may have felt that he was losing status to a new breed of royal servant as the result of Westmorland's advance. For all the stability which was introduced into northern society in these years there may have been growing a resentment of change and a wish among those losing out to oppose those responsible for creating it.

The establishment of social peace and the effectiveness of the rule of law have received considerable attention from historians in recent years. The issue of civil disorder is considered in an analysis of the reaction to the Lollard revolt led by Sir John Oldcastle, Lord Cobham, between early 1414 and his capture and execution late in 1417. True to form, the king had originally been reluctant to act against the rising threat of ideas presented by Oldcastle, a man of some military experience well known to Henry. However, the failure of the Lollard conspiracy against the king and the court in January 1414, and the growth of sympathy for heterodox ideas among many, including the gentry, called for the force of the secular law to assume the task of arresting and dealing with the heretic/rebel. It took nearly four years to achieve this, Oldcastle being finally captured in Wales before being tried by his peers in London, after which execution quickly followed. However, in keeping with Henry's appreciation of the importance of conciliation, rather than that of violent reaction, as the preferred means of maintaining peace within society, Lollards then experienced a general softening of attitude towards them. Nonetheless, inquiries into their attitudes went on, and suspects continued to be held, often without charges being brought against them.

While the general story of Henry's treatment of Lollards is familiar, Maureen Jurkowski presents us with an unfamiliar Henry V when she argues that the king showed little regard for the rights of the accused under the common law. Lollards taken at the time of the emergency in January 1414 were indicted by paid jurors assembled before the events of which they stood accused had even taken place, while Lollard commissioners were issued with pro forma indictments of treason, which showed scanty respect for normal judicial processes. Jurkowski accuses the king of uneven levels of justice; some men were executed, while others were spared. While the sale of general pardons in December 1414 brought in much-needed money, it clearly did the reputation of the common justice system little good. The broadening of a policy favoured by some of Henry's royal predecessors will have been regarded as an abuse of the royal prerogative of mercy.

More serious, however, is the charge levelled at Henry that under his rule some suspected of Lollard sympathies were imprisoned without being allowed access to due legal process, in disregard of a basic principle of common law. Does this suggest that by 1414 Lollardy, and support given to it, were no longer regarded as simply concerns of ecclesiastical courts, but that the view being taken of it as treason made it right for it to be tried in secular courts? Detention of those suspected of supporting rebels, the denial of the right to justice until those accused had posted bonds, and the detention without charge of persons suspected of Lollard activity were to become a permanent feature of the last years of Henry V's reign. Men had suffered like this under Richard II, but the practice had been halted by Henry IV, only to be resumed under the rule of his son, and continued into the early years of Henry VI's reign.

Henry V has long been regarded as a king under whose rule justice flourished. Contemporaries, in particular the French, thought of him as a king of justice, while in mid fifteenth century England the chronicler John Hardyng would express a similar opinion. Today, his willingness to undermine the protection of the liberty given to every individual by the law, the evidence for which is to be found in contemporary records, has been given the light of publicity. Has the whistle has been blown on the 'exemplar of justice'? The attitudes which underpinned such activities were not those which might reasonably be associated with the man. As such, they represent something of a challenge to our understanding of, and sympathy for, the king.

Alison McHardy's chapter introduces us to aspects of the life at court surrounding the king, and to the spiritual life of the king himself. She draws attention to the existence of the chapel royal, 'not so much a place as a travelling organization', which reminds one that the spiritual needs of the king and of those close to him had to be cared for wherever the king happened to be, whether at home or pursuing war abroad. The chapel was a way of underlining the importance attributed to religion and its practice, so that the provision of spiritual support, through the Church's services, was an important part of its raison d'être. Both its personnel and its workings are clear indicators of who were the churchmen closest to the king, and of the religious support which he expected them to give. The provision of music played a significant part in the work of the chapel royal in this reign. A number of its personnel were among the leading composers of the age, some enjoying reputations extending beyond the kingdom's boundaries. These men were supported by Henry's brothers, Thomas, duke of Clarence and John, duke of Bedford, as well as by the king, who showed himself to be among the leading patrons of musicians at this time. The fact that Henry may himself have written music is not beyond the realm of possibility. Of one thing we may be sure: English music was held in high regard at this period, and the chapel royal played a leading role in securing and assuring that reputation.

One of the chapel's chief members was Bishop Stephen Patrington, the king's Carmelite confessor, who, McHardy argues, may have been the author of the anonymous *Gesta Henrici Quinti*, written between 1415 and late 1417. He was, she proposes, a man close to the king, a theologian with a profound knowledge of the Bible (the *Gesta* is full of Old Testament quotations), who was probably present at Agincourt. These and other points are presented to make what is a reasoned case for Patrington's authorship. The proposal that the text should have been the work of a particular member of the chapel royal who was a close associate of the king is, at the very least, one which merits serious attention. If nothing else, it is a challenge to another scholar to do better.

A major theme to which four chapters make substantial contributions is that of finance or, to be more precise, how Henry V was able to manage the funding of his wars. Taxation, direct or indirect, was not the only method of raising money to support a war. A rather unusual aspect of how a late medieval king might do this is presented in Jenny Stratford's chapter, which describes the way Henry secured the financial means required to guarantee part of the wages of those taking part in his first expedition into France in 1415. While kings in the past had pledged items from their treasuries to corporate or individual supporters for particular purposes, never before had they done so directly with the captains (more than 250 of them) of the retinues raised to accompany them on campaign. The value to the historian of the evidence left by this process is considerable. Students of royal finances will not be alone in what they can learn from the evidence of the royal treasure, accumulated over the years from different sources, some of them French, and now being used to raise the money required to make war against France. Irony indeed. The process reflects the king's very personal commitment to the resumption of the conflict with the French, which demanded that he be ready to risk some of the crown's most 'personal' possessions in that cause; hence the order that it be done 'by the king's special command'. While the pledging of the crown's jewels and plate may suggest a rather last-minute attempt to rectify a miscalculation of the estimated costs of the expedition and, in particular, of the time it would take for the money to be collected and made available for use, Henry's difficulties may have been only the exacerbation of difficulties resulting from active diplomacy aimed at reducing piracy and its adverse effects upon indirect taxation in the first year or so of his reign. By the early spring of 1415 it had become evident that the money required to pay the army bound for France would not be available in the second quarter. The processes used to raise the money, including the innovative one described by Stratford, remind us how far the successful waging of war depended on taxation (the scheme in question here brought in the equivalent of a full lay subsidy) and on it being collected by the date agreed between the king and parliament. The rescheduling of subsidies, with all the difficulties which that caused, was to be a recurring theme of this reign.

An instance of this is to be found in the events which took place in Cheshire early in 1416 when opposition to the rising of a tax (or 'mise') in a part of the country which, as a palatinate, did not contribute to taxation voted in parliament, burst into the open. The demand for a tax by the king (otherwise earl of Chester) led to protests based on local solidarity. Michael Bennett argues for the existence of some coordination among the protesters who, he claims, showed an appreciation of events and developments beyond their county's boundaries, not least in France where contingents of Cestrians had only recently been fighting. This awareness, leading to written demands formally being made by them, might have led to a conflict between the king, representing the nation's needs, and themselves, as representatives of local solidarity. The way in which the matter was resolved tells us much about the methods used by Henry to win over those resisting his demands. A meeting of the county court (the assembly at which public issues were traditionally discussed, and at which those who bore much of the fiscal burden were heavily represented) which the king himself would attend was arranged for March 1416. Here, in return for a rescheduling of the timetable for the payment of the tax, Henry received the community's consent to its collection. The king's financial needs, allied to his determination to make the traditional tax-raising system function properly, and his willingness to travel to Cheshire to discuss, negotiate and even make concessions, are a graphic illustration of how Henry was able to obtain the financial support he required for the war he planned to fight in France.

Expressing high regard for the king's ability to raise the moneys required for war, Mark Ormrod digs deep into the reasons why Henry was so successful. Essentially, these can be reduced to two factors. The king worked within the existing fiscal system, introducing no new taxes, demanding that people pay according to their ability to do so, while granting fewer exemptions (other than to the very needy) than had been the practice in the past. Secondly, if the 'middling sort' bore the brunt of taxation (a view supported by Bennett), it fell upon a class which, generally speaking, could afford to pay, although this was not achieved without protest at the size of the burden the country was being asked to shoulder. On more than one occasion during his reign Henry was obliged to accept delays in the payment of taxes voted by parliament. These constitute evidence of the king's realistic appraisal of the country's financial position, and of the difficulties which his frequent demands for financial support created for those who bore the main burden of taxation. Granted, as Ormrod shows, that direct taxation was raised at an exceptionally high-level in 1416–17, it causes little surprise that there should have been protests in Cheshire at that time. It was to everybody's credit that these did not lead to major confrontations as they had, on more than one occasion, in the preceding century or so. It was, rather, what Ormrod regards as the nation's 'deep engagement', as well as his successes, which allowed the king's successful pursuit of the war in France.

Setting out to show why Henry V merited the title 'Flower of Chivalry', Craig Taylor emphasizes that, unlike his father who had earned a reputation as a crusader (in eastern Europe) and frequenter of tournaments, Henry V came to earn his chivalric reputation by another route and for other reasons. While he showed masculinity and great personal courage (at Agincourt, for example), it was for the qualities and characteristics of his leadership at the head of an army that the king stood out. A firm believer in truth and justice who accused the duplicitous French of deceit and of withholding, contrary to justice, what was not theirs, Henry went to war determined to claim his rights, launching an invasion which resembled a crusade of a new kind, a war inspired by vengeance.

The chivalry which Henry practised required that leaders act with ruthlessness, even brutality, quite unlike the modern romantically inspired view of chivalry. A further difference to today is the manner in which prisoners taken in battle were to be treated. Taylor contextualizes and, to an extent, defends the king's decision to have French prisoners taken at Agincourt killed while the battle still raged, and the English army was still in danger. Contemporary opinion does not appear to have been shocked by the event, and even the great 'chivalric' chronicler, Jean Froissart, writing only a generation earlier, could report similar actions without condemning them. The implicit warning is that we should not judge past decisions by the standards of today. More in keeping with modern ethical values is the picture of Henry V inspiring order and discipline (very Roman military virtues) upon his army, punishing acts of treason while rewarding loyalty, and always being ready to show mercy once his aim had been achieved. Respect for the commander, one feels, involved both the recognition of inspired leadership and a certain element of fear of the consequences if men fell into disobedience.

In both the process of conquest and in the establishment of Lancastrian rule in France, the treatment meted out to towns was a factor of the greatest practical importance. Neil Murphy's chapter is concerned with such matters. Towns were centres of judicial and financial administration in which royal officers lived and worked; some were military centres, others major points of economic contact and activity, others still were diocesan centres. Almost all were defended with walls. In some cases their capture had taken time; walls had had to be destroyed at Caen before the town capitulated, while at Rouen the king, anxious to preserve the city's defences, eventually starved it into surrender. A walled town was always a visible challenge to an invading army. But its fall was often the signal for the collapse of local resistance and the imminent surrender of settlements in the surrounding region.

The importance of towns often depended upon their geographical position. Caen, for instance, was at the very heart of lower Normandy, while Rouen guarded the river Seine between Paris and the sea, a task which it shared with Mantes, where there was a strategically sited bridge over the Seine to be fought over more than once in the years to come. The importance of such centres was reflected in the fact that some were placed under the care and command of English captains while, within Normandy at least, the *baillis*, chief royal administrative and judicial officers in each *bailliage*, were at first chosen from among Englishmen known to the king. Frenchmen, however, continued to hold the less important offices in the administrative and judicial hierarchies. By generally following a policy of conciliation, rather than by acting as a conqueror, Henry did what he could to encourage the return of peace and social conditions which would underpin a revival in economic enterprise and prosperity.

Other steps were taken to achieve a return to normality in French towns. Their importance was openly recognized through the confirmation of ancient privileges and charters granted by Henry's predecessors as kings of France. The return to their homes of those who had fled before the advancing English army was encouraged, each person who returned reflecting a decision that life under new rulers was possible. More important, however, was the boost which such persons gave to the restoration of manufacture and trade once the process of conquest was over. English men and women were also encouraged to settle in certain Norman towns; they would soon be found living in some numbers in Caen and Harfleur, which had lost a sizeable proportion of their populations as a result of the English invasion.

Going further, Murphy shows how the economic recovery of Normandy and other parts of northern France was encouraged through a revival of trade, which involved re-establishing economic relations with Brittany, Italy and England as early as 1419–20. The English invasion had done considerable harm to the economic prosperity of northern France, in the case of Caen probably aggravating an already evident economic decline. But the application of the treaty of Troyes was to lead to France having to accept a greater share of the burden of paying for war. In such circumstances the English administration had to make it possible for taxation in France to reflect an economy which might bear the demands made upon it. By pursuing a coherent economic policy Henry was able to alleviate with success some of the worst effects of war. This made the task of John, duke of Bedford, his de facto successor as ruler of Lancastrian France, easier than it might otherwise have been.

Finally, in a turn in the direction of historiography, I draw attention to what may be the earliest history (in the 'modern' sense) of the reign of Henry V, published by Thomas Goodwin in 1704. *The History of the Reign of King Henry the Fifth*, the work of a son of a well-known Cromwellian sympathizer and divine, reflects important changes taking place in the writing of history in the late seventeenth and early eighteenth centuries. Goodwin's work reflected a new approach to history. While interested in kings and great events, the author was ready to use many kinds of evidence, notably the records of government, to write history not largely to glorify or criticize kings and princes, but (in this case) to clarify how Henry V had ruled, what problems had confronted him, and how he had dealt with them. The king thus became a recognizably 'human' figure, faced with the difficult choices which those who conduct government have to face, above all when placed in the context of the many changes, political, religious and social, which were occurring in his day. Although the king's personality emerges from these pages, Goodwin's work was essentially a history of the reign, its achievements and what there was about it which brought fame to the king himself.

Two points may be emphasized. The picture of Henry conveyed to the reader is that of a king anxious to maintain good relations with his people, ready to listen to what they have to say, wishing to act for their good, which it is within his power to do. The work looks like an assessment of monarchy that a man of Whiggish sympathies could easily have written, evidence of how historians can impose the ideals of their own day in describing persons and events of the past.

The second point is the significance of the intellectual milieu in which Goodwin lived, and which clearly influenced him greatly. Ever since Tudor times, scholars (often described as antiquarians) had become increasingly interested in the material evidence upon which history might be based. Notable collectors of documents such as Sir Robert Cotton had amassed large quantities of records emanating from different branches of the royal household and administration. These would now contribute to the creation of a historical narrative which was all the more credible because of the number and nature of the sources being used. It added a further element which gave the reader an opportunity to be involved in the words which he read. As Goodwin wrote more than once, while it was the writer's task to make the evidence supporting what he wrote available to the reader (hence his lavish use of marginal notes giving references much as we do today), it was the privilege of the reader to decide whether or not it supported the case being made. The use of critical faculties was now becoming part of both writing and reading history.

1

The Making of a Prince:
The Finances of 'the young lord Henry', 1386–1400

Anne Curry

With such high levels of success as king as well as a substantial apprentice-ship as Prince, it is easy to overlook the fact that Henry V was not born into the royal purple. Until his circumstances changed around the time of his thirteenth birthday in the autumn of 1399, his future was that of a peer.[1] Even though his long-term prospects were promising – he was heir not only to his paternal Lancaster inheritance, but also to a share of that of the Bohuns through his co-heiress mother – he would have had to wait to enjoy these resources. In the shorter term, therefore, he was a landless youth dependent upon the financial support of his family.

His life and his financial resources were transformed by his father's usur-pation of the throne. On 15 October 1399, two days after the coronation of Henry (Bolingbroke), the young Henry was created Prince of Wales, duke of Cornwall and earl of Chester, and was acknowledged as heir to the throne should his father die. On 23 October the title duke of Aquitaine was added, and on 10 November that of duke of Lancaster.[2] With the first group of titles went a substantial landed endowment defined by precedent – the earldom of Chester; the principality of Wales, which fell into two groups of coun-ties in North and South Wales; and the south-western lands of the duchy of Cornwall, as well as its 'foreign manors' outside Devon and Cornwall which comprised scattered holdings in the midlands and south of England.[3]

---

[1] There has been debate on Henry's date of birth but 16 September 1386 is now accepted (Allmand, *Henry V*, pp. 7–8; I. Mortimer, *The Fears of Henry IV: The Life of England's Self-Made King* (London, 2007), p. 371).

[2] *PROME*, VIII, 33, 35, 37.

[3] A. Curry, 'The Demesne of the County Palatine of Chester in the Early Fifteenth Century' (unpublished MA dissertation, University of Manchester, 1977); A. Curry, 'Cheshire and the Royal Demesne 1399–1422', *Transactions of the Historic Society of Lancashire and Cheshire* 128 (1978), 113–35; W. R. M. Griffiths, 'The Military Career and Affinity of Henry, Prince of Wales, 1399–1413' (unpublished M.Litt. dissertation, University of Oxford, 1980); J. Hatcher, *Rural Economy and Society in the Duchy of Cornwall 1300–1500* (Cambridge, 1970), especially pp. 148–55. Although Hatcher sheds much light on economy and

At least 111 account rolls survive concerning Henry's landed income and his expenditure between the creations of October 1399 and his accession to the throne on 21 March 1413. Although the distribution of these financial records is uneven across both time and space, and there is a relative lack of household accounts,[4] further study of this large corpus would enable a reasonably detailed assessment of the Prince's finances. This, in turn, could inform study of his personal, political and military ambitions as he matured from youth to full manhood.

As the first stage of such a project, I am concentrating in this essay on two topics: first, Henry's situation before he became heir to the throne; and second, the creation of his appanage in the aftermath of his father's usurpation. The first topic sheds light on how younger members of a noble family were supported in their early years, and raises questions on how family strategy was applied in terms of financial and landed sustenance. The second topic has extra significance because of the installation of a new dynasty on the throne in 1399. There is the immediate interest of Henry's position during the exile of his father. Was he treated by Richard as a hostage? What place did he have in the establishment of the new regime? At one level, the need to re-establish the appanage of an heir to the throne after more than twenty years of royal occupation of such lands added to the problems which Henry IV faced in securing royal authority. It required decisions to be made on whether to continue Richard II's disbursements (such as annuities) and alienations, and on whether to replace his officials or not. At another level, it assisted the intrusion of a new dynasty by creating the vested interest of its second generation. Given that the young Henry was still a minor in 1399, we should not be surprised to see his father's close involvement in the setting up of the appanage, and in the decisions on policy and patronage in the early years of the new reign. Future work on the lands and finances of Prince Henry after 1400 will indicate at what point he took direct control, and the impact that had on his own choices concerning expenditure and patronage.

---

society there is still a need for an analysis of the Prince's income from the duchy more fully, and to date, there has been no dedicated study of its foreign manors.

4   Most of the surviving material for the household relates to 1400–5 (TNA, E 101/404/16; E 101/404/23; E 101/404/24; E 101/405/1; E 101/405/26). There are some daily expenses from 1407–8 (TNA, E 101/405/17) and 1409–10 (E 101/406/2), and a handful of warrants for 1412–13 (E 101/406/7). There are also seventeenth-century transcripts of extracts from wardrobe accounts (BL Harleian 4304 fols. 20r–21v) but these are haphazard in content. It is also possible to use the surviving accounts of the receiver-general of the duchy of Cornwall to show something of expenditure. Particularly useful here are TNA, SC 6/813/23 and 24 (8–9 and 9–10 Henry IV).

The Young Henry

As we might expect, money spent on Henry before 1399 came out of the coffers of his father and grandfather, as is revealed by the accounts of their various officials. One of the earliest is the purchase of a demi-gown in the account for the year from 1 October 1387 to 31 September 1388.[5] Over the years which followed, there are further references to expenditure on clothing, books and other items for Henry, described as 'the young lord Henry' (*iuvenis dominus Henricus*, as in the 1387–8 account), or as 'Lord Henry, son of the earl of Derby' (*dominus Henricus filius comitis Derb'*). Other historians have already cited several of these.[6] The same financial records enable us to trace something of the young Henry's itinerary. Like other aristocratic families, frequent moves between relatives and houses were made. For instance, just before the date assigned for his father's duel with Thomas Mowbray in September 1398, both he and his next eldest brother, Thomas, were sent from Kenilworth to Pontefract, where John of Gaunt was at this time, before returning to their father who was at Kenilworth.[7]

From the mid-1390s the young Henry was beginning to be present at major events. The account of Gaunt's receiver-general for 1396–7, for example, notes the purchase of four saddles with silver gilt fittings for Henry 'for the journey to Calais in the previous year' (*pro viagio usque Calesiam in anno precedente*), which suggests that he was present at Richard's marriage to Isabella of France.[8] In the negotiations which preceded this event, there had been some thought of a marriage between Henry and Isabella's younger sister, Michelle.[9] According to the account of William Loveney, the clerk of the Wardrobe of the earl of Derby, Adam Garston was sent from Hertford to London in September 1397 concerning robes for Henry and his brother Thomas for the parliament. Earlier in the year Garston had arranged robes for Henry for the 'obit' of the earl of Kent, who died on 25 April 1397 and was buried in Lincoln.[10]

---

5   Wylie, *Henry the Fourth*, IV, 157. The original document is TNA, E 101/28/2, account of Hugh Waterton of the receipts and expenses of the household and wardrobe of the earl and countess of Derby.

6   K. B. McFarlane, *Lancastrian Kings and Lollard Knights* (Oxford, 1972), pp. 115–16; Allmand, *Henry V*, pp. 9–11. The appendices of the fourth volume of Wylie's biography contain several extracts from relevant accounts.

7   TNA, DL 28/1/10 fol. 28r. I am grateful to Prof. Chris Given-Wilson for this reference.

8   TNA, DL 28/3/5 fol. 14r.

9   This is known through the reply of Charles VI in June 1396 to a now lost letter of Richard II: Archives Nationales J 644/2, cited in *Diplomatic Correspondence of Richard II*, ed. E. Perroy, Camden Series, 3rd Series 48 (London, 1933), p. 169. Allmand, *Henry V*, p. 10, writes of negotiations in 1395 for a possible marriage with Marie, daughter of John IV, duke of Brittany.

10   TNA, DL 28/1/6 fol. 36v, 36r. The parliament opened at Westminster on 17 September but was prorogued on 29 September and reconvened at Shrewsbury between 28 and

Elsewhere in the same account, relating to business carried out in July 1397, Garston is described as Henry's tailor (*sissor robarum iuvenis domini Henrici*).[11] This may suggest the development of a designated group of household servants for Henry around this point, perhaps partly shared with his brother Thomas, since Garston is also seen as providing clothes for him. More significantly, from 1 July 1397 Simon Bache, treasurer of the household of the earl of Derby, paid wages of 12*d.* per day to Peter Melbourne in the service of 'Henry, son of the lord'.[12] We shall see subsequently why this link with Melbourne is significant.

Henry did not have any income of his own. Save within the direct royal line, there was no automatic allocation of estates or titles to heirs within their father's lifetime even when they came of age. Indeed, the financial dependence on the father might continue for some time and was a reason why military service to the crown was attractive for the heirs of peers and even more for their younger siblings. When Richard of York (later earl of Cambridge) was chosen to attend Henry IV's daughter Philippa as she went to Denmark for her marriage, it was noted that he was of 'poor estate' (*povre estat*), and could not go on the journey without royal financial assistance.[13] Even in the royal family this was relevant. Henry's next brother, Thomas, was supported after the accession of Henry IV by an appointment as lieutenant in Ireland and by wages for service at sea. In 1409 it was suggested that if he did not want to go to Ireland he could nonetheless take 2,000 marks from its revenues as well as a further 1,000 marks from the king so long as the king would not have to bear any of the costs of Thomas and his household.[14] It was useful for the crown that there were valuable military commands for younger sons. We can speculate that Prince Henry's appointment to the wardenship of the Cinque Ports in 1409 and to the captaincy of Calais in March 1410 was partly pecuniary.[15]

---

31 January 1398. It was on 30 September that Henry's father, elevated at the end of the Westminster session as duke of Hereford, presented his bill against Thomas Mowbray, who had been similarly elevated as duke of Norfolk.

11 TNA, DL 28/1/6 fol. 11r. I have not so far found references to Garston serving Henry when Prince. Amongst many other payments in this account we also see that Stephen Ferbour was paid a shilling for a new scabbard for Henry's sword (fol. 36v).

12 TNA, DL 28/1/9 fol. 22v. A reference on folio 14v records a payment to Melbourne for his wages in the earl's court from 5 July 1396 to 1 July 1397 but without mentioning service to the young Henry. We see on 6 June 1397 a payment to the widow of John Marchall, *scutifer domini* for his services outside the household of the earl when in the house of the duke of Lancaster in the service of Henry, son of the lord. This suggests that the young Henry had been staying with his grandfather before July 1397.

13 *POPC*, II, 294 (8 July 1406).

14 Ibid., II, 320.

15 From my researches to date on the accounts of the receiver-general of the duchy of Cornwall for 1407–9, it seems that Henry's income from these estates had decreased compared with 1404.

Had Bolingbroke been allowed to inherit the duchy of Lancaster at the death of his own father, John of Gaunt, in February 1399, his son might subsequently have had specific estates allocated to him. As precedent, in 1333 Henry, third earl of Lancaster (d.1345), had given a life grant to his eldest son, Henry of Grosmont (d.1361), of much of the family inheritance in South Wales including the lordship of his birthplace as well as two manors in Yorkshire and the profits of the eyre of the forest of Pickering.[16] That said, Henry of Grosmont was already in his early thirties and had already been involved in military activity under Edward III. Also his father had apparently lost his sight around 1330 and therefore other factors could have occasioned the grant. Significantly, it was not until March 1337 that Henry of Grosmont was given a title, that of earl of Derby, which entitled him to £20 per annum in lieu of the traditional third penny from county pleas.[17] The Lancaster inheritance, including the earldom of Derby, passed via Henry of Grosmont's daughter, Blanche, to John of Gaunt. Following the precedent of 1337, John's eldest son, Henry (Bolingbroke), was created earl of Derby in 1377 at the age of eleven. It is possible, therefore, that this title would have been accorded to the young Henry within a few years of his father's inheritance of the duchy of Lancaster had events in 1398–9 not caused complete dislocation. To speculate even further: had Richard remained in power, the young Henry might have benefited from Richard's propensity to create 'duketti'. With his father as duke of Lancaster, might he have been created in due course as duke of Hereford, a title which Richard had granted Bolingbroke in September 1397, and which came from the latter's Bohun inheritance?[18]

Given these past precedents it is likely that by his late teens, or at least from the date of any marriage, Henry would have had a title and some estates or revenues to support him. It had been at the point of his own father's marriage in February 1381 that Gaunt allocated a number of manors to Bolingbroke in order to support the household of the newly married couple.[19] Use might also have been made of the young Henry's maternal inheritance. Even so,

---

[16] TNA, DL 25/1128, cited in R. Somerville, *History of the Duchy of Lancaster: Volume 1, 1265–1603* (London, 1953), p. 38, note 2.

[17] *CPR, 1334–8*, p. 400; *Complete Peerage*, VII, 401.

[18] This title came through Bolingbroke's deceased wife as co-heiress of Humphrey de Bohun (d.1373). There were also other titles: Northampton had been assigned in 1384 to Mary de Bohun although it had previously been held by Thomas of Woodstock who had married Mary's elder sister Eleanor. Hereford had initially looked as though it would be given to Woodstock but was accorded to Bolingbroke in 1397. A further Bohun title, Essex, appeared to have gone to Thomas of Woodstock in 1374 (*Complete Peerage*, VI, 474–5).

[19] I am grateful to Prof. Given-Wilson for discussion on this point. See also Mortimer, *Fears of Henry IV*, p. 41: 'thus we know that Henry's income of £426 9s. in 1381–2 came predominantly from three manors which John had allocated him: Passenham, Soham and Daventry, plus an allowance from his father's Norfolk estates'.

the young Henry would have had, like other noble heirs-in-waiting, limited resources until he came into his main paternal inheritance.[20]

Enough, however, of the 'what if?' In October 1398 Richard II aborted Bolingbroke's proposed duel with the duke of Norfolk at Coventry, sending the former into exile for ten years and the latter for life. On 3 or 4 February 1399 John of Gaunt died at Leicester. Richard is alleged by Froissart to have extended Bolingbroke's exile to life but this is not supported by the evidence. The king was certainly determined, however, that Bolingbroke should stay away for the full ten years. At his departure from England, Bolingbroke had been granted letters patent to allow his attorneys to sue for any inheritance arising during his exile. On 18 March 1399, however, these were revoked by the king, acting on the advice of a parliamentary commission set up at the end of the previous parliament, on the grounds that they were contrary to the judgements which had been made at Coventry.[21] Some duchy of Lancaster lands were thereafter granted out temporarily to others, but Richard did not envisage a permanent state of confiscation or disinheritance unlike the forfeiture of Thomas of Woodstock, duke of Gloucester, following his fall in 1397.[22] The grant made on 20 March 1399 to Edward, duke of Aumale, of the duchy of Lancaster honours of Leicester, Pontefract, Higham Ferrers and Bolingbroke, as well as other lands in Leicestershire and Lincolnshire, was to be held from the death of Gaunt 'until Henry [Bolingbroke] or his heir should sue them out of the king's hands'.[23]

At the time of Gaunt's death, the young lord Henry was around twelve-and-a-half years old. Allmand suggests tentatively that he was taken to Richard's

---

[20] This was even true for the direct royal line. Soon after the accession we see Henry IV granting his younger sons revenues from specific manors to support their estate (e.g. for Thomas, *CPR, 1399–1401*, p. 69 (14 November 1399); for Humphrey, ibid., p. 148 (2 December 1399); for John, ibid., p. 155 (16 December 1399)). The manors were a mixture of royal demesne and forfeitures. Note that Henry IV did not rush to give titles or major landholdings to any other of his sons. Thomas was twenty-four by the time he was created duke of Clarence and earl of Aumale on 9 July 1412, in advance of the expedition which he had been appointed to lead to France. John came of full age (twenty-one) in 1410 yet did not get a title until 16 May 1414 when created duke of Bedford and earl of Kendal, with the earldom of Richmond being added on 24 November 1414. Humphrey came of age in 1404 yet was only created duke of Gloucester and earl of Pembroke on 16 May 1414.

[21] *PROME*, VII, 398–9; A. Dunn, *The Politics of Magnate Power: England and Wales 1389–1413* (Oxford, 2003), p. 72. Noted also in *Johannis de Trockelowe et Henrici de Blaneford monachorum S. Albani necnon quorundam anonymorum, chronica et annales*, ed. H. T. Riley, Rolls Series 28 (London, 1866), pp. 232–3, 265.

[22] Dunn, *Politics*, pp. 59–62.

[23] *CFR, 1391–9*, pp. 293, 297. Note also that Katherine Swynford successfully petitioned in March and May for her dower and other lands which had initially been confiscated as part of the Lancastrian holdings (*CPR, 1396–9*, pp. 516, 555; *CCR, 1396–9*, pp. 365, 476). I am grateful to Becky Holdorph for this point.

court following his father's exile as a surety for the latter's good behaviour.[24] Kingsford gives a different interpretation, placing this royal action after the death of Gaunt. 'Richard, who, whatever other faults he possessed, was a kindly man, took the boy under his own care and kept him about his Court.'[25] In fact, Henry's whereabouts are not at all certain. To date, no mention of him in Richard's court or presence has been found. If he was with Richard, should we take it that he moved around with the king, whose itinerations over the winter and spring of 1398–9 were extensive?[26] The earliest reference to Henry is found on the issue roll for the Michaelmas term, under the date 21 February 1399, a few weeks after Gaunt's death, which had occurred at the beginning of February. Here we find a payment to 'Henry, son and heir of the duke of Hereford', of £20 out of £500 per annum, to be taken from the royal exchequer during royal pleasure.[27] This sum was reasonably generous and appropriate given Henry's status. By way of comparison, in 1395–6 we find annuities of 200 marks to the earl of Nottingham and to Thomas Holland, son of the earl of Kent, 350 marks to Richard of York (later earl of Cambridge, then aged about twenty), and 500 marks to Edmund, duke of York.[28]

The grant of the annuity was not surprising in that Henry otherwise had no potential source of support other than the revenues of his father and grandfather, and their status was problematic at this point, even though it was not until 18 March that the decision to prevent Bolingbroke's premature suing for his inheritance was announced.[29] This was two days after the burial of Gaunt at St Paul's.[30] Saul suggests that, in his decisions over the terms of the restoration of the Lancaster inheritance, Richard saw the young Henry as 'the object of his hopes'. To this end, any grants made of the lands in the interim included the clause 'until Henry of Lancaster, or his heir, shall have sued the same out of the king's hands according to the law of the land'. However, this was standard formula. The young Henry would have come of age before his father's exile ran to its full term. He was still too young to inherit in 1399. Within five months Richard would be deposed. Therefore, we can only speculate whether Richard would have allowed him to hold any of the lands or enjoy their revenues in the future. There is nothing to suggest any 'special relationship' between the king and Henry at this point. There was no need for one. But the grant of the annuity was a clear sign that the king did not intend to disparage his cousin's son. In that respect it was

---

[24] Allmand, *Henry V*, p. 12.

[25] C. L. Kingsford, *Henry V: The Typical Medieval Hero* (London, 1901), p. 16.

[26] N. Saul, *Richard II* (London, 1997), pp. 473–4.

[27] TNA, E 403/561, m. 14.

[28] C. Given Wilson, *The English Nobility in the Late Middle Ages* (London, 1987), p. 155.

[29] Saul, *Richard II*, p. 404.

[30] The assumption is that the young Henry would have been present, but so far this has not been proved.

an important statement of intent, which was continued, as we shall see, by further support towards the Irish campaign and a dubbing to knighthood.

On 5 March 1399, a further £10 of the £500 annuity was paid to Henry by Peter Melbourne (*per manus Petri Melbourne scutiferi*).[31] A further payment of £40 out of the annuity was made on 6 May via Melbourne.[32] Identification of Peter Melbourne (d.1418) is helpful here, not least as we have already noted his connection with the upbringing of Henry before 1399. He was an official of the duchy of Lancaster as well as an executor of the will of John of Gaunt.[33] He had entered into a life indenture with the duke in 1376,[34] and had become an esquire of his household in the 1380s.[35] He also had strong connections with Bolingbroke, receiving a life annuity from the early 1390s, and accompanying him not only to Prussia in 1392 but also to the Holy Land as one of only a handful of intimates. Melbourne was also used to collect payment of the royal pension due to Bolingbroke. At the point he collected the payment at the exchequer for the young Henry in March 1399 he was constable of the duchy of Lancaster castle at Melbourne (Derbyshire), as well as steward of the lordship.[36] It has been suggested that the payment was in reality from the revenues of the Lancaster and Hereford estates.[37] Yet the entries in the issue rolls were for direct payments at the exchequer not for assignments from another source, unless the *per manus Petri Melbourne* can be taken to imply that the latter was diverting the money from sequestrated Lancastrian funds he held at Melbourne.[38] However, we would expect the source of funds to be made clear in an issue roll entry, and, significantly, there

---

31 TNA, E 403/561 m. 16.

32 TNA, E 403/562 m. 8.

33 Somerville, *Duchy*, p. 377, citing *John of Gaunt's Register, 1379–1383*, ed. E. C. Lodge and R. Somerville, 2 vols. (1937–8), II, 10. Gaunt had made his will at Leicester castle on 2 February 1398. Somerville, *Duchy*, p. 67 note 3; S. Armitage Smith, *John of Gaunt* (London, 1904), p. 404. For a biography of Melbourne see *HP*, III, 712–4. This mentions also that his mother had been 'a leading member' of the household of Gaunt and his second wife. For the point that this Derbyshire and Staffordshire area of the Duchy was well represented in Gaunt's household see H. Castor, *The King, the Crown and the Duchy of Lancaster: Public Authority and Private Power 1399–1461* (Oxford, 2000), pp. 195–6.

34 N. B. Lewis, 'Indentures of Retinue with John of Gaunt, Duke of Lancaster, Enrolled in Chancery 1367–1399', Camden Miscellany 22 (Camden 4th series 1, 1964), no. 5; TNA, DL 42/15 m. 1v, cited in S. Walker, *The Lancastrian Affinity* (Oxford, 1990), p. 275.

35 East Sussex Record Office GLY 3469 mm. 1–5, cited in Walker, *Lancastrian Affinity*, p. 217 note 194.

36 TNA, DL 29/6154.

37 Allmand, *Henry V*, p. 12: 'the recipient of £500 from Hereford's revenues'.

38 Biggs claims that other payments made to Henry Bolingbroke during his exile, via the hands of John Leventhorpe, his receiver-general, and Richard Ramsey, came 'ironically, from the surplus income of John of Gaunt's estates': see D. Biggs, *Three Armies in Britain: The Irish Campaign of Richard II and the Usurpation of Henry IV 1397–9* (Leiden, 2006), p. 84. This might theoretically be the case, but all these payments were recorded on the issue roll as being made from exchequer funds directly rather than from assignments.

was no effort to reconcile these payments in the later account rolls of the exiled duke's officials. By contrast, after the usurpation, efforts were made to make repayments to such officials for money they had spent on the support of the younger members of the family, John, Humphrey and their sisters, who had been housed at Eaton Bray (Beds.) whilst their father was abroad.[39]

The timing of the royal grant to Henry – 21 February 1399 – suggests that he was not at court before this point, and it is unclear why he would have needed an explicit personal grant of funds if he was resident at court. It is likely, therefore, that he had been with his grandfather at Leicester, with Melbourne in his service much as before Bolingbroke's exile.[40] By 21 February, the date of the first payment to Henry, Richard II had decided on an expedition to Ireland. On that very day, the controller of the royal household, Sir John Stanley, made a payment of £1,333 6s. 8d. to the keeper of the Wardrobe to make provision for the household of the king against his *adventum* into the land of Ireland.[41]

It remains likely, however, that Henry remained in the care of Melbourne elsewhere, even if it had been decided by 21 February that both should go on the royal campaign to Ireland.[42] Richard was at Great Haywood in Staffordshire on 21 February,[43] not so far removed from Leicester, and even closer to Melbourne. There is no doubt that Peter Melbourne was well rewarded after the usurpation, which suggests that he was deemed to have provided good service to the young Henry. One of Bolingbroke's first acts as king (2 October) was to confirm Peter in office at Melbourne. In the next month his annuity was increased from £10 to 100 marks, and there were further grants in February 1400 of forfeitures in Derbyshire which had formerly belonged to Thomas Merck, bishop of Carlisle, who had spoken out against Henry's seizure of the throne.[44] Furthermore, Peter was in office as chamberlain to

---

[39] TNA, DL 28/4/1, fol. 6: account of John Leventhorpe 'receiver of the king's [i.e. Henry IV's] possessions which were his before the coronation, from the Feast of the Purification 22 Richard II (11 February 1399) to the same feast in the following year'. Thomas accompanied his father into exile and returned with him.

[40] How soon was Peter, as executor, able to pass on to Henry the *hanap d'or* which John of Gaunt had bequeathed in his will to his grandson? For the duke's will see Armitage Smith, *John of Gaunt*, p. 428. Henry's younger brother, John, was also bequeathed a *hanap d'or* in his grandfather's will. Melbourne is not listed amongst the executors given powers on 20 March 1399 'for the speedier execution of the will of the king's uncle whereof the king is supervisor' (*CPR, 1396–9*, p. 502).

[41] TNA, E 403/561 m. 14.

[42] Bolingbroke had been given by the king 2,000 marks per annum during his exile, which was collected at the exchequer by John Leventhorpe (TNA, E 403/561, m. 4, 11 November 1398, E 403/562 m. 2, 15 April 1399), so a payment did not need the actual recipient to be at court or even in England.

[43] Saul, *Richard II*, p. 474.

[44] TNA, DL 42/15 fol. 1v, 2 October 1399; Somerville, *Duchy*, pp. 377, 381; *CPR, 1399–1401*, p. 195.

Henry, Prince of Wales, by at least December 1401,[45] and may have held this office from the start of the new reign. He was also commissioned with other members of the Prince's council (John Stanley and Hugh Mortimer, who later succeeded Melbourne as chamberlain) with taking the Cheshire men into grace after the battle of Shrewsbury in 1403.[46] Henry, both as Prince and king, showed him much largesse.[47] A grant made at the accession of 1413 mentioned Melbourne's continuous service to the Prince 'from his youth up'.[48]

Melbourne's position in the months preceding the Lancastrian usurpation gives further insights into the complex politics of this period. On 8 April 1399 he had his annuities confirmed by Richard II in return for giving up the offices of constable of Melbourne and keeper of its park and forests.[49] This suggests some kind of deal with Richard, or else an effort to keep one foot in the Lancastrian and one in the royal camp, a gesture all the more significant if he had the keeping of the young Lord Henry. Might this indicate the time, therefore, when Melbourne and his young charge came to Westminster in preparation for the Irish campaign?[50] On 20 April Melbourne was accorded letters of protection in anticipation of his service on Richard II's expedition.[51] Preparations were also made around this point to equip Henry for his participation in the campaign. In addition to the £40 payment of the annuity made via Melbourne on 6 May, the issue roll for the Easter term of 1399 also records the payment on 2 May to Henry, again via the hands of Melbourne, of £100. This was not part of the annuity but of the sum of £148 15s. 9d. ordered by the king for Henry's apparel, armour and other necessities for the expedition. The remaining £48 15s. 9d. was paid by the hands of John Frenyngham, skinner of London.[52] Whilst purchases were often made at a distance, this may also indicate Henry's presence in London in late April/early May. Peter's responsibility for Henry may have continued into the

---

45 'Calendars of Recognizance Rolls of the Palatinate of Chester', *Annual Report of the Deputy Keeper of the Public Records* [henceforward *DKR*], XXXVI (London, 1875), p. 304.

46 TNA, E 101/405/1 (Indentures and warrants relating to the treasury of the prince of Wales, 4–6 Henry IV 1402–5). Melbourne served in the wars in Wales and continued to hold some role in the Prince's household until at least September 1403.

47 *HP*, III, 713.

48 *CPR, 1413–16*, p. 13.

49 *CPR, 1396–9*, pp. 522–3.

50 The king was in London/Westminster in mid-March (at the time of Gaunt's funeral) and Canterbury in early April before returning to Westminster by 16 April. Thenceforward, he moved slowly westwards via Windsor, Oxford, Gloucester and Cardiff, before reaching Milford Haven on 27 May (Saul, *Richard II*, p. 474).

51 *CPR, 1396–9*, p. 525.

52 TNA, E 403/562 m. 7. On the same day, Humphrey, son of the late duke of Gloucester, was given £100 for the same purpose by the hands of Thomas Burgh. Edmund Holland, son of Thomas, duke of Surrey, was also given £100 on the same date but the entry does not say that this was for military costs.

campaign. Henry was not in receipt of royal wages for the expedition as he had not indented directly with the king, nor does he seem to have been serving within another retinue. Under such circumstances he would have been entitled to *bouche de court* of Richard on the campaign. This might also have been the case for Peter Melbourne although he received military wages. It is worth noting that several others of Bolingbroke's affinity were also on the campaign. The politics of these months are more complicated than we might think. The usurpation deceives us into assuming that there was ubiquitous and constant anti-Ricardian feeling across the Lancastrian group.

The wording of the St Albans chronicles – 'he also took with him boys of noble birth, the sons of the dukes of Gloucester and Hereford, whose relatives he especially feared'[53] – has been taken to suggest that Richard deliberately took to Ireland both Henry and Humphrey, son of the late duke of Gloucester (then aged about seventeen), as hostages for the good behaviour of their relatives.[54] If true, the tactic did not work! These chronicle accounts were undoubtedly written with pro-Lancastrian hindsight. It was very common for noble boys to be taken on campaign, even if they were not old enough to indent in person or to bring their own retinue. There had been plans to take Richard on campaign in 1377, at the age of ten. Opportunities to be blooded in actual warfare were few and far between. It would be extremely unlikely that the campaign to Ireland would not be used for this purpose for Henry and for other young men around his age. It does not require Richard to have a penchant for the prepubescent, or to have taken Henry with him deliberately as a way of keeping his father in check. Richard did not think that he needed to keep Bolingbroke in check, but assumed that the exile would continue for the prescribed time. Richard's knighting of Henry, as described by Creton, can be interpreted as an act of honour towards the Lancastrian line, the invocation of the military reputation of his forebears, irrespective of current issues with Bolingbroke.[55] If the account is to be believed, it took place just before an anticipated engagement with the Irish rebels, exactly the setting we would expect, and was accompanied by other dubbings of young men, including, it seems, Alan Buxhill, then aged eighteen.[56]

---

[53] *Duxerat autem secum nobiles pueros filios ducum Gloverniae et Herefordiae quorum affines praecipue verebatur.*

[54] *Johannis de Trockelowe*, p. 239; *The Chronica Maiora of Thomas Walsingham 1376–1422*, trans. D. Preest, with introduction and notes by J. G. Clark (Woodbridge, 2005), p. 306.

[55] *Apres fist il de vray cuer sans amer/Le filz du duc de lancastre mander/qui est bel et jeune bachelor/et avenant;/et puis le fist chevalier en disant/Mon beau cousin, soiez preu et vaillant/ desoremaiz, car pou avez vaillant/sans conquerir*: *A Metrical History of the Deposition of Richard II attributed to John Creton*, ed. J. Webb, *Archaeologia* 20 (1824), 1–423 (p. 299, translation p. 289).

[56] Ibid., translation, p. 152, writes of 'the son of the countess of Salisbury ... and many others'. There is an implication that Janico Dartasso was also knighted on the campaign.

Even according to the pro-Lancastrian sources, it was not until Richard had heard the news of Bolingbroke's invasion and had decided to return to England that he imprisoned Henry as well as the son of Gloucester in Trim castle.[57] Here Henry seems to have remained, thirty miles to the north-west of Dublin. The date of his return to England is uncertain. According to Adam Usk, 'the duke sent to Ireland for his eldest son Henry and for Humphrey the son of the duke of Gloucester who had been imprisoned by King Richard in Trim castle; and they were sent back to him together with a large collection of the king's treasure'.[58] This passage comes immediately after the chronicler's account of Bolingbroke's presence in Chester (9–20 August) and his move to London with the captive king (with an estimated arrival date of 1 September), and is preceded by the linking phrase 'in the meantime'. This wording suggests, therefore, that arrangements to bring the young Henry back were initiated before Bolingbroke left Chester.[59] Usk adds that Henry came back safely, 'bringing with him in shackles Sir William Bagot',[60] but that Humphrey, son of the duke of Gloucester, died in Anglesey on the way back, having being poisoned in Ireland by Lord Despenser. The alleged location of Humphrey's death suggests that the boys were to be brought back via Chester. This is also implied in a warrant for issue of 5 March 1401 in favour of Henry Dryhurst of 'West Chester'.[61] Here Dryhurst was recompensed for the cost of wine which he had provided to Bolingbroke's household whilst in Chester. It also paid Dryhurst 20 marks for the freightage of a ship from Chester to Dublin, and 'for sailing from the same place and back again to conduct the Lord the Prince, the King's son, from Ireland to England, together with the furniture of a chapel and its ornaments which formerly belonged to the late King Richard the Second, deceased'.

Whether Henry was back in Chester before his father left the city is unclear. It is a possibility if the location of Humphrey's death was Chester or Coventry, as put forward by other chroniclers.[62] Bolingbroke and Richard passed through Coventry on 26 August.[63] The young Henry carried the sword of justice at the coronation of Henry IV on 13 October, having been knighted

57 *Johannis de Trockelowe*, p. 248; Walsingham, *Chronica Maiora*, p. 308. Humphrey seems to have died on the way back from Ireland but details are unknown. He was buried at Walden Abbey, Essex (*Complete Peerage*, V, 729).

58 *The Chronicle of Adam Usk 1377–1421*, ed. C. Given-Wilson (Oxford, 1997), pp. 60–1.

59 This was also Kingsford's view (*Henry V*, p. 19).

60 Bagot was tried during the parliament in October.

61 TNA, E 404/16/394; *Issues of the Exchequer*, ed. F. Devon (London, 1837), p. 281.

62 *Complete Peerage*, V, 729. According to the *Traison et Mort*, Bolingbroke entrusted Richard to Humphrey and to the heir of the earl of Arundel at Chester on 19 August: *Chronicles of the Revolution 1397–1400*, ed. C. Given-Wilson (Manchester, 1993), p. 151. Another chronicle gives Humphrey as being drowned on the return from Ireland (*Historia Vitae et Regni Ricardi Secundi*, ed. G. B. Stow (Pennsylvania, 1977), p. 155.

63 *CPR, 1396–9*, p. 593, letters patent issued *Teste Rege* at Coventry on 26 August.

by his father the evening before.[64] He may have been present when Richard 'abdicated' on 30 September, although this is not noted in the official Record and Process.

Henry the Prince

With his father's acceptance as king, Henry was on the verge of transformation from a landless noble heir to prince. On 15 October, two days after the coronation, it was announced in parliament by the archbishop of Canterbury that it was proposed to create him Prince of Wales, duke of Cornwall and earl of Chester. The Lords and Commons were asked whether they wished to consent to this and to accept him as heir to his father to the crown of England. They did.

> The king, sitting on his throne in full parliament, placed a coronet on the head of the said Henry, his eldest son, and placed a gold ring on his finger, and put a golden staff into his hand, and then kissed him, and gave him his charter concerning these things. And thus he made him prince of Wales, duke of Cornwall, and earl of Chester, and then he caused him to be led, thus arrayed by the duke of York, uncle to our said lord the king, to the seat ordained and assigned to him in parliament by reason of the aforesaid principality.[65]

There was no precedent for this simultaneous creation or such a ceremony. The king was intent upon ensuring that the new royal line was authenticated by all means possible. On 23 October, again within parliament, Henry IV gave his son another title.[66] The lords were asked by the archbishop if the Prince should be styled duke of Aquitaine. All agreed that he should. Behind this creation lay the baggage of the past, especially the granting of the duchy to John of Gaunt in 1390. Henry wished to assure all that there was no intention of alienating Aquitaine outside the main royal line. By creating Henry duke of Aquitaine it also confirmed the Lancastrians as the royal dynasty since the duchy had been held by the heirs of previous kings. Yet Henry did not hold the duchy in the same way as these predecessors. He never possessed any lands in, or gained any revenues from, the duchy. Nor did he ever visit it, although that may have been the initial plan which had provoked the creation at this point.[67]

---

[64] *Chronicle of Adam Usk*, ed. Given-Wilson, pp. 71–3.
[65] *PROME*, VIII, 33–4.
[66] Ibid., 34–5.
[67] All Souls College, Oxford, MS 182, fol. 197b, printed in H. G. Richardson and G. O. Sayles, 'Parliamentary Documents from Formularies', *BIHR* 11 (1933–4), 147–62. 'The points of the articles discussed between the lords and commons of parliament on the eve

On 10 November it was also agreed in the parliament that the Prince should hold the title 'duke of Lancaster'. The argument here was that since Henry IV had become king, he could not include the title duke of Lancaster in his style. Yet he wished to continue the title since it had been borne by his father and many illustrious forebears. The king therefore ordained, with the assent of the Lords and Commons, that his son should have the title, and also the liberties and franchises held by his predecessors as dukes and earls of Lancaster, to hold for himself and his heirs 'completely separated from the crown of England'. A charter was shown in the parliament and given to Prince Henry.[68]

Yet as with Aquitaine, the Prince never actually held the lands of the duchy of Lancaster or enjoyed its value in the same way as his grandfather had done. Henry IV retained the revenues for himself, despite the fact that the parliamentary grant said that he should hold the liberties and franchises of the duchy *disseverez de la corone dEngleterre quitement et entierment*.[69] Only on 15 June 1411 was the Prince granted any landed interest in the duchy. This came in the form of a life grant of some duchy lands in Lincolnshire.[70] Their value, at £168 per annum, was small, especially compared with the value of his estates in Wales, Chester and Cornwall. However, their location is significant in the light of the location of some of the foreign manors of the duchy of Cornwall in the same county. It is also noteworthy that the grant was made when the Prince was prominent on the royal council. It might point to the Prince's increased financial needs at this stage of his life. He also seems to have had some unspecified interest in the duchy of Lancaster manor of Knaresborough. It is listed in a valor of the Prince's estates of 1404 and valued at £500 but with the note that it was 'in the hands of the king as of the duchy of Lancaster, and there is no revenue' (*in manibus Regis ut de ducatu Lancastrie et remanet nichil*). Whilst Henry's landed and financial interests in the duchy of Lancaster were limited, his itinerary shows that he took advantage of his

of All Saints [31 October], to be shown to our most dread lord the king by the aforesaid lords. Item, touching the eldest son of the king, who has been created prince in this parliament, that it be entered and enrolled as of record that this was done by assent of the commons in parliament, for greater security, etc. Item, the said prince should not leave the realm at such a tender age until peace has been more securely established within the kingdom, etc.'

68 *PROME*, VIII, 37–8. For the charter, see *Charters of the Duchy of Lancaster*, ed. W. Hardy (London, 1845), pp. 102–40.

69 *PROME*, VIII, 37. The seal used by the king in the duchy was termed *Sigillum Henrici dei gratia regis Anglie de ducatu Lancastrie* (Somerville, *Duchy*, p. 145).

70 TNA, DL 29/731/12016; TNA, DL 42/16 part 2, fol. 61v, noted in Castor, *King, Crown and Duchy of Lancaster*, p. 32 (although in Somerville, *Duchy*, p 165, the reference is given as TNA, DL 42/16 fol. 102v, 15 June 1411). Humphrey was given the profits of Castle Donington and of Risley and Allerton wapentakes on 15 January 1410 (TNA, DL 42/16 fol. 60v, cited in Somerville, *Duchy*, p. 165). These areas had been alienated to Edmund, earl of Kent, and his descendants, but returned to the duchy in 1408 (ibid., p. 173).

father's duchy holdings by spending a great deal of time in the principal seats, not least Kenilworth and Leicester. Indeed he spent more time in duchy castles and houses, and at Westminster, than in his own lands. That said, we also see Henry IV at places within the Prince's possessions, such as Wallingford, Kennington and Berkhamsted.[71]

Henry had become Prince unexpectedly. He did not have any of the trappings expected of a prince of the realm, and may not, on his return from Ireland, have had many servants. This had to be rectified. Although this is an assumption based on an undated and damaged membrane in the Chancery Miscellanea, it could be that there was an early emergency arrangement made for the establishment of his household and stable, allocating two gentlemen with eight horses, two yeomen with six horses and one groom.[72] In material from the privy council records, also undated but undoubtedly early in the reign, we have a report that the Prince was not provided with *toute manere arraye* as appropriate for his household. A list follows: *chapelles, chambres, sales, stoff pur sa garderobe, panetre, buter, cusyne, squiller, saucer, almoigner, avoigner, et generalement de toutes choses et necessaries apurrtenantz a menage.*[73] The relevant officers of the royal household were instructed to fulfil the council's orders to remedy this situation. We have a further insight into how the Prince's accoutrements were built up thanks to the fall-out of a usurpation: in February 1400 forfeited plate was given to him at royal command.[74] On 11 November 1399, Henry IV exempted his son from payment of issues of the seal in chancery.[75]

The creations of Henry as Prince, earl and duke in parliament in October–November 1399 were deliberate efforts to confirm, as Lancastrian, not only the present but also the future. This was by necessity as much as intention, since the Prince was underage. Indeed, his youth could be seen as offering political advantage to Henry IV in the early years of the reign. The Prince would technically be the holder of the lands which were associated with his titles, since the feudal rules of minorities did not apply to lands held by the heir to the throne. But parental interference in the establishment of the Prince's appanage was wholly to be expected given his age and the circumstances under which the new dynasty had come to power.

It is also important to remember that some actions concerning his future lands had occurred before his appanage was established. Bolingbroke's intervention pre-dates even the deposition of Richard II. This was hardly surprising in the case of the earldom of Chester which had been courted by Richard and elevated into a principality, and over which Henry needed to

---

[71] See, for instance, the places of issue noted in *Calendar of Signet Letters of Henry IV and Henry V*, ed. J. L. Kirby (London, 1978).

[72] TNA, C 47/3/53/14. This document also refers to John and Thomas.

[73] *POPC*, II, 42.

[74] *CPR, 1399–1401*, p. 198.

[75] Ibid., p. 86.

impose immediate control. John Trevor, bishop of St Asaph, was appointed as chamberlain of Chester, Flintshire and North Wales on 16 August, whilst Henry was at Chester.[76] On 1 November, a month after the accession of Henry IV, Trevor was confirmed in office, but by the king not the Prince. Henry Percy (Hotspur) was appointed by the king as justiciar of Chester on 29 October 1399 but had occupied the office from at least 13 October.[77] The Prince's confirmation of this appointment under the seal of the earldom dates to 14 May 1400. There were further early changes at demesne level where offices had previously been granted by Richard as instruments of patronage. At Macclesfield, for instance, Peter de Legh (captured and executed on 12 August at Chester as he tried to escape disguised as monk) was replaced as steward by Sir Thomas Wensley. The initial appointment was made by the king on 13 October and enrolled in the patent rolls, and was confirmed by the Prince under the seal of the earldom on 20 January 1400.[78] These examples reflect the state of emergency both before and after the usurpation, and the time needed to establish administration in the name of the Prince after his titles had been assigned. A similar situation prevailed in the duchy of Cornwall. Here too the appointment of a Lancastrian nominee predated Richard's deposition. On 29 September, 'Teste rege ... by the advice of duke of Lancaster and with the assent of the council', John Wynter (or Winter) was appointed as steward of the duchy of Cornwall.[79] Wynter was confirmed in this office by Henry IV on 5 October. On 10 October Peter Hatton was appointed controller of what was still the king's receipt of the duchy.[80]

Until the grants to the Prince were made and implemented, Henry IV had a legal right to interfere, since, following Richard's deposition, all the lands of the subsequent princely appanage had come into his hands. This was to lead to some confusion. For instance, Henry IV granted William Beauchamp the manor and park of Cheylesmore (Warws.) 'by word of mouth', but on 2 December 1399 had to compensate him with a grant of a manor in Worcestershire, because the king had, since his grant to Beauchamp, given Cheylesmore (which was within the foreign manors of the duchy of Cornwall) to his son the Prince.[81] There were also several legal and financial nice-

---

[76] *CPR, 1396–9*, p. 591. TNA, CHES 2/73 m. 9 (4), *DKR*, XXXVI, 99, for appointment of Trevor 16 August, confirmed by the king on 1 November 1399 (TNA, CHES 2/74 m. 1 (1), DKR, XXXVI, 100). For his biography see J. Tait, 'John Trevor (d. 1410/1412)', rev. R. R. Davies, *ODNB*.

[77] TNA, CHES 2/74 m. 7 (4), *DKR*, XXXVI, 379. Confirmed in office by Prince Henry on 14 May 1400 (TNA, SC 6/774/11 m. 3).

[78] P. Morgan, *War and Society in Medieval Cheshire 1277–1403*, Chetham Society, 3rd series 34 (Manchester, 1987), p. 204; *CPR, 1399–1401*, p. 31; confirmation, TNA, SC 2/255/3 m.2; TNA, CHES 2/74 m. 2d (6), *DKR*, XXXVI, p. 312,.

[79] *CPR, 1396–9*, p. 595.

[80] *CPR, 1399–1401*, pp. 1, 10.

[81] Ibid., p. 118.

ties to transact in order for the lands of the Prince's appanage actually to pass into his control and for their revenues to fall to him. On 15 October, the date on which he was accorded his main titles, the king had to grant him separately the custody of lands arising from minorities and wardships in the principality of Wales and counties of Chester and Flint which Henry IV had enjoyed to that point as king.[82] On 8 November, the king granted his son all arrears he had received from these parts of his appanage save for those he had granted to other persons in the interim.[83]

It seems, however, that this was slow in taking effect, and had to be reissued a year later on 9 November 1400.[84] Enrolments of letters patent over the first nine months of the new reign demonstrate Henry IV's continuing involvement in the Prince's lands, even after it is known that the Prince had his own seals. It was the king who chose which of Richard II's annuities, payable out of the revenues of Chester, Wales and the duchy of Cornwall, to confirm.[85] The same applied to the alienations of manors. For instance, on 28 October, Margaret Sarnesfield was confirmed by the king in the Ricardian grants of the manor of Helstone and the boroughs of Bossiney and Trevere made in 1389 and 1395, as well as other annuities from the duchy of Cornwall.[86] These royal actions had an effect on the revenues which the Prince might enjoy from his lands in the future.

Royal involvement is also seen in the choice of the Prince's officials. Unless Richard's officials were continued in office, which happened at the lower levels of demesne administration, Lancastrians were placed into key roles in the Prince's new lands. We have seen this already with Peter Melbourne who appears as the Prince's chamberlain. Sir Thomas Wensley, whose appointment as steward of Macclesfield has already been noted, was a member of the retinue of Gaunt and subsequently of Bolingbroke, and was one of a large group of Derbyshire gentry who welcomed the latter on his arrival in July 1399. As well as Macclesfield, he had also been granted two stewardships in the duchy of Lancaster (High Peak and Chesterfield).[87] John Wynter, steward of the duchy of Cornwall, had been receiver of the duchy of Lancaster estates in Norfolk from 1396, and had married the sister-in-law of Bolingbroke's butler, John Payn.[88]

---

82 Ibid., p. 114.
83 Ibid., p. 61.
84 Ibid., p. 373. It was reissued again on 23 August 1401 (ibid., p. 544).
85 For two examples out of Cheshire revenues: Matthew Sweeteham, granted 12 June 1391, confirmed by Henry IV on 14 October 1399 (ibid., p. 47); Richard Redman, granted 2 October 1397, confirmed by Henry IV on 31 October 1399 (ibid., p. 47).
86 Ibid., p. 39.
87 *HP*, IV, 807–9. Somerville, *Duchy*, p. 136 note 5, thinks he was in exile with Bolingbroke and returned with him.
88 Castor, *King, Crown and Duchy of Lancaster*, p. 62. For his full biography see *HP*, IV, 929–31.

Another good example is Simon Bache. From 16 October 1400 he was treasurer of the Prince's household:[89] he continued to hold this post until at least 23 February 1404, appearing as controller of the Prince's Wardrobe in 1404–5.[90] Bache had been treasurer of the household of Bolingbroke from 1385 to 1399. Indeed it is possible that he retained this office until 20 May 1400.[91] As with Wensley and Wynter, we also see links with the duchy of Lancaster estates. Immediately after the usurpation (and perhaps also before it) Bache was receiver of the honour of Leicester. He continued to hold receiverships within the duchy of Lancaster estates, including Leicester, at the same time as he was treasurer of the Prince's household.[92] He probably knew Prince Henry from the moment of his birth. Mortimer notes that Bolingbroke spent the late summer of 1386 at Monmouth with close companions, including Bache, his treasurer.[93] The young Henry junior was born at Monmouth on 16 September 1386. Bache, like Melbourne, was a true Lancastrian.

There was undoubtedly a high-level of continuity in the Lancastrian family firm before and after the usurpation. There was also a transitional phase whilst the Prince's household metamorphosed from that of his father as duke. This may have taken up to a year. It is not until October 1400 that we have the first list of *prestita diversorum officiariorum hospicii domini Henrici principis Wallie* which shows the full range of officers and servants of the various parts of the princely household.[94] Until Bache was appointed as treasurer of the Prince's household, all payments from the various parts of the Prince's lands were made to Thomas More, 'receiver general of moneys coming from the lands and possessions of Henry, prince of Wales'.[95] More had been receiver of Queen Anne in the previous reign, and was appointed royal treasurer of the king's household in 1402.[96]

---

89 TNA, E 101/404/16 m. 2.
90 TNA, E 101/404/16: Particulars of account of Simon Bache as treasurer of the household of the Prince of Wales (m. 2, 16 October 1400 to 30 September 1401; m. 3 1 October 1401 to 30 September 1402; m. 4, 1 October 1402 to 30 September 1403; m. 5, view of account 1 October 1403 to 24 February 1404). See also TNA, E 101/404/23 for his fuller account as treasurer of the Prince's household from 1 October 1402 to 30 September 1403. He was still in office as controller of the Prince's Wardrobe in 1405 (E 101/405/26).
91 Somerville, *Duchy*, p. 386.
92 *CPR, 1399–1401*, p. 21 (21 October 1399). Somerville, *Duchy*, p. 562. He remained in this office until at least 8 November 1401. See also Somerville, *Duchy*, pp. 565, 588, for his accounting as receiver of Leicester castle and of Higham Ferrers and other manors 1400–2. His support was well rewarded. On 5 October 1399 he was granted, as king's clerk, the prebendary of Thame in the cathedral of Lincoln (*CPR, 1399–1401*, p. 1). On 4 July 1401 he was amongst those whose good estate was to be prayed for in the chantry at St Martin's Leicester alongside the king and his children (*CPR, 1399–1401*, p. 371).
93 Mortimer, *Fears of Henry IV*, p. 64.
94 TNA, E 101/404/16, m. 2.
95 TNA, SC 6/1222/9 m. 4 (South Wales); SC 6/774/11 m. 3d; 791/1 m. 11 (Chester).
96 TNA, SC 6/805/1 m. 3; SC 6 805/5 m. 4; Wylie, *Henry the Fourth*, I, 301.

What of the Prince's financial position in the first year of the new reign? Further detailed research is needed on the surviving accounts, as well as interpolations from earlier and later accounts to fill gaps in knowledge, but some basic points can be made. It is apparent that the income from Prince Henry's newly acquired lands was constrained by past and current decisions. Richard II, in common with subsequent kings without male heirs of their body, tended towards an arm's-length approach to the principality of Wales, duchy of Cornwall and earldom of Chester. This led to alienations, even in the duchy despite the charter of its creation laying down that its estates were never to be dismembered or granted to anyone other than the duke.[97] Richard had retained most of the deer parks in Cornwall (of which there were seven),[98] and its castles, but had shown little interest in the assessionable manors.[99] Therefore only nine of the seventeen passed to Prince Henry.[100] The rest had been granted by Richard to his half-brother, John Holland, earl of Huntingdon (d.1400), and his wife, Elizabeth, sister of Henry IV (d.1425). Despite her husband's involvement in the Epiphany plot of 1400, Elizabeth kept these manors as her jointure. This situation was not resolved until April 1404, when, in parliament, Elizabeth recognized the lands as belonging to the Prince, and he granted them formally to her and her new husband, Sir John Cornwall, whom she had married before December 1400.[101] The net receipts from the duchy in the last year of Richard's reign were just over £549.[102]

There is relatively little surviving information for the foreign manors of the duchy. We know that Henry IV had alienated the manor of Isleworth

---

[97] Hatcher, *Rural Economy and Society*, pp. 6–7.
[98] Ibid., p. 179 sq.
[99] Ibid., pp. 6–7, 137.
[100] Ibid., pp. 149–50. These were widely scattered with three in the south-east, Rillaton, Climsland and Liskeard; two in the north-east, Helstone-in-Triggshire and Penmayne; two in the centre, Tybesta and 97 acres at Talskiddy; and two in the west, Tywarnhail and Helston-in-Kirrier.
[101] The Prince was still under age at this point, therefore his warranty was not effective in law to give a secure title to Elizabeth and her husband. As a result, he pledged before king and parliament that when he came of age he would give secure title to them for Elizabeth's lifetime. His brothers made a similar oath in case they were ever to come into possession of the duchy. The king confirmed the grant made by the Prince: *PROME*, VIII, 248–50. These lands were Tremanton, Calstock, Asborough, Restormel, Penlyn, Penknyth, Lostwithiel and Camelford, Tewynton, Moresek, Tintagel and the fishery of the Fowey. Sir John had right to keep them after Elizabeth's death in return for 100 marks (Hatcher, *Rural Economy*, p. 198, citing TNA, SC6/813/22). John Holland had also held, by Richard II's grant, the town of Northwich within the earldom of Chester but this had been exchanged for other lands before 1399. On 12 May 1418 it was 'restored' to Elizabeth and her son John (d.1447), who had recently been restored by Henry V to the earldom of Huntingdon (Curry, 'Demesne of the County Palatine', p. 235 sq).
[102] SC 6/813/17 m. 3.

(Middlesex) to Henry Bowet on 13 October, before the grant of the duchy of Cornwall to his son. This reduced the potential income by 100 marks,[103] but gross income from the foreign manors in Berkshire and Oxfordshire in the first year of the Prince's control was £210. Of this, £129 was spent on fees and annuities, leaving little profit.[104] Richard had remitted half of the Wallingford fee farm for twenty years from June 1396 because of the plague and poverty of the town. This was confirmed by Henry IV on 5 February 1400.[105] Other manors had been alienated by Richard, or by Henry IV, although in the case of Watlington, the holder, Thomas Gloucester was forced to pay arrears because his letters of royal grant were invalid, having been made after the creation of the Prince – another example of confusion caused by the new king's initial involvement. Many Ricardian annuities were confirmed and continued, including that to Thomas Chaucer which reduced the income from the Wallingford fee farm by a further 20 marks. It was Henry IV himself who had made the confirmation on 23 October 1399.[106] This was also the case in the earldom of Chester where twenty-one existing annuities were confirmed, including three which dated back to the time of the Black Prince.[107] But the change of dynasty also led to new disbursements in patronage. We see a particularly poignant grant of 100 shillings from the revenues of Carmarthen on 4 May 1400 to Joanna Waryn, formerly nurse to Prince Henry, and her husband John.[108]

The earldom of Chester, along with Flintshire, paid £353 out of the net income of £530 to the Prince's receiver-general in the first year of the reign, plus £100 from old debts.[109] In North Wales, Robert Parys was appointed as chamberlain under the Prince's seal on 6 July 1400.[110] In South Wales, John Merbury acted as receiver but his account only starts on 31 March 1400.[111] This again suggests some delay in the transition of regimes. We can gain some idea of potential income from the accounts of 1397–8. North Wales had an income of £542 from demesne receipts and £200 from taxation, which produced a net income after expenses of £455.[112] South Wales saw total demesne receipts of £1,544 but the expenses section of the account is incomplete.[113]

Such evidence as survives suggests that the Prince's income in the first

103   *CPR, 1399–1401*, p. 195.
104   TNA, SC 6/1096/14.
105   *CPR, 1399–1401*, p. 201.
106   Ibid., p. 33. Chaucer was confirmed as constable of the castle on 16 October (ibid., p. 15), and steward of the honour on 26 October (ibid., p. 34).
107   Curry, 'Demesne of the County Palatine', p. 241.
108   TNA, SC 6/1222/9 m. 3.
109   TNA, SC 6/774/11 m. 3d, SC 6 /791/1 m. 11.
110   TNA, SC 6/1216/1.
111   TNA, SC 6/1222/9.
112   TNA, SC 6/1215/10.
113   TNA, SC 6/1222/8.

year of his father's reign was at least £1,500, with unknown income from South Wales and most of the foreign manors of the duchy of Cornwall. There is evidence, however, of some paternal assistance. For instance, he was still being supplied with hay and oats at royal expense in July and November 1400,[114] and being paid sums from the exchequer.[115] Whilst he had his own residences, most notably at Kennington, he also had a suite at Westminster with its own chapel.[116]

Conclusion

The establishment of the appanage of Prince Henry was therefore an integral part of the establishment of the Lancastrian dynasty. Not surprisingly, given the age of the Prince and the circumstances of the usurpation, the hand of Henry IV is seen at every point, and most noticeably in appointments made to the Prince's household and administration. The Prince could simply reflect on his good fortune and on the potential which his lands would offer in the future, both in support of his lifestyle and in the exercise of his own patronage in due course. It was not expected, of course, that the Prince would face, over subsequent years, serious financial difficulties as well as huge responsibilities in the defence of his lands. The Welsh wars had a major effect on the Prince's revenues. In this respect, yet also helpful in providing an idea of the financial potential of his lands more broadly, we are fortunate to have a valor for the Prince's estates which was drawn up between November 1403 and June 1404. This put the gross annual value of his lands at £10,758 12s. 9¾d.[117] Demesne expenses and annuities immediately consumed £2,742 10s. 1¾d. of this. However, by this point in time, the Welsh rebellion had caused the loss of all of the Prince's revenues from North and South Wales and Flintshire, a loss which was deemed to total £5,613 17s. 6d. As a result, only £2,404 7s. 1½d. remained, out of which Henry was expected to meet the usual expenses of his household and Wardrobe and to maintain his castles and manors in England, as well as to ensure the adequate defence of his castles and towns in Wales.

---

114 *CPR, 1399–1401*, pp. 327 (28 July, 200 cartloads of hay, possibly for the Scottish campaign), 372 (13 November, 400 qtrs of oats to be taken to Kennington). See also ibid., p. 412 for provision of carriage of harness and victuals of the Prince from London to Chester.

115 *CPR, 1399–1401*, p. 523, pardon to the Prince of £200 paid to him by the king in May 1401 and delivered to his esquire, Robert Castell. That said, the issue rolls for the first two years of the reign do not record any payments to the Prince from the royal exchequer.

116 *CPR, 1399–1401*, p. 388.

117 TNA, SC 11/862, abstracted in Curry, 'Cheshire and the Royal Demesne', Appendix. For the dating of the valor see Griffiths, 'Military Career', p. 71, and Curry, 'Demesne of the County Palatine', p. 288 sq.

The same valor gave the cost of garrisoning and victualing these Welsh places as £2,903. Therefore he was in deficit to the tune of £500 12s. 10½d. even before he began to meet his regular expenses.

The solution which was applied was the diversion of Cheshire revenues to support some of the Welsh costs.[118] This was only made possible by the raising of taxation in Cheshire as a fine for the involvement of men of the county in Hotspur's rebellion of 1403. It also necessitated an aggressive campaign to increase demesne revenues in the earldom and to collect arrears. It also meant that some annuities were allowed to go unpaid. Cheshire revenues were not enough, however, to cover all the costs: expenses exceeded receipts in four of the remaining years of the reign. Some moneys were paid into the Chester exchequer by John Waterton, keeper of the Prince's secret treasury, in order to assist with Welsh garrison expenses, but these were small-scale compared with the costs.[119] Revenues from Flintshire were disrupted to 1406 at least, but the income from that area increased considerably after 1407, being boosted also by fines for participation in the revolt. Revenues in north Wales recovered slowly. In 1408 John Bolde as constable of Conway still continued to receive part of his fee from Chester, although it was now possible for £60 to be payable at Caernarvon. Payments to the Prince's household from Cheshire revenues could be resumed in 1409–10, and in 1411 money could be drawn on the Cheshire exchequer for support of the Prince's troops which he was sending with the earl of Arundel to the duke of Burgundy.[120]

This is, of course, taking the picture into years well beyond the first establishment of the Prince's appanage, but it provides a useful contrast with the relatively easy transfer of the lands to the Prince in 1399–1400. As is well known, Prince Henry was chronically short of funds when campaigning in Wales, even though exchequer funds were paid for his support.[121] His household was running a deficit of over £360 in the spring of 1404.[122] The Prince shared fully in the financial difficulties of his father's reign. What effects this had on his relations with his father, and on his ability to finance the creation of his own affinity, remain important questions to pursue. Much research still remains to be done, but there is no doubt that the financial records can provide important insights. For instance, an initial study of new grants of

---

118 Curry, 'Demesne of the County Palatine', pp. 284–96.
119 TNA, SC 6/775 m. 2.
120 TNA, SC 6/775 m. 12.
121 *POPC*, II, 62–3. Between 17 April and 14 July 1403, for example, the exchequer contributed £5,323 6s. 8d. to his costs in comparison with the £1,851 from his own resources (TNA, E 101/404/24 fol. 2). For general discussion see R. R. Davies, *The Revolt of Glyn Dŵr* (Oxford, 1995), p. 260, and for further detail R. Griffiths, 'Prince Henry, Wales and the Royal Exchequer 1400–13', *Bulletin of the Board of Celtic Studies* 32 (1985), 202–16; and R. Griffiths, 'Prince Henry's War: Armies, Garrisons and Supply during the Glyndŵr Rising', *Bulletin of the Board of Celtic Studies* 34 (1987), 165–74.
122 TNA, E 101/404/16 m. 5.

annuities from his estate revenues reveals that Prince Henry began to spend much more on patronage from the autumn of 1407. Fifty-one new grants of annuities were made in the year following Michaelmas 1407, the average for the previous six years being less than ten per annum.[123] We can suggest, therefore, that it was not until he turned twenty-one that a truly independent prince was made.

---

[123] Griffiths, 'Military Career and Affinity', Appendix, with additional input from a study of surviving account rolls for the various parts of the Prince's lands.

2

Henry V's Establishment: Service, Loyalty and Reward in 1413[1]

Gwilym Dodd

> That I have turn'd away my former self;
> So will I those that kept me company.
> (William Shakespeare, *Henry IV*, pt II, Act V, scene v)

To whom did Henry V turn to help establish his rule in the early years of his reign? This, in essence, is the question which I shall address in the following discussion. It centres on the dynamics of the transition of power and the relative balance between continuity and change that can be observed by considering who the 'winners' and who the 'losers' were in 1413. The subject of who Henry retained in his company once he became king holds special interest in light of his reputation as a play-boy Prince who kept bad company and lived a life of excess. There is the well-known account in the *Brut* which suggested that Henry had a lot of growing up to do in 1413. Fully aware of his shortcomings, Henry is said to have purged himself of those who had led him astray during his more carefree days as Prince – men who had addressed him with the sort of inappropriate familiarity for which Richard II had been criticized at the end of his reign – before surrounding himself with only those individuals who he could count on to give him sound advice and counsel. The passage is worth citing at length because it has clearly influenced historical interpretations of Henry (beginning, most notably, with Shakespeare's creation of the well-known fictional character, Sir John Falstaff, to whom Henry addressed the words quoted above), and because it encapsulates precisely the issues which I would like to explore in this chapter:

> And before he was Kyng, what tyme he regnyd Prince of Walyes, he fylle
> & yntendyd gretly to ryot, and drew to wylde company ... & lykewyse all
> his meyne of his housolde was attending & plesyd with his governaunce,

---

[1] I would like to thank Christopher Allmand, Shelagh Mitchell, John Milner, Tony Pollard, Anthony Tuck and Matt Ward for kindly reading through and commenting on earlier drafts of this chapter.

out-sept iij men of his howsolde, which were ful hevy and sory of his governaunce ... And thane he beganne to regne for Kyng, & he remembryd þe gret charge & wourship þat he shulde take upon hym; And anon he comaundyd al his peple þat were attendaunt to his mysgovernaunce afore tyme, & al his housolde, to come before hym. And whan they herde þat, they were ful glad, for they subposyd þat he woolde a promotyd them in-to gret offices, & þat they shulde a stoned in gret favyr & truste with hym, & nearest of counsel, as they were afore tyme ... some of them wynked on hym, & some smylyd, & thus they made nyse semblaunte unto hym, meny one of them. But for al þat, þe Prynce kept his countynaunce ful sadly unto them, And sayde to them: 'Syrys, ye are þe peple þat I have cherysyd & mayntynyd in Ryot & wylde governaunce; and here I geve yow all in commaundment, & charge yow, þat from this day forward þat ye forsake al mysgovernaunce, & lyve aftyr þe lawys of Almyhety God, & aftyr þe lawys of oure londe ... And thus he voydyd al his housolde, saving tho iij personys þat he hatyd most, whiche were ful sory of his governaunce; & them he lovyd aftyrward best, for þere good counsayle and good governaunce, & made them aftyrward gret lordys'.[2]

The account finishes by stating that the king repopulated his household with twelve men of 'good disposicyoun' sent to him by his grandmother Joan, countess of Hereford.[3] There may be good grounds to suspect that this story is in large measure apocryphal, for it too conveniently closes the door on the more controversial earlier part of Henry's life, whilst paving the way to his later achievements and glory. What is more, Henry is shown to have affected this crucial transition himself, thus saving his honour and reputation: he had become a new man, fit for a new reign *of his own volition*.

Tracing the origins of the story suggests other perspectives, however. This particular account was included in a version of the *Brut* written anonymously sometime in 1478–9.[4] The tale was not entirely without precedent, for earlier works included briefer references to the change that apparently overtook Prince Henry's character at his accession. William Caxton alluded to it in his own continuation of the *Brut*, probably written after 1470, which described how the Prince turned from a 'wild and recheles' youth into 'a new man ... entent to lyve vertuously'.[5] Yet the story had earlier precedents. John Hardyng, writing in the 1450s, included an account of the transformation of

---

[2] *The Brut or The Chronicles of England*, ed. F. W. D. Brie, 2 vols., EETS OS 131 and 136 (London, 1908), II, 594–5.

[3] The author confuses Joan Bohun for Catherine Swynford.

[4] The original manuscript is Lambeth Palace Library (MS 84). For a description, see L. M. Matheson, *The Prose* Brut: *The Development of a Middle English Chronicle* (Tempe AZ, 1998), pp. 309–11.

[5] *Brut*, II, 494. See L. M. Matheson, 'Printer and Scribe: Caxton, the *Polychronicon*, and the *Brut*', *Speculum* 60 (1985), 593–614 (esp. pp. 607–9).

the Prince's character.[6] It is also to be found, briefly, in the *Vita Henrici Quinti*, written by the Italian humanist Tito Livio in 1437–8, as well as in the *Vita et Gesta Henrici Quinti* which is now thought to have been written slightly earlier than Livio's work in the mid-1430s.[7] The earliest explicit reference is to be found in the chronicle of Thomas Walsingham, which recorded: '[i]n truth, no sooner did he [Henry V] assume the honours of kingship than he became a changed man, dedicated to honour, propriety, and dignity of demeanour, ignoring no kind of virtue even when he did not desire to make it his own'.[8] There is a hint – though not much more of a hint – of a change in Henry's character in the *Gesta Henrici Quinti*, written *c.*1417, which suggested that it was only upon his accession to the throne that Henry displayed the piety that was expected of a man of his royal status:

> For this prince, after he had first taken his seat upon the throne of the kingdom, wrote out for himself the law of Deuteronomy in the volume of his breast.... For from the very beginning of his assumption of governance, so fervently had he been devoted to the hearing of divine praises and to his own private prayers that once he had begun them there was not anyone, even from amongst his nobles and magnates, who was able by conversation, however brief, at any time to interrupt them.[9]

These remarks, and especially Walsingham's, indicate that the idea that 1413 marked an important change in the quality of Henry's character existed before the king's death in 1422. Indeed, they may indicate contemporary unease about his actions before the accession; Walsingham clearly felt this period of the king's life needed to be addressed and explained.

Interestingly, the author of the *Brut* manuscript seems to have been the first to articulate the more elaborate version of the tale which sees the Prince change the people with whom he had associated: this detail does not appear in the chronicles of Hardyng or Walsingham, nor in the *Vita et Gesta* or Livio's *Vita*. It was, however, included in *The First English Life of King Henry the Fifth*, written anonymously in 1513–14.[10] The relevant passage in this work reads as follows:

---

6   *The Chronicle of John Hardyng*, ed. H. Ellis (London, 1812), p. 372
7   *Titi Livii Foro-Juliensis Vita Henrici Quinti, Regis Angliae*, ed. T. Hearne (Oxford, 1716), p. 4; *Thomae de Elmham vita et gesta Henrici quinti ...*, ed. T. Hearne (Oxford, 1727), p. 12. For a general description, see C. L. Kingsford, *English Historical Literature in the Fifteenth Century* (New York, 1913), chapter 3. For the dating of the *Vita et Gesta*, see D. Rundle, 'The Unoriginality of Tito Livio Frulovisi's *Vita Henrici Quinti*', EHR 123 (2008), 1109–131.
8   Thomas Walsingham, *The St. Albans Chronicle, Volume II, 1394–1422*, ed. J. Taylor, W. R. Childs and L. Watkiss (Oxford, 2011), pp. 620–1.
9   GHQ, p. 155.
10 *The First English Life of King Henry the Fifth*, ed. C. L. Kingsford (Oxford, 1911).

amongst the first acte of his Coronacion called unto him all those younge Lordes and gentlemen that were the followers of his younge acts, and had tofore bin most familiar with him, to everie of whome severally he gave right rich and bounteous giftes, whereby they were all right greatkly inhaunced in substaunce. And then he commaunded them that they that woulde change theire life and conversacion in like manner as he intended to doe shoulde abide with him and continewe in his Court. And to all them that woulde persever in their former light conversacion he gave expresse commaundement upon paine of theire heads never after that daye to come to his presence.[11]

A significant portion of *First English Life* was translated from Livio's *Vita Henrici Quinti*.[12] But this passage evidently was not.[13] Instead, it seems likely to have derived from a now lost account of the reign of Henry V compiled by, or at the behest of, James Butler, earl of Ormond (1392–1452).[14] The *First English Life* contains a number of stories which the compiler directly attributes to Ormond, and at the start of the section that deals with the Prince's ill-starred youth, he affirms the veracity of his account by referring to Ormond as well as the 'common fame' of the ensuing tale. It is quite possible that the author of the *Brut* manuscript cited above also drew on the same source. That the story of the Prince's unsuitable companions originated in an account penned by the earl of Ormond gains a measure of plausibility when we consider that Ormond served with the Prince's brother, Thomas, duke of Clarence, in the latter's expedition to France in 1412–13. Clarence had been given command of the expedition after the Prince had disgraced himself by seeming to plot a coup against the king.[15] The sentiments expressed in the *Brut* and *First English Life* thus resonate with a view that could well have been prevalent within Clarence's circle; that is to say, that Prince Henry's rash and ill-considered political machinations in the closing years of his father's reign were a consequence of his mixing with bad company. The *Brut* adds a further important detail by alluding to three persons whom Henry was said to have 'hated most' when he had been Prince, but who then became 'great lords' during his reign. The obvious candidates are Henry's three younger brothers – Thomas, John and Humphrey – who were not close to Henry before 1413, but who showed great loyalty to their older brother thereafter.[16] Although

---

[11] Ibid., p. 19.

[12] Ibid., pp. xiv–xv.

[13] The modern edition is unclear on this, for the story falls between sections ascribed to 'Titus Liuius' and the 'Translator' respectively. A comparison with the *Vita Henrici Quinti* confirms the point, however.

[14] *First English Life*, ed. Kingsford, p. xvii.

[15] P. McNiven, 'Prince Henry and the English Political Crisis of 1412', *History* 65 (1980), 1–16.

[16] Given the input which Humphrey is considered to have had in the compilation of Livio's *Vita* it is noteworthy that no suggestion was made in this work that Prince Henry gathered

Thomas was made duke of Clarence by Henry IV in 1412, it was not until 1414, when Henry V was on the throne, that John and Humphrey received the titles which befitted their status as princes of the royal blood, that is to say, as the dukes of Bedford and Gloucester respectively.[17]

If these deductions are correct then we have the source for this story but not necessarily the proof of its accuracy. Ormond may simply have conveyed a sense of bitterness felt by Clarence and a sizeable portion of the political community at the wilful and irresponsible actions of the young Prince at the end of Henry IV's reign. Blaming unnamed and unsuitable companions, whom the Prince was said to have banished anyway, was a convenient way of letting him off the hook whilst upholding the underlying impropriety of his actions. On the other hand, we should not assume that the tale was simply literary flourish. By 1413, largely as a result of his military leadership in Wales, the Prince was surrounded by a sizeable and well-defined group of close friends and associates.[18] But the Prince's own record was mired in controversy, and it is quite possible that he felt under pressure to shed some of his former associates in order to regain political credibility as well as public confidence at the time of accession. Certainly, Henry's position in 1413 was not an easy one. Notwithstanding the earl of Cambridge's botched rebellion in 1415, his dynastic position appears to have been fairly secure, but he inherited a political community whose unity and sense of common purpose had, largely as a result of his own actions, come under severe strain, and especially in the final months of his father's reign there were worrying signs of political fracture. There is a particularly telling remark from a contemporary chronicler who claimed that Henry V was crowned (*only*) 'with the agreement of the greater part of the lords of the realm'.[19] Perhaps this is why, within three days of his accession, but over two weeks before the coronation, there occurred a highly unusual form of reconciliation between the new king and members of the political community, then gathered for parliament, in which the latter swore oaths of allegiance to their new sovereign and Henry himself promised

around him unsuitable companions whilst shunning his brothers, so if Clarence held this view it does not seem to have been shared by his youngest brother: R. Weiss, 'Humphrey duke of Gloucester and Tito Livio Frulovisi', in *Fritz Saxl, 1890–1948*, ed. D. J. Gordon (London, 1957), pp. 218–27; A. Petrina, *Cultural Politics in Fifteenth Century England: The Case of Humphrey Duke of Gloucester* (Leiden, 2004), pp. 327–32.

[17] For the precise dating and full titles see p. 16, fn. 20 of Anne Curry's chapter in this volume.

[18] The key work on the Prince's affinity is W. R. M. Griffiths, 'The Military Career and Affinity of Henry, Prince of Wales, 1399–1413' (unpublished M.Litt. thesis, University of Oxford, 1988). Griffiths estimates that at least 150 men received annuities from Henry of Monmouth in the course of his father's reign, and eighteen individuals were formally retained (p. 185). For an account of the Prince's activities in Wales, see R. Griffiths, 'Prince Henry and Wales, 1400–1408', in *Profit, Piety and the Professions in Later Medieval England*, ed. M. Hicks (Gloucester, 1990), pp. 51–61; Allmand, *Henry V*, chapter 3.

[19] Kingsford, *English Historical Literature*, p. 284.

to rule for the honour of God and the prosperity of the whole realm.[20] Gerald Harriss's comment that 'Henry V began his [rule] acutely conscious of the insecurity of his position' may well have a considerable ring of truth in it.[21]

Thus we should not be lulled into thinking that the smooth transfer of power between father and son which occurred in 1413 made decisions about who should retain their positions and who could be displaced by 'new men' especially straightforward. Coming to the throne in the prime of his life with a ready-made entourage, whose members – or at least those whom Henry chose to keep – could neatly slot into the broader framework of royal governance, put Henry V at a distinct advantage in comparison to kings like Richard II and Henry VI, whose bonds of friendship and trust had to be forged in the far more complex circumstances of their personal rule, but it also inevitably meant that many of those who had enjoyed positions of favour and influence under Henry IV would probably be displaced by the Prince's own men. This was not without some risk, as the case of Sir Thomas Grey illustrates. His involvement in the Southampton Plot of 1415, as one of the earl of Cambridge's key accomplices, is probably to be explained by the financial hardship he was suffering as a result of Henry's decision not to renew the annuity of £40 which he had received from Henry IV.[22] Henry's position in 1413, on succeeding his father, was thus not wholly dissimilar to the position his father faced in 1399: he needed to generate broad-based political consensus by expanding the basis of his support. He also needed to prove that he possessed the kingly virtues necessary to make his rule a success. At the same time, however, he had to reward those who had become his close friends and followers in the years before he came to power, because these were the men whose loyalty and service he could count on most.

What follows is based around a series of underlying questions, of which the most important is whether 1413 marked a significant turning point – both for Henry and for the scores of men who sought his grace and favour. Is there evidence that Henry turned his back on key supporters and friends when he became king? In more general terms, to what extent did the Lancastrian 'establishment' fundamentally reconfigure itself around the Prince's entourage? Or did the structures created under Henry IV remain essentially intact in 1413 because only a relatively small number of the Prince's men were brought in by the new king? This last question raises a number of subsidiary questions about the nature of political affiliation in this period. Above all, was there still, in 1413, a meaningful entity that we can describe as the Lancastrian 'establishment', whose collective sense of common purpose and iden-

---

20 *Vita et Gesta*, ed. Hearne, p. 16; *Vita Henrici Quinti*, ed. Hearne, p. 5; *First English Life*, ed. Kingsford, p. 18. Allmand regards this incident in a rather more optimistic light (*Henry V*, p. 64).

21 Harriss, *Cardinal Beaufort*, p. 68.

22 Pugh, *Southampton Plot*, pp. 102–5.

tity, forged in the crucible of usurpation, was strong enough to transcend the tensions and difficulties which had occurred at the very end of Henry IV's reign? Or did these tensions mark out new patterns of loyalty, to the extent that Henry consciously sought to exclude men who had shown unwavering loyalty to his father (or to Clarence)? Finally, how far did personal connections count in this period? Whilst we may expect the Prince to have promoted his closest associates to positions of importance in his regime, how far did these personal connections extend further down the line, to influence who belonged to the much broader group of individuals who considered themselves to be the 'king's men' – that is to say, those who belonged to what might loosely be termed the 'royal affinity'?

Charter Witnesses

A brief consideration of the witnesses to royal charters in the first months of Henry's reign provides the basis for some preliminary thoughts on these questions.[23] As a number of historians have shown, the names of the witnesses provide a good indication of the men who stood at the very centre of power, for there was probably a very close correlation between the names of the witnesses and the identity of the king's principal councillors.[24] The witness lists for the first twelve months of Henry V's reign not only show remarkable consistency – they also indicate that the senior members of Henry's regime were very much his own men. The chancellor, Bishop Henry Beaufort, and the treasurer, Thomas, earl of Arundel, feature in every list by virtue of their office: they were brought in by Henry to replace, respectively, Archbishop Arundel and Sir John Pelham.[25] This was straightforward political displacement: Archbishop Arundel and Pelham were key members of the 'court party' who had opposed the Prince from 1409, whereas Beaufort and Thomas Arundel could be counted amongst Henry's most important and loyal allies. The only other senior lay magnate to witness charters regularly in these early months was Richard, earl of Warwick, a nobleman who, along with Thomas Arundel, had developed very early associations with the Prince by virtue of his service in Wales.[26] He became his life retainer in 1410 (Thomas Arundel had achieved this distinction in 1407). The three bishops whose names regu-

---

[23] For a brief summary of the witnesses to Henry V's charters, see J. Catto, 'The King's Servants', in *Henry V*, ed. Harriss, pp. 88–9. The following paragraphs are based on my own survey of the original charter rolls for the first two years of Henry's reign (TNA, C 53/180–83).

[24] C. Given-Wilson, 'Royal Charter Witness Lists 1327–1399', *Medieval Prosopography* 12 (1991), 35–93 (p. 44).

[25] For Arundel, see G. L. Harriss, 'Fitzalan, Thomas, Fifth Earl of Arundel and Tenth Earl of Surrey (1381–1415)', *ODNB*. For Pelham, see *HP*, IV, 39–44.

[26] C. Carpenter, 'Beauchamp, Richard, Thirteenth Earl of Warwick (1382–1439)', *ODNB*.

larly appear on the charters – Thomas Langley of Durham, Nicholas Bubwith of Bath and Wells and Henry Chichele of St David's – also had a record of service to Henry, most notably as the three senior clerics who had been nominated to attend his council in May 1410 when Henry IV had withdrawn from the affairs of state due to illness.[27]

The two household officers regularly witnessing charters were Thomas Erpingham, who had been made steward of the new king's household in the place of Sir John Stanley, and Henry, Lord FitzHugh, who took the place of Richard, Lord Grey of Codnor as chamberlain. Erpingham's prominence is readily explained by the fact he had been an annuitant of the Prince since 1409.[28] On the other hand, nothing is known of FitzHugh's connections to Henry before 1413, which makes his almost instantaneous promotion especially impressive. FitzHugh was also appointed constable of England at the accession – an office usually held by a senior member of the nobility – and later, in 1415, he acted as one of the king's executors.[29] At fifty-five years old FitzHugh was a man of Henry IV's age, and was perhaps regarded as an important link to the older generation. He may even have been, to some extent, a substitute father figure for the young king, the latter anxious to draw on the wise counsel and experience of such a venerable member of the Lancastrian political elite.[30] FitzHugh may not have had the connections to the Prince to explain his promotion in 1413, but he certainly seems to have had personal qualities which would have appealed to Henry once he became king. For FitzHugh was the very personification of the chivalric knight, combining martial excellence (he was made a Knight of the Garter in 1408), with a strong crusading ethos (he went on campaign – like Henry IV – to Prussia in 1408–9, and then travelled to Rhodes in 1409–10 to aid the Knights of St John of Jerusalem).[31] He was exactly the sort of individual with whom the young king might have wished to have been associated, and the favour he was shown clearly indicates Henry's willingness to expand the group of individuals who formed his intimate circle. Some indication of the regard with which FitzHugh was held is shown by the fact that he was almost certainly the driving force behind Henry V's decision to establish the first Bridgettine house of nuns at Syon in March 1415.[32] Finally, of the great offices of state,

---

27 Allmand, *Henry V*, pp. 45–6. Langley did not serve and was replaced by Chichele. Beaufort, Warwick and Thomas Arundel also served.

28 S. Walker, 'Erpingham, Sir Thomas (*c.* 1355–1428)', *ODNB*; and A. Curry, 'Sir Thomas Erpingham: A Life in Arms', in *Agincourt 1415: Henry V, Sir Thomas Erpingham and the Triumph of the English Archers*, ed. A. Curry (Stroud, 2000), pp. 53–77. For FitzHugh, see A. C. Reeves, *Lancastrian Englishmen* (Washington DC, 1981), pp. 65–138, esp. pp. 84–6.

29 Wylie and Waugh, *Henry the Fifth*, I, 15, fn. 2. See also discussion on FitzHugh by Mark Arvanigian in this volume, p. 83.

30 I am grateful to Tony Pollard for this suggestion.

31 Reeves, *Lancastrian Englishmen*, pp. 80–1.

32 Allmand, *Henry V*, pp. 274–6.

only the keeper of the privy seal office, John Prophet, remained in place when Henry came to power. He too regularly witnessed charters in this period.

It should be evident then that Henry surrounded himself with men he knew and could depend on. These were not, however, men rashly promoted to positions for which they were unprepared or unqualified. Like Henry himself, all – without exception – had proved their mettle in the reign of Henry IV. They were experienced statesmen and capable administrators. Having a connection to the Prince appears to have been an important qualification, but this did not preclude those with a record of loyal service to his father: Bishops Langley, Bubwith and Chichele, as well as the earls of Arundel and Warwick, had all served as Henry IV's councillors in the final years of his reign.[33] Erpingham had occupied key positions in the previous king's household in the early 1400s. Moreover, those individuals who were 'dropped' did not retire in disgrace, but continued to serve the new king, even if they were now somewhat removed from his person: Sir John Pelham was employed as an ambassador to France in the summer of 1414 and in the following year was entrusted with the safekeeping of no less a person than James I of Scotland;[34] Sir John Stanley retained his lordship over the Isle of Man and was reappointed (he had previously held the post from 1399 to 1401) lieutenant of Ireland in June 1413 in place of Clarence, though he died shortly afterwards in January 1414;[35] and Richard, Lord Grey of Codnor, became one of Henry V's most trusted diplomats and was directly involved in the negotiations for the king's marriage to Catherine of Valois in 1414–15.[36] Both Stanley and Codnor had at some point under Henry IV served the Prince, so their removal from Henry V's household was hardly the act of a political purge: it was more akin to a cabinet reshuffle.[37]

This aside, the one notable absentee from the witness lists was Thomas, duke of Clarence, the king's brother. There is no obvious explanation: Clarence had been in Aquitaine when Henry IV died on 20 March 1413, but

---

[33] See D. Biggs, 'Royal Charter Witness Lists for the Reign of Henry IV, 1399–1413', *EHR* 119 (2004), 407–23 (pp. 422–3).

[34] *HP*, IV, 39–44.

[35] See M. Bennett, *Community, Class and Careerism: Cheshire and Lancashire in the Age of Sir Gawain and the Green Knight* (Cambridge, 1983), pp. 216–17; Wylie and Waugh, *Henry the Fifth*, I, 58–9.

[36] C. L. Kingsford, 'Grey, Richard, Fourth Baron Grey of Codnor (*c.* 1371–1418)', rev. R. A. Griffiths, *ODNB*.

[37] The analogy might also apply to the replacement by Sir William Hankeford of Sir William Gascoigne as chief justice of the king's bench in 1413. Historians have looked in vain to find any basis of truth in Shakespeare's account of Gascoigne's imprisonment of Prince Henry for contempt of court to explain the judge's apparent dismissal in 1413, but at Henry's accession Gascoigne was sixty-three years old, he had been chief justice since 1400, and his departure may simply have been the honourable retirement of a faithful old servant of the Lancastrian regime: E. Powell, 'Gascoigne, Sir William (*c.*1350–1419)', *ODNB*.

he had hastened home and was back in London by 14 July.[38] Nothing else is known about his activities until the following spring when his name began to appear regularly in the witness lists.[39] Henry V had showed his brother the respect he deserved as a royal Prince, by granting him a pension of 2,000 marks in July 1413, but the suspicion must be that in the early months of the reign Clarence was deliberately sidelined as a way of underscoring the new political structure and the subservient place he now held within it.[40] Perhaps this was because he was now heir presumptive. Certainly, his rather perfunctory dismissal as captain of Calais on 3 February 1414, when he was replaced by the earl of Warwick,[41] suggests that the new king was not in an especially generous or reconciliatory frame of mind.

The Knights and Esquires of the Household

My principal interest, however, lies not in the king's relationship with his senior nobles and officeholders, who have already been subjected to scrutiny in published work,[42] but with the larger group of men who enjoyed a favoured position in Henry's regime by virtue of their membership of the royal household. I choose my words carefully because disagreement about the use and definition of terms such as household, retinue and affinity makes this tricky terrain through which to navigate.[43] My concern is specifically with the knights and esquires who retained a special connection to the king by virtue of their receipt of a royal annuity or lucrative office. These were the *familiares regis*, the '*king*'s knights' and '*king*'s esquires' who were marked out from the greater mass of men who enjoyed similar rank because they were entitled to wear the royal livery. The key point is that it was of the household knights and esquires that the king demanded the greatest levels of loyalty and service, domestically (as attendants to the king in person), politically (as his trusted agents in the localities) or militarily (as the captains in his armies). The quid pro quo was that the household knights and esquires

---

38 Wylie and Waugh, *Henry the Fifth*, I, 116–19.
39 TNA, C 53/181.
40 *CPR, 1413–16*, p. 94.
41 Wylie and Waugh, *Henry the Fifth*, I, 40, fn. 2.
42 G. L. Harriss, 'The King and His Magnates', in *Henry V*, ed. Harriss, pp. 31–51; Catto, 'King's Servants'; and Allmand, *Henry V*, chapter 16.
43 For general discussion, see C. Given-Wilson, *The Royal Household and the King's Affinity: Service, Politics and Finance in England 1360–1413* (New Haven, 1986), pp. 202–3; and R. Horrox, *Richard III: A Study in Service* (Cambridge, 1989), pp. 12–21 and chapter 5. Henry V's retinue has been discussed by David Morgan, but he does not discuss the personnel in detail: see D. Morgan, 'The Household Retinue of Henry V and the Ethos of English Public Life', in *Concepts and Patterns of Service in the Later Middle Ages*, ed. A. Curry and E. Matthew (Woodbridge, 2000), pp. 64–79.

tended to enjoy the greatest share of royal patronage, so membership of this elite was not only highly prestigious, but also extremely lucrative. We can assume that the decision about who became a household knight or esquire ultimately rested with the king since this affinity, like any affinity, described a fundamentally personal relationship between the king and his closest and most reliable supporters. Who was invited to join Henry's household and what their record of service was before 1413 thus takes us to the very heart of the questions posed at the start of the chapter.

In the account book of the treasurer of the royal household, Thomas More, dating to Henry's first regnal year, seven knights of the chamber are listed (see Appendix 1).[44] Chamber knights belonged to the king's inner circle: they were amongst the most important household men who spent much of their time personally attending to the king's domestic needs.[45] Of the men listed in 1413, none had served as chamber knights for Henry IV.[46] This indicates the very personal nature of their selection. A good king, at least, could not pick and choose who amongst his nobles shared in the exercise of power, but he had a much freer hand when it came to choosing individuals from the knightly classes who were to be regularly in his company. A common factor for many was their military service to the king when he had been Prince. Sir John Phelip, for example, had entered the Prince's household as early as 1401 and, following a distinguished record of service in the Welsh Marches, was awarded an annuity of 40 marks by the Prince in 1406.[47] Likewise, Sir John Skydmore played a key role in suppressing the Welsh under Henry IV: he held a series of constableships of castles and by 1405 had become an esquire formally attached to the Prince's household.[48] Sir Robert Whitney also served the Prince and by 1407 was in receipt of an annuity.[49] From about the same time Sir John Grey also received an annuity from the Prince.[50] Service to the Prince was not the only consideration, however: at least three chamber knights had served Thomas Arundel (Umfraville, Phelip and Gray) and a fourth, Roland Leynthale, was married to one of Arundel's daughters. Gilbert Umfraville and John Phelip, in particular, had made names for themselves during Arundel's campaign against the Armagnacs in 1411.[51] Umfraville had no apparent connection to Henry prior to 1413, but in 1409, at the age of

---

[44] TNA, E 101/406/21. This may not be a comprehensive list: see Given-Wilson, *Royal Household*, pp. 208–9.
[45] Ibid., pp. 206–11.
[46] Ibid., Appendix VI.
[47] *HP*, IV, 68–70.
[48] *HP*, IV, 391–4.
[49] *HP*, IV, 840–1.
[50] Pugh, *Southampton Plot*, p. 104.
[51] For background, see A. Tuck, 'The Earl of Arundel's Expedition to France, 1411', in *Reign of Henry IV*, ed. Dodd and Biggs, pp. 228–39; for Umfraville's participation, see Wylie, *Henry the Fourth*, IV, 63. For Phelip, see *HP*, IV, 69.

nineteen, he was one of three English champions who had jousted for three days against their French counterparts at Lille.[52] Henry's decision to promote Umfraville into this elite circle of knights, like his decision to appoint Henry, Lord FitzHugh as his chamberlain, sent a clear message about the martial ethos of the men whose company he valued most.[53]

In the same account book, More also lists the esquires of the chamber – twenty-three in total. Similar patterns of service can be found amongst a large proportion of the individuals included. A number had clearly been key members of the Prince's entourage. William Porter was a member of the Prince's household by 1403, and by 1409 was one of his esquires of the body.[54] He also accompanied Arundel on the latter's expedition to France in 1411. Robert Lovell could similarly boast a long and distinguished career in the service of the Prince, stretching back to 1404: by 1410 he had become one of the Prince's esquires.[55] Louis Robessart had also started his career in the household of the Prince, apparently as early as 1403, and subsequently gained considerable military experience in Wales.[56] Nicholas Merbury was an usher of the chamber and master of arms in the Prince's household, and in 1411 was acting as receiver of the chamber, a position he later acquired in the royal household.[57] John Chetwynd had received annuities from both Henry IV and the Prince, as duke of Cornwall, and was an esquire of the Prince's chamber before the end of Henry IV's reign.[58] The Prince had entrusted him with the keepership of Snowdon forest. Robert Morton's inclusion amongst the esquires of the chamber is probably to be explained by the fact that Henry was godfather to his son.[59] Morton's career had gone nowhere under Henry IV, so his elevation into the king's household in 1413 is a good example of the efficacy of personal connections: by October 1413 he had been made keeper of the royal falcons. John Cheyne had not served the Prince directly, but he was no doubt well known to the Prince as a member of his father's council. However, it was probably Cheyne's diplomatic activities during the period when the Prince headed government in 1410 and 1411 which persuaded the

[52] C. Given-Wilson, '"The Quarrels of Old Women": Henry IV, Louis of Orléans, and Anglo-French Chivalric Challenges in the Early Fifteenth Century', in *Reign of Henry IV*, ed. Dodd and Biggs, p. 40. See also, H. Summerson, 'Umfraville, Sir Robert (d. 1437)', *ODNB*.

[53] The point applies more generally to his household officers, for which, see Allmand, *Henry V*, pp. 356–7.

[54] *HP*, IV, 118–21.

[55] *HP*, III, 632–4.

[56] H. Collins, *The Order of the Garter 1348–1461: Chivalry and Politics in Late Medieval England* (Oxford, 2000), p. 120.

[57] Griffiths, 'Military Career and Affinity', p. 198.

[58] Allmand, *Henry V*, p. 36; *HP*, II, 544, fn. 1.

[59] *HP*, III, 790–2.

new king of his usefulness to the regime.[60] The case of Christopher Strange demonstrates a different dynamic at play. There is no record of service to Henry before 1413, but his father, Sir John Strange, was a noted 'Lancastrian' whose political credentials included support for the Appellants in 1388, supervision of Henry Bolingbroke's estates during the latter's exile in 1399, and appointment to the position of controller of Henry IV's household between 1405 and 1413.[61] More importantly, Sir John Strange could count amongst his associates the steward of Henry V's household, Sir Thomas Erpingham, as well as one of the king's long-standing supporters, the chamber knight Sir John Phelip: these connections may well have been decisive in thrusting Christopher into Henry's orbit. From Henry's point of view, employing the 'next generation' made perfect sense: it ensured a break with the past and enabled him to become the focus of the new men's loyalties. It was also probably the least objectionable way of discontinuing the service of men who had shown great commitment and loyalty to the Lancastrian regime in his father's reign.

Amongst the broader group of household knights and esquires, the men who had no specific function or office to perform within the household itself, but who nevertheless were regarded as household men, similar patterns can be observed. But here we confront a significant methodological problem that is worth exploring in some detail. Until recently it was thought that household knights and esquires could be readily identified in the calendars of patent and close rolls where particular names were prefixed or suffixed by the terms 'king's knight' or 'king's esquire'. However, Shelagh Mitchell has shown that these terms were used inconsistently by the editors of the published calendars and in fact they bear no relation to the terminology employed in the original chancery rolls.[62] In these rolls, and particularly where grants are recorded, a different diplomatic style was used to distinguish household knights and esquires from other knights and esquires. Knights of the household were referred to as *dilecto et fideli militi nostro N[ame]*, whereas 'ordinary' knights were referred to as *dilecto et fideli nostro N[ame] militi*. The same diplomatic conventions applied to esquires. Everything hinged on where an individual's rank was specified in relation to his name, and its position in relation to the all-important possessive pronoun *nostro*. Mitchell's research fundamentally changes the way in which household knights and esquires are defined, so that the crucial factor is no longer office-holding in the household or receipt of an annuity, but the form of the address used to identify knights and esquires as specifically *royal* knights and esquires. The body of knights

---

[60] *HP*, II, 549–52.

[61] *HP*, IV, 500–2.

[62] S. Mitchell, 'Some Aspects of the Knightly Household of Richard II' (unpublished D.Phil. thesis, University of London, 1998), chapter 1. I would like to thank Dr Mitchell for the extremely helpful communication we have had on this subject and for her generosity in permitting me to draw on her research in this chapter.

and esquires who can be considered to have been 'royal' or 'of the household' was therefore much larger than previously thought, and incorporated a large part of what used to be described as the extended royal affinity. There is much merit in this new approach, not least because it explains the curious anomaly by which royal esquires, and not royal knights, are to be found listed in the account books: this is not because the household was filled only with esquires, it was simply indicative of different accounting methods.[63]

Appendix 1 presents the results of a survey of the household knights and esquires of the first two years of Henry V's reign. Since no livery rolls exist for the early years of the reign,[64] my investigations have necessarily depended entirely on the methodology outlined above. Such a survey holds intrinsic historical value for showing the size and composition of the king's extended household retinue before the Agincourt campaign of 1415. There were sixty-eight knights and 186 esquires. Not surprisingly, there was a mixture of 'old' and 'new' men. I estimate that thirty-eight out of the sixty-eight household knights (56 per cent), and ninety-four out of 186 household esquires (i.e. just over half) were formerly retained by Henry IV.[65] This did not, however, make them exclusively the former king's men. For much of Henry IV's reign there was an evident fluidity surrounding service and loyalty, so that it was perfectly possible for individuals to consider themselves servants and annuitants of the king as well as associates of the Prince.

In fact, it is striking how many of the men whose annuities were confirmed in 1413 had gravitated towards the Prince in the course of the 1400s. In the early part of Henry IV's reign, for example, Sir Roger Leche had been made an esquire of the royal body, but later in the decade, as a result of service in Wales, he had entered the Prince's household and eventually became its steward.[66] In 1401, Sir Thomas Chaworth had become a knight of the royal body, but in 1411 he, Leche and others were imprisoned in the Tower of London for their part in trying to persuade Henry IV to abdicate.[67] Sir William Bourchier had his annuity confirmed by Henry IV in 1400, but by 1401 was serving as a knight of the Prince's chamber.[68] Thomas Chaucer was another key supporter of the Prince. He had initially benefited from Henry IV's benevolence (he was

---

[63] I.e. Esquires were paid out of the wardrobe; knights were paid from the exchequer. Given-Wilson makes the point that since the fees and robes allowances paid to esquires were lower than for knights, it made sense for the king to pay them through his Wardrobe: *Royal Household*, p. 212.

[64] The earliest dates to 3–4 Henry V: TNA, E 101/406/26.

[65] For Henry IV's reign I have consulted D. Biggs, '"Then you perceive the body of our kingdom": The Royal Affinity of Henry IV, 1399–1413' (unpublished D.Phil. thesis, University of Minnesota, 1996), pp. 541–93.

[66] *HP*, III, 570–3. See also H. Castor, *The King, the Crown, and the Duchy of Lancaster: Public Authority and Private Power 1399–1461* (Oxford, 2000), pp. 32, 204, 211 and 223–4.

[67] *HP*, II, 533–6.

[68] *HP*, II, 315–17.

made chief butler in 1402), but soon became a stalwart of the Prince's faction and achieved particular distinction by advancing the Prince's interests as Speaker in the parliaments of 1407, 1410 and 1411.[69] John Waterton had links to Henry IV possibly going as far back as 1391; he had been made a royal esquire by 1402, but in 1400 he was made receiver of the duchy of Cornwall by the Prince and campaigned with him in the following years.[70] Many other individuals fitted this profile: Sir John St John, for example, had begun Henry IV's reign in receipt of a 100 mark annuity, but by 1406 was retained as a knight of the body by the Prince;[71] the esquire, Hugh Mortimer, also enjoyed a royal annuity (£60) from Henry IV, but focused his activities on service to the Prince, for whom he acted as chamberlain between 1403 and 1411;[72] and John Merbury was one of Henry IV's esquires, but came within the purview of the Prince by virtue of his position as chamberlain, and later receiver, in South Wales.[73] This evidence suggests that the Prince had effectively taken over a large part of his father's affinity from roughly the middle years of the reign. This may have been partly by design, but it may also have been the natural consequence of the heavy engagement of many of Henry IV's annuitants in the Welsh conflict which inevitably pushed them into the sphere of the young Prince, where lasting bonds of friendship and loyalty were established.

On the other hand, not all the men incorporated into the wider affinity could boast of such an impressive record of commitment to the Prince. Many were no doubt included because of their experience and abilities. Men like Sir John Etton, Sir Alexander Lounde and Thomas Strickland were key members of the northern gentry and seasoned campaigners against the Scots.[74] Sir John Cornwall had served extensively on the Welsh Marches, and between 1404 and 1406 had been joint controller of the musters there.[75] Sir John Blount had a distinguished military career which included no less a feat than capturing the marshal of France in 1412,[76] whilst Richard Clitheroe had been heavily involved under Henry IV in naval affairs and from 1410 had been responsible for victualling Calais.[77] Sir Robert Corbet and Sir Walter Hungerford were not so much military men as key players in the administration of their respective counties.[78] It is a measure of Henry's pragmatism, as well as perhaps his eagerness to build bridges, that he retained Sir John Tiptoft, one of his

---

69   *HP*, II, 524–32.
70   *HP*, IV, 784–87.
71   *HP*, IV, 280–3.
72   *HP*, III, 783–6.
73   *HP*, III, 716–20.
74   *HP*, III, 36–8; 629–30; IV, 513–16.
75   *HP*, II, 661–3; Reeves, *Lancastrian Englishmen*, pp. 139–202.
76   *HP*, II, 256–7 note.
77   *HP*, II, 598–602.
78   *HP*, II, 654–6; III, 446–53.

fiercest opponents in the last years of Henry IV's reign – but then Tiptoft was one of the most experienced politicians of his age and Henry would have been foolish not to utilize his talents.[79] Similar considerations almost certainly account for Henry's continuation of his father's policy of retaining men who had begun their service in the household of Richard II, providing a useful reminder that the Lancastrian 'establishment' continued to draw on elements of the former Ricardian regime even now, a generation removed from the usurpation in 1399.[80]

Of the newcomers to the affinity, some men were promoted as a result of their service to the Prince. Sir Humphrey Stafford, Sir Robert Whitney and the esquire Peter Melbourne fall into this category.[81] Others were younger sons of fathers who had served Henry IV loyally but who had perhaps reached an age where they wished to retire gracefully from public service. There are enough examples of this to suggest that this was a clear policy. Sir Nicholas II Montgomery was the son of a distinguished Lancastrian supporter, Sir Nicholas I, who lived until 1424 when he must have been almost eighty years old.[82] Sir Ralph Shirely was made one of Henry V's knights at the age of twenty-two, though in his case his father had been killed at the battle of Shrewsbury.[83] Sir Philip Leche joined his father, Sir Roger Leche (d.1416), as one of Henry's knights.[84] Shirley and Leche were both knighted on the eve of Henry's coronation.

It is now possible to show that Henry's early affinity was not exclusively a military affinity. This much is obvious by exploiting the information available from the medieval soldier database[85] to show the proportion of knights and esquires who went on to serve in Henry's army at Agincourt. Of the esquires, ninety-nine (53 per cent) are recorded to have accompanied the king to France in 1415. Of the knights, forty-four (64 per cent) went on this campaign. As one would expect, a much greater proportion of knights than esquires served as captains in the army. The overwhelming majority of knights and esquires who served individually were assigned to the retinues of either Sir Robert Chalons (one of Henry's household knights) or John Burgh (an interesting character, whose career was made in the service of Thomas, earl of Arundel, under

79 *HP*, IV, 620–8.
80 For example: Sir Thomas Barre; Sir Edmund Noon; Sir Richard Redmayne; Sir John Routhe; and Sir John St John, all of whom were household knights of Richard II (as well as Henry IV). I am very grateful to Shelagh Mitchell for pointing these connections out to me.
81 *HP*, IV, 439–42; 840–1.
82 *HP*, III, 762–4.
83 *HP*, IV, 366–8.
84 *HP*, III, 569–70.
85 AHRC-funded database www.medievalsoldier.org, accessed 28 February 2012. I have also consulted the list of those individuals who indented to serve on the 1415 campaign published in Curry, *Agincourt: A New History*, Appendix D.

whose authority he worked as under-treasurer in the exchequer from March 1413).[86] A total of 62 per cent of the men *newly appointed* to Henry's household affinity crossed the Channel with the king in 1415. A slightly smaller proportion (i.e. 50 per cent) of the men who had belonged to Henry IV's household affinity served at Agincourt.

The infamous heretic Sir John Oldcastle, an old friend and trusted retainer of the king, is the obvious absentee from these lists.[87] His omission appears to confirm the observation made by the author of the *Vita Henrici Quinti* that Henry turned Oldcastle out of his household before coming to the throne in 1413.[88] Interestingly, Oldcastle may not have been alone in this respect. In his research on Henry's princely household, William Griffiths identified fourteen men below the rank of baron who had been retained for life by the Prince.[89] *None* of these individuals appears to have been taken on by Henry once he became king.[90] Are we to suppose that these men were the 'wylde company' noted in the *Brut*, and the 'misleaders' of Shakespeare's play? Perhaps. It does seem strange that the men who, along with Oldcastle, appear to have enjoyed a large measure of the Prince's confidence were not then accorded any favour when Henry became king – and none of them (other than Oldcastle) is known to have been tainted by association with the Lollards.[91]

One other group of men who do not feature in the lists of Henry's knights and esquires of 1413 are the individuals who served with Thomas, duke of Clarence, in August 1412, when the latter embarked for France in pursuit of his father's foreign policy aims.[92] These were now emphatically aligned with the Orléanists after a period in which the Prince of Wales, as effective head of the English government in 1410 and 1411, had pursued an alliance with John the Fearless, duke of Burgundy. There are listed in the French rolls letters of protection for some seventy-five individuals, including a good number of knights and esquires, who accompanied Clarence on this expedition. Yet only

---

[86] *HP*, II, 419–22.
[87] See discussion in this volume by Maureen Jurkowski.
[88] *Vita Henrici Quinti*, ed. Hearne, p. 31.
[89] Griffiths, 'Military Career and Affinity', p. 205. These were Sir Thomas Grey; John de Legh, esquire; William Walweyn, esquire; Geoffrey Arden; John Baskerville; John Bodenham; Thomas Bromwich; Thomas Burghope; Walter Devereaux; Philip Dumbleton; Thomas de la Hay; Walter de la Hay; Thomas Holcot; and Richard Wyseham.
[90] There is very little trace of these men in the printed records, a sure sign that little value was placed on their service by the crown.
[91] In fact three – Thomas de la Hay, John Bodenham and Thomas Holcot – were appointed in January 1414 to investigate the incidence of Lollardy in Herefordshire: *CPR, 1413–16*, p. 177.
[92] See J. D. Milner, 'The English Enterprise in France, 1412–13', in *Trade, Devotion and Governance: Papers in Later Medieval History*, ed. D. J. Clayton, R. G. Davies and P. McNiven (Stroud, 1994), pp. 80–101; and more recently J. Milner, 'The English Commitment to the 1412 Expedition to France', *The Fifteenth Century XI: Concerns and Preoccupations*, ed. L. Clark (Woodbridge, 2012), 9–23.

a handful – John Kyghley, John Fastolf, Sir John Cornwall and Sir William Bardolf – were subsequently recruited into Henry V's affinity.[93] This raises two points of interest. First, it establishes the not altogether surprising fact that, with the exception of Cornwall, none of the Prince's men chose to associate themselves with the new direction taken by English foreign policy under the revived authority of Henry IV. The fact that hardly any of the men who fought for Clarence were subsequently incorporated into the royal affinity does not necessarily indicate that these men were in some way 'punished' for the service they had performed for the new king's brother, but it does underline the personal nature of recruitment, and the diminished chances of securing the Prince's favour if military service had not been performed directly for him or in his interests. The expedition led by the earl of Arundel in the previous Autumn, on this occasion in fulfilment of the *Prince's* foreign policy aims, presents an instructive contrast, for of those known to have accompanied the earl, three – Sir John Phelip, Sir John Oldcastle and William Porter – were annuitants of the Prince, and another four – Sir William Bardolf, Sir Gilbert and Sir Robert Umfraville and Sir John Grey – went on to occupy key positions in Henry V's household.[94]

The second point is in many ways more significant, however. In 1413, as we have seen, Henry V created a new household affinity by amalgamating the core elements of his own retinue with his father's. What is striking is not so much the omission of the Prince's men from Clarence's army, but the almost complete absence in this force of men from his father's affinity. Clarence's expedition was a royal expedition, but it appears that the royal affinity stayed at home. It is not difficult to see why this might have been. At precisely the time when preparations were being made for the embarkation of Clarence's expedition to the continent, in the summer months of 1412, relations between the Prince and Henry IV had deteriorated to such an extent that the Prince, with 'a considerable body of supporters', was reported to have marched on London at the end of June to air his grievances with his father.[95] Some contemporaries evidently thought the Prince was raising an armed insurrection.[96] Although the crisis had passed by the time Clarence left for France, it is quite understandable that Henry IV might have wished to keep his supporters close at hand in case his elder son threatened further instability. This indicates the gravity of the situation and suggests, in particular, that Henry IV did not have absolute faith in the intentions of his eldest son. With tensions running so high in the summer of 1412, it is an intriguing

---

93 TNA, C 76/96; and Wylie, *Henry the Fourth*, IV, 74, fn. 1. I would like to thank John Milner for his generosity in discussions we have had on this subject.

94 Wylie, *Henry the Fourth*, IV, 55, 47, 62; Tuck, 'Arundel's Expedition', p. 232.

95 McNiven, 'Prince Henry' (quotation at p. 6).

96 This was reported in the Prince's letter to his father: see Walsingham, *St. Albans Chronicle, 1394–1422*, p. 613.

thought that many of the men who came together in 1413 as part of the newly configured royal affinity might have been called upon to fight each other in a civil conflict less than twelve months previously.

The Coronation Livery Roll

There is a document, hitherto unnoticed, which provides further perspective on the people Henry V looked to for support in 1413. BL MS Stowe 440 contains a seventeenth-century transcription of a contemporary issue roll, now apparently lost, which lists the names of those men who received special coronation liveries of scarlet cloth on the eve of Henry V's coronation on 9 April 1413. The main feature of this list is its sub-division into a graduated series of groups, each defined by a certain length (i.e. an *ell*) of cloth awarded according to the status of the recipient (see Appendix 2). There is an especially full record of the distribution of special liveries to mark the coronation of Henry IV where it is clear that the cloth was used to make up robes, gowns or hoods, depending on the length of cloth distributed (and the status of the recipient).[97] The distribution of robes – or in this case, of different lengths of luxury fabric to be displayed on a state occasion – was a common method of conferring honour on selected individuals and to demarcate status and hierarchy within the political community.[98] This document provides new evidence to show who was held in particular esteem by Henry V. Apart from the senior nobility, all of whom are included in the list apart from Clarence, who was still in Aquitaine, and Prince Humphrey, who was omitted presumably because of his appointment as chamberlain of England, the remaining individuals represented only a proportion of the social or professional groupings from which they were drawn, so their selection was evidently a special mark of favour: this was a public show of the people who really mattered to the new king. The inclusion in this list of men of many different ranks, representing a broad cross-section of the whole political community, also emphasized the universal nature of the consent in Henry's accession to the throne.

As one would expect, the greatest dignity was reserved for the most senior nobles who received twelve lengths, though an interesting distinction in the order of seniority was drawn between Henry's closest supporters, the earls of Arundel and Warwick, who had served the king when he had been Prince, and a larger band of younger, inexperienced noblemen who had yet to prove

---

[97] *The Coronation of Richard III: The Extant Documents*, ed. A. F. Sutton and P. W. Hammond (Gloucester, 1983), pp. 92–9.

[98] F. Lachaud, 'Liveries of Robes in England, c. 1200–c. 1330', *EHR* 111 (1996), 279–98 (esp. pp. 288–9).

themselves.[99] Prince John clearly belonged to the highest tier as the king's younger brother. Westmorland, on the other hand, was placed in the second tier, with the youngsters, perhaps because he had no close ties with the king or court.[100] The archbishop of Canterbury was in the first tier, as primate of England, as was Henry Beaufort, as the chancellor. In the third and fourth tiers, receiving eight and six lengths respectively, were mainly men who held baronial rank. These were evidently a select band, for only nineteen out of the thirty-two barons summoned to attend Henry's first parliament in May 1413 were included.[101] Those *excluded* from the list, but summoned to parliament, included Hugh Stafford, fifth son of Hugh, earl of Stafford (d.1386);[102] William Ferrers de Groby (though his *fourth* son, Edmund, evidently was);[103] John, Lord Welles;[104] Ralph, Lord Cromwell;[105] Thomas, Lord Dacre of Gilsand;[106] Robert, Lord Willoughby (though his uncle, Thomas, Lord Willoughby, was);[107] Ralph, Lord Greystoke[108] and John Neville, Lord Latimer.[109] Since none of these men could boast anything approximating to a distinguished career in the service of the Lancastrian crown it seems likely that they were excluded because they were not yet known to, or especially valued by, the new king. Some of these individuals, like Hugh Stafford and Robert Willoughby, had only just come into their inheritance, whilst others, like John, Lord Welles and Ralph, Lord Greystoke, were old men who had long since given up public office, whilst others, like Ralph, Lord Cromwell and Thomas, Lord Dacre, had never shown any interest in service to the crown.

By contrast, many of the barons who received livery had established positions in the Lancastrian regime, and some had especially close ties to the new king. Henry Scrope, lord of Masham, had proved himself an immensely valuable servant of the crown in Henry IV's day, fighting at Shrewsbury in 1403, helping to subdue the Welsh rebels and latterly serving on important

---

99 See Harriss, 'King and His Magnates', pp. 31–51. Of the earls of Somerset, Norfolk, March, Salisbury and Huntingdon, Thomas, earl of Salisbury was the oldest, at the age of twenty-five.

100 A. Tuck, 'Neville, Ralph, first earl of Westmorland (*c.*1364–1425)', *ODNB*.

101 *Report from the Lords' Committees touching the Dignity of a Peer*, 5 vols. (London, 1820–9), IV, 817.

102 D. Richardson, *Magna Carta Ancestry: A Study in Colonial and Medieval Families* (Baltimore, 2005), p. 765.

103 Ibid., p. 209.

104 *Complete Peerage*, XII, Part 2, 441–3.

105 Ibid., III, 552.

106 Ibid., IV, 7.

107 For Robert, see *Complete Peerage*, XII, Part 2, 663–5 and G. L. Harriss, 'Willoughby, Robert (III), sixth Baron Willoughby (1385–1452)', *ODNB*; for Thomas see *HP*, IV, 871–3.

108 K. Dockray, 'Greystoke Family (per. 1321–1487)', *ODNB*; *Complete Peerage*, VI, 195–6.

109 *Complete Peerage*, VII, 476–7.

diplomatic missions.[110] He was also treasurer at the time when the Prince controlled his father's government between January 1410 and December 1411.[111] Reynold Grey of Ruthin, a Marcher lord in Wales, had similarly been closely involved in the Welsh conflict in the 1400s, serving under the command of the Prince,[112] as had Edward Charleton, lord of Powys, who had spent long periods in the 1400s helping to put down the Welsh rebellion where his estates lay.[113] Richard Grey of Codnor had also served in Wales and was appointed the king's lieutenant there in 1401. In addition, he was made Admiral of the North in 1402, royal chamberlain in 1406 and 1410, and negotiated on behalf of the Prince for his proposed marriage to Anne, daughter of the duke of Burgundy, in 1412.[114] Hugh, Lord Burnell also fought with the Prince in Wales, and became a key member of the Prince's council in 1410 and 1411.[115] Like Richard Grey, Henry, Lord Beaumont had acted in a diplomatic capacity on behalf of the Prince in 1410–11; he had become chamberlain of the duchy of Lancaster from 1409, and was in receipt of an annuity from Henry by 1410.[116] William, Lord Zouche was an annuitant of the Prince (from 1408), and had also served as a member of Henry IV's council. He was acting as lieutenant of Calais by May 1413.[117] John Talbot, Lord Furnivall, who had seen more or less continuous service on the Welsh borders, again under the command of the Prince, was made lieutenant of Ireland in February 1414.[118] William, Lord Roos de Hamelak, the only baron to receive ten lengths of cloth, alongside the senior nobility, was a pillar of the Lancastrian establishment, though he had not acted within a close orbit of the young Prince. He had served in the royal council for most of Henry IV's reign and was treasurer between 1403 and 1404; the annuity of 100 marks he had enjoyed under Henry IV was confirmed by Henry V in October 1413.[119] Similarly, as we have

---

[110] B. Vale, 'Scrope, Henry, Third Baron Scrope of Masham (c. 1376–1415)', *ODNB*. See also Wylie, *Henry the Fourth*, II, 412 (and fn. 2), 446; III, 100, 354.

[111] Wylie, *Henry the Fourth*, III, 284 and note 5, 314; IV, 51.

[112] Ibid., I, 142, 144, 250, 305; R. I. Jack, 'Grey, Reynold, Third Baron Grey of Ruthin (c. 1362–1440)', *ODNB*.

[113] T. F. Tout, 'Charlton, Edward, Fifth Baron Charlton of Powys (1370–1421)', rev. R. A. Griffiths, *ODNB*.

[114] Wylie, *Henry the Fourth*, I, 173, 286–7, 306 (fn. 6); II, 428; III, 305–6; *Complete Peerage*, VI, 127–9. For the marriage, see Tuck, 'Arundel's Expedition', p. 236.

[115] Wylie, *Henry the Fourth*, I, 245, 375; II, 427; IV, 246; Allmand, *Henry V*, p. 45; Harriss, 'King and his Magnates', p. 33.

[116] Wylie, *Henry the Fourth*, IV, 37 (fn. 3); R. Somerville, *History of the Duchy of Lancaster, Volume One 1265–1603* (London, 1953), p. 417; Griffiths, 'Military Career and Affinity', pp. 194, 205.

[117] Wylie and Waugh, *Henry the Fifth*, I, 39–40, and note 2 (p. 40).

[118] A. J. Pollard, 'Talbot, John, First Earl of Shrewsbury and First Earl of Waterford (c. 1387–1453)', *ODNB*; Allmand, *Henry V*, p. 35 (fn. 88).

[119] Wylie and Waugh, *Henry the Fifth*, I, 268 (fn. 3), 402, 406, 414; II, 112, 427. See also *Complete Peerage*, II, 102–3.

seen, Henry's chamberlain, Henry, Lord FitzHugh (eight lengths of cloth), did not directly serve the king when he had been Prince, but he could boast an impressive record of military, diplomatic and administrative service to Henry IV.[120] Thomas, Lord Berkeley had served on the councils of both his father and Richard II and was appointed as Admiral of the South and West in 1403 and Warden of the Welsh Marches in 1404.[121] Along with Lords Grey of Ruthin, Morley and Edward Charleton, lord of Powys, he was nominated to the serve on the regency council in April 1415 when Henry left for France.[122]

The picture that emerges, then, is of a large group of barons who had proved their worth either to the king in person, when he had been Prince of Wales, or more generally to the Lancastrian regime in his father's reign. It is striking how many provided vital services to the king subsequently, not least in the Agincourt campaign of 1415, where almost a dozen of those named on the coronation livery roll are known to have served in the English army.[123] All the barons who attended the meeting of the great council in April 1415, which took the fateful decision to mount the Agincourt campaign, were included in the coronation livery roll.[124] Eight of them were already Knights of the Garter,[125] and a further three, together with two knights, would win places in the Order later in Henry V's reign.[126] Particular honour was accorded to the only three men of non-baronial rank to receive eight lengths of cloth: Sir William Harrington, Sir Thomas Erpingham and Sir Gilbert Umfraville. Erpingham had earned his place as a result of years of continual and valuable service to the crown, and because of the trust and faith with which Henry evidently still held him (he was appointed steward of the household at the outset of the reign).[127] Umfraville and Harrington were both fighting men. Harrington had connections with the Prince going back to 1403, and had been

[120] Reeves, *Lancastrian Englishmen*, pp. 69–85; A. C. Reeves, 'Fitzhugh, Henry, Third Baron Fitzhugh (1363? – 1425)', *ODNB*; and see discussion above p. 42.

[121] Wylie, *Henry the Fourth*, I, 377, 384, 432; II, 33, 55, 296, 302; *Complete Peerage*, II, 130–1.

[122] Wylie and Waugh, *Henry the Fifth*, I, 455, and fn. 8.

[123] I.e. Botreaux; Bourchier; Camoys; Clifford; Clinton; Ferrers; FitzHugh; Mautravers; Scrope; Talbot; and Zouche: *Soldier in Medieval England* database (see note 85 above), and Curry, *Agincourt: A New History*, Appendix D.

[124] *POPC*, II, 156. The barons attending the council meeting were: Botreaux; Bourchier; Cammoys; Clifford; Clinton; Ferrers; Grey of Codnor; Grey of Ruthin; Harrington; Mautravers; Morley; Poynings; Willoughby; and Zouche. For discussion of this meeting, see Mortimer, *1415: Henry V's Year of Glory*, Appendix 2.

[125] I.e. Lord Grey of Codnor (1403); Lord Roos (1403); Sir John Stanley (1404); Lord Lovel of Titchmarsh (1405); Lord Burnell (1406); Lord FitzHugh (1408); Lord Scrope of Masham (1410); and Lord Morley (1411): Collins, *Order of the Garter*, pp. 292–3.

[126] I.e. Sir John Dabrichecourt (1413); Lord Camoys (1414); Sir William Harrington (1415); Lord Zouche (1415); Lord Clifford (1421): ibid.

[127] See above note 28.

paid an annuity by the Prince from 1406;[128] whilst Umfraville, a knight of great distinction and renown, having served in the Anglo-Burgundian expedition of 1411, was clearly held in great favour by the king: in 1415 he was bequeathed a golden bowl in Henry's will.[129]

If political significance can be attached to the fact that only a proportion of the barons who received personal summons to parliament were accorded the honour of wearing the king's special livery at his coronation, there is constitutional significance in the fact that almost a dozen of the men who were chosen to wear the king's livery at his coronation, and were termed *domino* to signify their baronial rank, were not in fact included in the list of barons summoned to the parliament which met less than a week after the coronation on 15 April 1413.[130] This is significant because it is generally understood that by the early fifteenth century the baronage had developed into a homogenous social group defined, above all, in institutional terms by the hereditary right to receive a personal summons to parliament.[131] In one sense, the existence of these 'non-parliamentary' barons actually proves how closely defined the criteria determining eligibility for personal summons were, for whilst most of these men had some grounds for claiming baronial status, none quite made the mark. For instance, William, Lord Bourchier was grandson of Robert first Lord Bourchier, but his father, as a younger son, had not inherited the title.[132] In 1409, the elder branch of the Bourchier family became extinct through lack of male heirs, but the baronial title theoretically remained with William's cousin Elizabeth until her death in 1433, when finally it passed to William's son Henry (William himself had died in 1420). William therefore had no legal or tenurial claim to the barony even if, as the sole male representative of the extended family, there was some logic behind his use of the title. A very similar situation pertained to Richard, Lord Bergavenny who was sole heir to the Bergavenny barony, but was prevented from entering his inheritance when his father died in 1411, because the lands had been left in their entirety to his mother Joan Beauchamp.[133] Since the right of individual summons was tied to the tenure of a barony, which in this case was in possession of his

---

[128] Griffiths, 'Military Career and Affinity', pp. 188, 210. See also, R. Horrox, 'Harrington Family (per. c.1300–1512)', *ODNB*.

[129] Summerson, 'Umfraville, Sir Robert'.

[130] *Dignity of a Peer*, IV, 817.

[131] See J. E. Powell and K. Wallis, *The House of Lords in the Middle Ages* (London, 1968), pp. 309–15, 323–5; K. B. McFarlane, *The Nobility of Later Medieval England* (Oxford, 1973), pp. 124, 269; C. Given-Wilson, *The English Nobility in the Late Middle Ages* (1987), p. 58. See also K. E. Fildes, 'The Baronage in the Reign of Richard II, 1377–1399' (unpublished D.Phil. thesis, University of Sheffield, 2009), chapter 2 (pp. 38–54).

[132] Powell and Wallis, *House of Lords*, pp. 467–8; *HP*, II, 315–17.

[133] *Complete Peerage*, I, 26–7; C. Carpenter, 'Beauchamp, William (V), First Baron Bergavenny (c. 1343–1411)', *ODNB*.

mother, Richard had no right to attend parliament as a peer (that is, until he was made earl of Worcester by Henry V in 1420).

A rather different set of circumstances explains Richard, Lord Despenser's ambiguous position, for it was not the vagaries of inheritance law but the forfeiture of the barony by Henry IV, as a result of his father's attainder for treason in 1400, which barred him from attendance at parliament as a peer.[134] Despenser's inclusion in the coronation roll clearly indicated Henry V's intention to rehabilitate him, but he died in October 1414, and the attainder was not in fact reversed until 1461. Edward, Lord Hastings, John, Lord Mautravers and William, Lord Moleyns fit into the category of men who claimed baronial status, all in contentious circumstances, but had not received definitive judgement on their respective cases, though their receipt of liveries equivalent to baronial rank, and their designation as *domino* at the coronation, suggests that the crown was hedging its bets.[135] Hastings's claim rested on the outcome of a dispute with Reynold, Lord Grey of Ruthin, who was tactfully placed in a senior position in the scale of livery distribution. The inclusion of Lord Mowbray amongst the barons receiving eight lengths of cloth was presumably a scribal error, for the office of Earl Marshal was restored to John Mowbray in 1412 (after his brother's execution and forfeiture in 1405) and he was included amongst the senior nobles receiving ten lengths of cloth in this capacity, presumably because the office was considered to be of such importance in the coronation ceremony.[136]

There were thus good constitutional reasons for these men to be omitted from the list of parliamentary summons, but the fact that the king chose to ignore these factors and include them on the coronation roll alongside those whose baronial status was secure indicates a surprising degree of flexibility

---

134 *Complete Peerage*, IV, 278–82; Harriss, 'King and His Magnates', p. 36.

135 For Hastings, see M. H. Keen, 'Hastings, Sir Edward (1382–1438)', *ODNB*; and M. H. Keen, 'English Military Experience and the Court of Chivalry: The Case of Grey and Hastings', in *Guerre et Société en France, en Angleterre et en Bourgogne, XIVe – XVe siècle*, ed. P. Contamine, M. H. Keen and C. Giry Deloison (Lille, 1991), pp. 123–42. For Molyns, see *Complete Peerage*, IX, 41–2; Powell and Wallis, *House of Lords*, pp. 476–7. In 1414 John Mautravers presented a petition asserting his right to be called to parliament and attend royal councils, by virtue of his claim to earldom of Arundel. This directly challenged the claims of John Mowbray who successfully blocked Mautravers' aspirations, though later in 1433 Mautravers finally achieved his goal (though he died shortly afterwards whilst serving in France). His only personal summons to parliament had been in 1429, though he was here noted as 'knight'; see *PROME*, XI, 70 and 117–22. The original petitions, referring back to 1414, are TNA, SC 8/26/1280 (1433) and 130/6454 (1433), from Mowbray's son and heir, John; and SC 8/88/4396 (1433) from John Mautravers, styling himself as John, earl of Arundel.

136 However, he had to wait until 1425 before he recovered the title of duke of Norfolk, for which see R. E. Archer, 'Parliamentary Restoration: John Mowbray and the Dukedom of Norfolk in 1424', in *Rulers and Ruled in Late Medieval England: Essays Presented to Gerald Harriss*, ed. R. E. Archer and S. Walker (London, 1995), pp. 99–116 (esp. pp. 104–5).

to the question of rank and status. In some of these cases it seems clear why the king chose to flout the conventions in this way. William, Lord Bourchier had served with the Prince from 1401 when he was made a knight of his chamber. He was a man who had enjoyed the new king's confidence from the very start and, besides, his clandestine marriage in 1403 to Anne, countess of Stafford, granddaughter of Edward III, placed him very firmly in the upper reaches of the English nobility. Sir John Stanley had similarly proved to be of great value to the king before 1413. He was retained from 1400 and served as steward of the Prince's household between 1403 and 1405. In common with many of the other barons, Stanley had proved himself more widely as an able administrator and an extremely capable soldier.[137] His grant in 1405 of the lordship of the Isle of Man pushed him more closely towards baronial rank, and probably explains his inclusion in the coronation list amongst men with this status, but it was not until 1456 that his grandson, Thomas, formally entered the peerage having received a personal summons to parliament.[138]

Given the apparently winning formula of baronial rank together with a track record of service to the crown, and especially *military* service in Wales in the 1400s, as key qualifications for inclusion in the list of those receiving scarlet robes in 1413, there is the curious omission of Gilbert, Lord Talbot to consider. Talbot was summoned to Henry V's first parliament in May 1413 and yet, in spite of the fact that he had a strong record of service to the Lancastrian regime, and was a Knight of the Garter,[139] he was not given the honour of wearing the king's scarlet robes at the coronation. There is no ready explanation for this. Talbot was the older brother of John Talbot, Lord Furnivall (who did receive robes).[140] Both Talbot brothers had seen extensive service in Wales by virtue of the fact that their estates lay in the regions affected by the rebellion. Both men had served under the Prince of Wales, but Gilbert if anything had been closer to the Prince, becoming a member of his household in 1403. John had entered his inheritance in 1408 (succeeding his stepfather, Thomas Neville, Lord Furnivall) earlier than his brother had fully entered into the Talbot inheritance on their mother's death in 1413, but Gilbert had been summoned to parliament as a baron since 1404 – earlier than John. Perhaps it came down to what the brothers could offer Henry as king, for it is noticeable that whilst John was soon given a position of immense responsibility with his appointment as lieutenant of Ireland (after the death

---

[137] For what follows see, *Complete Peerage*, XII, Part 2, 248–9; Griffiths, 'Military Career and Affinity', p. 215; *HP*, IV, 455–6.

[138] Powell and Wallis, *House of Lords*, p. 500.

[139] Collins, *Order of the Garter*, p. 292.

[140] For background and discussion of the Talbot family in the early fifteenth century, see A. J. Pollard, 'The Family of Talbot, Lords Talbot and Earls of Shrewsbury in the Fifteenth Century' (unpublished D.Phil. thesis, University of Bristol, 1968), pp. 12–22.

of John Stanley), Gilbert's roles under Henry V were far less impressive.[141]
On the other hand it may simply have been the case that Gilbert was ill and
unable to attend the coronation. The omission from the list of John Oldcastle
is easier to explain, but certainly no less significant. There can be no question
that this was a deliberate snub. He would be summoned as Lord Cobham
to the parliament which met in May 1413, so his standing as a peer of the
realm was not yet in doubt. Oldcastle not only met, but far exceeded, the
criteria apparently necessary for a baron to receive the king's special coronation livery: above all he had proved himself to be exactly the sort of successful
high-status military man to whom Henry looked from the outset of his reign.
Oldcastle's omission from the coronation list provides further evidence to
suggest that Henry had already, before he ascended the throne, determined
on a policy of distancing himself from this controversial figure.

Below the rank of baron, the list includes a good number of the knights
and esquires who belonged to the royal affinity (marked in bold in Appendix
2). Besides Erpingham, Harrington and Umfraville, Sir Simon Felbrigge,
Sir Roger Leche and Sir Thomas Chaucer were singled out for the highest
honours, receiving six lengths of cloth each. It was also within this tier of six
lengths that senior administrators within royal government begin to appear.
These included: John Prophet, keeper of the privy seal (continuing in a post
he had held since 1406); John Burgh, under-treasurer; William Lasingby, chief
baron of the exchequer; and John Wakering, keeper of the chancery rolls. Two
key duchy of Lancaster officers, John Wodehouse, who became chancellor
on Henry's accession, and Sir Roger Leche, who became chief steward of
the northern parts, also received six lengths.[142] There were also key household men, including: Richard Courtenay, treasurer of the chamber (a very
close friend of the king's);[143] John Spenser, cofferer of the household (another
individual close to the king, with a long record of service when he had been
Prince);[144] Thomas Carnika, keeper of the Great Wardrobe (he had served as
the king's General Receiver when he had been Prince);[145] John Icklington,

---

141 As Pollard suggests (ibid., p. 22), 'proven loyalty rather than outstanding ability
     commended him most to the king'.
142 John Leventhorpe, the only key duchy of Lancaster official to retain his position from
     the previous reign, received four lengths. Interestingly, the two other principal duchy
     officials appointed by Henry V – Hugh Mortimer (chamberlain) and Sir Walter Hunger-
     ford (chief steward of the southern parts) – did not receive a coronation livery. For
     office-holding, see Somerville, *Duchy of Lancaster*, pp. 389, 397–8, 405, 417, 419, 428.
     Biographies of these men can be found in *HP*, III, 591–5 (Leventhorpe); IV, 885–7 (Wode-
     house); III, 783–6 (Mortimer); III, 570–3 (Leche); and III, 446–53 (Hungerford). See also
     discussion of these appointments in Castor, *King, Crown, and the Duchy of Lancaster*,
     p. 37.
143 R. G. Davies, 'Courtenay, Richard (c. 1381–1415)', *ODNB*.
144 *HP*, IV, 417–19.
145 Wylie and Waugh, *Henry the Fifth*, I, 28.

former treasurer of Henry's household when he had been Prince;[146] and Edmund Lacy, dean of the royal chapel.[147] The inclusion of the London mayor, William Waldern, is a good indication of the special status held by the capital city, not least because it played host to the coronation proceedings themselves (the coronation procession passed through London's streets).[148]

Members of the royal affinity appear in the remaining tiers, but perhaps not in the numbers one might expect. In fact, in these last groups there is a veritable mixture of royal knights and esquires, other knights and esquires with no apparent connection to the crown, and a wide range of other royal servants. Edmund Hastings, Adam Peshale and Thomas Willoughby were not members of the royal affinity, as far as I know, but they were all important landowners and very influential in their respective regions, and so were the sort of men upon whom the king might have wished to bestow honours.[149] Richard Tempest was a seasoned campaigner who, at the age of fifty-nine, indented to accompany Henry to France in 1415.[150] Sir John Wiltshire was a key member of the earl of Arundel's affinity.[151] It is interesting to see John Pelham and John Tiptoft, erstwhile supporters of the 'court faction' against the Prince, receiving higher honours (i.e. five lengths) than John Leventhorpe, the receiver-general and attorney-general of the duchy of Lancaster.[152] In Leventhorpe's group, receiving just four lengths, was an eclectic mix of low-level crown servants, including Robert Preston, one of the king's farriers;[153] William Buxton, David and Owen Kawardyn and Thomas Porter, all king's yeomen;[154] William Halyday, one of the king's minstrels;[155] Richard Appleton, auditor of accounts in the exchequer;[156] and Thomas Cavendish, a servant of the royal cellar.[157] No doubt, Sir John Strange was included in recognition of the long service he had performed for the king's father as controller of the royal household between 1405 and 1413 – in 1413 he was sixty-five years old and his son, Christopher, had recently taken his place in the royal household. The same might be said of Sir John Greyndore, a loyal servant of the duchy of Lancaster from the early 1390s and a seasoned campaigner in

[146] Ibid., 469, fn. 11.
[147] N. Orme, 'Lacy, Edmund (*c.*1370–1455)', *ODNB*.
[148] *HP*, IV, 745–7.
[149] *HP*, III, 317–19; IV, 61–4; IV, 871–3.
[150] *HP*, IV, 573–5.
[151] *HP*, IV, 874–5.
[152] *HP*, III, 591–5.
[153] *CPR, 1413–16*, p. 129.
[154] TNA, E 101/406/21 mm. 27d, 28.
[155] *CPR, 1413–16*, p. 96.
[156] Wylie and Waugh, *Henry the Fifth*, I, 303, n. 5.
[157] *CPR, 1413–16*, p. 248.

Wales throughout the 1400s.[158] At Henry's accession he was made constable of Monmouth. The reason for John Russell's inclusion almost certainly lay in his long record of providing legal counsel for the duchy of Lancaster, which stretched back to 1403;[159] and Nicholas Gerard, another lawyer, had his annuity confirmed in 1413, as well as his position as clerk of the statute merchant at Shrewsbury.[160] It is interesting to note the appearance of John Kemp in this same group, a sign perhaps of the high regard which the future archbishop and cardinal had already acquired early in his career.[161]

There was also a 'Calais connection', a reminder that between March 1410 and October 1412 Henry had been captain of this vitally important strategic town and in that time had forged valuable associations with military men: his lieutenant there, Sir Thomas Pickworth,[162] received five lengths; and four lengths respectively were given to John Montgomery, bailiff of the Calais 'Eskenage',[163] and John Gerard, captain of the Lancaster Tower in the town.[164] The new king's martial interests were also indicated by the inclusion within the group receiving four lengths of cloth of seven royal heralds.[165] Heralds appeared in an English context at the end of the thirteenth century, offering advice on heraldic matters and presiding over ceremonies for their noble or royal masters. Over time, they were increasingly regarded as the arbiters of the right of individuals to bear arms, and Henry V notably attempted in 1417 to bring the whole system within the auspices of the crown by appointing a supreme herald, Garter 'king of arms of the English', to preside over the armorial office and to ensure the regulation of all heraldic affairs.[166] At the coronation, only a selection of a much larger group of heralds was accorded the honour of wearing the king's livery. Henry quite understandably excluded the private heralds of the nobility;[167] but he also chose only a

---

158 Griffiths, 'Military Career and Affinity', p. 186; Allmand, *Henry V*, p. 354; *HP*, III, 243–6.
159 *HP*, IV, 246–8.
160 *HP*, III, 174–5.
161 R. G. Davies, 'Kemp, John (1380/81–1454)', *ODNB*.
162 Wylie, *Henry the Fourth*, III, 306; and Wylie and Waugh, *Henry the Fifth*, I, 329, n. 1.
163 Ibid., 38, n. 2.
164 Ibid., 42–3.
165 As first noted by John Anstis in *The Register of the Most Noble Order of the Garter*, 2 vols. (London, 1724), I, 328, fn. 't'. It is not clear whether Anstis had consulted the original document or the copy now held in the British Library. He simply notes that the names derived from a record then held in the Pell Office.
166 J. W. Armstrong, 'The Development of the Office of Arms in England, c. 1413–1485', in *The Herald in Late Medieval Europe*, ed. K. Stevenson (Woodbridge, 2009), pp. 9–28 (esp. pp. 16–25); and A. Ailes, 'Royal Grants of Arms in England before 1484', in *Soldiers, Nobles and Gentlemen: Essays in Honour of Maurice Keen*, ed. P. Coss and C. Tyerman (Woodbridge, 2009), pp. 85–96 (p. 89).
167 For which see A. R. Wagner and H. S. London, 'Heralds of the Nobility', in *Complete Peerage*, XI, Appendix C, 39–104 (esp. pp. 51–92).

proportion of the royal heralds for this special role.[168] Almost all had demonstrably close ties to the king and more broadly to the Lancastrian dynasty. The Leicester and Lancaster Heralds had originally been in the service of Henry's grandfather John of Gaunt; the Hereford Herald had been associated with Humphrey de Bohun, earl of Hereford, before serving Henry Bolingbroke, who had inherited the Hereford title by virtue of his marriage to de Bohun's daughter; the Derby Herald had served Henry Bolingbroke, as earl of Derby, since 1393; and the Cornwall Herald was directly linked to Henry as Prince of Wales and duke of Cornwall.[169] The Nottingham Herald must have reverted to the crown after the forfeiture for treason of Thomas Mowbray, duke of Norfolk (and earl of Nottingham) in 1405; and the Leopard Herald was the creation of Henry himself, or possibly his father, rather poignantly invoking the leopards (or lions) on the royal coat of arms.[170] Finally, Guyenne, King of Arms, though still in receipt of four lengths of cloth, was noted separately from the other heralds. The Leicester and Lancaster Heralds were also 'kings of arms',[171] but only the Guyenne Herald was accorded this title in this record, an honour which probably reflected Henry's high regard for William Bruges who held the office and in 1417 was promoted as the first Garter King of Arms.[172]

What qualified all these individuals to be included on this roll, and what duties they performed at the coronation, are questions with no clear-cut answers. Overall, the list contains only a proportion of the baronage, a minority of household men, a fraction of the king's wider affinity, a proportion of his heralds and a rather curious mixture of gentry, clerks and servants whose reasons for inclusion remain a matter of conjecture. Henry V appears to have exercised much greater selectivity in the people he chose to wear scarlet livery than his father in 1399 when more of a spectacle was made of this part of the coronation proceedings.[173] Political expediency and social convention must account for some of Henry's choices. However, given the relatively high preponderance amongst the representatives of the royal affinity of men who had known the king when he had been Prince (e.g.

---

168 E.g. Windsor, Carlisle, Nazers, Chandos, Northampton, Ireland, Bordeaux, Chester, Wales were not included: see A. Wagner, *Heralds of England: A History of the Office and College of Arms* (London, 1967), p. 55.

169 W. H. Godfrey et al., *College of Arms Monograph* (London, 1963), pp. 130, 248, 249, 266, 270–1; H. Paston-Bedingfield, 'The Heralds at the Time of Agincourt', in *Agincourt 1415*, ed. Curry, pp. 133–8 (esp. pp. 133–4).

170 Godfrey, *College of Arms*, p. 271.

171 Wagner, *Heralds of England*, p. 55.

172 Godfrey, *College of Arms*, p. 40; H. S. London, *The Life of William Bruges: The First Garter King of Arms*, Harleian Society old ser. 111–12 (1970), esp. pp. 12–18; Armstrong, 'Development of the Office of Arms', p. 22.

173 *Coronation of Richard III*, ed. Sutton and Hammond, pp. 92–9.

Harrington, Stanley, Leche, Cheyne, Spenser, Merbury, Porter, Wodehouse, etc.), and similarly of barons who had associated with Henry in the years before 1413, it is possible that personal considerations also came into play and that many of these men were singled out from their peers because they were individuals whose friendship and service the king valued most. These men formed the very core of Henry's 'establishment'; they were the men who most helped the king to establish his rule in 1413.

Conclusion

As hard as they might try, historians will continue to struggle to overturn the basic view that Henry V was an extraordinarily capable and successful king. This chapter offers no significant reappraisal of this orthodoxy, but it does provide further support for the idea that the seeds of this success lay in the circumstances of his father's reign and in the support he was able to cultivate amongst a large number of military-minded young men. No other late medieval English king, at the point of their succession, hit the ground running quite as well as Henry V did in 1413. This was because a network of men who had proven their loyalty and their abilities to the Prince was already well established when he became king. For it was not just Henry who had cut his teeth in Wales, but a whole generation of Englishmen who had fought alongside Henry or for his father. On his accession Henry V thus became head of a Lancastrian establishment that was deeply imbued with a warrior ethos and whose members – or a large number of them – probably felt a keen sense of expectation that the king would provide new opportunities for martial exploits. Henry's personal leadership skills were undoubtedly highly evolved, but even the most ardent devotee of this king's achievements must acknowledge the good fortune which attended the Prince in the 1400s, giving him the chance to hone his man-management and leadership qualities, as well as to forge friendships and associations which became politically important in later years. In 1413 Henry was able to promote these men to positions of great prominence without running the risk of being accused of favouritism because they had already proved their worth by giving valuable service to the English state. Thus, from the outset, the crucial link between service, and especially military service, and reward was established.

In 1413, the political elite underwent a reshuffle rather than wholesale change. In his chamber and in the upper echelons of government, Henry replaced his father's men with his own, but this was to be expected of any king wishing to get the most out of the servants and advisers who served him. In the ranks of household knights and esquires, there was a higher level of continuity, as well as evidence that 1413 was used as an opportunity to introduce a new generation of men from families with a proven Lancastrian pedigree. Although it is possible that some lower status individuals who had served Henry in Wales when he was Prince, but who were not subsequently favoured when he became king, formed the basis of the story of Henry's purging of his court in 1413, there is no other evidence to suggest that he turned his back on his former associates, and the story with which I began this chapter may simply have had its origins in the inevitable transformation of Henry's entourage from the relatively small, exclusive 'private' affinity of a Prince into a much enlarged and inclusive 'public' affinity of a king.

Investigation of Henry's royal knights and esquires raises important methodological as well as political points of interest. Trawling through original writs and chancery rolls to identify members of the household affinity produces a more reliable and apparently more comprehensive (though not necessarily definitive)[174] list of household knights and esquires than reliance on the published calendars, but it does nothing to obviate the impression that relatively little importance was attached by contemporaries to establishing and clearly demarcating exactly who belonged to this select group of individuals. Whilst the special formula proposed by Mitchell to identify household knights and esquires holds true in the majority of cases, it is still important to recognize that it was only used in certain types of record, and even then usually only where grants of patronage were noted. It is also significant to note, from Mitchell's research, that only a proportion of knights who were eligible to receive the king's robes – and were duly recorded on the livery rolls – evidently chose to do so, though it is likely that rather less elaborate visual markers such as badges or collars were more widely used to signify membership of the royal household.[175]

These points raise important questions about the distinctiveness of the body of household knights and esquires, and the particular value attached to the various modes and means of identifying the men in this group. Though association with the royal household was undoubtedly a source of great prestige and individual aspiration, the opaqueness of the records shedding light on the identity of these men, as a distinct collective entity, lends support to the observation by Rosemary Horrox that 'such imprecision was characteristic of a society which regarded service as open-ended and personal'.[176] This, indeed, is where the coronation livery roll is so instructive, for it indicates how the net was cast far wider than the royal household when it came to the distribution of personal honour and liveries by the king. The coronation

---

174 There is no indication that Sir John Greyndore was one of Henry V's household knights, even though the fact that he had been a household knight under Henry IV and had been attached to the household of the Prince of Wales since 1403, had held high office in the duchy of Lancaster in 1413 and was in receipt of an annuity, strongly suggests he might have been: *HP*, III, 243–6.

175 Mitchell, 'Aspects of Knightly Household', p. 71 calculates that only eleven out of a possible thirty-nine knights of the household received robes in Richard II's reign. For discussion of badges and collars, see Given-Wilson, *Royal Household*, pp. 237–43.

176 Horrox, *Richard III*, p. 227.

livery roll underlines the very personal nature of service and reward in the late medieval polity and the importance which the king placed not on hierarchies defined by constitutional convention or social rank, but by the loyalty and friendship of individuals he was counting on most to help him rule his kingdom.

APPENDIX 1:
HENRY V'S HOUSEHOLD KNIGHTS AND ESQUIRES 1413–14

Methodology

The account of Thomas More for 1 Hen. V (**TNA, E 101/406/21**) has been used to identity the knights and esquires of the chamber, and a large number of royal esquires. King's knights and additional royal esquires have been identified by searching for the phrase *dilecto et fideli militi/armiger [N]* or *a nostre chier et foial chivaler/esquier [N]* in the following records: privy seal writs sent to chancery (**TNA, C 81**); privy seal writs sent to the exchequer (**TNA, E 404**); and the patent rolls (**TNA, C 66**). It is not clear why the wardrobe accounts do not list royal knights, nor why only a proportion of royal esquires should be listed.

Names in bold indicate a knight/esquire of the chamber. Names in italics are listed in E 101/406/21 only.

The three columns indicate, respectively, whether the individual had been retained by Henry IV ('ac' indicates where an individual had his 'annuity confirmed' by Henry V), whether he had served or had any connection to Henry V when he was Prince (as an annuitant, retainer or office-holder), and/or whether he served in the Agincourt campaign of 1415. For Henry IV's retainers I have consulted Douglas Biggs, '"Then you perceive the body of our kingdom": The Royal Affinity of Henry IV, 1399–1413', (unpublished D.Phil. thesis, University of Minnesota, 1996), pp. 541–93 in conjunction with my own survey of TNA C 66 (patent rolls). For the Prince's affinity I have used William Rhidian Morris Griffiths, 'The Military Career and Affinity of Henry, Prince of Wales, 1399–1413', (unpublished M.Litt. thesis, University of Oxford, 1988), for details on the Prince's annuitants. For the Agincourt campaign I have consulted the AHRC-funded 'The Soldier in Later Medieval England Online Database', www.medievalsoldier.org for muster rolls (M). Information on the involvement of other individuals has been obtained by consulting the database for letters of protection (P), and Anne Curry, *Agincourt: A New History* (Stroud, 2005), Appendix D for indentures of service (I), though in neither case do these sources provide actual proof of service. Where given, the names of the captains under whom a knight or esquire served is indicated. If the individual themselves served as a captain this is shown as 'capt.'

Royal Knights

	NAME	Henry IV	Prince	Agincourt
1	Florys van Alkemade			Yes (I)
2	Richard Arundel	Yes		Yes (I)
3	John de Assheton	Yes?		Yes (M) capt.
4	William Bardolf			
5	Thomas Barre	Yes (ac)		
6	Walter Beauchamp			Yes (M) capt.
7	William Beauchamp	Yes (ac)		Yes (M) duke of Gloucester
8	John Blount	Yes		Yes (I)
9	William Bourchier	Yes	Yes	Yes (M) capt.
10	Thomas Broke	Yes		
11	George Chadelyche			
12	Robert Chalons	Yes		Yes (M) capt.
13	Thomas Chaworth	Yes		Yes (I)
14	William Clifford	Yes	Yes	
15	Hortonk van Clux	Yes		Yes (M) capt.
16	Robert Corbet	Yes		Yes (M) earl of Arundel
17	John Cornwall	Yes	Yes	Yes (I)
18	*William Courtenay*			Yes (M) capt.
19	William Cromwell			Yes (M) capt.
20	John Dabrichecourt	Yes (ac)		Yes (M) capt.
21	Thomas Dutton	Yes (ac)	Yes	Yes (M) capt.
22	Thomas Erpingham	Yes	Yes	Yes (M) capt.
23	John Etton	Yes		
24	John Fastolf			Yes (M) de la Pole
25	Simon Felbrigge			Yes (M) capt.
26	Thomas Greseley	Yes		Yes (M) capt.
27	**John Grey**	Yes	Yes	Yes (M) capt.
28	Stephen de Guyar			
29	William Harrington		Yes	Yes (M) capt.
30	Richard Harrington			
31	Thomas Hauley			Yes (I)
32	Walter Hungerford	Yes		Yes (M) capt.
33	Roger Leche	Yes	Yes	Yes (I)
34	Phillip Leche			Yes (I)
35	**Roland Leynthale**			Yes (M) capt.
36	John Littlebury	Yes (ac)		
37	Alexander Lounde	Yes (ac)		Yes (I)
38	Thomas Lucy	Yes		

NAME	Henry IV	Prince	Agincourt
39 William Lyle, junior	Yes (ac)		
40 Laurence Merbury			
41 Nicholas Montgomery			Yes (I)
42 Charles de Navarre			
43 Edmund Noon[1]	Yes		
44 Thomas Percy	Yes (ac)		Yes (M) capt.
45 Edward Perrers	Yes (ac)		
46 **John Phelip**	Yes	Yes	Yes (M) capt.
47 William Phelip	Yes		Yes (M) capt.
48 John Popham			Yes (M) duke of York
49 Richard Redmayne	Yes	Yes	
50 John Robertsart	Yes (ac)		Yes (M) capt.
51 Ralph Rochefort	Yes (ac)		
52 John Rothenhale			
53 John Routhe	Yes (ac)		Yes (M) H. Lord FitzHugh
54 John St. John	Yes	Yes	
55 Simon Sandeford			
56 Ralph Shirley			Yes (M) capt.
57 *John Skydmore*	Yes	Yes	Yes (I)
58 Humphrey Stafford		Yes	
59 **Hugh Standissh**		Yes	Yes (I)
60 John Stanley	Yes (ac)	Yes	Yes (M) capt.
61 Edmund Thorp	Yes		
62 John Tiptoft	Yes (ac)		Yes (I)
63 Roger Trumpington	Yes		Yes (M) capt.
64 Thomas Turnstall		Yes	Yes (I)
65 **Gilbert Umfraville**			Yes (I)
66 Robert Umfraville			
67 Thomas West			Yes (M) capt.
68 *Robert Whitney*		Yes	

[1] Noted as both a knight and esquire.

Royal Esquires

	NAME	Henry IV	Prince	Agincourt
1	Nicholas Alderwych	Yes (ac)		Yes (M) capt.
2	*Thomas Appulton*			Yes (M) Robert Chalons
3	*Nicholas Ashton*			Yes (I)
4	*Thomas Aston*		Yes	
5	*John Astoo*			Yes (M) John Burgh
6	*William Atherton*		Yes	
7	John Auncell	Yes (ac)		
8	Robert Babthorpe	Yes (ac)		Yes (M) capt.
9	*William Bank*			Yes (M) John Burgh
10	John Barry			
11	John Belle	Yes		Yes (I)
12	Simon Blackebourne	Yes (ac)		
13	William Blackebourne			Yes (M)
14	John Blaket	Yes (ac)		Yes (I)
15	James Blount			Yes (M)
16	Robert de Bolton/Bolren			Yes (M) earl of Suffolk
17	Henry Bowet	Yes (ac)		
18	*Thomas Bowet*	Yes		Yes (M)
19	William Bowes			Yes (M) capt.
20	Richard Boynton	Yes (ac)		
21	William Bradwardyn		Yes	Yes (M) John Burgh
22	Hugh Broart			
23	John Brocart	Yes (ac)		
24	William Brokesby	Yes (ac)		Yes (M)
25	Thomas Brounflete	Yes (ac)		
26	Robert Brut			Yes (I)
27	William Burton			Yes (M)
28	**John Butler**			Yes (M)
29	Simon Campe	Yes		
30	*William Castelyn*			Yes (M) Robert Chalons
31	John Cavendish			Yes (M) duke of Glouc
32	William Chancellier	Yes (ac)		
33	Thomas Chaucer	Yes	Yes	Yes (M) capt.
34	**John Cheyne**	Yes		Yes (M) capt.
35	**John Chetwynd**		Yes	Yes (M)
36	*John Clement*			Yes (M) Robert Chalons
37	Richard Clitheroe	Yes (ac)		Yes (P)
38	John Clifford		Yes	Yes (M) Robert Chalons

	NAME	Henry IV	Prince	Agincourt
39	William Clinton	Yes (ac)		Yes (P)
40	John Clipsham	Yes (ac)		
41	Richard Clopton	Yes (ac)		
42	John Cope	Yes (ac)		
43	John Courroys			
44	Thomas Corbet			Yes (M) Robert Chalons
45	John Credy	Yes (ac)		
46	Richard Cressy	Yes (ac)		
47	*John Curson*	Yes		Yes (P) Thos Erpingham
48	James Dartas	Yes (ac)		Yes (I)
49	John Durham	Yes (ac)		
50	*Thomas Easton*			Yes (I)
51	John Elmham			Yes (M)
52	John Esmond	Yes (ac)		Yes (M)
53	Richard Etton/Eaton			Yes (M) John Burgh
54	Laurence Everard			Yes (M) Robert Chalons
55	Henry Filongley	Yes (ac)		Yes (I)
56	Richard Filongleye	Yes (ac)	Yes	
57	William Fitz Henry			Yes (M)
58	Simon Flete			
59	*John Folville*			Yes (M)
60	Henry Fowler	Yes		Yes (I)
61	Bertram de France	Yes (ac)		Yes (M) John de Burgh
62	John Fynbargh			
63	Richard Gardemewe	Yes (ac)		Yes (I)
64	Arnold de Ghent	Yes		
65	Robert Gloucester		Yes	Yes (I)
66	John Golafre	Yes (ac)		
67	Thomas Goter	Yes (ac)		
68	*John Gra*			Yes (M) capt.
69	*Andrew Grey*			Yes (M)
70	Sampson Greenwich	Yes (ac)		
71	Richard Halsam			Yes (M) Robert Chalons
72	Roger Harbrik			
73	William Hardegrove			Yes (P) Henry V
74	James Harrington	Yes (ac)		Yes (I)
75	Richard Hay	Yes (ac)		Yes (M) capt.
76	John Hawkeswell	Yes (ac)		
77	Nicholas Haywode	Yes (ac)		Yes (M) Robert Chalons
78	*Robert Heron*			Yes (M) John Lumley

	NAME	Henry IV	Prince	Agincourt
79	*John Hertishorne*		Yes	
80	Thomas Hethey			
81	Robert Heton		Yes	Yes (M) John Grey
82	John Hobildod	Yes (ac)		Yes (M) Robert Chalons
83	*Anthony Hoby*		Yes	
84	James Hoget	Yes		Yes (I)
85	William Hoghwyk	Yes (ac)		
86	**John Holland**			Yes (M) capt.
87	Nicholas Holland		Yes	Yes (M) Robert Chalons
88	John Horsey	Yes (ac)		Yes (I)
89	John Hotoft		Yes	
90	*John Hull*			
91	Gerard Hune	Yes (ac)		Yes (M) Robert Chalons
92	William Hunte	Yes (ac)		
93	John Ireby [?Freby]			Yes (I)
94	Nicholas Jerard	Yes (ac)		
95	Louis John			Yes (M)
96	Henry Kirkestede	Yes (ac)	Yes	
97	John Knyght	Yes (ac)		
98	John Kyghley			
99	Nicholas Lary			Yes (M) John Burgh
100	Thomas Lathe	Yes (ac)		
101	Peter Laward		Yes	
102	William atte Lee			Yes (M) capt.
103	Robert Litton	Yes (ac)		
104	John Liverpool	Yes (ac)		
105	Henry de Lounde	Yes		Yes (M) capt.
106	Geoffrey Louther	Yes (ac)		
107	William Louther	Yes (ac)		
108	**Robert Lovell**		Yes	Yes (I)
109	William Loveneye	Yes (ac)		
110	Hugh Malgrave	Yes (ac)		
111	Nicholas Mandit			
112	Richard Marbroke			
113	Richard de la Mare	Yes (ac)		
114	Richard Mawardyn			
115	Peter Melbourne		Yes	
116	John Merbury	Yes (ac)	Yes	Yes (I)
117	**Nicholas Merbury**		Yes	Yes (M) capt.
118	John Mersk	Yes (ac)		

	NAME	Henry IV	Prince	Agincourt
119	John Molton	Yes (ac)		
120	Henry Morley	Yes (ac)		
121	Hugh Mortimer	Yes	Yes	
122	**Robert Morton**	Yes (ac)		Yes (M) duke of York
123	*William Mounteney*			Yes (M) Henry V
124	Edmund Noon[2]	Yes (ac)		
125	John Norbury	Yes	Yes	
126	William Norton	Yes (ac)		
127	John Nowell			Yes (I)
128	Robert Passmere			Yes (M) Robert Chalons
129	Thomas Percy			Yes (M) Robert Chalons
130	**Nicholas Petche**	Yes		
131	*John Pilkington*			Yes (M) capt.
132	*John Pole*			
133	Thomas Pomeroy	Yes (ac)		
134	Ralph Pope	Yes (ac)	Yes	Yes (M)
135	**William Porter**	Yes (ac)	Yes	Yes (M) capt.
136	John Pyryent	Yes (ac)		Yes (I)
137	*Thomas Radcliff*			
138	*John Ramsey*			
139	Ralph Ramsey	Yes (ac)		Yes (I)
140	John Rider	Yes (ac)		Yes (M)
141	*Louis Robessart*		Yes	Yes (M)
142	*John Rothenale*		Yes	Yes (I)
143	John Routh	Yes (ac)		Yes (M) d. of Clarence
144	*Roger Salveyn*		Yes	Yes (P)
145	Robert Saperton	Yes (ac)		
146	Hugh Say			
147	Nicholas Saxton			
148	Urian Seinpiere	Yes (ac)		
149	John Selby	Yes		Yes (M) capt.
150	Thomas Shepey	Yes (ac)		
151	Robert Sherwynd	Yes (ac)		
152	William Sherwynd			
153	**Robert Shotesbroke**	Yes	Yes	Yes (M) capt.
154	John Skelton			Yes (M) duke of York
155	John Spenser	Yes (ac)	Yes	
156	Gerard Spronk	Yes		Yes (I)

[2] Also noted as a knight.

	NAME	Henry IV	Prince	Agincourt
157	Ralph Standissh	Yes (ac)		
158	Thomas Staunton			Yes (M) Robert Chalons
159	Thomas Strickland	Yes (ac)		Yes (M) capt.
160	Richard Stucle			
161	**John Stiward**			Yes (M) capt.
162	Thomas Strange			
163	***Christopher Strange***			
164	Matthew Sweetenham		Yes	
165	*John Swillington*			Yes (M) capt.
166	*Simon Sy*			Yes (P) Henry V
167	Nicholas Talbot	Yes (ac)		
168	Thomas Talbot	Yes (ac)		Yes (M) earl of Hunt.
169	*John Tempest*			
170	Rees ap Thomas	Yes (ac)	Yes	
171	*William Tirwhit*			Yes (I)
172	Robert Tyntour	Yes (ac)		
173	John Topcliff			Yes (M) capt.
174	William Tropnell			Yes (I)
175	**William Troutebeck**	Yes		Yes (I)
176	Robert Twyford	Yes (ac)		Yes (M) J. Dabrichecourt
177	*John Upton*		Yes	Yes (P) earl of March
178	John Vale		Yes	Yes (I)
179	Thomas Warde		Yes	Yes (M) capt.
180	Phillip Walwayn	Yes (ac)	Yes	
181	John Waterton	Yes	Yes	Yes (M) capt.
182	*Robert Wodeford*			
183	John Wodehouse		Yes	
184	Walter Wilcotes			
185	Henry Wilymot			
186	Richard Wydeville	Yes (ac)	Yes	

APPENDIX 2:
A ROLL OF THE RECIPIENTS OF SCARLET CLOTH
AT HENRY V's CORONATION (BL MS STOWE 440)

* Names in bold indicate membership of the royal affinity (see Appendix 1).
I have inserted noble titles where relevant.

12 lengths

Thomas Arundel, archbishop of Canterbury; Prince John; Henry Beaufort,
bishop of Winchester, chancellor; Thomas, earl of Arundel, treasurer of
England; Richard, earl of Warwick

10 lengths

Edmund, earl of March; Ralph, earl of Westmorland; Thomas, earl of Salisbury; John, earl of Somerset; Earl Marshal; James, earl of Ormond; John, earl
of Huntingdon; William Lord Roos de Hamelak

8 lengths

Thomas, Lord Berkeley; Reynold, Lord Grey de Ruthin; Lord Mowbray;[1]
John, Lord Clifford; John, Lord Lovell of Tichmarsh; **Sir William Harrington**;
Thomas, Lord Camoys; Henry, Lord FitzHugh; Henry Scrope, Lord of
Masham; Lord Charlton; William, Lord Botreaux; **Thomas Erpingham**;
Gilbert Umfraville (earl of Kyme); Thomas, Lord Morley; Thomas, Lord
Willoughby; Richard Beauchamp, Lord Bergavenny; **William, Lord Bour-
chier**; John Talbot, Lord Furnivall; Hugh, Lord Burnell

6 lengths

Roger, son of the earl of March; Edward, son of the earl of Huntingdon;
Richard, Lord Despenser; Edmund, Lord Ferrers of Groby; William Bour;
Henry, Lord Beaumont; [illegible]; Richard, Lord Strange; **Simon Felbrigge**;
William la Zouche, Lord of Harringworth; **John, Lord Stanley**; Edward,
Lord Hastings of Elsing; Lord Grey de Wilton; Ralph Neville; William, Lord
Clinton; Henry Percy; Master Grey [of Codnor?]; Robert, Lord Poynings;
William, Lord Molyns; **Roger Leche**; Edmund, son of the earl of Devon; John,
Lord Mautravers; Master Richard Courtenay; Master John Prophet; Master
John Iklington; Thomas Carnika; **John Wodehouse**; John Wakering; William

---

[1] Presumably a scribal error: John Mowbray, brother of the rebel of 1405, came of age in
1413 and was noted above as the Earl Marshal (receiving 10 lengths).

Lasingby; John Burgh; Edmund Lacy; William Waldern, mayor of London;
Thomas Chaucer, butler

5 lengths

William Clifford; **Robert Corbet**; **William Harrington**; John Greyndore;
Walter Ufflett; Thomas Pickworth; Richard Tempest; Nicholas Longford;
Walter Langford; **John St John**; John Trumpington; Thomas Dynmok; Lord
Grey; **Thomas Gresley**; John Gresley; John Hused; John Pelham; **Thomas
Talbot**; **Sir Humphrey Stafford I**; John son of Lord de Grey de Codmore;
Thomas West; Bartholomew Verdon; **Hugh de Standissh**; John Wiltshire;
Robert Morley; Roger de Lovell; **John Dabrichecourt**; Adam Peshale; Baldwin
Straunge; John Bigot; **Thomas Tunstall**; John Fitz Leigh; **Thomas Brounflete**;
John Tiptoft; **John Cheyne**; Thomas Willoughby; Thomas Pouderey; Edmund
de Hastings; Thomas Grene; Thomas son of Lord Talbot; John Bushy; **Thomas
Barre**; Ralph Rotherford; John Colpepper; **Ralph Shirley**; **William Porter**;
John Stuard; **Nicholas Merbury**; **John Spenser**

4 lengths

John Strange; **John Chetwynde**; **Robert Morton**; John Savage; John Russell;
John Upton; William Leventhorp;[2] **John Cavendish**; Thomas Cavendish;
Thomas Dynmock; John Edmund; Thomas Stanley; John Shirley; John Gerard;
John Pyryent; John Colyer; John Wyot; Richard Appleton; John Montgomery;
John Walsingham; Thomas Derham; Geoffrey Colet; Ralph Bleverhayset;
Thomas Brook; **Nicholas Holand**; **Thomas Ward**; Magistro Nicholas Phisir;
Thomas Clynke; Guyenne King of Arms; **John Credy**; Walter Burton; **John
Bell**; Owin Kawardyn; David Kawardyn; Thomas Porter; William Halyday;
Robert Clew; Lancaster Herald; Leicester Herald; Derby Herald; Hereford
Herald; Nottingham Herald; Cornwall Herald; Leopard Herald; Richard
Lyndesey; John Gerard; William Warner; John Helds; William Woodhouse;
Nicholas Gerard; William Stilt; John Kemp; William Werbilton; **Thomas
Corbet**; Arnaldo Squyer; John Botsc...; John Hereford; William Brewster;
Hugh Bigg; John Burton; John Compton; William Preston; William Buxton;
Robert Preston; John Coventry

3 lengths

John Bott; William Pym; John Pye; John Middelton; John Pym; John Lurao;
John Lurao

---

[2]   Presumably a scribal error: *John* Leventhorpe.

3

Henry V, Lancastrian Kingship and the Far North of England

Mark Arvanigian

Historians of the English north in the late Middle Ages have recently engaged with a number of issues of importance to students of both the English regions and of the period. Of these, two stand out for the purposes of this chapter. The first considers the prospect of the 'far north' as a unique frontier society, sufficiently set apart from the main currents of English society by virtue of the dictates of border warfare and its close proximity to England's perennial enemy. This envisages a region bordered, roughly, by the Scottish borders to the north, and by the palatinate of Durham and the sparsely settled county of Westmorland to the south. Lancastrian influence, as a result of the efforts of John of Gaunt and Henry IV, now extended northwards into Durham and Westmorland from Yorkshire and Lancashire: Durham by the appointment of the Lancastrian clerk Thomas Langley as prince bishop, and Ralph Neville, by virtue of his marriage to John of Gaunt's daughter and Henry IV's half-sister, Joan Beaufort, and his commensurate elevation to the earldom of West-morland. By the second half of the reign of Henry IV, both counties were solid outposts of partisan Lancastrian power. That is to say, they were controlled by a group of men whose allegiance predated and transcended their fidelity to their lord king, by virtue of their shared allegiance to him as duke of Lancaster prior to 1399. Further north, this cannot be said to have been true. Cumberland and Northumberland remained the heart of the English 'far north', a sparsely populated border country governed not through the usual considerations of royal justice and administration, but instead by virtue of specially appointed military governors and with consideration of the region's many ancient liberties.

One central aim of this chapter is to consider the nature of authority in this remote region.[1] An example of the complexities involved in this exercise may

---

[1] C. J. Neville, *Violence, Custom and Law: The Anglo-Scottish Border Lands in the Later Middle Ages* (Edinburgh, 1998), esp. pp. 96–124; and C. J. Neville, 'Keeping the Peace on the Northern Marches in the Later Middle Ages', *EHR* 109 (1994), 1–25; R. L. Storey, 'The Wardens of the Marches of England towards Scotland, 1377–1489', *EHR* 72 (1957), 593–615;

be found in the broad legal and military remit given to the royal wardens of the Marches, creations of the Scottish wars and who carried a great weight of responsibility for the defence of the north.[2] Their necessity speaks to the region's unique character. In fact, this chapter will claim as its foundation a single supposition: that the far north had, for much of its history, been destabilized by twin curses, namely the frequent incursions of hostile Scots and the ambitions (and relative independence) of its own nobility. Enough ink has been spilled on both subjects in recent years to make the truth of both of these claims quite plain. Rather than revisit them here, this chapter builds on the strength of their arguments by exploring the idea that by the end of his reign Henry IV had to some extent resolved these challenges. He did this by creating a workable governing apparatus for the far north by combining the public infrastructure of royal government with important elements of the king's own private assets – drawn from the great Lancastrian patrimony – to create an early version of that modern notion, the 'public–private partnership'. The chapter further considers whether, in policy terms, the incipient reign of Henry V represented a kind of 'new start' in the region, or simply the continuator of the successful work of his predecessor. In doing so, it will reinforce Professor Pollard's claim that the Percys were a dominant force in the north only for the briefest of moments, and that in fact it is the Nevilles who should be regarded as the region's great traditional power, despite a good deal of historiography (and it is true, a few contemporary claims) to the contrary.

Pollard was interested primarily in the prominence of the two families as they came into conflict during the Wars of the Roses, from the 1450s onwards. Yet, in a region largely bereft of noble society and now in the absence of the Percys, it was the reigns of Henry IV and Henry V which gave the crown an opportunity to build a stronger presence there, and to reshape the region politically. Henry V was able to capitalize on his father's groundbreaking work and his own reputation for good governance in extending the scope of Lancastrian dominion in the far north. Rather than calling on a close cadre of Lancastrian householders and duchy officers to oversee his government, as Henry IV had done, he instead spread the benefits of royal office-holding and patronage more widely.[3] Evidence can be found in his parliaments, where he was broadly trusted by the Commons, more so after his military successes in

---

J. A. Tuck, 'The Emergence of a Northern Nobility, 1250–1400', *Northern History* 22 (1986), 1–17.

[2] An interesting approach is A. J. Macdonald, 'John Hardyng, Northumbrian Identity and the Scots', in *North-East England in the Later Middle Ages: Regions and Regionalism in History*, ed. R. H. Britnell and C. D. Liddy (Woodbridge, 2005), pp. 25–42.

[3] G. L. Harriss, 'The King and his Magnates', in *Henry V*, ed. Harriss, pp. 31–51. Harriss also seems to have coined the very apt term *familia* to denote the extended family and close friends at the core of the Lancastrian world.

France.[4] The Commons held the view that the regime was generally frugal and properly constituted, well counselled in the main, and possessed a proper sense of the role of kingship in the public arena.[5] Further evidence may be found in his openness toward those whose ancestors had once been disloyal (including many northerners), whom he reinstated and even patronized, where prudent. In doing so he completed the work begun by his father, and politically realigned the far north. Though this realignment was ultimately not to be an enduring one, it was nonetheless sufficient to provide Henry V with the short-term benefit of stability.

Background

Regional society and county administration were crucial indicators and well-springs of royal support – consider the role of Cheshire for Richard II, for example. It was the northern character of the king's private affinity which Henry IV exploited to establish his regime, maintain order in the northern March and ultimately defeat his many enemies.[6] Henry V was a beneficiary of that stability in the north, particularly with respect to the Scottish borders. Macdonald's excellent study elaborates on the effects of intermittent warfare in the region, and teases out its many connections to national politics.[7] One observation which might well be added to his own was that Lancastrian rule was in fact born of the hostilities between England and Scotland, in that Henry Bolingbroke achieved the throne through the support he gained from the region's military nobility and their retinues – much of it underwritten by the royal exchequer. To prevent this same elixir from threatening his own government, Henry recognized the wisdom of encouraging the Nevilles to form a bulwark to the Percys. This was the northern legacy left to his son, who enjoyed it *without* the political instability and echoes of royal usurpation that had dogged his father. This was a crucial step, because the security situation was much improved elsewhere. Wales had become quieter – in part because of the work done by the young Henry of Monmouth during his

---

4 Allmand points out that the king was present at five of the early parliaments, but attended just one after that of October 1416, when his military victories meant his absence and which also made his presence less necessary in ensuring the Commons' compliance: Allmand, *Henry V*, chapter 17, and esp. pp. 381–3. For the king's relationship with his parliaments, see also G. L. Harriss, 'The Management of Parliament', in *Henry V*, ed. Harriss, pp. 137–58 (pp. 145–7).

5 Ibid., pp. 142–3.

6 P. Morgan, *War and Society in Medieval Cheshire, 1272–1403* (Manchester, 1987), esp. chapter 5. For another view, see T. Thornton, 'Cheshire: The Inner Citadel of Richard II's Kingdom?' in *The Reign of Richard II*, ed. G. Dodd (Stroud, 2000), pp. 85–96.

7 A. Macdonald, *Border Bloodshed: Scotland and England at War, 1369–1403* (Edinburgh, 2000).

father's reign – while the situation in Ireland had also improved, and from the crown's perspective would continue to improve, following the appointment of John Talbot as king's lieutenant there in 1414.[8] There is little question that this significant improvement in England's regional stability, after decades of insecurity, played an important role in broadening the new king's horizons politically.

In this, the importance of the Percys cannot be overstated. Since late in the reign of Edward III, the north had been a source of considerable trouble to the crown. Though their ability to defeat the English in pitched battle was necessarily limited, Scottish Marcher lords had made a fine living from harassments and border raiding, which proved destructive enough to disrupt local society and merit the consistent attention of central government. The legacy of Scottish belligerence and the alliance between the Scottish and French crowns were disruptions to all facets of local life as the region became an embattled frontier society.[9] Practically, this resulted in some considerable loss of local autonomy, as the traditional authority of the landed community was now overshadowed by the Percys and their private ambitions as Marcher lords – and the needs of the crown for border defence. The most ubiquitous symbol of this latter requirement was the appointment of the two royal wardens of the Scottish Marches, vested with plenipotentiary civil and military authority, and possessed of command over the armed garrisons at a string of border fortresses under their command – all underwritten by royal government. Perhaps inevitably, given their local standing and web of retainers throughout the region, these commissions were usually made to the Percys – which only served to amplify the family's ambitions.[10]

It was in fact the interplay between these two elements which proved destabilizing; Percy power, extensive as it may have been by its own resources, was very much amplified by those of the crown. This was a long-standing problem for royal government, in that the most serious sources of political

---

[8] For the best complete treatment of the revolt in Wales, see R. Rees Davies, *The Revolt of Owain Glyn Dŵr* (Oxford, 1995). Irish lordship's early framework is set out in R. F. Frame, *English Lordship in Ireland, 1318–1369* (Oxford, 1982); while the Lancastrian period is surveyed in A. Cosgrove, *Late Medieval Ireland, 1370–1541* (Dublin, 1981). For Ireland as a specifically early Lancastrian pre-occupation, see K. Simms, 'The Ulster Revolt of 1404: An Anti-Lancastrian Dimension?' (pp. 141–60), and E. Matthew, 'Henry V and the Proposal for an Irish Crusade' (pp. 161–75), in *Ireland and the English World in the Late Middle Ages*, ed. B. Smith (London, 2009).

[9] This argument builds upon the question asked, most notably, in essays by S. Ellis, 'Region and Frontier in the English State: The English Far North, 1296–1603', in *Frontiers, Regions and Identities*, ed. S. G. Ellis, Raingard Eßer, J.-F. Berdah and Miloš ezník (Pisa, 2009); and A. King, 'Scaling the Ladder: The Rise and Rise of the Grays of Heaton, *c*.1296–*c*.1415', in *North-East England*, ed. Britnell and Liddy, pp. 57–73.

[10] A. Tuck, 'War and Society in the Medieval North', *Northern History* 21 (1985), 33–52; A. Goodman, 'Religion and Warfare in the Anglo-Scottish Marches', in *Medieval Frontier Societies*, ed. R. Bartlett and A. MacKay (Oxford, 1992), pp. 245–66.

disenchantment also originated in the northern counties. The Scottish wars had turned the far northern March into what amounted to a militarized zone, its string of fortresses now manned by permanent garrisons – England's only real standing army. With extensive, near vice-regal powers, and significant local retinues, the Percys and to a lesser extent the Nevilles had maintained the king's peace while simultaneously defending the realm against the Scots. Sizeable wages and remittances for expenses followed, and ensured the consistent engagement of the gentry community in this project.[11] This influx of money was also a source of undoubted easing of the financial hardships of the region's landed class: as Scottish raiding disrupted trade, agriculture and other land uses, their values naturally declined.[12] As local landed wealth was undermined, the importance of royal commissions and other employment grew, if only in relative terms. Also of growing importance was the alignment of the local gentry with the region's great families, who controlled much of this employment. The Percys could naturally call upon a group of border knights to assist with defence and staff the frequent royal commissions, and these relationships endured even following Hotspur's defeat at Shrewsbury in 1403 and the failure of Scrope's rebellion in 1405 – evidence surely of their powerful nature.[13] As a result, the usual ties of service, fealty and utility which so often characterized lordship and service were here amplified by the circumstances of border life. Thus, for Henry V, the absence of the Percys – following the disgrace and forfeiture of the family in his father's reign – presented a unique opportunity.[14] Success in this meant finding amenable alternatives to the Percys, and these came from the king's 'private' retinue – the Lancastrian affinity.[15] Modern historians have drawn a sharp distinction between Henry V's patronage pattern and that of his father, and to be sure, in the new administration, old Lancastrian retainers were less in evidence. Yet, as the years passed, demography also played a role in separating the new reign from its Lancastrian past.

---

[11] For the sums issued to the March wardens during the reign of Henry IV, see for example TNA, E 403/582.

[12] Evidence from inquisitions post-mortem and elsewhere demonstrates the degree to which lands in the border shires and liberties were brought to waste. See for, example, TNA, DURH 3/13.

[13] M. Arvanigian, 'Managing the North in the Reign of Henry IV, 1402–1408', in *Reign of Henry IV*, ed. Dodd and Biggs, pp. 82–104.

[14] The experience of Richard II is worth recalling in this regard. He attempted to circumvent the Percys by appointing others, including his favourites, as March wardens. In a short time, having proved unsuccessful, this strategy was abandoned, and as hostilities with Scotland became more acute, the Percys were duly reappointed to these posts: A. J. Macdonald, *Border Bloodshed*, p. 75; A. Tuck, 'Richard II and the Border Magnates', *Northern History* 3 (1968), pp. 27–52.

[15] S. Walker, *The Lancastrian Affinity, 1361–99* (Oxford, 1990), Appendix 1.

Lancastrian Northerners and Henry V's Early Council

Henry V's early councils show the degree to which he continued his father's reliance upon northerners; many were of old Lancastrian stock, men who had acted with the king against the Percys and afterwards assisted in the establishment of royal policy in the realm's four most-northerly shires. As Brown noted in his survey of fifteenth-century royal councils, evidence from this period is sparse. There is, however, evidence for the sessions of 1415, the first year with enough extant material sufficient for drawing any conclusions. In that year, nineteen different council members attended fourteen separate meetings. Of these participants, some attended only occasionally, while others – particularly the ecclesiastics and officers of state – were much more assiduous.[16] In these early sessions, attendance exceeded five or six councillors very rarely, and these tended to be servants, friends and kinsmen rather than representatives of the great families of the realm.[17] Of these, several old Lancastrians reappear in familiar roles. For example, Sir Thomas Erpingham was a long-time companion of Henry IV dating at least to the 1390s and probably earlier; he now appeared regularly on his son's council. Erpingham had long ago gained renown as a soldier-knight, and had been a trusted retainer first of John of Gaunt, and then as a companion knight to Henry Bolingbroke. He was among the first of the secular figures named to Henry V's council, and became a regular member, faithful in his attendance.[18] His nomination and regular attendance undoubtedly point to the king's belief in the enduring value of long and loyal service to his family, and along with Henry, Lord FitzHugh (see discussion below), his fidelity to these sessions was greatest amongst the secular members.

The far north was nonetheless the region best represented on the council. One name that appears consistently in these lists was Ralph Neville, earl of Westmorland. Just as he had been prior to 1413, Westmorland's services were much in demand in the north during Henry V's reign, and he was therefore only occasionally in attendance at council meetings. Yet, in spite of his absenteeism, he continued to be named to the council year-on-year, and like the council's other core members, was named in Henry V's frequent instructions from abroad with all of the council's other core members. Apparently, retaining his uncle's counsel was important enough to the new king for alternative arrangements to be made for the times when the earl could not attend in person: Westmorland was granted leave to continue the practice he had begun during Henry IV's reign of naming his own surrogates to the council.

---

[16] A. L. Brown, 'Kings' Councillors in Fifteenth-Century England', *TRHS* 19 (1969), 95–118 (p. 105).

[17] J. Catto, 'The King's Servants', in *Henry V*, ed. Harriss, pp. 75–96.

[18] T. E. John, 'Sir Thomas Erpingham', *Norfolk Archaeology* 35 (1973), 96–109; Walker, *Lancastrian Affinity*, Appendix 1.

The first of these had been his younger brother, Thomas, Lord Furnival, in 1405, who though he had little prior connection with the king or the Lancastrians, nonetheless was chosen to serve in the important office of treasurer of England until his death in 1408. Following his death, Furnival was replaced by Westmorland's associate and retainer William Heron, Lord Say, a member of an important Northumbrian family who soon afterwards became steward of Henry IV's household, probably also the result of his patron's sponsorship.[19]

In Henry V's reign, Westmorland's council representative was probably another northerner, Henry, Lord FitzHugh. FitzHugh's family had been neighbours and close allies of the Nevilles in the North Riding of Yorkshire, for the fathers of the two men had served together for decades in John of Gaunt's retinue. In addition to serving as a regular councillor in the new reign, FitzHugh was also named to high office, serving as constable at the new king's coronation, and then as Henry V's chamberlain – even though he was by now well into his fifties. Yet his presence was clearly required, and he was expected to be mainly present at court. It was probably for this purpose that he was granted an income from the vill of Harrow, to maintain his estate while resident at Kennington, Westminster and London – an indication of his value to the king.[20] Though he never achieved the heights of his neighbour, Lord FitzHugh's career nonetheless closely tracked that of Westmorland: both had strong connections with the duke of Lancaster and his retainers, both prized these connections above all others and both traded heavily upon these connections in their political ascent to careers in royal service. In due course, FitzHugh's son and heir married Alice Neville, Westmorland's granddaughter by Joan Beaufort, in a rather grand wedding ceremony at Raby castle. In the event, the wedding took place after the earl's own death in 1425, and was thus presided over by the dowager countess and her son (the bride's father), Richard Neville, the future earl of Salisbury. So, in the early years of the reign, Westmorland served Henry V as an absentee councillor and lieutenant in the north, just as he had done for the king's father, yet he also remained closely in touch with council proceedings through his connections to its other northern members – who tended also to be of long Lancastrian extraction.

This northern flavour was in evidence also amongst the council's ecclesiastics – and was in fact supplemented by the presence of Bishop Beaufort of Winchester, who as chancellor was the council's de facto chairman. Beau-

---

[19] M. Arvanigian, 'The Durham Gentry and the Scottish March, 1370–1400: County Service in Late Medieval England', *Northern History* 42 (2005), 257–73. The fact that a new treasurer was appointed almost annually during the reign, because of the hardship placed on them by the king's consistent financial shortfalls, made his tenure of service quite unusual; see J. L. Kirby, *Henry IV of England* (London, 1970).

[20] *Foedera*, IX, 13.

fort was also the countess of Westmorland's brother. He became chancellor immediately after the coronation, and as Henry V's mentor and confidant, was surely the council's guiding spirit. As Gerald Harriss has shown, his was the leading voice in the formation and execution of most royal policy, second only to the king himself.[21] Beaufort was joined by his old Lancastrian colleagues and long-time servants, Bishops Courtenay and Langley, along with Bishop Chichele. Courtenay was the scion of the great Devonian family, the son and brother of two earls of Devon, and while Courtenay's connections to Lancaster are murky before the ascent of Henry IV, thereafter the earl and his family were promoted in their region and consistently served the king's interests.[22] A true northerner, Langley's career stretches back to his service in John of Gaunt's administration, where he acted as the duke's household clerk, then as duchy chancellor. Archdeacon of York and twice nominated for other bishoprics by Henry IV, Langley was finally elevated to the see of Durham in 1406, then served as chancellor twice before the reign's end. Though the two men had long been acquainted, Langley's Durham appointment made him a much closer colleague and confidant of the earl of Westmorland, as the traditional Neville *caput* was at that time Raby castle in Teesdale, within the palatinate. The evidence of their relationship, begun in the court of John of Gaunt many years earlier, is by now well known, and for the purposes of this discussion it is enough to say that Langley – who was amongst the council's most faithful attendees – was generally in league with Westmorland, and as a close ally provided the earl with another window into council proceedings. The core of the working council, then, was clearly dominated by the Beaufort–Neville party and its allies. While Henry V was notable for his personal involvement in policy-making, the council very likely had extensive latitude in the execution of royal policies. Beaufort, Langley and a few others were amongst just a handful present at the majority of meetings – in fact, each of the bishops was far more likely to attend a given meeting than not.

Two points stand out from this glimpse into the council's workings. First, experience was clearly valued, overriding the undoubted temptation to make a 'fresh start' with a new, younger cohort – even though some of those who were proposed might be expected to be regularly unavailable by virtue of their other responsibilities.[23] Thus, for example, Henry placed great trust

---

21 Harriss, *Cardinal Beaufort*, pp. 68–90. Questions of agency are notoriously difficult when considering 'royal' governance. Amongst late medieval English kings, Henry V has a reputation for close management, yet even in this case his council and chancellor were clearly the driving forces behind the making and implementation of policy.

22 M. Cherry, 'The Courtenay Earls of Devon: The Formation and Disintegration of a Late-Medieval Aristocratic Affinity', *Southern History* 1 (1979), 72–97.

23 It would certainly have been a practical impossibility for the duke to rely on this group consistently, as fully half were to accompany the king to France and others on the Scottish March; see Brown, 'King's Councillors in Fifteenth-Century England', p. 106n.

in the 55-year-old Henry Fitzhugh to serve as constable of England, even though the office was usually held by a more senior, comital-rank member of the nobility; he was soon made household chamberlain, an office he held for the duration of the reign.[24] Henry V also trusted him to serve as a justice during the trial of Lord Scrope and the earl of Cambridge in 1415 to ensure that the council would be represented in the subsequent investigation into the Southampton Plot.[25] Jeremy Catto considered these early appointments pragmatic and apolitical, and the deep Lancastrian roots of the appointees of little relevance to their engagement.[26] Yet the evidence suggests otherwise, and instead points unmistakeably northward, where Fitzhugh, Westmorland, Langley, the duke of Bedford (prior to 1414) and others continued to enhance the Lancastrian hold over regional society. They were abetted by their allies on the council – Thomas Erpingham and Henry Beaufort (the countess of Westmorland's brother) – and extended their reach and that of the crown still further northward, in the process alleviating the long-standing problem of the power of the Percys in that region.[27] In this sense, the evidence suggests that the new king was not simply recruiting local men into royal service to achieve regional stability, nor was he recruiting as high-level administrators and officers of state men who had only recently found their *metier* in the service of the crown. Instead, he was reaching further back still to the household, court and retinue of his grandfather to ensure the early success of his regime. In the process he extended Lancastrian influence in the far north, a region which had proved so troublesome to his predecessors, by promoting, and exploiting, the service of family and close allies, notably those tied to the crown through a Beaufort connection.

Lancastrian Partisanship in the Far North: Extending the Orbit of Influence

This pattern of continuity between the reigns of the first two Lancastrian kings in the use of duchy retainers and other members of their 'private' circle in regional governance was explored by Helen Castor, who studied the phenomenon in several core areas of direct duchy of Lancaster landholding and interest. Yet, it was at least as evident, though more indirectly, elsewhere. In the northern borderlands there were of course just two active magnate

---

[24] Allmand, *Henry V*, pp. 352–3, 357. See also discussion by Gwilym Dodd in this volume, p. 42.

[25] Allmand asserts that his military background may have appealed to the king: ibid., pp. 352–3.

[26] Catto, 'The King's Servants', pp. 93–5.

[27] For Langley's episcopal career, see R. L. Storey, *Thomas Langley and the Bishopric of Durham, 1406–1437* (London, 1961).

families in the entire region: the Percys and the Nevilles. Their courts naturally served as political epicentres, and their quarrels with each other are well known to students of the later fifteenth century. Yet, during the period of royal transition after 1413, the fall of the Percys presented the crown with a political problem, a vacuum ready to be filled from any number of quarters. Moreover, it was here that the Nevilles became a fulcrum of *royal* authority in the north, which in the early years of the reign extended its reach northward, into the far reaches of the kingdom. This was possible only because of the unique origins of their loyalty to the king, which ran far deeper than simply the universal obligation of a subject to his sovereign. Instead, the family's loyalties – centred firmly on the person of the earl of Westmorland and Countess Joan – predated Lancastrian royal ascent, and had always been recognized as something more than a tie of service. The earl himself had long been referred to by Henry IV as his 'brother', though he had no blood relations to the king.[28] It seems that his marriage to Joan and his family's distinguished history of service was sufficient reason for such an impressive expression of royal affection.

As Pollard has shown, with so few aristocratic families of any kind active in the north-east, and with many of these in the hands of either minors or the elderly, the Nevilles became a logical focus for royal policy and the ambitions of regional society. Henry IV's policy of capitalizing on this is by now well known, and this only intensified after the downfall of the first earl of Northumberland and the final fall of the Percys in the 1400s: they had performed this leadership role in Northumberland for two generations and more. Across the Pennines, the story was much the same, as the absence of the Percys – holders of the great Lucy lordship of Cockermouth, and the barony of Egremont – was also felt there.[29] In the north-west, Henry V's governance if anything relied to an even greater extent on the earl of Westmorland's authority and connections in local society, through his family network and his focal point for gentry service. The value of these connections had already proved critical, following the string of rebellions by members of northern landed society during Henry IV's reign.

So who benefited from the new regime? To a great degree, the new reign brought little change in the character of regional society; those families whose members thrived in the early period of Henry V's reign were generally those boasting old Lancastrian ties, or those who had gone out of their way to create stronger links with the new royal line early in Henry IV's reign. For example, the former group might include Lords FitzHugh of Ravensworth and Roos of Hamelak, long-standing Lancastrian retainers.[30] Lord Roos had been a colleague of his neighbour, William, Lord Willoughby on Henry IV's

---

[28] For example, *CPR, 1401–5*, pp. 233, 258.

[29] Pollard, *North-Eastern England*, p. 94.

[30] Walker, *Lancastrian Affinity*, Appendix 1; M. Arvanigian, 'A Lancastrian Polity? John of

council, and the two men undertook several commissions and embassies in concert for the crown. With FitzHugh, the three men were entrusted with responsibilities far beyond their estate; all were amongst a trusted group associated with Bolingbroke and John of Gaunt, and all became stalwart royalists in the uncertain early years of the new regime. Such was the straightforward reward from Henry IV for long and loyal Lancastrian service.

Also of interest were members of the region's elite drawn into the extended Neville/Lancaster orbit through marriage, kinship ties and service – a kind of secondary royal tie. Consistent with the process elsewhere, the loyalties of the heirs of the rebels of Henry IV's reign were quite often reincorporated into the political community through marriage and the grant of wardship to old Lancastrians. Ralph Neville's comital status, his blood ties (via Joan) to the crown and the waning (non-) issue of Beaufort legitimacy made a marriage into the Neville clan an acceptable – indeed, welcome – prospect for even comital-rank peers. John Mowbray, brother and heir of the rebel Earl Thomas of 1405, was restored to his lands in 1413 by Henry V. Yet this took place only after his agreeing to (and carrying through with) his own marriage to Katherine Neville, eldest daughter of Westmorland and Countess Joan, in 1411.[31] Richard Despenser (son of Thomas, duke of Gloucester, the rebel of 1400) regained a portion of his inheritance and the family's title when he became fourth Lord Burghersh in 1409. He then contracted a marriage to Eleanor Neville, Westmorland's second Beaufort daughter, in May 1412; through this connection and his own good service, he became a Knight of the Bath in 1413, though he died in the following year. Amongst this generation of Neville children, perhaps the match that is best known to historians was that of the youthful Richard Neville, eldest Beaufort son and eventual heir to most of the earl of Westmorland's North Yorkshire and Cumbrian lands. His marriage to the daughter and heir of Thomas Montague, earl of Salisbury in 1409 brought the northern branch of the Lancastrian family a second earldom, and with it even greater prospects for long-term northern governance.

All of this took place, of course, in the vacuum created by the absence of the Percys from the political scene, though even their restoration saw the crown make best use of its political assets in curbing their authority. Intermarriage between the Neville and Percy families followed ancient precedent, but the new conditions of Lancastrian kingship invested the event with an added dimension of national politics. For this reason, the 1412 marriage between Eleanor Neville (her second) and the youthful Henry Percy, future earl of Northumberland, necessitates a moment's consideration. The Percy restoration loomed large over the field of northern politics, and while it certainly may well have been a sign of the king's magnanimity – scholarly

Gaunt, John Neville and the War with France, 1368–88', in *Fourteenth Century England III*, ed. W. M. Ormrod (Woodbridge, 2004), pp. 121–42.

[31] *CPR, 1413–16*, p. 138.

opinion seems to favour this interpretation – the matter is far from certain. Percy's suit for the restoration of his lands and title met with success only because it met with the assent of the king. Conditions were attached to his restoration, however; one was that he should marry a daughter of the earl of Westmorland, the marriage taking place at Berwick in 1414. Though forced to wait until the king's return from France in 1416 before receiving the crown's investment of his 'creation' as earl of Northumberland (forfeited lands and titles were not 'restored' to the heir, but instead the grant was made afresh), it was the marriage that took place two years previously that signalled the imminent return of the Percys to the rest of the political community. A key factor influenced royal motives. The Southampton Plot demonstrated to the king just how dangerous Henry Percy could be in *Scottish* hands, as a focus for a rebellion *in England*, centred on northerners sympathetic and loyal to the earl of Northumberland. Reconciled and restored, however, a Percy heir could be 'domesticated', tied to the crown through a Beaufort marriage and kept under the watchful eyes of Westmorland and perhaps the duke of Bedford – who continued to retain control of many of the first earl of Northumberland's border estates long after the young earl's restoration. Moreover, the old Percy estates in Yorkshire were never restored, nor were lands elsewhere that had been acquired by the old earl or his son. So the 'full restoration' of Henry Percy left him with significantly less landed wealth than his grandfather had possessed.[32] For these reasons, his ability to create mischief was significantly curtailed.

Beyond the unusual case of the Percys, a consideration of other important families of the far northern counties serves to confirm Henry V's preference for continuing the general policy of reconciliation practised by his father. Richard, Lord Scrope of Bolton, in Wensleydale, was an important landowner in North Yorkshire, a cousin of the Scropes of Masham and a well-respected figure in the north; he was just twelve years old at the time his uncle, the archbishop of York, led his ill-fated revolt in 1405. Yet royal service was also very deeply ingrained in the family: his renowned grandfather, Richard, had served under the Black Prince at Crécy and as treasurer of England in the 1370s, before becoming steward of the royal household during the earliest years of Richard II's reign. He later retired to the north and finished the construction and crennelation of the family seat of castle Bolton.[33] What is more, the elder Richard also was a long-time Lancastrian retainer, one of

---

[32] The first earl of Northumberland's remit and forfeitures are fully catalogued in a document transferring many of his possessions to John of Lancaster following the act of forfeiture of June, 1405. This is confirmed and repeated in a second document from sometime shortly after, in response to an undated petition of John of Lancaster. The formal inclusion in this latter document of Sir Robert Umfraville by name may suggest that it was created some years later, perhaps closer to 1411. See TNA, SC 8/184/9197.

[33] *CPR, 1377–81*, p. 369.

John of Gaunt's bannerets during his campaigns of the 1380s.[34] At the age of nine, his grandson stood to inherit the title from his father, Roger, who died in 1403; for the time being, his valuable wardship and marriage were granted by Henry IV to Ralph Neville. Upon reaching his majority, Richard Scrope married Westmorland's daughter Margaret (his daughter with his first wife, Margaret Stafford) at Raby in December 1413. Whether this union played a role in the treachery of Lord Scrope's cousin, Henry Lord Scrope of Masham, at Southampton, is at best uncertain, though for the Scropes of Masham, the encroaching power of the Neville–Beaufort clan in their sphere of influence was surely palpable.

Thomas, Lord Dacre of Gilsland, whose family estates were contiguous to his home at Naworth castle in Cumberland, came into his inheritance at the death of his father William in 1408.[35] He first received an individual summons to the parliament of 1412, in recognition of his majority and noble standing.[36] His grandfather, Hugh, Lord Dacre had been a Lancastrian retainer since at least 1372, and joined the elder Lord Scrope of Bolton as Gaunt's banneret in the 1380s.[37] By virtue of Thomas Dacre's marriage to Phillipa Neville, he himself now joined another select but expanding group of men tied to the Lancastrian crown through an alliance with the Nevilles. He too became son-in-law to the earl of Westmorland, sometime before 1410.[38] Though no record of a formal indenture survives, it is sensible to assume that all of Westmorland's sons-in-law were either already retainers or were soon to become such. Dacre and Neville served together three times on the Cumberland bench in 1413–14. Thomas Dacre may also have deputized for his father-in-law in other capacities in this early phase of the new reign, when the earl's many activities kept him away from Carlisle. Indeed, in the final decade or so of his life Westmorland gradually withdrew from many of his long-standing

---

[34] Walker, *Lancastrian Affinity*, pp. 27, 31, 47 and 281. He was amongst those who went abroad with Gaunt on his first campaign abroad, to France in 1359. His early annuity of £40 was therefore consistent with his high standing in Yorkshire, though later annuitants of lesser import received greater sums (ibid., pp. 262–84).

[35] His lands were the substance of a series of enfoeffments-to-use; *CPR, 1408–13*, p. 355.

[36] The records for the 1412 session do not survive.

[37] Walker, *Lancastrian Affinity*, pp. 47, 157 and 268. The Dacres lost some of their holdings in Lancashire during the late 1370s to Gaunt's palatine steward, Robert Plessington. However, an argument that this might have driven them away from the duke is difficult to sustain, as Plessington later loaned them over 1,000 marks in cash. Moreover, Lord Hugh followed in his own father's shoes by serving as warden of the west March from 1379 to 1382. This was a coveted appointment, one that Dacre clearly owed to his connection to Gaunt, who had just accepted command of the Scottish border. Dacre's command ended in 1382 – with his arrest on suspicion of murdering his brother, Randolph.

[38] The date of their marriage is uncertain, though the birth of their son and heir, William, was in 1410.

royal commissions, and was replaced by his retainers and children; Dacre, for example, succeeded him as chief forester of Inglewood in 1420.[39]

The Far North

Perhaps nowhere was the encroaching Lancastrian ascendancy so late in coming as in the north-west, and especially Cumberland, for while his estates lay principally in the North Riding and Durham, it was here that the earl of Westmorland settled into his role as the king's governor of the far north-west. Serving as royal warden of the west March with Scotland and keeper of Carlisle by the start of the reign, he had already constructed an impressive infrastructure of personnel, offices and landed interests in the region – in spite of significant Percy inroads in the previous decades. Yet these inroads have been somewhat overstated: they were, after all, relatively recent arrivals to both border shires. The Percys were even more recently arrived in Cumberland, as their great lordship of Cockermouth was gained only through the old earl's (second) marriage in 1384 to Maud Lucy, who was sometimes styled countess of Angus and was heiress to many of the old Umfraville lands. As the king's agent in the north-west, Westmorland now superseded old Percy ties and gained control of Cockermouth and Egremont from the crown, together with the substantial Percy lands in Allerdale: these were effectively translated to his growing corpus of border country estates. Amongst them were the baronies of Burgh-by-Sands and Liddell, both former Lancastrian estates comprising the Dunstanburgh lordship that was overseen by Westmorland; and the earl's own honour of Penrith and Inglewood Forest, his great stronghold in the north-west hard by its capital, Carlisle. To this great Lancastrian foothold should also be added the duke of Bedford's earldom of Kendal, granted to John of Lancaster along with his ducal promotion in May 1414.[40] Bedford, of course, was never interested in being a northern territorial magnate, and the lands were now being overseen by Westmorland following the duke of Bedford's move to London.

Other evidence of royal governance in the far north seems vaguer, though it can be made sense of if understood within the context offered here. In 1414, for example, Neville was replaced as March warden by his eldest son, John (sometimes inaccurately styled 'Lord Neville'), yet this was clearly for the purpose of the earl taking part in Bedford's regency council in London, convened to govern during the king's absence on campaign in France. In fact, naming his son as his successor reflected Westmorland's considerable

---

[39] *CPR, 1413–16*, p. 417; *CPR, 1416–22*, p. 316.
[40] Indeed, this half of the barony of Kendal became known as the 'Richmond fee', because it became a part of the earldom of Richmond and was henceforth passed down along with the honour.

latitude in determining such matters. Yet it also served as a reminder that the region was still unstable, a fact aptly demonstrated by the size of the force brought to bear on the occasion of the battle of Yeavering, in July 1415, where the Scots brought some 4,000 troops into Northumberland.[41] By November of that year, Henry V had made Bedford earl of Richmond, a title which Westmorland had lobbied for and coveted during Henry IV's reign in vain, even though he controlled its *caput*, the honour of Richmond, after 1398. This obviously had more to do with the building of Bedford's estate than any loss of favour on the part of Westmorland. Yet it also seems clear that the crown was unwilling to alienate the title outside the royal family. In any case, the overall picture is clear: through Bedford and especially Westmorland, royal interests and authority were being secured in the north-west, and with Ralph Neville's earldom of Westmorland and its appurtenances, his control of Penrith and Carlisle, and Bedford's control of much of the former Percy estates plus the barony of Kendal, together they had little trouble replacing the Percys as leaders of the military aristocracy. In this way, the absence of the Percys helped to clarify the Nevilles as a potential focus for local loyalties.

Percy roots were unquestionably deeper, however, in Northumbrian soil. Here, Henry IV had been surprised at the effort required to retake their castles, along with those which had long been under their command as March wardens. Following the battle of Shrewsbury and the death of Hotspur, and Scrope's rebellion and the flight of his father, the captains of several of these fortresses remained loyal, and refused to hand them over to the crown. As captains of Berwick and lords of Alnwick and Warkworth, and the most significant landowners in the county, the Percys were always the natural choices to serve as March wardens, whether as governors of an east or a 'middle' March. With commensurate authority over the great string of castles from Roxburgh to the coast, including their own castles and those of Newcastle and Berwick, their authority was obviously made of sterner stuff.[42] Perhaps because of this, Henry V's policy proved to be a departure from his father's. Henry IV had remained resolute throughout the second half of his reign in keeping in place the attainder of the young earl of Northumberland, and while his eventual restoration may perhaps have been a sign of Henry V's magnanimity, as Allmand notes, practical politics was more likely the cause. Even for a king of his stature, the distance between the south and

---

[41] John Neville was the eldest son of Lord Ralph and Margaret Stafford, the earl's first wife. Precariously placed in terms of his inheritance, because the earl and Joan Beaufort were in the process of disinheriting him in favour of their Beaufort children, he continued nonetheless to serve the crown in his father's company, and later as a soldier on Henry V's French campaigns.

[42] M. Weiss, 'A Power in the North? The Percies in the Fifteenth Century', *Historical Journal* 19 (1976), 501–9; J. A. Tuck, 'Richard II and the Border Magnates', *Northern History* 3 (1968), 27–52.

Northumberland had in no way contracted, and the king's writ still brought with it rather less force there than elsewhere.[43]

Perhaps too Henry V was now in a position to be magnanimous: the passage of time had meant that more of the region was solidly in the hands of the extended royal family than had ever been the case. For a decade their focus had been Henry IV's young son John, who had come north in 1403 at the age of fourteen nominally to serve as warden of the east March and the keeper of Berwick, but more probably as an apprentice to his uncle, the earl of Westmorland. Yet he was also an important symbol of Henry IV's commitment to peace and security in the Scottish March – a posting similar to those of his brothers to Wales and Ireland, perhaps. Under Henry V, a more mature duke of Bedford was now warden of the east March in his own right, and held authority not only over such castles as royal Bamburgh and Lancastrian Dunstanburgh, but also many of the attainted Percy fortresses along the Northumbrian border with Scotland as well. Dunstanburgh, substantially rebuilt and re-fortified by John of Gaunt, together with Bamburgh, Norham, Berwick and Roxburgh, gave Bedford a foothold from which he could oversee the Percy estates.[44] Perhaps the magnitude of this responsibility explains why Bedford's responsibilities in the north remained largely unchanged right up to the time of his appointment as protector of the realm, prior to the king's absence on campaign in France. Yet his shift southward to tend to national affairs did not lead to a decline in Lancastrian influence in the far northern counties.

There were several reasons for this. Lancastrian influence gained undoubted traction with the elevation of the king's clerk, Thomas Langley, to the see of Durham in 1406. Along with the bishop's power in the palatinate, which no doubt would have radiated northward in any event, came his control over the two north Durham liberties of Islandshire and Norhamshire, and the castle at Norham. As Storey showed, while normally absent from the palatinate, Langley was nonetheless an active bishop who made several important reforms of his palatine administration, giving particular regard to the centralization of financial administration and the steward's judicial authority. In Ralph Eure, Langley had found a sound partner who governed Durham with a good deal of authority and skill, maximizing profits from the temporalities and ensuring local loyalty even in the face of such upheavals

---

43 Allmand, *Henry V*, pp. 311–12.

44 John of Lancaster was made warden of the east March in 1403, following the battle of Shrewsbury. At that time, his age (he was just fourteen) made real custody or leadership a practical impossibility. Given that all of his deputies in the north-east were associates and members of the Neville affinity, and that it was the earl of Westmorland himself who faced down the rebels at Shipton Moor in 1405, the proper conclusion is that he and not John of Lancaster was the real power in the borders at this early stage: *CPR, 1401–5*, pp. 258, 324.

as the Percy and Scrope rebellions.[45] With the extensive Durham holdings of the Nevilles, Eure, and the influential local families of Claxton and the Strangeways (both Neville retainers), Lancastrian interests in Durham were if anything strengthened over time.[46]

Prominent members of the gentry community of the far north also came into the royal orbit through its network of family, friends and service. Here, along with the usual commissions of the peace and array, and the bench, opportunities for service also extended to the defence of the borders – again, of special import in the absence of Percy leadership. Most of the highest offices in the region – the shrievalties of Yorkshire, Northumberland and Cumberland, along with the Durham palatine steward, and the March wardens and its main lieutenancies – were already in the hands of partisan Lancastrians and retainers by the start of the reign. Amongst these offices, those of the March wardens were especially critical; they were held by the king's brother John of Lancaster (now duke of Bedford) and his uncle the earl of Westmorland. By the end of Henry IV's reign and with his royal backing, the two had assembled a trusted group of active and able lieutenants. Chief amongst these was Sir Ralph Eure, an important landowner in Durham and the North Riding, and a long-time servant of the regime. Probably the foremost character amongst the landed but untitled, he was returned by the Commons electors of both the North Riding and Northumberland on several occasions. Trusted by the crown, Neville and his lord bishop, he was in fact hosting the earl of Westmorland at his castle of Witton-le-Wear in Durham at the outbreak of Archbishop Scrope's rebellion in 1405; the two men responded together and ultimately quashed the revolt.[47] A frequent royal commissioner throughout the region and the bishop of Durham's palatine steward, Eure had also been an important Lancastrian and Neville retainer from the very start of Henry IV's reign. His landed status, ability and wide scope of action that covered virtually the whole of the north made him unique amongst the region's gentry.

Only two others approached Eure in terms of his stature as an administrator and political significance, and both appear regularly as commissioners in Henry IV's early reign. Thomas Rokeby, the sheriff of York, and Sir Robert

---

[45] Not a single member of the Durham gentry is known to have joined and fought for the rebels. Storey, *Thomas Langley*, makes no mention of any Durham men joining with the archbishop's cause, nor do the Durham or national records suggest it. See also M. Arvanigian, 'Landed Society and the Governance of the North in the Later Middle Ages: The Case of Sir Ralph Eure', *Medieval Prosopography* 22 (2001), 65–87.

[46] Christian Liddy has outlined the Neville holdings in Durham, and shown the extent of their network of interests there. If anything, he has understated their influence, and the influence of the Lancastrian crown, within the palatinate: C. D. Liddy, *The Bishopric of Durham in the Late Middle Ages: Lordship, Community and the Cult of St. Cuthbert* (Woodbridge, 2008), pp. 76–123.

[47] Arvanigian, 'Landed Society', 65–87.

Umfraville of Redesdale were both experienced military men who skilfully kept the peace in their counties and fought to repel incursions along the border. From an important Yorkshire family, Thomas Rokeby gained a certain renown for leading the royal army to victory over the earl of Northumberland at Bramham Moor in 1408, and for this was granted the Percy manor of Spofforth, with Leathley and Linton, by the crown for the term of his life.[48] He went to France with Henry V on the Agincourt campaign, and campaigned with the king again in 1417; he is thought to have died in France sometime around 1418.[49]

Also critical was the six-year appointment in 1411 of Sir Robert Umfraville to serve as John of Lancaster's chief lieutenant, and a sort of 'sub-warden' of the ancient middle March (now no longer operating as a formal, distinct jurisdiction) with custody of the castle at Roxburgh; Umfraville was a trusted knight of the king, and had formerly served at his side as Prince of Wales.[50] Although it no doubt owed much to the period of the Prince's ascendancy on Henry IV's council in 1410 and 1411, the appointment nonetheless far outlasted it. The Umfravilles were an important border family, particularly in Redesdale, where they owned much land and had once been styled lords of Angus, though they had recently come under twin curses that had led to their diminution. Like many other border landowners, they suffered from the decline in land values that accompanied frequent Scottish raiding – a regular feature of border culture during the Scottish wars; and their claim to regional leadership had lately been eclipsed by greater rivals. The move northward in the fourteenth century by the Nevilles and Percys, from home bases in Yorkshire and Durham, respectively, changed the political dynamic of the region very much to the detriment of its long-established families – including the Umfravilles.[51] As they became subsumed by these – Sir Robert himself had served his minority as a ward in the tutelage of the earl of Westmorland during the reign of Henry IV, while some of his family's former lands had gone with the widowed Maud Lucy into the hands of the earl of Northumberland – their natural response was to resort to service. Here, they met with notable success: the chronicler Harding tells of the earl of Westmorland making Sir Robert keeper of Warkworth castle, as a reward for his exploits in

48 *Fœdera*, VIII, 529.

49 Wylie, *Henry the Fourth*, III, 147 and 154–8. For Umfraville, see below.

50 *Calendar of Documents Relating to Scotland Preserved in Her Majesty's Public Record Office*, ed. J. Bain, 4 vols. (Edinburgh, 1881–8), IV, 163.

51 An example of the disruption possible when magnate families became active in the land and marriage markets can be seen in the first earl of Northumberland's marriage to Maud Lucy, which changed the political dynamics of the far north-west. The marriage brought the Percys the lordship of Cockermouth and the barony of Egremont – setting the stage for even greater political shifts.

bringing it to heel following the earl of Northumberland's death at Bramham Moor.[52]

In some sense, this was the path Umfraville used to recover some of his family's lost prestige. His good service led to his becoming a household knight of Henry IV, who thereafter appointed him on many occasions – often in the company of Robert Tempest, sheriff of Northumberland – to inquire into local matters of interest to the crown.[53] In due course, and in keeping with the northern strategy of the Lancastrian establishment, Umfraville married yet another of the earl of Westmorland's daughters, cementing their relationship and his ties to the crown. For Robert Umfraville, in this new context, old truths remained: royal service, local administration and the defence of the realm continued to be part of the family's responsibilities as Marcher lords. Service to the Lancastrian regime was the route by which he regained much of his family's past prominence, and his apprenticeship with Westmorland and subsequent royal service were useful methods of ensuring his independence from the Percys, who though reinstalled in 1416, continued to remain political outsiders for some time afterwards.[54] As the adopted ward of the king's trusted uncle, and with a strong attachment to both Henry V and Bedford at Roxburgh and Warkworth, he was a clear choice when the time came to strike at the French. He was summoned by name by the king to bring a company of men and join the royal party at Southampton for the Agincourt campaign.

A Northern Dimension to the Southampton Plot

Further evidence of the king's policy in the far north may be drawn from a more unexpected source. The scholarly tradition surrounding the Southampton Plot has it that Henry, Lord Scrope of Masham, joined this group of conspirators, led by the earl of Cambridge and another co-conspirator, Sir Thomas Gray of Heaton (Northumberland), for reasons which remain largely unknown; Scrope was a close confidant of the king and at the very centre of power. Yet all titled lordship has its roots in local power and authority – authority that was somewhat autonomous even from the intrusions of the king, provided all was working as it should. In this quite distinct moment in northern politics, it is likely that the revolt of Scrope's uncle, the archbishop,

---

52 Harding was, of course, a retainer of Sir Robert Umfraville, who soon after this granted him custody of Warkworth castle. Harding fought under Umfraville's banner at Agincourt in 1415.

53 See, for example, *CPR, 1413–16*, pp. 420, 422.

54 Henry Percy's recovery of his family's former stature took place only very slowly, over several years; he was never allowed the sort of free chase in the region enjoyed by his father or grandfather.

and his own receding ability to exercise traditional lordship in Yorkshire, in the face of the ongoing Neville–Beaufort ascendancy – may have shown Scrope that in time this would come to dominate the lower nobility, in favour of Westmorland and his numerous offspring. The earl himself had, after all, been the instrument of the demise of Archbishop Scrope, whose emerging cult surrounding the church of York must in some sense reflect local sympathy, as well as a general antipathy toward the execution of so senior a churchman as Scrope. Though Scrope's rebellion was probably not part of any more general conflict between the Scropes and the rising Nevilles, it is nonetheless true that the Nevilles were brought great rewards by the Lancastrian crown, such as having the lordship of Richmond within their sphere of influence, while the Scropes gained none, in spite of Lord Henry's good service at court. Scrope's rebellion may in part have reflected discontent in some sense against the crown's remaking of northern society, which involved improperly bypassing some traditional families, like Mowbray and Scrope, in favour of others with closer ties of family and service.

From this perspective, the participation of Thomas Gray can be explained by the similar circumstances of his being overshadowed in his own back-yard. He very likely found himself isolated within the emerging polity of the Lancastrian north. Gray's origins were significant enough, and his ances-tors of sufficient repute, to indicate for him a leadership role in local society, similar to the one he and his family had enjoyed in times past. Yet his role was if anything diminishing. His connection to the Southampton Plot has perplexed scholars, beyond his son's betrothal to Cambridge's daughter – a powerful motive perhaps.[55] Sir Thomas Gray the younger was brought into Lancastrian service by his father, a retainer of the earl of Westmorland from 1396 at least, and extending through Richard II's downfall. Soon after West-morland's marriage to Joan Beaufort and the corresponding increase in royal patronage in the far north, including the grant of Richmond and the resettling of his great Yorkshire lordships of Middleham and Sheriff Hutton on his new family, Thomas Gray the elder, seeing clearly what the future might hold, became attached to the new earl of Westmorland, and in so doing received a significant annuity and a command on the Northumbrian border with Scot-land, namely Gray's home at Wark castle on the river Tweed – a command purchased for him by the earl. Wark sat at the centre of Gray's own Northum-berland estates, yet as his inquisition post-mortem shows, they were badly decayed in value.[56] Scottish incursions into north Northumberland had taken a significant toll, and as a result Gray became even more heavily dependent

---

[55] National issues have been posited, as has the connection by marriage of the children of Cambridge and Gray; see Pugh, *Southampton Plot*, pp. 160–77. E. F. Jacob, *Henry V and the Invasion of France* (London, 1947), pp. 56–7, claims simply that Gray's involvement owed to his connection to the Percys.

[56] The indenture itself is enrolled as TNA, E 326/3515; see also TNA, DURH 3/13.

upon the wages received from royal commissions and the like – especially those along the border. He even abandoned the stewardship of Durham to do this, indicating its potential for reward, and also accepted a commission from the bishop of Durham to oversee his Northumbrian castle and liberty of Norham, near the Scottish border.[57] Scholars have considered various reasons for Thomas Gray the younger being drawn into the plot hatched by Scrope and Cambridge, and have concluded that he probably retained a lingering loyalty to the Percys. Surely this much was true – after all, the families were close, and Gray himself had been born at their home of Alnwick castle, in 1384.

Yet for all that, Thomas Gray's participation in such a desperate and unlikely scheme as the one hatched by the conspirators of 1415 remains elusive from the perspective of national affairs. An explanation of simple discontent with his position is belied by the improved standing of his family as important administrators and border commanders during the Scottish wars of the previous century – he was from a famous and important border clan.[58] The elder Thomas Gray had been the object of Neville preferment as early as the 1390s, and was formally retained by the earl of Westmorland shortly before his own demise in 1400. Yet the loyalty of his family had more recently shifted in the direction of Neville. Like his father and grandfather before him, the younger Sir Thomas had made much of the royal commissions and offices available in the region, and like them, he too had shown himself to be useful to those with patronage to offer. Like his father, too, he served occasionally as constable of Bamburgh and Roxburgh castles, two very important commands, and more regularly acted as a justice of the peace and keeper of the truce in Northumberland.[59] The younger Sir Thomas had also been loyal to the regime right through the rebellions of Richard II's partisans – and even those of the Percys – during Henry IV's reign. Gray had not been a party to the barons' revolt of 1400, though his northern neighbour Ralph, Lord Lumley, was among its leaders. Nor is there evidence that he was present at Shrewsbury, or at any of the sites of subsequent skirmishes led by the earl of Northumberland and his associates over the following half-decade. Yet the conventional wisdom of historians explaining his participation in the Southampton Plot has focused on his family's long historical attachment to the Percys, arguing that their rivalry with the house of Lancaster, exacerbated by the execution of Archbishop Scrope and the formation of a cult in his memory

---

[57] A. King, 'Scaling the Ladder: The Rise and Rise of the Grays of Heaton, c.1296–c.1415', in *North-East England*, ed. Liddy and Britnell, pp. 57–74.

[58] He received a warrant for payment of his retinue in 1415 prior to departing Southampton; *Foedera*, IX, 259.

[59] TNA, E 326/3515.

centred at York, led this proud northerner to harbour royal antipathy afresh.[60] And yet, if Jacob and others are correct that Percy sympathies lay behind Gray's involvement in the Southampton Plot, surely his discontent would have been manifest at an earlier date. What is more likely is that the younger Thomas Gray became disenchanted with the growing stature of the Nevilles, and that this discontent was the source of his enmity toward the crown in 1415, and the key to his involvement with the conspirators of 1415. Like Lord Scrope, Gray and others were affected by the rise of the Nevilles and their followers, which limited the prospects of those used to having ample opportunities in the far north. Because he was the father of over twenty surviving children (by two women of noble standing) and the commander of a growing military complex in the borders, members of Westmorland's family – such as John Neville, from his elder Stafford brood, and his eldest Beaufort son, Richard, along with his numerous sons-in-law – were rapidly assuming leadership positions there. As a result employment which would once have been taken up by the region's traditional landed families was beginning to concentrate in royalist, Neville hands. The fact that, in spite of this, many of the Neville offspring were yet very young children who would in due course also compete for such patronage, must have been a source for grave concern, giving other northerners reason to consider their futures.[61]

A cursory investigation of royal commissioners named during this period in the far north confirms a reliance upon old, reliable ties of kinship and a history of service over any preference for the established families in the region. A few examples here will suffice. William Gascoigne was appointed chief justice of king's bench at Henry's coronation, only to find the judge retired home to the north one week later.[62] As an old retainer of the duchy of Lancaster, Gascoigne was an architect of the Neville/Beaufort trust, the device used by Westmorland after 1397 to repatriate lands through conveyance to use, in favour of his Beaufort offspring and to the great detriment of his elder children by his deceased wife, Margaret Stafford.[63] William Gascoigne was a trustee himself of important Neville estates on several occasions, as was his brother Richard and some of their associates. This coincided with the growing maturity of Richard Neville, Westmorland's eldest Beaufort son and prospective heir. Given the crown's abiding interest in seeing the earl retain his lands for the exclusive use of the ever-loyal Beauforts, the

---

[60] J. W. McKenna, 'Popular Canonization as Political Propaganda: The Cult of Archbishop Scrope', *Speculum* 45 (1970), 608–23; P. McNiven, 'The Betrayal of Archbishop Scrope', *BJRL* 54 (1971), 173–213.

[61] Richard Neville, the eldest *male* child of this union, was born in 1400 but as befitted his noble kinfolk, his brothers-in-law could surely expect to receive a certain amount of patronage from the family and the crown. All had the potential to displace others outside the family, even within their own expected spheres of influence.

[62] Wylie and Waugh, *Henry the Fifth*, I, 14.

[63] Ibid., 19.

renewed attention of the crown's finest lawyer to these matters is intriguing. Certainly, Judge Gascoigne's departure was not a retirement, and may have been something more of a strategic move to bolster Lancastrian control of the north. He continued his active political and judicial career, and accepted several important royal commissions over successive months, each involving significant travel. These included appointments to the commissions of the peace for Cumberland, Northumberland and the North Riding as well as for the East Riding, and for Beverly and Ripon.[64] He also served irregularly as a justice of *oyer et terminer* for York, and clearly provided leadership while adding his experience and gravity.[65] An example of the latter would be in politically sensitive cases, such as when he served as a judge in the matter of the kidnapping of Lady Scrope, along with the theft of a large sum of money belonging to Henry Lord Scrope from Faxflete, in the spring of 1413.[66] More critical still was his involvement with the commission sent to investigate the kidnapping of Murdoch of Fife, the son of the king of Scotland, which was the prelude to the Southampton Plot (foiled by its alleged principal, the earl of March himself) as the king made plans to cross to France. Murdoch was intercepted by Lord Scrope of Masham, for the purpose of exchanging him with the Scots for the young Henry Percy – at that time a guest of the Scots in exile – so as to raise the men of the north against Henry V in the name of Percy and Mortimer, clearly an attempt to echo the character of the rising against Henry IV of 1403.[67]

It is also interesting to note one further judicial appointment, that of Richard Norton, who became chief justice of the court of Common Pleas in 1413, which coincided directly with Gascoigne's departure from king's bench.[68] Norton was the son of Adam Conyers of the North Riding village of Norton Conyers, and like his kinsman John Conyers, was a protégé of Judge Gascoigne. He was, in fact, one of several northern jurists, all with connections to Gascoigne, who rose to prominence in Lancastrian, then royal, service. Like Conyers, Norton sat on the North Riding bench, and like Conyers he was an important trustee of the earl of Westmorland.[69] Conyers was conveyed a number of the earl's Durham lands, while Norton was among those enfeoffed of some of his North Yorkshire estates, with reversion to the use of the earl, Countess Joan and their Beaufort children – again, very much at the expense of his elder children with Margaret Stafford. Norton rose to become the chief justice of the bishop of Durham's palatine liberty before his eventual elevation to

---

[64] *CPR, 1413–16*, pp. 417–26.

[65] *CPR, 1413–16*, p. 65.

[66] The value of goods taken from the two locations was recorded as £5,000. *CPR, 1413–16*, p. 65.

[67] Allmand, *Henry V*, pp. 309–10.

[68] *CPR, 1413–16*, pp. 3, 40.

[69] See, for example, *CPR, 1408–13*, pp. 497, 500.

the Westminster bench, yet like Conyers his critical connections were Neville connections.[70] Members of the Neville clan had already enjoyed generations of service from the Conyers, and by the time he was appointed chief justice of Common Pleas several of Norton's kinsmen had already been members of the Neville household and retinue. In fact, his own father had once acted as receiver at Raby for the earl's father, John Neville, while John Conyers served Westmorland in the same capacity.[71] Later generations of the family would go on to serve in similar capacities, now in the households of Richard Neville, future earl of Salisbury, and Joan Beaufort, respectively.

Based upon their local standing, men like Thomas Rokeby and Sir Richard Redman, who were themselves landowners of substance in Westmorland and the North Riding, might well have expected careers of local leadership for themselves, and by virtue of their own standing. Yet instead it was the trust placed in them by the Lancastrian regime and its northern, Beaufort agents which caused them to be elevated above their neighbours, and reach the apex of northern gentry society. Redman served as the Speaker for the Commons in the parliament of 1415, when in a remarkable gesture of either largesse or goodwill, that body granted the king the wool staple for life, free and clear and without further condition.[72] This unprecedented act may of course have been due to the king's newfound fame and his recent military success; it would not be sensible, however, to dismiss the effectiveness of the speaker-ship of Redman, who was so thoroughly enmeshed in Lancastrian service, and who had benefited so much from the growth of Lancastrian interest in his region.[73]

Clearly, in managing the political landscape of the far north, Henry V made use of the full array of his personal assets and those which fell to him with the royal coronation. He employed with great efficiency the Beaufort/Neville clan in the tempestuous region, and like his father before him, gave the earl of Westmorland and his associates his full trust in managing their bailiwick, along with the significant authority and resources which accompanied various offices and commissions – including those of the March wardens. This group was well placed to continue to provide order and defence, as they had done since the unrest of the prior reign. At the core of this cadre was an almost ideal combination of old Lancastrian associates and servants on the one hand, and those like Robert Umfraville and Richard Norton on the other, who enthusi-astically served the Lancastrian crown as a new generation of retainers and knights. With the fall of the antagonistic Percy and Lumley families in the previous decade, and with the great northern sees of Durham and York now

---

[70] TNA, DURH 20/14/8; Durham University Library, Church Commission Bishopric 189809.

[71] TNA, DURH, 20/2.

[72] Harriss, 'Management of Parliament', pp. 137–58, 145–7.

[73] Redman's presentation as Commons Speaker is found in *PROME*, IV, 63, m. 4.

in the safe hands of Lancastrian partisans, the Nevilles and their Lancastrian associates were in a unique position to deliver stability to the crown and keep the peace in the Scottish borderlands. The process of political reconfiguration was not, of course, without its victims; the discontent with their northern policies which were partially responsible for the rebellions of the previous reign make clear that many were uneasy – and more – over these changes. Certainly, as this chapter has sought to demonstrate, the changes amounted to far more than a simple reshuffling of personnel for the Lancastrian administration. Extending northward from areas of established Lancastrian influence further south, particularly in Yorkshire, Durham and Lancashire, the establishment of family and retainers in the far north amounted to nothing less than a political reconfiguration of this border region along royalist lines. This in turn temporarily ended the instability and political unrest that had provided the region with its outsized importance during the period of the Scottish wars.

4

Henry V's Suppression of the Oldcastle Revolt

Maureen Jurkowski

At the time of Henry V's unexpected demise in August 1422 contemporary commentators were fulsome in their praise of his qualities as a ruler and, above all, his achievements in the administration of justice. *Exemplar justicie* was among the personal attributes listed in the minutes of a meeting of the king's council just after his death,[1] and a similar compliment was paid in the inscription *Civitas Regis iusticie* spotted on a wall over the entrance to London Bridge during the celebrations of his victory at Agincourt in 1415.[2] French chroniclers in particular sang his praises as a paragon of justice, and the English writer John Hardyng lauded his success in law enforcement, albeit after the decades of chaos that followed his demise and with no small hankering after that comparative golden age.[3] Was this reputation deserved? In his appraisal of criminal justice under Henry V, Ted Powell argued that, by and large, it was, although not in a conventional sense, and not through Henry's use of the existing common law channels, but often by extra-legal means, and above all, through the sheer force of his personality.[4] This chapter will test this reputation further by examining closely how Henry dealt with what was the first, and arguably most profound, domestic challenge to his rule: the threat posed by the Lollard uprising led by Sir John Oldcastle in January 1414 and its aftermath – that is, the period during which the latter remained a fugitive from justice. How effectively did he deal with this threat and what were the means that he used? These are the questions that will be addressed here, before considering what bearing the answers have on an assessment of the accuracy of his reputation.

---

[1] ('Exemplar of justice') POPC, III, 3, quoted in E. Powell, *Kingship, Law and Society, Criminal Justice in the Reign of Henry V* (Oxford, 1989), p. 269.
[2] ('City of the king of justice') GHQ, p. 103, cited in Allmand, *Henry V*, p. 412.
[3] Powell, *Kingship*, pp. 269–70.
[4] Ibid., pp. 269–75; E. Powell, 'The Restoration of Law and Order', in *Henry V*, ed. Harriss, pp. 60–74.

Oldcastle: Soldier and Heretic

In origin a Church reform movement based upon the ideas of the Oxford theologian John Wyclif, the Lollard heresy had evolved into a religious sect that was gaining in strength in the early fifteenth century. Since the 1380s it had been spread largely by itinerant preachers, several of whom were Oxford-trained and enjoyed the patronage of members of the gentry.[5] Sir John Oldcastle was himself such a patron. Born *c.*1370 to Sir Richard Oldcastle of Almeley, Herefordshire, and his wife Isabel, he was probably influenced by Lollard preachers as a young man.[6] Two of the sect's most eloquent exponents operated in his midst around 1390: the much-travelled William Swinderby, who is believed to have preached in Almeley and its surrounding villages, and Walter Brut of Pipe and Lyde (near Hereford), where Oldcastle's family owned lands.[7] He also had connections with the band of soldiers and courtiers known as the 'Lollard knights'; he acted as an executor of the will of Sir Lewis Clifford (d.1404), lord of the nearby castle of Ewyas Harold.[8]

Oldcastle embarked upon a military career at an early age. As an esquire he took part in the earl of Arundel's naval expedition of 1387 and received letters of protection to accompany his uncle Thomas Oldcastle to Ireland in 1397 in the service of Roger Mortimer, earl of March.[9] In 1400 he campaigned in Scotland with Henry IV, by which time he had been knighted. A seventeenth-century pedigree of the Oldcastles names his mother as *domina de Gray de Codnore* (Lady Grey of Codnor) and even if unsubstantiated, it may indicate some sort of kinship with Richard, Lord Grey, with whom he evidently had a close relationship.[10] He served in the latter's retinue at Roxburgh castle in 1401 and as his deputy when Grey was charged with the defence of the town of Brecon and county of Herefordshire from the Welsh rebels in 1405.[11]

---

5   For a summary of their activities, see: M. Jurkowski, 'Lollard Networks', in *Wycliffite Controversies*, ed. J. P. Hornbeck and M. Bose (Turnhout, 2011), pp. 261–8.

6   C. Kightly, 'Sir John Oldcastle (*c.* 1370–1417), of Almeley, Herefs. and Cobham, Kent', in *HP*, III, 866.

7   Both men had influential supporters in the county: M. Jurkowski, 'Who Was Walter Brut?' *EHR* 127 (2012), 285–302; A. Hudson, 'The Problem of Scribes: The Trial Records of William Swinderby and Walter Brut', *Nottingham Medieval Studies* 44 (2005), 80–104 (pp. 84–94).

8   Clifford did not name him as an executor in the will, but he was clearly serving in that capacity by 1413: TNA, E 403/612, m. 7 (printed in F. Devon, *Issues of the Exchequer* (London, 1837), p. 323). For the Lollard knights, see: K. B. McFarlane, *Lancastrian Kings and Lollard Knights* (Oxford, 1972), pp. 139–232.

9   TNA, E 101/40/33, m. 1d; *CPR, 1396–9*, p. 170.

10 BL MS Lansdowne 259, fol. 35r; and see below.

11 TNA, E 101/42/40, m. 1; W. R. M. Griffiths, 'The Military Career and Affinity of Henry, Prince of Wales, 1399–1413' (unpublished M.Litt. dissertation, University of Oxford, 1981), p. 146; TNA, E 364/39, m. 5; PSO 1/4, no. 40; *Calendar of Signet Letters of Henry IV and Henry V*, ed. J. L. Kirby (London, 1978), no. 453.

Oldcastle in fact played a large part in the suppression of this uprising, under the command of Henry, Prince of Wales, not only locally, but in Kidwelly, Carmarthen and at the siege of Aberystwyth.[12] For this service he was well rewarded and his local prominence was enhanced considerably. He sat in the parliament of 1404 as a knight of the shire, was a peace commissioner in 1404, 1405 and 1406, and held office as county sheriff in 1406–7.[13] His fortunes were significantly raised with his marriage by June 1408 to Joan, the thrice-widowed granddaughter and sole heir of John, third Lord Cobham, who had died earlier that year. It has been suggested that the marriage was arranged by Prince Henry himself,[14] as further remuneration for Oldcastle's services, but it is more likely to have come about through the influence of Lord Grey, whose estates at Hoo and Halstow in Kent adjoined the Cobham seat of Cooling castle. Sir John began to be summoned to the House of Lords as Lord Cobham in October 1409.[15]

His active support for the Church reforms advocated by the Lollards is first evident in the following year. In April 1410, a month after the burning at the stake of the Evesham tailor John Badby for refusing to abjure his heretical views,[16] Archbishop Arundel took steps against a chaplain named John residing with Oldcastle. He ordered the dean of Rochester to cite him and place the churches in which he had been preaching heresy – Cooling, Hoo and Halstow – under interdict.[17] Undaunted, Oldcastle had the ban lifted and continued to maintain Lollard preachers on his estate, among them Robert Chapell alias Holbeche.[18] In September he wrote to the prominent Bohemian nobleman Woksa von Waldstein, applauding his support for the Hussite reformers, and in the following year to King Wladislas of Bohemia, advo-

---

[12] Kightly, 'Sir John Oldcastle', p. 866; W. T. Waugh, 'Sir John Oldcastle', *EHR* 20 (1905), 434–56, 637–58 (pp. 436–7); TNA, C 66/374, mm. 26d, 30d.

[13] He was granted an annuity of £40 from two duchy of Lancaster manors in Gloucestershire and a further 40 marks from the fee farm of Monmouth lordship in April 1406, both for life: TNA, DL 42/16, pt. 2, fols. 23v, 203. In February 1407 he received a share in the royal lease of the Mortimer lordship of Dinas in Breconshire: Kightly, 'Sir John Oldcastle', p. 866.

[14] N. Saul, *Death, Art and Memory in Medieval England: The Cobham Family and their Monuments, 1300–1500* (Oxford, 2001), p. 29.

[15] Waugh, 'Sir John Oldcastle', pp. 438–9.

[16] For Badby, see P. McNiven, *Heresy and Politics in the Reign of Henry IV* (Woodbridge, 1987), esp. chapter 11.

[17] London, Lambeth Palace Library, Register of Thomas Arundel, Archbishop of Canterbury, Reg. II, fols. 13v–14r (printed in *Concilia Magna Brittaniae*, ed. D. Wilkins, 4 vols. (London, 1737), III, 328–31; BL Cotton MS Faustina C. v, fols. 125r–126r.

[18] C. Kightly, 'The Early Lollards: A Survey of Popular Lollard Activity in England, 1382–1428' (unpublished D.Phil. dissertation, University of York, 1975), pp. 372–5. Chappell, who was forced to abjure heresy in 1416, was apparently an Oxford graduate: Emden, *BRUO*, I, 388; *The Register of Henry Chichele, Archbishop of Canterbury, 1414–1443*, ed. E. F. Jacob and H. C. Johnson, 4 vols., Canterbury and York Society 42, 45–47 (Oxford, 1938–47), III, 15; IV, 155–8.

cating the same cause.[19] Despite his religious views, Oldcastle continued to enjoy the Prince's support and in the autumn of 1411 was given a command in the expedition sent to France by the Prince to assist the Burgundians against their Orléanist rivals.[20]

Arundel's crackdown on Lollardy had meanwhile continued apace, particularly in Oxford. In 1409 his *Constitutions* restricted theological debate in the universities and an academic committee was appointed to draw up a list of errors in Wyclif's writings. A list of 267 errors was presented to convocation in March 1411 and a book burning was held at Carfax, perhaps around this same time.[21] On the first day of the following convocation, convened in March 1413, John Lay of Nottingham, a chaplain strongly suspected of heresy, was summoned before the archbishop's registrar. Lay admitted that he had celebrated Mass in London that morning before Oldcastle and the registrar demanded to see his certificate of ordination and licence to preach, ordering him to produce them on the following day. This incident, in K. B. McFarlane's view, suggests that Oldcastle was being watched.[22] Henry IV's death later in the month then put all further moves against Oldcastle on hold.[23]

In June 1413, however, during the next meeting of convocation, the archbishop obtained further evidence against him. A raid on a London illuminator's shop uncovered some unbound quires belonging to Oldcastle that contained several short heretical tracts. A clerical disputation visited Henry V at his palace in Kennington and, in Oldcastle's presence, read out the most extreme of the views that the tracts expressed. The king, however, refused to take action against his favourite. Arundel persisted, however, and after failing to convince his friend to renounce his heretical opinions, Henry V

---

[19] The first letter was to be forwarded to Wladislas of Zwierzeticz, a prominent academic reformer, in the event of von Waldstein's absence: Waugh, 'Sir John Oldcastle', pp. 442–4. Both letters are printed in Josef Loserth, 'Über die Beziehungen zwischen englischen und böhmischen Wiclifiten', *Mitteilungen des Instituts für österreichische Geschichtsforschung* 12 (1891), 254–69 (pp. 266–7). For the date of the second letter, see: M. Van Dussen, 'Conveying Heresy: "A Certayne Student" and the Lollard-Hussite Fellowship', *Viator* 38 (2007), 217–34.

[20] P. McNiven, 'Prince Henry and the English Political Crisis of 1412', *History* 65 (1980), 1–16.

[21] It is worth noting that a comment made by one of the twelve compilers of the list appears to allude to Oldcastle's patronage of preachers: A. Hudson, 'Notes of an Early Fifteenth-Century Research Assistant, and the Emergence of the 267 Articles against Wyclif', *EHR* 118 (2003), 685–97 (p. 690). For the Oxford crackdown, see also J. I. Catto, 'Wyclif and Wycliffism at Oxford 1356–1430', in *The History of the University of Oxford*, II: *Late Medieval Oxford*, ed. J. I. Catto and R. Evans (Oxford, 1992), pp. 175–261 (pp. 244–53).

[22] He was perhaps the same preacher named John reportedly living with Oldcastle in 1410: K. B. McFarlane, *John Wycliffe and the Beginnings of Non-Conformity* (London, 1952), p. 163. For preaching licences, see: I. Forrest, *The Detection of Heresy in Late Medieval England* (Oxford, 2005), pp. 60–8.

[23] *Concilia*, III, 338; Waugh, 'Sir John Oldcastle', p. 446.

wrote to the archbishop in August, sanctioning ecclesiastical proceedings against him.[24] Oldcastle refused to be summoned at his castle at Cooling, and it was only after his excommunication for contumacy that he evidently gave himself up, producing at his heresy trial a written statement of his opinions.[25] Even after his condemnation to death on 25 September, Henry V gave him a respite of forty days to recant, remanding him to the Tower, and he was reportedly freed from his shackles upon a promise to do so.[26] All the while, however, he was mobilizing his local supporters to post hand-bills around the city protesting against his wrongful conviction, and on the evening of 19 October he escaped with their aid. One of his accomplices was the parchmener William Fisher alias Parchmener alias Hampden, at whose house on Turnmill Street in Clerkenwell, just outside the city walls, Sir John resided for the next three months, plotting a revolt against the king and his government.[27]

Uprising and Suppression

News of Oldcastle's escape may initially have been concealed from Henry V and he took no action until 28 October, when he dismissed the keeper of prisoners in the Tower, Sir Robert Morley, from his post and ordered the sher-iffs of London to make proclamations forbidding anyone from harbouring him.[28] Archbishop Arundel had already taken steps to publicize Oldcastle's conviction for heresy around the kingdom by sending copies of the proceed-ings against him to the bishops of the southern province with instructions that the official condemnation of his opinions be read out in English in all churches.[29] On 10 December, moreover, he publicly excommunicated the fugi-tive knight and his supporters at St Paul's Cross.[30] Such publicity may have been counterproductive, however, as there is evidence to suggest that when the news became known, support for Oldcastle began to increase in various parts of the country, particularly where Lollard preachers had been active. In

---

[24] *Concilia*, III, 352–3.

[25] For the trial, see: *Concilia*, III, 353–7; *Fasciculi Zizaniorum*, ed. W. W. Shirley (London, 1858), pp. 433–49; Reg. Arundel, II, fols. 27r–v, 142v–145v.

[26] *GHQ*, pp. 6–7.

[27] For Fisher and his house, see M. Jurkowski, 'Lollard Book Producers in London in 1414', in *Text and Controversy from Wyclif to Bale: Essays in Honour of Anne Hudson*, ed. H. Barr and A. M. Hutchison (Turnhout, 2005), pp. 201–26 (pp. 205–8, 219).

[28] *CPR, 1413–16*, p. 103; TNA, E 404/29, m. 136; *CCR, 1413–19*, p. 41; *Calendar of the Letter-Books of the City of London A–L*, ed. R. R. Sharpe, 11 vols. (London, 1899–1912), *Letter-Book I*, p. 119.

[29] Forrest, *Detection of Heresy*, p. 148; *Fasciculi Zizaniorum*, ed. Shirley, pp. 448–50.

[30] *A Chronicle of London from 1089 to 1483*, ed. N. H. Nicolas and E. Tyrrell (London, 1827), pp. 96–7.

Derbyshire, for example, even members of the local gentry were preaching Lollard views publicly.[31] Oldcastle sent messengers with handbills to Lollard sympathizers around the country, making known his plans.[32]

Henry V and his ministers knew that something was afoot, but had no details of the plot or of the exact whereabouts of Oldcastle. A lead was provided when Philip Okore (or Okeover), deputy keeper of the Tower under the new warden Sir John Dabriggecourt, reported a visit to other Lollard prisoners in custody there by the wife of the London tailor Richard Wrothe on 26 November and recommended that Wrothe be arrested as an accessory to Oldcastle's escape.[33] Wrothe may have yielded further information; certainly, by 11 December the undersheriff of Middlesex had been paid to assemble a panel of jurors in anticipation of a Lollard insurgency.[34] The real breakthrough came on 5 January, however, when two of the conspirators betrayed to the king a plot to kidnap him and his brothers by insurgents disguised as mummers during the Twelfth Night celebrations at Eltham palace.[35] The king immediately alerted the mayor of London, who ordered the aldermen to keep special watch in their wards, and on the following evening the mayor himself went to the 'signe of the Axe' outside Bishopsgate, where he arrested the carpenter John Burgate and seven others, including an esquire of Oldcastle. He brought these plotters to the king at Eltham where they revealed plans for a large-scale muster at St Giles's Fields on 10 January.[36]

The king and mayor now became aware that Oldcastle was staying with Fisher in Clerkenwell, and attempted to arrest him there. Sir Robert Morley, the disgraced former keeper of the Tower, sent his valet John Barton and others to keep a watch on Fisher's house,[37] and a constable of Smithfield made a search of the premises at night, finding Lollard books, but not Oldcastle or Fisher,[38] who had doubtless learned of Burgate's arrest and moved to another safe

---

[31] M. Jurkowski, 'John Fynderne of Findern: An Exchequer Official of the Early Fifteenth Century, His Circle and Lollard Connections' (unpublished Ph.D. dissertation, Keele University, 1998), pp. 301–5.

[32] *The Chronica Maiora of Thomas Walsingham (1376–1422)*, ed. and trans. D. Preest with J. G. Clark (Woodbridge, 2005), p. 393; *The Chronicle of Adam Usk 1377–1421*, ed. C. Given-Wilson (Oxford, 1997), pp. 246–7; and see below.

[33] *Select Cases in Chancery A.D. 1364 to 1471*, ed. W. P. Baildon, Selden Society 10 (1896), p. 109.

[34] The king gave him a gift of one mark for his efforts and the jurors were paid £7 for their costs and expenses and for waiting at Westminster: TNA, E 403/614, m. 9.

[35] The turncoats were John de Burgh and Thomas Kentford, both London carpenters, each of whom was rewarded with an annuity of 10 marks for life: *CPR, 1413–16*, p. 157; TNA, E 208/12, unnumbered writs; Kightly, 'Early Lollards', p. 484.

[36] *Calendar of Letter-Books, I*, p. 119; Kightly, 'Early Lollards', p. 485.

[37] They were paid a special reward of 20s. by the king: TNA, E 403/614, m. 13. Morley, who had been briefly imprisoned for his negligence, was perhaps attempting to exonerate himself: *CCR, 1413–19*, p. 41.

[38] TNA, E 403/614, m. 12.

house. It was perhaps at this point that the king deployed a spy (*explorator regis*), Thomas Burton, to snoop around Clerkenwell, listening under eaves and hanging around the inns and taverns, and he evidently picked up some valuable information.[39]

On 7 January Henry issued a writ to all sheriffs in England ordering them to make proclamations warning against unlawful assemblies and arrest all offenders, and on the following day he rode discreetly with his lords from Eltham, through London, to Westminster.[40] Meanwhile, rebel contingents were descending on the capital from the north, west and east. After an initial muster at Ware, Hertfordshire, the men from Derbyshire were told to seek further instructions from one of the Leicestershire insurgents at the 'Wrastelers on the Hope' tavern in Smithfield.[41] The plan was then to assemble at St Giles's Fields, half way between London and Westminster, with the intention of marching on the king. Armed with his knowledge of this stratagem, Henry V decided to ambush them on the evening of 9 January while many were en route to the muster, reportedly acting against the advice of many of his councillors, who felt it too dangerous to proceed without reinforcements, as they were expecting to face a Lollard force numbering some 25,000.[42] Together with his brothers, the earl of Warwick, Archbishop Arundel and other lords, he 'took the field' near the priory of St John, Clerkenwell, intending to intercept the rebels approaching from the north. This bold strike was accompanied by another key strategic move: he ordered that the city gates be shut and armed guards placed at them to prevent the London contingent from joining their fellows. His action proved decisive; as Kightly notes, many of the Londoners known to have taken part were from extra-mural areas of London.[43] Specific details are lacking, but it appears that little actual fighting occurred, and only a few rebels were reportedly killed.[44] Henry's forces captured more than eighty men,[45] while others successfully escaped the scene, but were later taken into custody in their home counties, or en route there.

---

[39] The king paid him a reward of £5 for discovering the Lollards' plans: TNA, E 403/614, m. 16. Spies were commonly employed in military and diplomatic contexts, although little is known of their domestic activities: J. R. Alban and C. T. Allmand, 'Spies and Spying in the Fourteenth Century', in *War, Literature, and Politics in the Late Middle* Ages, ed. C. T. Allmand (Liverpool, 1976), pp. 73–101.

[40] *CCR, 1413–19*, pp. 114–15; Kightly, 'Early Lollards', pp. 488–9.

[41] Jurkowski, 'Lollard Networks', p. 270. The Wrestlers on the Hoop was almost certainly located close to the 'wrestling place' near the Clerk's Well in Clerkenwell, for which, see: W. J. Pinks, *The History of Clerkenwell* (London, 1881), pp. 7–8; TNA, SC 6/HenVIII/2120, fol. 4. The Essex rebels met at the 'Hors on the Hoop', probably further east: TNA, KB 9/204/1, m. 9.

[42] *Chronica Maiora of Walsingham*, pp. 394–5; C. L. Kingsford, *English Historical Literature in the Fifteenth Century* (New York, 1962), p. 293.

[43] Kightly, 'Early Lollards', pp. 489–91.

[44] *Chronica Maiora of Walsingham*, ed. Preest and Clark, p. 395.

[45] Kingsford, *English Historical Literature*, p. 293.

The first place searched for fleeing rebels was naturally Clerkenwell, the acknowledged headquarters of the revolt. Oldcastle himself eluded capture, but two horses and two red robes lined with gold belonging to him were found on St John's Street in the custody of Matthew Toly, a barber, and John Joynour, ironmonger. They later claimed that an unknown esquire had left them for safekeeping on the morning of the uprising.[46] Also initially escaping from the king's forces were Robert Harley, esquire, William Morley, a brewer from Dunstable, and John Purvey, an important Lollard writer and former secretary to John Wyclif himself. They were quickly discovered, however, at the Cock Inn on Turnmill Street in the lodgings of three sympathizers, and by 12 January were in the custody of the sheriffs of London in Newgate prison.[47]

Punishment and Pardon of Insurgents

On the morning of 10 January, meanwhile, proceedings were put in place to indict, try and convict those in custody. The king appointed two of his most reliable lords and councillors, William, Lord Roos of Hamlake, and Henry, Lord Scrope of Masham – both men of unimpeachable orthodoxy – to head a small commission of oyer and terminer, comprised of the mayor of London and three royal justices.[48] They sat down to a hearty breakfast at the Tower and then got down to the business of convicting some sixty-nine rebels of treason, with the help of the jurors impanelled in December, each of whom was paid a reward on the king's orders.[49] On 13 January thirty-eight of the convicted insurgents were transferred from the custody of the earl Marshal to the sheriffs of London and taken by them for execution to St Giles's Fields.[50]

---

[46] When summoned before the king's bench in 1415, Toly and Joynour reported that the mayor had confiscated these goods, and he was in turn distrained to answer the king for them. He subsequently pleaded a royal pardon and deposited the goods in the exchequer: TNA, KB 27/618, rex rot. 34; KB 29/54, rot. 13.

[47] TNA, E 368/187, m. 300. For 'the Cock' on Turnmill Street, still extant in 1842, where no. 67 now stands, see: Jurkowski, 'Lollard Book Producers', pp. 218–19; *Survey of London, South and East Clerkenwell*, XLVI, ed. P. Temple (New Haven, 2008), figs. 228, 230, 234.

[48] Namely, Hugh Huls, John Preston and John Martyn: *CPR, 1413–16*, p. 175. For the piety of Roos and Scrope, see M. Jurkowski, 'La Noblesse anglaise de la fin du Moyen Age: Pour ou contre la défense de l'orthodoxie religieuse?' in *Le Salut par les armes. Noblesse et défense de l'orthodoxie (XIIIe – XVIIe siècles)*, ed. F. Mercier, A. Boltanski and J.-P. Genet (Rennes, 2011), pp. 227–38 (pp. 232–3).

[49] Kingsford, *English Historical Literature*, p. 293; TNA, E 403/614, m. 9. The jurors received a gift of £6: TNA, E 403/614, m. 12. The legal breakfast was then considered a legitimate form of bribery. For an extravagant example, see M. Jurkowski, 'Lancastrian Royal Service, Lollardy and Forgery: The Career of Thomas Tykhill', in *Crown, Government and People in the Fifteenth Century*, ed. R. E. Archer (Stroud, 1995), pp. 33–52 (p. 42).

[50] All thirty-eight were hanged and seven were also burnt, probably as relapsed heretics or for refusing to abjure: *CCR, 1413–19*, pp. 56–7; Kingsford, *English Historical Literature*, p. 293.

Four others, among them a 'textwriter' from St John's Street, were reportedly executed on 19 January.[51] In the absence of the justices' oyer and terminer file of the proceedings,[52] it is uncertain why only 60 per cent were executed. To be sure, they included key figures in the uprising: Robert Harley, Richard Morley, the Gilbert brothers of Kibworth Harcourt – leaders of a Leicestershire contingent – and William Reynham, son and heir of Sir Edmund Reynham of Burnham Westgate, Norfolk.[53] Although there was a clear intention to punish the ringleaders, a number of lesser men were also hanged – for example, John Purvey's servant Henry Corbrigge, three Derbyshire rebels of little means and a group of prosperous Buckinghamshire tradesmen.[54] Meanwhile Purvey himself, together his long-time companion John Parker and the other remaining convicted insurgents, were left in Newgate to await the king's will. They may have been targeted as those most likely to provide information that would lead to the capture of Oldcastle.[55]

Some of the captured rebels, indeed, had already furnished the names of their patrons, since the commission sitting at the Tower indicted both rebels who had fled the scene and others known to have been complicit in the revolt, including several members of the gentry.[56] Two of the latter were lawyers from the Derby area: Thomas Tykhill, the king's attorney in the court of Common Pleas, and Henry Bothe, attorney for the duchy of Lancaster in

---

[51] They included the carpenter John Burgate, an unnamed 'glover on London Brigge' and the priest John Beverley: Kingsford, *English Historical Literature*, p. 293. Beverley was apparently a figure of some standing among the Lollards and was later regarded as a martyr: J. A. F. Thomson, *The Later Lollards* (Oxford, 1965), pp. 28–30. The glover may have been John Canwell, glover, a rebel whom the London escheator reported had no goods or chattels to be confiscated: TNA, E 357/24, rot. 49. No other judicial proceedings against Canwell have been found.

[52] Only three membranes survive from the file written up by the king's bench clerk John Corff: TNA, KB 9/991; E 403/614, m. 13.

[53] For the preacher William Gilbert, who had also preached in the Derby area, and his brother Nicholas, see: M. Jurkowski, 'Heresy and Factionalism at Merton College, Oxford in the Early Fifteenth Century', *Journal of Ecclesiastical History* 48 (1997), 658–81 (pp. 666–7); and Jurkowski, 'Lawyers and Lollardy in the Early Fifteenth Century', in *Lollardy and the Gentry in the Later Middle Ages*, ed. M. Aston and C. Richmond (Stroud, 1997), pp. 155–82 (pp. 159–60). For Reynham, see M. Jurkowski, 'Lollardy and Social Status in East Anglia', *Speculum* 82 (2007), 120–52 (p. 128); *CCR, 1413–19*, pp. 318–19.

[54] For the value of goods forfeited by Roger Benvyle of High Wycombe, glover; John Horewode, taverner, Richard Turnour, baker, John Fletcher, John Wynchester, weaver, and Walter Young, all of Amersham; and John Fynche of Little Missenden, see: TNA, E 357/24, rots. 67–67d; Powell, *Kingship*, p. 161. For the possessions of the executed Derbyshire men (John Maysham, brazier alias scythemaker; and Peter Clifton and William Scot, both corvisers), see Jurkowski, 'John Fynderne', pp. 306–8. For Corbrigge, see note 55 below.

[55] For Purvey and Parker, see M. Jurkowski, 'New Light on John Purvey', *EHR* 110 (1995), 1180–90.

[56] TNA, KB 27/611, rex rots. 13–13d.

Derbyshire. It later came to light that they had sponsored Lollard preachers there in the years leading up to the revolt.[57] Three others were prominent king's knights: Sir Thomas Chaworth of Wiverton, Nottinghamshire, Sir Thomas Beauchamp of Whitelackington, Somerset, and Sir Thomas Broke the younger, of Holditch, Dorset, husband of Oldcastle's stepdaughter Joan Braybrooke.[58] The Middlesex sheriffs were ordered to produce their bodies before the king's bench on 24 January, together with Oldcastle and nineteen others indicted before the commission.[59] Most of them, predictably, did not appear when their names were called, but Edward, duke of York, constable of the Tower and the earl of Arundel came before the justices and reported that Chaworth, Beauchamp, Tykhill and three others – Sir Roger Cheyne of Drayton Beauchamp, Buckinghamshire, his son and heir John, and John Bryan of (High) Wycombe – were all in his custody in the Tower, 'by special order of the king, for the said treasons and felonies, so that they could neither appear nor surrender themselves to stand to the deliberation [of the court] in this matter'. In order words, their right to defend themselves at common law was denied to them. They were forced to remain prisoners within the Tower at Henry V's will and proceedings against them were temporarily suspended.[60] Meanwhile outlawry proceedings were swiftly begun against the fugitive suspects and writs were issued to the county escheators for inquests into their goods and chattels.[61]

In early February Chaworth, Beauchamp and Tykhill, together with Bothe and Broke, who had by now joined them in the Tower, posted bonds of 1,000 marks each to guarantee their good behaviour while in custody. Backed by four mainpernors each, all of whom were also under pain of 1,000 marks, they undertook not to attempt to escape, while the king agreed that they

---

57 TNA, KB 27/614, rex rots. 15–15d, 24. The weaver John Grene of Chaddesden, Derbyshire, captured at St Giles's Fields and convicted of treason, but spared execution, may have given them up in exchange for leniency: Jurkowski, 'John Fynderne', pp. 305–8. For Tykhill and Bothe, see Jurkowski, 'Career of Thomas Tykhill', pp. 33–52; Jurkowski, 'Lawyers and Lollardy', pp. 157–61; TNA, DL 42/16, fol. 65.
58 The evidence for Lollard sympathies on the part of Beauchamp and Broke, who were neighbours and close associates, is solid enough, but as regards Chaworth, an avid owner of English devotional texts, the matter is less certain: R. W. Dunning and L. S. Woodger, 'Sir Thomas Beauchamp (d. 1444) of Whitelackington, Som.', in *HP*, II, 156–8; J. S. Roskell and L. S. Woodger, 'Sir Thomas Brooke (*c.* 1391–1439), of Holditch, Dorset and Weycroft, Devon', in *HP*, II, 375–7; C. Rawcliffe, 'Sir Thomas Chaworth (d. 1459), of Wiverton, Notts. and Alfreton, Derbys.', in *HP*, II, 533–6; Jurkowski, 'John Fynderne', pp. 328–9; T. Turville-Petre, 'Some Medieval English Manuscripts in the North-East Midlands', in *Manuscripts and Readers in Fifteenth-Century England: The Literary Implications of Manuscript Study*, ed. D. Pearsall (Cambridge, 1983), pp. 125–41 (pp. 132–3).
59 TNA, KB 37/4/1/4, unnumbered writ. I thank Dr James Ross for this reference.
60 TNA, KB 27/611, rots. 13–13d.
61 For example, TNA, E 153/2450B, m. 5; E 153/1842, m. 8; E 153/800, m. 9; E 143/21/4, m. 20.

could live unchained in houses within the Tower 'needful and fitting'.[62] Perhaps it was because they did not personally take up arms against him that Henry V was inclined to treat them with relative leniency, while locking them up for some months probably also served another purpose: it prevented them from lending support to the fugitive Oldcastle. On 12 May the constable of the Tower was ordered to bring Chaworth, Bothe and Tykhill before the king.[63] Sometime within the following ten days, all three, and perhaps also Thomas Broke, were released from custody after posting further bonds of 1,000 marks each, again backed by four prominent mainpernors who pledged matching sums. The mainpernors undertook to have them before the king in chancery, upon a reasonable warning, to answer whatever charge might be laid against them on the part of the king in future.[64] Beauchamp, however, remained in the Tower until 13 September, when the king authorized his release after he had given sufficient security that he would present himself for trial when ordered to do so.[65] It was not until the autumn of 1414 that all five were finally allowed to enter a plea to the indictments made against them in January. Having surrendered themselves to the marshal, they pleaded not guilty in the king's bench on 18 October and were released on the recognizance of mainpernors during the summoning of the jurors. The trial took place remarkably quickly and all were acquitted and released on 27 October, probably on the instructions of a king's serjeant-at-law, who was noted as having been present.[66]

Fewer details are available of Henry V's treatment of the three prominent rebels from Buckinghamshire in the Tower – Sir Roger Cheyne, his son John and John Bryan – all of whom were in custody by 18 January,[67] but the first two, certainly, appear to have been more harshly dealt with, perhaps because they did not have the means to post the same extortionate bonds or had played a greater role in the uprising. There is no indication that they were extended the same privileges as the other prisoners, and according to his inquisition post-mortem, Sir Roger died on 14 May 1414, probably while in the Tower.[68] His son John was still a prisoner there until November

---

62 Beauchamp's bond was posted on 12 February and those of the others on 8 February. All of their mainpernors were either members of the gentry or wealthy Londoners: *CCR, 1413–16*, pp. 116, 121; TNA, C 259/7, m. 2.

63 *CCR, 1413–19*, p. 124.

64 Chaworth's bonds were given on 22 May, and the others were presumably posted between 12 May and that date: TNA, C 259/7, m. 6.

65 TNA, C 81/1364/18.

66 TNA, KB 27/614, rex rots. 15–15d, 24.

67 *CCR, 1413–19*, p. 54. However, Sir Roger's younger son Thomas, also indicted, remained at large and was eventually pardoned: ibid., p. 177; TNA, C 67/37, m. 58.

68 *CIPM*, XX, nos. 176–9. The Buckinghamshire antiquarian Browne Willis recorded that he was buried in the Tower chapel, although Sir Roger's simple memorial brass tomb lies today in the parish church of Cassington, Oxfordshire, where he was lord of the manor.

1414, when he pleaded a pardon before king's bench and was acquitted and released.[69] Bryan, a prominent burgess of High Wycombe who may have been well connected in the London merchant community, was luckier.[70] He bought his pardon on 18 May, procured the necessary letters of validation on 10 June and was a free man by the time that he was acquitted by pardon, on 3 October 1414.[71]

Also able to buy his freedom was Ralph Garton, a wealthy mercer of Coventry who had backed a contingent of rebels from that city. Having also been indicted before Lords Roos and Scrope, Garton was taken into custody in Coventry by its mayor on 13 January and brought before the king's bench at Westminster on 8 February. He escaped further imprisonment after his attorney argued that because he was 'broken by debility and old age', a spell in a hard prison would surely kill him. He was instead released to the custody of eight mainpernors who, under bonds of 1,000 marks, undertook to produce him at his trial, and Garton himself posted an additional 1,000 marks.[72] At length he too acquitted himself by pleading a general pardon.[73] Other rebels who had been indicted by the commissioners and initially avoided capture were not treated so leniently when finally discovered. Walter Blake, the chaplain who had led the Bristol contingent, was very quickly tracked down and arrested in Oxford with five others, and by 27 January he was in the Marshalsea. Employed by a prominent family of Bristol merchants, Blake was well armed and equipped and was clearly perceived as a ringleader; he was hurriedly tried and convicted of treason on that day and was

---

Browne Willis incorrectly gives the date of his death as 4 May 1415, however: BL MS Additional 5840, fol. 20; Kightly, 'Early Lollards', p. 393n. Sir Roger was the patron of the Lollard priest Thomas Drayton, rector of Drayton Beauchamp, who was also implicated in the revolt. Drayton was subsequently tried twice for heresy: M. Jurkowski, 'Lollardy in Coventry and the Revolt of 1431', in *The Fifteenth Century, VI, Identity and Insurgency in the Late Middle Ages*, ed. L. Clark (Woodbridge, 2006), pp. 145–64 (pp. 146–7); A. Hudson, *The Premature Reformation: Wycliffite Texts and Lollard History* (Oxford, 1988), pp. 125–6.

69 TNA, KB 145/5/2/1, unnumbered writ; *CPR, 1413–16*, p. 244; TNA, KB 27/614, rex rot. 41.

70 He was the first-named attestor of the parliamentary election indentures in the borough of High Wycombe in 1420, 1421 and 1422: TNA, C 219/12, no. 4, m. 4; no. 6, m. 4; C 219/13, no. 1, m. 5. (I am grateful to Dr S. J. Payling for the latter reference.) He was perhaps related to John Bryan (d.1418), citizen of London and son of the prominent fishmonger John Bryan, who owned estates in Buckinghamshire, Middlesex and London: *CCR, 1385–9*, pp. 322–3, 487; TNA, C 147/135B; Prerogative Court of Canterbury, Wills, 42 Marche (Image Ref. 162); Kingsford, *English Historical Literature*, p. 295.

71 *CPR, 1413–16*, p. 188; TNA, KB 27/614, rex rot. 3. For the acquittal by pardon procedure, see below.

72 TNA, KB 27/611, rex rots. 13–13d.

73 His involvement with the Lollards seems to have continued; certainly, his wife was executed for her part in the 1431 uprising, see: Jurkowski, 'Lollardy in Coventry', pp. 150–4, 158–63.

later drawn through the streets of London and hanged at St Giles's Fields.[74] Taken into custody not long afterwards was Sir Roger Acton of Sutton-by-Tenbury, Shropshire, a crown retainer and one of Oldcastle's more important lieutenants.[75] He was sent to the Tower on 8 February, in accordance with his higher social status, and was quickly tried, convicted and executed in like manner.[76]

While the seizing of these men was no doubt of importance in the suppression of the revolt, what Henry V was most anxious to know was the whereabouts of Oldcastle, who continued to elude capture. The work of finding him had begun immediately after the revolt. On 11 January a proclamation was sent to every sheriff, to be read out in all cities and boroughs, advertising a reward for his capture.[77] Anyone providing information that led to his arrest would receive 1,000 marks of gold, an annuity of £20 for life and permanent exemption from all forms of taxation.[78] Oldcastle's friends and associates were approached for information, among them Sir Hugh Luterell, a feoffee of his estates in Norfolk and Suffolk, to whom a king's messenger had been sent with all possible haste.[79] It was important to freeze Oldcastle's assets, so to speak, and his lands were quickly taken into the king's hands, along with those of the other fugitive rebels. The inquests into his lands in Kent, held from 5 to 10 February, include a room-by-room inventory of goods in his residence of Cooling castle, which, while wonderfully informative of the number and layout of rooms, suggests that all objects of high value had been removed before the escheator's arrival, leaving only beds and other heavy furniture, basic utensils and stock and grain stores.[80] The escheator John Darell was later paid a special reward for taking possession of these goods while accompanied by a large posse of men, in case of resistance from his adherents.[81] Efforts to cut off Oldcastle's income were not entirely successful, however. It later came to light that some of his tenements in the city of Hereford had been concealed from the escheator by friends who presumably passed on the

---

[74] TNA, KB 27/611, rex rot. 7; Kingsford, *English Historical Literature*, p. 293. For the panel of jurors who convicted him, see TNA, KB 37/4/1/4, unnumbered writ. For Blake and the More family who employed him, see Kightly, 'Early Lollards', pp. 240–50.

[75] For Acton, who had sponsored at least one Lollard preacher, see M. Jurkowski, 'The Arrest of William Thorpe in Shrewsbury and the Anti-Lollard Statute of 1406', *Historical Research* 75 (2002), 273–95 (pp. 289–91).

[76] *CCR, 1413–19*, p. 54; TNA, KB 27/611, rex rot. 7; Kingsford, *English Historical Literature*, p. 293.

[77] *Foedera*, IX, 89; TNA, E 403/614, m. 12.

[78] For a copy of the proclamation, see: TNA, E 175/3, no. 15.

[79] TNA, E 403/614, m. 13. Luterell was the choice of Joan Cobham's former husband Sir Reginald Braybrooke, and was not necessarily on the best terms with Oldcastle: TNA, E 368/187, rots. 80–80d.

[80] TNA, E 153/1008, m. 3 (Dartford), m. 4 (Cooling), m. 5 (Cobham), m. 6 (Canterbury).

[81] TNA, E 403/633, m. 3; Devon, *Issues of the Exchequer*, p. 353.

rents to him, and additional funds were allegedly hidden for him by other associates.[82]

On 11 January Henry V also appointed commissioners of inquiry throughout England to track down fugitive rebels in their home counties and reveal the activities of other Lollards who had not taken part in the revolt, all of which would facilitate the search for Oldcastle. The commissions were headed by local peers or reliable members of the gentry, who were instructed, unusually, to return their indictments directly to Henry V in chancery.[83] Sixteen commissions were issued covering London, Bristol and twenty counties,[84] with returns surviving from ten counties and Bristol.[85] In two counties, Hampshire and Nottinghamshire, the jurors made no presentments, submitting blank returns, and, indeed, there is no indication that any of the rebels came from either (apart from Sir Thomas Chaworth), although there was a history of Lollard agitation in both.[86] No returns at all survive from the remaining counties.[87]

To preside over these commissions Henry V again relied upon the service of William, Lord Roos; he sat personally at every session in Derbyshire, Leicestershire and Nottinghamshire, and Richard de Vere, earl of Oxford, did the same in Essex.[88] Jurors made two distinct types of indictment: (1) of treason against the king for complicity in the revolt; and (2) of being a Lollard and/or holding Lollard opinions. In the latter category were four women: Agnes, wife of Thomas Tykhill, Eleanor Warde of Daventry, and Christina More and the wife of John Kenfeke, both of Bristol.[89] In some cases, suspects were accused of both treason and Lollardy, but more commonly of one or the other. Since heresy was not a criminal offence but a violation of Church law, suspects accused of Lollardy were liable to arrest and delivery to the bishop of their diocese to purge themselves of heresy. If they did not undergo purga-

---

82 TNA, E 159/195, Michaelmas *communia*, rots. 1–1d, 3–3d, 13d; Devon, *Issues of the Exchequer*, pp. 352–3.
83 Powell, *Kingship*, p. 153; TNA, KB 27/613, rex rot. 6.
84 *CPR, 1413–16*, pp. 177–8.
85 TNA, KB 9/204/1 (Derbyshire, Essex, Hertfordshire, Leicestershire, Northamptonshire, Nottinghamshire, Worcestershire); KB 9/205/1, mm. 51–57 (Oxfordshire), 81–85 (Bristol and Gloucestershire); *CIM* VII, 462 (Hampshire); Powell, *Kingship*, p. 152.
86 In 1440 and 1514 there was a community active at Odiham, Hampshire, where Wyclif's disciples had preached in 1382: Thomson, *Later Lollards*, pp. 63–5, 88–9; Jurkowski, 'Lollard Networks', pp. 262, 275. For Lollards in Nottingham in the late 1380s and early 1390s, see ibid., p. 269.
87 Namely, Bedfordshire, Buckinghamshire, Devon, Dorset, Kent, Herefordshire, London, Shropshire, Somerset and Warwickshire.
88 TNA, KB 9/204/1, mm. 1–12, 20–83, 128–145.
89 Jurkowski, 'Thomas Tykhill', pp. 37–40, 48; M. Jurkowski, 'Lollardy in Oxfordshire and Northamptonshire: The Two Thomas Compworths', in *Lollards and Their Influence in Late Medieval England*, ed. F. Somerset, J. C. Havens and D. G. Pitard (Woodbridge, 2003), p. 91; Kightly, 'Early Lollards', pp. 245–8.

tion, then they could be arrested by royal officials to secure their appearance before the king's bench. In practice, there were anomalies in the indictment and purgation procedures, with variation both locally and according to the social standing of the suspects.

In Leicestershire, commissioners sat from 4 to 7 February at Melton Mowbray, Leicester and Loughborough. Five Leicestershire men had been captured and convicted of treason at St Giles's Field. The jurors at these sessions indicted one of them and eleven others who had risen with Oldcastle, for treason. While twelve others were accused of Lollardy, only four men in total were indicted for both treason and Lollardy. The jurors were unusually forthcoming about the heretical views that the latter had expressed. They described Ralph Friday of Wigston, for example, as an excellent speaker against the pope and his power, and memorably quoted him as having asserted that 'Thomas Arundell archbishop of Canterbury is one of the disciples of the anti-Christ and a murderer of men.'[90] They indicted Thomas Ile alias Scot, a scrivener of Braybrooke, Northamptonshire (close to the Leicestershire border), of both Lollardy and copying and distributing handbills sent to him by Oldcastle, but not of treason, perhaps because he took no part in the revolt.[91] Nine indicted only for Lollardy in Leicestershire had been taken into custody and imprisoned in the Marshalsea by 16 June, when Henry V ordered their delivery to the bishop of Lincoln for purgation.[92] Thomas Ile, meanwhile, had been separately arrested by the constable of Braybrooke and imprisoned in Northampton castle, where he remained until freed by the king's justices of gaol delivery on 18 February 1415, having secured the king's pardon two months earlier. Curiously, however, he was not required to recant his beliefs.[93]

Similar inconsistencies occurred in the treatment of rebels and Lollards in neighbouring Derbyshire. Five of the Derbyshire insurgents had escaped capture, including one of their leaders, the chaplain William Ederyk. He was sheltered by the Tykhills in February 1414, before fleeing to Warwickshire, where he was eventually arrested with two others. Ten rebels in all were indicted for treason, in addition to Tykhill and Bothe. Of these, only Ederyk was also charged with Lollardy, but two of the others were nevertheless

---

[90] Similar sentiments were also uttered by John Belgrave of the same town: TNA, KB 9/204/1, m. 141. For Friday and Belgrave, see Jurkowski, 'Lawyers and Lollardy', pp. 162–3. Both men had been exposed as Lollards during Bishop Repingdon's visitation of the archdeaconry of Leicester in the previous year: see J. Crompton, 'Leicestershire Lollards', *Transactions of the Leicestershire Archaeological and Historical Society* 44 (1968–9), 11–44; Forrest, *Detection of Heresy*, pp. 207–30.

[91] They also presented the rector of Braybrooke (Robert Hoke) as a Lollard: TNA, KB 9/204/1, mm. 130, 134, 141. For Hoke, a notorious heretic, see McFarlane, *Lancastrian Kings*, pp. 195–6; Hudson, *Premature Reformation*, pp. 80n., 90–1, 164, 207.

[92] TNA, KB 27/613, rex rot. 6.

[93] TNA, JUST 3/52/16, mm. 10, 12; Kightly, 'Early Lollards', pp. 139–40.

required to purge themselves of heresy. Eight persons in all were presented as Lollards, six of whom were members of the gentry. All had to undergo purgation, but none were arrested, and consequently they did not appear before the bishop for some years; a few, apparently, never did.[94] The indictments followed a like pattern in Bristol, which produced the largest number of both rebels and Lollards,[95] and Northamptonshire, where there is evidence of the coercion of at least one juror.[96] Similarly, one of the five panels of jurors in Colchester uniquely refused to indict anyone.[97] It is also clear that several of the indictments – in Derbyshire, Essex and Bristol – incorporated an official text to which local details were added.

On 28 March, with most of the principal insurgents having been captured, tried and executed, Henry V offered a general pardon to all fugitive rebels who surrendered themselves to the courts by midsummer, with a few named exceptions. Both the men tried and convicted at St Giles's Fields and still imprisoned in Newgate or the Marshalsea, and those indicted before the Lollard commissions sitting in their localities, could now purchase charters of pardon, which would acquit them of all indictments.[98] It was not as simple a matter as it seemed, however, since two documents had to be procured from chancery: the pardon itself (costing 13*s*. 4*d*.) and a writ of *non molestatis* certifying that the suspect had posted a bond guaranteeing his future behaviour and ordering the king's justices to proceed no further with the charges.[99] In practice there was sometimes a long gap between a defendant's purchase of a pardon and the posting of the necessary security, presumably due to lack of collateral to secure the bond, during which he remained in prison. John Grene of Derbyshire, for example, who had been captured, tried and convicted at St Giles's Fields, was imprisoned in the Marshalsea until 23 July 1414, when he was transferred to Newgate. On 15 December 1414 he procured a general pardon, but a few days later he was sent back to the Marshalsea, where he remained until able to obtain the writ of *non molestatis* on 6 May 1415. Only then did he appear before the king's bench, and plead his pardon and writ, upon which he was acquitted and released.[100] Most of the indicted rebels were at length able to acquit themselves by this process, but some were not

94 Jurkowski, 'John Fynderne', pp. 301–15.
95 Kightly, 'Early Lollards', pp. 241–9.
96 Thomas Spryggy refused to serve and complied only after he was fined for contempt. His brother John was amerced for refusing to open Thomas's door to the mayor: TNA, KB 9/204/1, m. 103; Jurkowski, 'Lollardy in Oxfordshire and Northamptonshire', pp. 91–2.
97 It is surely no coincidence that John Abraham, later burnt at the stake for heresy, was on the panel: TNA, KB 9/204/1, mm. 8–12; Jurkowski, 'Lollardy and Social Status', p. 131.
98 *CCR, 1413–19*, pp. 176–7; *Foedera* IX, 119–20.
99 Powell, *Kingship*, p. 84.
100 TNA, KB 27/616, rex rots. 23–23d; Jurkowski, 'John Fynderne', pp. 314–15.

so lucky. The Lollard writer John Purvey, his companion John Parker, and Richard Knyght of Burton, Somerset, all died awaiting pardons in Newgate – where conditions were notoriously bad – within a few months of the revolt.[101]

Oldcastle as Fugitive: Abortive Plots and Summary Arrests

Meanwhile, the search for Oldcastle continued, and a new statute enacted in the parliament held at Leicester in May 1414 provided additional powers to secular officials to aid this effort and allow for more effective policing of heresy generally. Firstly, sheriffs and other crown officers were required to swear an oath on taking office that they would do their utmost to extirpate heresy and Lollardy, and put themselves at the service of the ecclesiastical authorities to this end whenever necessary. Justices of the peace and all other itinerant royal judges were vested with the authority to arrest and indict heretics and then hand them over to Church officials, and a new penalty of forfeiture of lands and goods for convicted heretics was instituted.[102] Nevertheless, Oldcastle remained at large throughout 1415 while Henry V planned his campaign in France, efficiently quashing an abortive dynastic revolt in Southampton in the days just prior to setting sail in August.[103]

By that time rumours had begun to circulate that Oldcastle was planning another insurrection and the king reportedly left some of his most loyal troops behind for this reason.[104] Sir John seems to have been based in the midlands at that time; in August 1415 John Prest, the vicar of Chesterton, Warwickshire (near Coventry), sheltered him there,[105] and in December 1415 he allegedly attempted to instigate a second uprising near Malvern, Worcestershire. The chronicler Thomas Walsingham reports that he sent a threatening letter to the local peer, Richard Beauchamp, Lord Abergavenny, who responded by raising a large force of men at Hanley castle, and Oldcastle hastily withdrew. Five of his accomplices were said to have been captured, however, together with a cache of money, weapons, painted banners and a standard depicting a chalice and loaf of bread – reminiscent of the Hussite chalice motif.[106] It is not

---

[101] They died on 16 May, 16 April and 10 May, respectively: TNA, E 368/187, rot. 300. For conditions in Newgate, see C. M. Barron, *London in the Later Middle Ages* (Oxford, 2004), pp. 164–6.

[102] *SR*, II, 181–3.

[103] See Pugh, *Southampton Plot*.

[104] *GHQ*, pp. 20–1.

[105] TNA, KB 9/209, m. 40. He was possibly the same John Preest of Northampton who despatched letters to Oldcastle just prior to the revolt: TNA, KB 9/204/1, mm. 99–100; Jurkowski, 'Lollardy in Oxon. and Northants.', pp. 91–2.

[106] *Chronica Maiora of Walsingham*, ed. Preest and Clark, pp. 405–6; Kightly, 'Early Lollards', pp. 293–5. For the Hussite chalice motif and its use on military banners, see T. Fudge,

clear how many men Oldcastle had had at his disposal; two from Coventry were later indicted for raising troops for him on that occasion.[107]

In October 1416 Oldcastle was in Piddington, Oxfordshire, where he was said to have been harboured by the chaplain John Whitby, who was later hanged for this crime.[108] In the same month the London sheriffs finally succeeded in arresting William Fisher, with whom Oldcastle had planned the 1414 revolt. He was swiftly tried and convicted of treason and executed. His arrest occurred just days after yet another conspiracy had been uncovered, in which Benedict Wolman and Thomas Bekeryng were implicated, and the two events were probably related. Wolman was a veteran anti-Lancastrian plotter, ostensibly with some Lollard beliefs, and, together with his co-conspirators, had written to Sigismund, Holy Roman Emperor, inviting him to invade England, install a Ricardian impostor on the throne, and confiscate the temporalities of the Church. Their faith in Sigismund proved misplaced; he betrayed the plot to Henry V.[109] Also involved was Thomas Lucas, a common lawyer and former fellow of Merton College, Oxford, who had probably composed the letter. He was not indicted until March 1417, however, for his part in this plan, which involved distributing handbills in the streets of London and Canterbury. He was acquitted at trial a few months later.[110]

There were other reported, but not wholly reliable, sightings of Oldcastle elsewhere in the midlands towards the end of 1416. Robert Rose alias Smith, a felonious chaplain from Hartshorne, Derbyshire, who turned approver, claimed on 4 February 1417 to have met him before that date on Swarkestone Bridge, near Derby. He rode three or four leagues with him and they ate and drank together.[111] In December 1416 a Nottinghamshire lawyer, John Howes of Howes, reportedly gave him succour at Hickling Rise in the same county.[112] The crown became increasingly anxious to secure his capture and in January 1417 Henry V ordered a new proclamation to be made in counties where Oldcastle was known to enjoy support, renewing the offer of a reward

---

The Magnificent Ride: The First Reformation in Hussite Bohemia (Aldershot, 1998), pp. 245–51.

107 TNA, KB 9/209, mm. 35–36; Jurkowski, 'Lollardy in Coventry', p. 151.

108 TNA, KB 9/209, mm. 62–62d. Whitby was probably the same man of this name summoned before the bishop of Durham in 1402 for preaching heresy: Jurkowski, 'Lollard Networks', p. 264.

109 Jurkowski, 'Lollard Book Producers', pp. 208–9; M. Aston, 'Lollardy and Sedition, 1381–1431', in M. Aston, *Lollards and Reformers, Images and Literacy in Late Medieval Religion* (London, 1984), 1–47 (pp. 27–9). Among Wolman's goods was 'part of a psalter glossed with English': TNA, E 136/108/13. For his career as a conspirator, see Jurkowski, 'Lollardy in Oxon. and Northants.', pp. 84–5.

110 Jurkowski, 'Heresy and Factionalism', pp. 675–6. Handbills had also appeared in St Albans, Northampton and Reading: Thomson, *Later Lollards*, pp. 16–17.

111 Among other crimes, Rose stood accused of distributing Lollard handbills found in nearby Burton on Trent, Staffordshire: TNA, JUST 3/56/14, m. 14; JUST 3/195, rot. 50d.

112 TNA, JUST 3/195, rot. 37. For Howes, see Jurkowski, 'Lawyers and Lollardy', p. 163.

for his capture, with the additional inducement that the captors would find the king 'henceforward very generous in their affairs, and in every lawful and honest suit of theirs'.[113]

By the summer of 1417 Oldcastle was in Northamptonshire. In May he was reportedly at Silverstone with two co-conspirators – Sir Thomas Talbot of Davington, Kent, and John Walmesley, a yeoman from Walmesley, Lancashire – and in the following month Ralph Clerk, a chaplain from Coventry, allegedly armed himself and rode off to join them.[114] It is clear that another uprising was planned, perhaps timed to coincide with the king's imminent departure for France. On 15 July, Oldcastle, now also in the company of John Langacre of High Wycombe, was received at Byfield by William atte Well and his wife Beatrix, and at Silverstone by Hugh Frayn and his wife Joan.[115] The plot seems to have been disrupted, however, and he departed the area abruptly, leaving a steel chest of armour in the Frayns' possession.[116]

On 22 July, a week after this latest episode, the king appointed an oyer and terminer commission to investigate Lollardy in nine counties.[117] His justices sat in late August and early September at Coventry, Oxford and Northampton, at which several of the indictments discussed above were made, but Oldcastle remained at large.[118] From an inquest held a year after his capture, it is clear that by 20 August he had retreated to his Herefordshire estates, but Henry V did not know this and the threat of insurrection still loomed, especially as the latter was abroad.[119] The autumn of 1417 saw the implementation, therefore, of a new policy of summary arrest and imprisonment in the Marshalsea of suspected Lollards – many never before indicted for Lollardy

---

[113] The offer was to be proclaimed in Warwickshire, Leicestershire, Shropshire, Gloucestershire, Nottinghamshire, Derbyshire, Northamptonshire, Herefordshire, Oxfordshire, Berkshire, Staffordshire, Worcestershire, Somerset, Dorset and Bristol: *CCR, 1413–19*, p. 379.

[114] TNA, KB 9/994, rot. 42; KB 27/630, rex rot. 13d; KB 9/209, m. 34. For Clerk and his patron, the wealthy Coventry widow Elizabeth Meryngton, see Jurkowski, 'Lollardy in Coventry', pp. 152–4.

[115] Langacre had previously been indicted, imprisoned and pardoned for his part in the revolt: Jurkowski, 'Lollard Book Producers', pp. 206–7; *CCR, 1413–19*, p. 148; 'Lollardy in Oxfordshire and Northamptonshire', pp. 92–3.

[116] The chest of armour, explicitly stated to have belonged to Oldcastle, contained a pair of 'close bristeplattes', a steel 'paunce', chain mail and another breastplate 'cum lez wyngges', all of which had been confiscated by Sir Thomas Grene: TNA, E 153/1281, m. 3.

[117] Namely, in Northamptonshire, Bedfordshire, Buckinghamshire, Oxfordshire, Berkshire, Hertfordshire, Middlesex, Leicestershire and Warwickshire: TNA, KB 9/209.

[118] TNA, KB 9/209, mm. 1–27 (Northamptonshire), mm. 28–50 (Warwickshire), mm. 51–62 (Oxfordshire). No indictments seem to have been made in Berkshire or Middlesex, although jurors were impanelled in the former, nor in Bedfordshire, Buckinghamshire, Hertfordshire or Leicestershire: TNA, KB 9/209, mm. 63–71.

[119] H. G. Richardson, 'John Oldcastle in Hiding, August–October 1417', *EHR* 55 (1940), 432–8.

or treason – who had the means to offer Sir John shelter or financial support. The detention orders themselves are not recorded in any crown records, and the arrests were only brought to light after Oldcastle's capture and execution, when these Lollard suspects petitioned for their release.

Oldcastle had lived discreetly at his manor of Almeley until 12 October, when he set off for North Wales to meet up with Gruffyd, son of Owain Glyndŵr, presumably to seek out an alliance with him. He was intercepted near Welshpool in late November by four tenants of Sir Edward Charleton, Lord Powys and brought to Westminster where parliament was in session. On 14 December he was formally condemned by the Lords and immediately executed.[120] Lord Powys then claimed the 1,000 mark reward, either on behalf of his tenants, or as their overlord, but died on 14 March 1421 before any of it was paid over. It was left to his widow and executors to stake their claim, and on 3 February 1422 Lady Powys took receipt of a one-third share.[121]

The threat of Oldcastle having subsided, the king and his ministers were now willing to listen to the petitions of the Lollard suspects detained in the Marshalsea – who numbered at least thirteen – for their release. Gaining their freedom earliest were the wealthiest and most prominent among them, who could afford to post the most expensive penal bonds. William Marshall, a gentleman of Stretton-en-le-Field, Derbyshire, who had been imprisoned on suspicion of Lollardy and was released on 8 December 1417, was not particularly prominent, but he was backed by powerful members of the local gentry, led by Sir Richard Vernon of Haddon, who undertook to produce him in court in future, if required.[122] On 1 February 1418 Joan, widow of Robert Burdet, esquire, of Baddisley Clinton, Warwickshire, was released after posting a bond of £500 in chancery a week earlier, backed by five gentry mainpernors posting identical bonds, to guarantee that henceforth she would not maintain anyone heretical nor lead any unlawful assemblies.[123] A few days later, on 4 February, Henry Jeke, a burgess of Tamworth, Staffordshire, posted a bond of £200 and was freed to the custody of four men, who, at £100 each, undertook to produce him before the king's bench whenever requested. He was

120 *CCR, 1419–22*, p. 196; *CPR, 1416–22*, p. 145; *PROME*, IX, 210–15, 218.
121 Devon, *Issues of the Exchequer*, pp. 370–1; TNA, E 42/260. For Lord Powys's death, see *CIPM*, XXI, nos. 826–7.
122 TNA, KB 27/626, rex rot. 28d. He had been indicted for preaching heresy at Stretton on 1 October 1413 and was ordered to stand correction before his ordinary, which, ostensibly, he never did: TNA, KB 9/204/1, m. 66; KB 27/699, rex rot. 5. He was involved in a local dispute in 1417 as well, and his mainpernors had already posted bonds of 100 marks each before the king's bench on 20 November that he would keep the peace against a local enemy; Marshall himself gave surety for 200 marks: TNA, KB 27/626, rex rot. 28. For the dispute, see Jurkowski, 'John Fynderne', pp. 436–48. He had been in the Marshalsea since at least 22 November: TNA, KB 9/210, m. 39.
123 TNA, KB 27/627, rex rot. 9; *CCR, 1413–19*, pp. 454–5. For the Burdets, see Jurkowski, 'Lollardy in Coventry', pp. 147–8.

said to have been lately imprisoned on suspicion of Lollardy and complicity with Oldcastle.[124] On 10 March William Glasier of Barton under Needwood, Staffordshire, and Thomas Praty of Solihull, who had been detained for the same reason since at least 21 November 1417, were released to four mainpernors under similar conditions, each man posting a bond of £100.[125]

It was with the freeing of six lesser men, on 11 July 1418, that the procedure for these releases was made clear. The royal writ of 7 July ordering their delivery clearly incorporated a quotation from their (no longer extant) petition, which complained that they had been arrested 'pur suspicion deresie nient enditez nappellez de treson ne dautre cryme sunt este ia long temps et uncore sont detenuz en prisone de la mareschialcie' ('for suspicion of heresy, not indicted nor appealed of treason or of any other crime, have been for a long time now and are still detained in the prison of the Marshalsea'). William Coston, a chaplain of Baddisley Clinton, John Clement, a London tailor, John Barnaby, a gentleman of York, Henry Parmonter, a bottlemaker of Worcester, Nicholas Taillour, a tailor of Leicester and John Grene of Chaddesden, Derbyshire, were released to the custody of six mainpernors, who promised, with 20 marks each, to have them before the king's bench from time to time to respond to whatever might be laid against them.[126] Although Taillour was one of the Leicestershire men indicted for Lollardy and sent to the Marshalsea in 1414, he had been delivered to Bishop Repingdon for purgation, while Grene, as we have seen, had been released and pardoned in 1415. The other four had no demonstrable involvement with the revolt, although Clement had connections with known Lollards.[127] John Belgrave of Wigston, another of the Leicestershire men indicted for Lollardy in 1414, was also a prisoner in the Marshalsea in November 1417 and he too may have been summarily arrested.[128]

The unusual circumstances of the release of Thomas Briklesworth, a 'gentleman' of Brixworth, Northamptonshire, are revealed by an entry on the king's bench controlment roll. He had been indicted for insurgency in February 1414 and was acquitted on 20 April 1415 by a general pardon.[129]

---

124 He agreed not to violate Church law nor support anyone who held heretical opinions: TNA, KB 27/627, rex rot. 12. For Jeke, see Jurkowski, 'Career of Robert Herlaston', pp. 116–20.

125 TNA, KB 145/5/6; Jurkowski, 'John Fynderne', pp. 322–3.

126 TNA, KB 145/5/6; KB 27/629, rex rot. 17d; and see Jurkowski, 'John Fynderne', pp. 323–6.

127 See notes 92 and 100 above. For Clement, see Jurkowski, 'Lollard Book Producers', pp. 214–16.

128 He was in custody from at least 20 to 22 November: TNA, KB 9/210, m. 39. In 1414 he had also been imprisoned there, but had been delivered, like Nicholas Taillour, into the hands of Bishop Repingdon: see notes 90 and 92 above. For Belgrave, see further Jurkowski, 'Career of Robert Herlaston', pp. 118–10.

129 TNA, KB 9/204/1, m. 93; KB 27/616, rex rot. mm. 1–1d (pardon dated 20 January 1415).

Nevertheless, Briklesworth – known variously as a mercer and a chapman, who also used the surnames Gylour, Fauconberge and Burton – was back in the Marshalsea 'on suspicion of treason and Lollardy' by 20 November 1417.[130] His release did not come about until 2 December 1418, when four London tradesmen came before the king's bench and posted bonds of 20 marks each guaranteeing that if the court would deliver him to their custody, he would travel to Normandy with all haste, properly armed and arrayed, and accompanied by a valet and page. There he would serve the king in his wars until given royal licence to come back to England, which he was to produce in court upon his return, but nothing further is recorded.[131] Although no such other cases relating to imprisoned Lollards have been uncovered, sending troublesome individuals to fight in the French war was common practice under Henry V; he used this tactic of redeploying the bellicose proclivities of feuding gentry on a number of occasions.[132]

After the demise of Oldcastle, Henry V's treatment of his erstwhile supporters notably softened in the few remaining years of his reign. Although in December 1418 he ordered an inquiry in Herefordshire into the activities of nine men suspected of having colluded with Oldcastle in his final months in 1417, they were ultimately shown leniency. Four were found not guilty by the court and the cases of the others – mostly from Almeley – were referred to the king's council, who chose to believe their claims that they had acted under duress and acquitted them.[133] Similarly, John Prest, the vicar of Chesterton who had sheltered Oldcastle in 1415, was at length pardoned for this crime in June 1421.[134] Nonetheless, investigations into the activities of those who had aided and abetted Oldcastle continued, generally in the form of commissions

---

[130] He served as a juror at inquests into the deaths of fellow prisoners on at least four occasions between that date and 14 February 1418: TNA, KB 9/210, m. 39; KB 145/5/6. For his aliases, see TNA, C 237/38, m. 180; CP 40/603, rot. 291d.

[131] The four mainpernors were Nicholas Ive and Nicholas Novell, both mercers, John Westowe, cutler, and William Harry, draper, while Briklesworth himself gave an undertaking of £40: TNA, KB 29/55, rot. 23. Westowe had also put himself forward as a mainpernor for the six men released in July 1418, although he was not selected: TNA, KB 145/5/6; see above. He was prominent enough to be elected junior warden of the Cutlers' Company in 1420: C. Welch, *History of the Cutlers' Company of London*, 2 vols. (London, 1916–23), I, 243, 298.

[132] Powell, *Kingship*, pp. 232–40.

[133] Richardson, 'Oldcastle in Hiding', pp. 432–8. Two of the four initially acquitted – Walter Harald, a chaplain of Wigmore, and his brother Nicholas – may have come to the king's attention as Lollards, since they had been compelled to swear an oath against heresy in chancery in February 1418: *CCR, 1413–19*, p. 459.

[134] *CPR, 1416–22*, p. 372. It is not known how long he had been imprisoned; he was still being sought at the end of 1418: TNA, KB 27/630, rex rot. 2. Even after his pardon was secured he probably remained in custody until July 1421 when four mainpernors posted a bond of £100 to guarantee that he would henceforth hold no heretical opinions and would appear before the council upon request: *CCR, 1419–22*, p. 206.

of inquiry,[135] and there was an unsated appetite for the lurid accusations of approvers such as the counterfeiter William Carswell, the Irish scrivener John Fitzharry and John Wodecock, known as 'the baron of Blacmore'.[136]

Moreover, the practice of arresting suspected Lollards without charge carried on, although the detainees were almost certainly now fewer in number. A barker from Tamworth, William Halweton, for example, was arrested on suspicion of holding heretical opinions on 3 January 1419 and spent eleven months in custody before his release on 23 November 1419.[137] Indeed, in the first parliament of Henry VI's reign in November 1422 the Commons presented a petition urging that all prisoners being held on suspicion of Lollardy be handed over to their ordinaries for examination in compliance with the Lollard statute of 1414.[138] In an individual petition addressed to the duke of Gloucester and other lords of the same parliament, Thomas Payn of Glamorgan, described elsewhere as 'sometyme clerk and chief conseillor' to Sir John Oldcastle, similarly complained that he had been 'detained for a long time in a hard prison without indictment, impeachment or other reasonable cause, but by suspicion, without being able to respond', and asked to be tried in parliament. The lords ordered that the record of the case be reviewed, but its ultimate outcome is unknown.[139]

Conclusion

When we consider Henry V's response to the Lollard threat as a whole, we find that the ruthless treatment of Oldcastle's suspected collaborators by

---

[135] For example, TNA, KB 9/994, mm. 41–3; KB 9/83, mm. 2, 51; KB 9/215/1, m. 27.

[136] For Carswell, who died in the Marshalsea on 3 April 1420, and Fitzharry, see: Powell, *Kingship*, pp. 260–1; TNA, KB 145/5/8. I am obliged to Dr Hannes Kleineke for the latter reference. For Wodecock, see TNA, KB 9/203, mm. 5, 27.

[137] The details of his arrest are revealed uniquely in the records of the county escheator, who had confiscated his messuage in Tamworth: TNA, E 357/25, m. 87; E 136/209/15. For Halweton, see Jurkowski, 'Career of Robert Herlaston', p. 119.

[138] *PROME*, X, 22.

[139] TNA, SC 8/24/1186 (printed in *Rotuli Parliamentorum, 1278–1503*, 6 vols. (London, 1783–1832), IV, 196). He had been in custody since at least November 1419 by order of the king's council. He escaped from the Tower in April 1422 with Sir John Mortimer and other prisoners but was swiftly recaptured. Together with Mortimer he was then charged with treason. Although both men were acquitted by jury of what appears to have been trumped-up charges, they were returned to prison. Mortimer was sent to the Tower and Payn to Newgate: E. Powell, 'The Strange Death of Sir John Mortimer: Politics and the Law of Treason in Lancastrian England', in *Rulers and Ruled in Late Medieval England: Essays Presented to Gerald Harriss*, ed. R. E. Archer and S. Walker (London, 1995), pp. 83–97; Thomson, *Later Lollards*, pp. 17–18; TNA, SC 8/198/9871; 198/9872. For the colourful story of Payn's initial capture in 1419, see *An Anthology of Chancery English*, ed. J. H. Fisher, M. Richardson and J. L. Fisher (Knoxville, 1984), no. 159.

the king and his council manifest at the end of his reign – after years of rumours and abortive uprisings – was far from Henry's attitude at the beginning. Indeed, one could even conclude that he had been slow to act, certainly against Oldcastle. Whether it was because he looked benignly upon the foibles of his friend and comrade in arms, or had once felt some sympathy with his advocacy of Church reform – or, more likely, both – can only be conjectured and is a subject for another occasion.[140] What is certain is that it was Archbishop Arundel who made all the early running, and when Henry was finally compelled to move against his erstwhile favourite, he seems to have taken his cue from the prelate. Arundel had obtained his evidence against Oldcastle by having him followed and Henry similarly made use of spies and informers to seek him out after his escape from the Tower. When it came to dealing with the events of the planned insurrection itself, Henry had some luck when a few of the plotters betrayed the plan, but his handling of the suppression of the revolt itself was highly efficient and provided a foretaste of the military tactical flair that would serve him well in France. His bold, expeditious ride with few troops from Westminster to Clerkenwell to intercept the insurgents before they had mustered, and the sealing off of the city from the revolt, preventing Londoners from joining in, were absolutely key to his successful rout of the rebels.

Nevertheless, however effective it may have been, his dispensing of justice to the rebels in the law courts too often showed scant regard for their rights under the common law. Firstly, the captured insurgents were indicted by paid jurors who had been assembled for this purpose well before the uprising had even taken place; they were not eyewitnesses to the event. In mitigation, the normal procedure for impanelling jurors usually occasioned much delay and many of those judged at the Tower on 13 January had been caught red-handed, so to speak. It could also be argued that in a national emergency a pre-assembled jury was a decisive and effective strategy dictated by the need to restore order quickly.[141] Similarly, the circulation to Lollard commissioners of pro forma treason indictments was either efficient or slightly disingenuous, depending upon one's point of view, but it was comparable to the

---

140 His interest in Church reform – some of it certainly inspired by the Lollard challenge to the Church – has been well documented, see: J. Catto, 'Religious Change under Henry V', in *Henry V*, ed. Harriss, pp. 97–115; *Documents Illustrating the Activities of the General and Provincial Chapters of the English Black Monks 1215–1540*, ed. W. A. Pantin, 3 vols., Camden Society 3rd Series 45, 47, 54, (1931–7), II, 97–134.

141 Early fifteenth century jurors, moreover, often had no first-hand knowledge of a case tried before them and were drawn commonly from outside the immediate locality where the crime was committed: E. Powell, 'Jury Trial at Gaol Delivery in the Late Middle Ages: The Midland Circuit, 1400–1429', in *Twelve Good Men and True, The Criminal Trial Jury in England, 1200–1800*, ed. J. S. Cockburn and T. A. Green (Princeton, 1988), pp. 78–116 (pp. 82–9).

contemporary practice of putting prepared indictments before juries which they merely rubberstamped with the words 'billa vera'.

Finally, his policy in sparing some convicted insurgents and executing others was certainly not even handed, and it is not clear on what basis some were spared – possibly, as I have suggested above, because they could be pumped for valuable information – but hanging the ringleaders and showing leniency to the rest was standard modus operandi in suppressing a rebellion. It was certainly how the great majority of the participants in the Peasants' Revolt of 1381 had been treated, although Mark Ormrod has argued that this perceived leniency was in fact forced upon Richard II's government by financial and political considerations.[142] Selling pardons – and large numbers of the king's subjects did, in fact, purchase the general pardon offered in December 1414, not just insurgents – as well as placing men and women under the constraints of enormous penal bonds, also had financial benefits for the king, even if it made a mockery of the criminal justice system. The issuing of general pardons was not a new idea in government; Henry V's predecessors had used the practice for financial ends periodically since the fourteenth century, but he broadened its terms and the policy was widely seen as an abuse of the royal prerogative.[143]

His innovations did not always weaken the existing common law. The statute against Lollardy enacted in his first parliament significantly strengthened the powers of the state to apprehend suspected heretics, by giving authority to arrest to local keepers of the peace and itinerant justices and treating heresy as a crime against both Church and State by instituting the penalty of forfeiture to the crown of lands and goods. The passage of this law had an instant impact, leading to the arrests of the aforementioned John Claydon and the London baker Richard Gurmyn alias Baker by the mayor of London in the following year – when both men were burnt for heresy – and many others subsequently.[144]

However, Henry's propensity to lock up suspected Lollards without charge, denying them access to justice, showed a flagrant disrespect for the principles of the common law. This removal of the right to justice had begun in the immediate aftermath of the revolt, with his detention of members of the gentry who had sponsored contingents of rebels, not allowing them to appear in court to answer charges until they had posted extortionate bonds. It continued with the practice of detaining suspects without charge during

---

142 W. M. Ormrod, 'The Peasants' Revolt and the Government of England', *Journal of British Studies* 29 (1990), 1–30 (pp. 22–3).

143 Powell, *Kingship*, pp. 83–5; and see TNA, C 67/37.

144 For Claydon and Gurmyn, see *Reg. Chichele*, IV, 132–8; A. Hudson, *Premature Reformation*, pp. 211–14; Aston, 'Lollardy and Sedition', pp. 32–3; TNA, E 368/188, rot. 404. For later arrests by royal officials, see Powell, *Kingship*, p. 162; Thomson, *Later Lollards*, pp. 24, 99, 143–4; Jurkowski, 'Lollard Networks', pp. 277–8.

the latter stage of Oldcastle's flight from justice and seems to have become a permanent feature of his rule. He was not the first English king, of course, to make such arrests. Four men had been detained in the Tower without charge for years during Edward III's reign; an investigation in 1351 into the reasons for their arrests could only proceed by interviewing the men themselves, since there were no records to consult.[145] Richard II famously arrested several Lollards in 1395 and sent them to languish in the castles of Beaumaris and Conwy in North Wales.[146] Similarly, in 1394 he had ordered the detention of the royal esquire John Croft of Croft, Herefordshire, imprisoning him in Windsor castle for nearly a year until he had sworn an oath against heresy.[147] His bishops were also guilty of keeping Lollard suspects in custody without being charged – of which complaint was made in at least two Wyclifite tracts.[148] Indeed, the bishop of Lincoln ordered six men who had been the subject of a heresy investigation in Northampton in 1393 to be imprisoned afterward in the town's castle, where they remained for some time, apparently without charge, as alleged in a petition for their release sent to the chancellor.[149] Henry IV released the men held in the Welsh castles immediately after his accession, probably regarding them as victims of Richard's tyranny, and seems to have halted the practice.[150]

The revival of the policy of arbitrary arrest under Henry V was an unfortunate legacy that he bequeathed to his young son's regime. In the parliament of 1425 the Commons were again compelled to present a petition complaining that many persons arrested for treason, felony and Lollardy had been sent by the king's command to the Tower and other castles, where they remained a long time without any legal process against them, and asking that they appear quickly before temporal or spiritual judges and be either released or punished.[151] A case in point is that of John Grace, an itinerant preacher who preached in a Coventry park for five days in November 1424, drawing large

---

[145] One of them, indeed, claimed that he knew only that his arrest had been ordered by the chancellor and not the reason why: *Select Cases in the Court of King's Bench*, ed. G. O. Sayles, 7 vols., Selden Society 55, 57, 58, 74, 76, 82, 88 (London, 1936–71), VI, no. 47. I am again indebted to Simon Payling for knowledge of this case.

[146] The detainees included four fellows of Merton College, Oxford, John Claydon of London and at least nine men from Shrewsbury: Jurkowski, 'Heresy and Factionalism', pp. 661–5; Aston, 'Lollardy and Sedition', pp. 22–3; Jurkowski, 'Arrest of William Thorpe', p. 289.

[147] Jurkowski, 'Who Was Walter Brut?' pp. 296–7.

[148] *Four English Political Tracts of the Later Middle Ages*, ed. J-P. Genet, Camden Society 4th Series 18 (1977), pp. 17–18; *Remonstrance against Romish Corruptions*, ed. J. Forshall (London, 1851), pp. 156–7, the latter quoted in Hudson, *Premature Reformation*, p. 217.

[149] TNA, C 1/68/46; A. K. McHardy, 'Bishop Buckingham and the Lollards of Lincoln Diocese', in *Schism, Heresy and Religious Protest*, ed. D. Baker, Studies in Church History 9 (Cambridge, 1972), 131–45 (pp. 138–45).

[150] *CPR, 1399–1401*, p. 75.

[151] TNA, SC 8/24/1197 (printed in *PROME*, X, 270 from the enrolled petition).

crowds at a time when there was much unrest in that city. The king's council sent a royal serjeant-at-arms to arrest and convey him to the Tower, where he was still in custody in 1430; he was probably one of the prisoners to whom the Commons' petition referred.[152] In delivering a final verdict on the accuracy of Henry V's reputation as a king of justice, we must acknowledge that the protection of personal liberty under medieval common law was not what it ought to have been. No legal remedy for imprisonment without charge by the crown was yet available, as the king was regarded as having a royal prerogative to detain whomever he wished. It was not until the gross abuses of this privilege by Henry VII's council that a new writ of *habeas corpus ad subjiciendum* was developed to challenge the legitimacy of arbitrary imprisonment by the crown. The invoking of the guarantee of personal freedom enshrined in *Magna Carta* was still further in the future.[153] It would not be too anachronistic to suggest, nevertheless, that if Henry V displayed scant regard for the existing common law, bending it to his personal will, he had even less respect for his subjects; it is not what we would expect from an 'exemplar of justice'.

---

152 Jurkowski, 'Lollardy in Coventry', p. 157; TNA, E 101/51/11, 12; E 101/531/32.
153 J. H. Baker, 'Personal Liberty under the Common Law, 1200–1600', in his *The Common Law Tradition* (London, 2000), pp. 317–47 (pp. 335–47); P. D. Halliday, *Habeas Corpus, From England to Empire* (Cambridge MA, 2010), pp. 11–38.

5

Religion, Court Culture and Propaganda: The Chapel Royal in the Reign of Henry V[1]

Alison K. McHardy

Henry V's religious outlook is well known: he was fiercely orthodox and the founder of two religious houses. The clergy who ministered to the king's spiritual needs have, however, received less direct attention. This chapter investigates the clerics closest to him, especially the members of his chapel royal, and asks how they were linked to Henry's overseas ambitions, and how the king's liturgical observance and spiritual support shaded into propaganda, because the private Christian was inseparable from the public ruler. It is hoped that, by bringing together information from diverse sources, it may be possible to observe a clearer picture of Henry's ecclesiastical milieu, and to suggest lines of further investigation. The chapter is divided into three parts: first, a prosopographical study of the named chaplains (especially those on the 1415 expedition) is undertaken, discussing such matters as recruitment, education, rewards and subsequent careers; the second part provides a more detailed description of those royal chaplains who were important composers; finally, the chapter asks whether any named member of Henry V's ecclesiastical milieu can plausibly be identified as the author of the anonymous *Gesta Henrici Quinti*.

The Chapel Royal and the King's Army Chaplains

A good starting point is Thursday, 6 June 1415, when those who had contracted to serve in the forthcoming expedition to France came to the exchequer to receive their advance wages; they numbered 256,[2] and a dedicated issue roll

---

[1]   Thanks are due to the other members of the symposium for their kindness, tact, help, suggestions and encouragement to a novice in this reign, and to Anne Hudson and Andrew Jotischky for their help and interest.
[2]   Cf. Curry, *Agincourt: Sources and Interpretations*, p. 411, who arrives at the figure of 210. I counted a number of times and arrived at the figure of 256 on each occasion.

was later created to record that day's business.[3] The final membrane contains thirty names of members of the chapel royal.[4] These were not the only clerics contracted to serve abroad, for, as well as the members of the chapel royal listed all together, there were a dozen more ecclesiastics recorded on earlier membranes, including even some who were described as clerks of the king's chapel.[5] They were not the only clergy closely associated with Henry V in 1415. Shortly before embarkation the king made his will and named eight ecclesiastical beneficiaries: his confessor (Stephen Patrington); secretary (John Stone); almoner (Stephen Payne); doctor (Nicholas Colnet); and four others, John Wickham, Henry Romworth, Thomas Rodburne and Richard Cassy, identified only as 'our chaplains'.[6] Of these only Colnet and Payne were named on the issue roll as drawing wages for the expedition to France, though some or all of the others may actually have joined the army.[7] We can add to these names a few more chaplains identified from other sources, including the medieval soldier database.[8]

The group identified together as the clerks of the chapel were headed by the dean, Master Edmund Lacy. Well educated and already well rewarded, Lacy would become a bishop before our story ends. On his consecration as bishop of Hereford in April 1417 he retired to his diocese, and was translated to Exeter two years later.[9] Next to him in rank and distinction was Master Stephen Morpath, a much more shadowy figure. He has not been linked to either university, though in 1409 he was granted licence to study for three years at an English *studium generale*. By then he had already been the rector of East Knoyle (Wilts.) for two years, and had begun to collect prebends in collegiate churches.[10] These two were not by any means the only graduates in

---

3   TNA, E 101/45/5. It was drawn up by John Burgh clerk of Roger Leche on 24 November 1416. Leche was appointed treasurer on 17 April 1416 but dismissed on 23 November the same year; *Handbook of British Chronology*, ed. E. B. Fryde, D. E. Greenway, S. Porter and I. Roy, 3rd edn (London, 1986), p. 106.

4   Henry V's chapel royal normally consisted of thirty-two priests and clerks, and sixteen boys: R. D. Bowers, 'Choirs and Choral Establishments', in *Medieval England: An Encyclopedia*, ed. P. E. Szarmach, M. T. Tavormina and J. T. Rosenthal (New York, 1998), p. 180.

5   John Burwell (Burell) and John Mildenhale, both clerks of the king's chapel, appear on TNA, E 101 45/5, m. 9d. On m. 6d we find Richard Beston and Robert Allerton subclerks of the kitchen. For Allerton see also, *BRUO*, I, 25–6.

6   *Feodera*, IX, 289–93.

7   Curry, *Agincourt: A New History*, p. 67.

8   Walter Burton, Thomas Morton, Robert Alderton: AHRC-funded database www.medievalsoldier.org, accessed 12 April 2012.

9   Emden, *BRUO*, II, 1081–3.

10 *The Register of Robert Hallum Bishop of Salisbury 1407–17*, ed. J. M. Horn, Canterbury and York Society 72 (1982), no. 761; *CPR, 1405–8*, p. 247. On 24 May 1414, when he was described as a king's clerk, he was presented to the deanery of the king's free chapel within Wallingford castle: *CPR, 1413–16*, p. 199.

the group, as we shall see. Two more individuals deserve comment here. Alan Hert and John Brotherton were both described as 'brother', but their order, or orders, cannot be identified,[11] though Hert may have been the Dominican Brother Alan de Hert of York who was ordained subdeacon by Archbishop Waldby's suffragan in York on 22 September 1397.[12] In the spring of 1415 both were presented to benefices by the crown, Brotherton to All Hallows Bread Street, London, on 3 May, and Hert to Hamerton church (Hunts.) on 8 May.[13]

In 1415, two bishops, Richard Courtenay of Norwich, and Benedict Nicolls of Bangor, are known from other sources to have accompanied the army.[14] These two men illustrate the difficulty of defining 'the chapel royal' or 'the king's chapel' with precision. Courtenay was aristocratic, well educated and clearly well liked by his king.[15] Although at Henry's side in the Welsh expedition of 1407 and in the early stages of this first French campaign, Courtenay's diverse career had seen him act as an ambassador, a councillor and now he was treasurer of the household and keeper of the king's jewels. Benedict Nicolls, though apparently much more of a churchman than Courtenay, can still not be pigeon-holed precisely.[16] The see of Bangor was in some turmoil at the time of his promotion; Benedict Nicolls was consecrated in London on 6 August 1408 but not enthroned in his cathedral until 12 October 1409. He was last recorded in his diocese in December 1412, and thereafter he was evidently resident in London, where he was active in the prosecution of Lollards. His episcopal register shows him conducting diocesan business in his London house from 8 June 1413 onwards, but he also conducted the business of Bangor diocese in the palace of Westminster on 18 November 1414.[17] The spring and summer of 1415 saw Nicolls again conducting routine diocesan business in his London house.[18] After his starring role in causing the submission of Harfleur, the bishop of Bangor did not, it seems, remain with the army thereafter, for his register shows him back in London and conducting business in his house there on 6 and 8 October 1415.[19]

---

[11] Neither appears on the London clergy database, which is drawn from ordination lists in London registers: see V. Davis, *Clergy in London in the Late Middle Ages: A Register of Clergy Ordained in the Diocese of London Based on Episcopal Ordination Lists 1361–1539* (London, 2000), introduction and CD ROM.

[12] *A Calendar of the Register of Robert Waldby Archbishop of York, 1397*, ed. D. M. Smith, Borthwick Texts and Calendars: Records of the Northern Province 2 (York, 1974), p. 44.

[13] *CPR, 1413–16*, pp. 182, 184.

[14] *GHQ*, p. 44 (Courtenay), p. 50 (Nicolls). Courtenay had obtained a letter of protection on 29 June 1415: AHRC-funded database www.medievalsoldier.org, accessed 12 April 2012.

[15] Emden, *BRUO*, I, 500–2; R. G. Davies, 'Courtenay, Richard (*c*.1381–1415)', *ODNB*.

[16] G. Williams, 'Nicolls, Benedict (*d.* 1433)', *ODNB* (very brief); and A. I. Pryce, 'The Register of Benedict, Bishop of Bangor, 1408–17', *Archaeologia Cambrensis* 77 (1922), 85–107.

[17] Ibid., p. 99. He admitted Richard Praty, clerk, to Llanddwyn church, Anglesey, at the king's presentation.

[18] As noted for 1 January 13 February, 12 March, 20, 23 May, 1, 3, 7 June: ibid., pp. 99–101.

[19] Ibid., p. 102.

Yet it is clear that the bishop of Bangor was in some sense a member of the chapel royal, for on 4 April 1416 he conducted an ordination ceremony within the palace of Westminster. This was a most unusual occasion for there were only four candidates. The single deacon was Alan Kirketon, and one of the three priests was William Bontemps. Both were members of the king's chapel, and graduates too.[20] A still more unusual ordination took place later that same month. On Easter eve (18 April 1416) Nicolls celebrated orders *in capella domini nostri Regis infra manerium de Lamheth, Wyntoniensis diocesis*, thus indicating that the chapel royal was not so much a place as a travelling organization, which on this occasion came to rest in the archiepiscopal manor of Lambeth, on the Surrey shore. Once again there were four ordinands. The two priests were the king's secretary John Stone, and the king's chaplain Alan Kirketon.[21] A further sign of Nicolls's links to the king was that he consecrated the foundation stone of Sheen Charterhouse.[22]

The Agincourt campaign provides us with the largest number of the names of Henry's travelling chaplains, but they were not the only chaplains who accompanied Henry V's armies to France on various occasions. In 1419 six singers were engaged to serve with the king in France,[23] and the following year a further six named men were recruited to join the chapel royal in the same theatre of war.[24] Nor was the king the only person to take chaplains on campaign with him. In 1415, his brother Thomas, duke of Clarence, took his chaplain William Allington (Alyngton) who fell ill at the siege of Harfleur, but recovered and later became treasurer-general of Normandy.[25] Another on the same sick-list was Lord Willoughby's chaplain John Wilkynson.[26] William Balne, clerk, was in the service of Humphrey duke of Gloucester in 1415.[27]

[20] Ibid., p. 103; TNA, E 101/45/5 m. 11; Emden, *BRUC*, pp. 25–6 (Bontemps); Emden, *BRUO*, II, 1055–6 (Kirketon).

[21] Pryce, 'Register of Benedict, Bishop of Bangor', p. 104.

[22] N. Beckett, 'Sheen Charterhouse from its Foundation to its Dissolution' (unpublished D.Phil. thesis, Oxford, 1992), p. 18.

[23] A. Wathey, *Music in the Royal and Noble Households in Late Medieval England* (New York, 1989), p. 137.

[24] They were: Robert Chirbury, John Berewey, Robert Chamberleyn, John Testwode, John Fitzwilliam and John Broune. See A. Buckle, 'An English Composer in Royal and Aristocratic Service: Robert Chirbury, c. 1380–1254', *Plainsong and Medieval Music* 15 (2006), 109–22 (esp. p. 114). Thanks are due to Dr Charles Fonge for sending me a copy of this most useful paper.

[25] TNA, E 101/44/30 m. 1. I am grateful to Anne Curry for drawing my attention to this document. Allington's account books in this post, 1419–21 and 1422 are in TNA, E 101/187/14, and TNA, E 101/188/7.

[26] TNA, E 101/44/30 m. 12.

[27] AHRC-funded database www.medievalsoldier.org, accessed 12 April 2012.

The names of other chaplains to aristocratic and baronial soldiers who served abroad may well come to light.[28]

So far we have identified a number of men who served the spiritual needs of Henry V, mainly as members of his chapel royal. Skirting between the Scylla of variant spellings, and the Charybdis of men who bore identical surnames, the sources enable us to identify around fifty named men who were clerics, and who accompanied Henry V on his foreign campaigns, particularly in 1415, and who provided liturgical drama and spiritual succour to the royal household.[29] Compared to the multitudes discussed in other chapters of this volume, this group is tiny, yet it contained men who were deeply valued by the king,[30] men who were versatile and talented, and some who have left lasting memorials which we can still appreciate today.

Perhaps not all were priests, and not all were primarily on this expedition for the spiritual benefits which they could provide. We should not, however, exclude from our discussion men who had other identifiable roles, for example, as administrators in the royal household,[31] or diplomats like Master Richard Hals.[32] Versatility was a feature of the lives and careers of these men, and not all individuals are easy to categorize. There is also abundant evidence that sheer weight of numbers greatly impressed contemporaries when considering the quality of religious observance.[33] In particular, lengthy processions were something of an English speciality, precisely regulated and with elaborate conventions.[34] This meant that, in addition to the

---

28 Systematic searching among licences for non-residence in bishops' registers would probably produce more names.

29 Excluded from this number are surgeons William Bradwardyn (TNA, E 101/45/5, m. 11; E 101/69/8) and Thomas Morstede (TNA, E 101/69/4/409) who were laymen, and the physician and cleric Mr Nicholas Colnet (TNA, E 101/45/5, m. 7d. E 101/69/8/527); also the minstrels John Cliff, who seems to have died on active service (TNA, E 101/47/23; E 358/6), and Guy Middleton (TNA, E 101/45/5, m. 11). For the doctors' careers see C. H. Talbot and E. A. Hammond, *The Medical Practitioners in Medieval England: A Biographical Register* (London, 1965), pp. 220–2 (Colnet), 350–2 (Morstede) and 387–8, (Bradwardyn). The named surgeons and minstrels were 'team leaders' of groups of men. Morstede took twelve other surgeons with him in 1415, and an unspecified number in 1416, while Cliff was accompanied by seventeen other royal minstrels in 1415: TNA, E 101/45/5, m. 11.

30 Henry's will contained, as well as legacies to named chaplains, the sum of £200 in gold to be divided equally among the clerks of his chapel: *Foedera*, IX, 292.

31 Like Robert Allerton and Richard Beston, subclerks of the kitchen: TNA, E 101/45/5 m. 6d. For Allerton see Emden, *BRUO*, I, 25–6.

32 TNA, E 101/45/5 m. 9d, and E 101/47/34; Emden, *BRUO*, II, 857.

33 C. Burgess, '"For the Increase of Divine Service": Chantries in the Parish in Late Medieval Bristol', *Journal of Ecclesiastical History* 36 (1985), 46–65.

34 'Although processions formed a part of religious ceremonial throughout Christendom, they seem to have been particularly elaborate and impressive in England', N. Sandon, 'Liturgy and Church Music', in *Medieval England: An Encyclopedia*, ed. Szarmach, Tavormina and Rosenthal, p. 453.

main performers of religious rituals, a large 'supporting cast' in the liturgical drama was considered highly desirable. Furthermore, processions were not confined to church buildings but often took place outside as well, thus making them evident to a wider group of people than would have attended the services.[35] This point is exemplified by the scene before Harfleur, on 18 September 1415, when the bishop of Bangor and the members of the chapel royal, fully robed, were employed as a psychological battering ram before the town walls.[36] Conversely, those who were not present primarily to provide liturgical skills, but who nevertheless were priests, were pressed into service to hear confessions on the eve of Agincourt, though even then they were not sufficiently numerous.[37]

Much could be said about the personnel of the chapel royal. The recruitment of its members is the most shadowy aspect of their lives. Some had served other masters. Thus John Kyngman, a clerk of the royal household chapel from 1402 to 1427, and a member of the Agincourt contingent, had served in the chapel of William Montagu, earl of Salisbury, until the earl's death in 1397.[38] Sometimes family connections explain an individual's presence. John Prentys was apparently a member of a distinguished family, and there is little doubt how he gained entry to crown service, since a Richard Prentys was dean of the chapel royal from 1 October 1402 to 3 October 1412.[39] Another Prentys, Edward, had a successful career spanning nearly fifty years.[40] Edward, like John, and another Prentys, William, were graduates whose careers coincided in the early decades of the fifteenth century.[41] University educations opened the doors for others to employment in the chapel royal which had links with both King's Hall Cambridge and Merton College Oxford.[42] On several occasions the chapel royal recruited personnel, both adults and children, from Lincoln cathedral.[43]

Something must also be said about chaplains' rewards. Collegiate prebends, especially those in royal free chapels, formed the standard currency, but

---

[35] A. K. McHardy, 'Some Reflections on Edward III's Use of Propaganda', in *The Age of Edward III*, ed. J. S. Bothwell (Woodbridge, 2001), pp. 171–89 (esp. pp. 177–8).

[36] *'venerabilis pater dominus Benedictus, episcopus Bangorensis, a tentoriis regiis, precedente tota capella regia processionaliter in capis, iussu regio, usque sub muris'*, GHQ, p. 50. Although reminiscent of the siege of Jericho, Joshua 6, there is no biblical quotation or reference.

[37] *'non erat tunc parcitas, nisi solum parcitas sacerdotum'*, ibid., p. 78.

[38] Wathey, *Royal and Noble Households*, p. 137; TNA, E 101/45/5 m. 11.

[39] Wathey, *Royal and Noble Households*, p. 284.

[40] *The Cartulary of St. Mary's Collegiate Church, Warwick*, ed. C. Fonge (Woodbridge, 2004), p. 439. Edward Prentys is not included in Dr Emden's volumes.

[41] Emden, *BRUO*, III, 1517.

[42] Wathey, *Royal and Noble Households*, pp. 171–2; A. B. Cobban, *The King's Hall within the University of Cambridge in the Later Middle Ages* (Cambridge, 1969), esp. pp. 19–22.

[43] Wathey, *Royal and Noble Households*, p. 141.

some men did much better, especially if they were well educated.[44] It seems that in the chapel royal, as elsewhere in crown service, such as the privy seal office, the early fifteenth century saw an increasing distinction in their rewards between graduates and others.[45] Two examples must suffice. John Arundel was an Oxford graduate and was already on the path to advancement before the 1415 campaign commenced.[46] The following year he became dean of St George's College, Windsor, a high-profile post he held, apparently with distinction, until his death in 1454. This was followed by benefices which included prebends at Wells and Hereford cathedrals.[47] His friend, the well-connected John Prentys, another Oxford graduate, already had a well-established ecclesiastical career by 1415, and he became dean of St Stephen's royal free chapel, Westminster, in 1418.[48] Since there is some evidence that membership of the chapel royal was augmented for special occasions, for example for military campaigns overseas or for such ceremonial events as Queen Catherine's coronation in 1421, it would be interesting to know where they were recruited from, and whether they later returned to their former place or places of employment.

How dangerous was campaigning for the army chaplains? Dysentery, the curse of besieging armies, cut a swathe through this group, as through every other. At one end of the social scale Richard Courtenay, bishop of Norwich, the king's friend and kinsman, died before Harfleur in mid-September 1415, in Henry's presence;[49] at the other end, John Mildenhale, a clerk of the king's chapel, is not heard of after 1415 (or before) and may have been another victim of the infection,[50] while John Burell, said to have fallen ill at the siege of Harfleur, later recovered.[51] It is remarkable how many of the 1415 chaplains survived and later flourished, though Alan Kirketon is the only one known to have made a career in France, where he found that ecclesiastical advance-

---

[44] Wathey thinks it likely that many of the king's chaplains were resident at court for only six months of the year, and undertook other tasks, whether as diplomats or administrators, for the rest of the time; ibid., p. 62.

[45] A. L. Brown, 'The Privy Seal Clerks in the Early Fifteenth Century', in *The Study of Medieval Records: Essays in Honour of Kathleen Major*, ed. D. A. Bullough and R. L. Storey (Oxford, 1971), pp. 260–81 (esp. p. 275).

[46] TNA, E 101/45/5 m. 11. On 20 June 1415 the new bishop of Coventry and Lichfield was ordered to give Arundel a pension until he presented him to a benefice: *CCR, 1413–19*, p. 279.

[47] Emden, *BRUO*, I, 49.

[48] Emden, *BRUO*, III, 1516; *CPR, 1416–22*, p. 132. For links between Arundel and Prentys see *CPR, 1399–1401*, p. 507, and TNA, C 1/6/197. Hoccleve disapproved of them both, calling them idlers, 'La Male Regle de T. Hoccleue', verse 40 (lines 321–8), *Hoccleve's Works I: The Minor Poems*, ed. Frederick J. Furnivall, EETS ES 61 (1892), p. 35.

[49] R. G. Davies, 'Courtenay, Richard (*c*.1381–1415)', *ODNB*.

[50] TNA, E 101/45/5, m. 9d.

[51] M. Bent, 'John Burrell', in *NGDM*, IV, 612.

ment in the new-won lands was remarkably problematic, involving him in litigation over five benefices.[52]

Music in the Chapel Royal

The members of Henry's chapel-on-campaign were not there to provide only the minimum of liturgical and spiritual support. The services in the king's chapel were intended to impress, and we know that they did so; on 28 August 1415 Raoul le Gay, a captured priest of Harfleur who was then in the custody of Bishop Courtenay, was taken by him to a service in the king's chapel and was 'astonished to hear such beautiful music'.[53] Anyone with pretensions to be the very model of a modern monarch in the early fifteenth century would have wanted their private services to be sung in a style more elaborate than plainchant. Henry V was certainly in the vanguard of musical patronage, and may even have been a composer himself; he would surely have expected polyphonic music to be sung in the chapel royal. At this period 'polyphony' usually meant three voices: tenor, middle and third part.[54] The meaning of 'third part' was vague, perhaps intentionally so, and could mean the use of another voice in the same register, for example, a second tenor or another alto. However, the compass of the music which was performed could be increased by the employment of a baritone, and widened by an octave through the use of boys, that is, choristers. Whether choristers accompanied the army in 1415 is unclear, and perhaps unlikely, but later campaigns evidently saw boys serving in the chapel royal abroad. For example, in January 1420 John Pyamour was commissioned to go to Lincoln and recruit two boys to serve with the chapel in Normandy.[55] This was probably intended to demonstrate that Henry's chapel royal in Normandy was to be of the same quality as his chapel in his other realm: England.

---

[52] TNA, E 101/45/5, m. 5; C. Allmand, 'Alan Kirketon: A Clerical Royal Councillor in Normandy during the English Occupation in the Fifteenth Century', *Journal of Ecclesiastical History* 15 (1964), 33–9; C. Allmand, 'Some Effects of the Last Phase of the Hundred Years War upon the Maintenance of Clergy', in *Studies in Church History III*, ed. G. J. Cuming (London, 1964), pp. 179–90; *English Suits before the Parlement of Paris 1420–1436*, ed. C. T. Allmand and C. A. J. Armstrong, Camden Fourth Series 26 (1982), pp. 282, 288; Emden, *BRUO*, II, 1055–6.

[53] Mortimer, *1415: Henry V's Year of Glory*, p. 347.

[54] I tried to provide a non-musicians' guide to the rise of polyphony in 'Careers and Disappointments in the Late-Medieval Church', in *The Ministry: Clerical and Lay*, ed. W. J. Sheils and D. Wood, Studies in Church History 26 (Oxford, 1989), pp. 171–8 (at pp. 120–2).

[55] Wathey, *Royal and Noble Households*, p. 141. John Pyamour (fl. *c.*1418, d. before March 1426) was a member of the chapel royal 1416–20 and was the first Master of the Chapel Children. A namesake served Bedford in France in 1427; B. Trewell, 'Pyamour, John', in *NGDM*, XX, 637.

We can observe the high quality of the king's music, even while on the march, by considering some of the men he took with him. Four of his army chaplains in 1415, John Burell, John Cook, Thomas Damet and Nicholas Sturgeon,[56] were composers whose distinction has subsequently led them, in our own day, to warranting individual entries in the *New Grove Dictionary of Music and Musicians*.[57] The evidence which lies at the heart of their claim to fame is contained in the Old Hall Manuscript.[58] This manuscript was compiled between about 1415 and 1421, almost certainly for the chapel of Henry's brother Thomas, duke of Clarence, and came into the king's possession after Clarence's death in March 1421. The arrangement of the pieces was governed by the order of the Mass: all the compositions relating to each section were grouped together. The manuscript is incomplete since all the Kyrie pieces are lost, leaving the Gloria, Credo, Sanctus, Benedictus and Agnus Dei sections. The Old Hall Manuscript was written in two stages, or 'layers' as musicologists call it. The first layer was written by a single scribe, almost certainly working within Clarence's household, while on the pages he left blank among these compositions, and on some pages inserted later, other scribes – perhaps seven in number – made additions during the early 1420s. These entries are known as the second layer.

The exciting thing about the Old Hall Manuscript, from a historian's standpoint, is that the composers of its works are named, thus giving us a kind of 'Who's Who' of English court composers (or those working very close to the court) from the 1370s to the mid-1420s. Especially interesting is the name *Roy Henry* beside two compositions in the first layer, and after considerable debate musicologists now believe that this is indeed Henry V. It looks as though, when the book came into the possession of the chapel royal in 1421, some of its members added their own compositions, perhaps in their own hands. Of the six composers in the second layer, as I have said, four (Burell, Cook, Damet and Sturgeon)[59] were members of Henry V's army in 1415.

Burell, whose Gloria and Credo, both in three parts, appear in the Old Hall second layer, was perhaps a Yorkshireman; he was precentor of York Minster for ten days in April 1410, but exchanged this for the church of Gilling East,

---

[56] TNA, E 101/45/4, m. 9d (Burell), m. 11 (Cook, Damet, Sturgeon).
[57] *NGDM*. The entries on Burell (IV, 612), Damet (t) (VI, 872–3) and Sturgeon (XXIV, 630) were written by Margaret Bent alone; she collaborated with Roger Bowers on Cook (VI, 387–8). The following paragraphs are derived from these entries, unless otherwise indicated.
[58] The manuscript owes its name to the college of St Edmund, Old Hall, near Ware (Herts.), its home for many years. It is now in the British Library. It was edited by Andrew Hughes and Margaret Bent, *Corpus Mensurabilis Musicae* 46 (1969–73). Professor Bent's article in the *NGDM*, XVIII, 376–9 is a summary of current scholarship on this manuscript. These paragraphs are an attempt to summarize her article for other non-specialists like myself.
[59] Of the other two, one was John Dunstable, ibid., 376.

in the North Riding.[60] Later, from 1416, he held a corrody at Meaux Abbey (North Yorks.). He was a royal chaplain from 1413, his campaign service was cut short by sickness contracted at Harfleur, but he recovered, and remained a royal chaplain until 1421.[61]

If John Burell might be confused with a namesake who lived into the 1430s, John Cook had an an even more common name. But a John Cooke contributed nine compositions to the Old Hall Manuscript, and these are in both layers of the manuscript. Intriguingly, 'serious attempts' were made to erase two of his pieces from the manuscript, and this, coupled with a curious blip in his ecclesiastical career at this time, suggests that he suffered 'a catastrophic fall from favour' in about 1419. Did Cook perhaps defect to Clarence's chapel in about 1419, returning to the chapel royal after Clarence's death? Cook is one of only two composers represented in both layers of the Old Hall Manuscript, the other being Lionel Power who is known to have been in Clarence's employ. According to Professor Bent, Cook's work is heavily influenced by Power's (perhaps he was a pupil) which would support the theory that John Cook the musician served two masters. It is possible that he resumed his ecclesiastical career in 1426, and he lived on until 1442.

Thomas Danet is also known by nine works, though all of them occur in the second layer.[62] We can trace his life almost from the cradle to the grave. Born in 1389 or 1390 he was the illegitimate son of a gentleman and attended Winchester College *c*.1403–7, but spent most of his life – that is, from 1413 to 1431 – as a royal chaplain. He probably retired into purely clerical life after that, and died late in 1436 or early the following year.

Another old Wykehamist was Nicholas Sturgeon, the most celebrated of our quartet, for whom seven compositions in the Old Hall Manuscript survive. As Margaret Bent remarks, his slightly unusual name allows us to be confident that we are dealing with a single person whose 'exceptionally well-documented career' took him, a Devonian of noble birth, from Winchester College in 1399, via New College, Oxford, to a life in the chapel royal where he served continuously from 1413 to 1452. Outside this institution he was exceptionally well rewarded for a royal chaplain, and in later life, during the decade 1441–51, he was especially concerned with the administration of St George's chapel, Windsor.

Sturgeon and Danet had other things in common besides having been at

[60] J. Le Neve, *Fasti Ecclesiae Anglicanae 1300–1541*, 12 vols. (London, 1962–7), VI (Northern Province), 11.

[61] He was dead by February 1423, so is to be distinguished from the John Burrell who held prebends at Chichester (Mardon ?–1424) and Hereford (Norton ?–1436): Le Neve, *Fasti Ecclesiae*, VII (Chichester), 35; II (Hereford), 39.

[62] He is confused with Thomas Danet, died 1483, by Emden, *BRUO*, I, 540–1.

the same school – if not necessarily at the same time.[63] The position and character of their works in the manuscript suggests a 'compositional relationship which can only be deliberate'.[64] More important for us, there are good grounds for thinking that some work of each was composed for or even sung in the London thanksgivings for the victory at Agincourt. In particular, Danet's setting of the text *Benedictus qui venit in nomine Domini*, words which were sung on this occasion,[65] has been linked to this celebration. Interestingly, Danet's will includes the bequest to his mother of 'a silver cup chased and engraved with writing, including the words "*Benedictus qui venit in nomine Domini*"'.[66] It would be pleasing to think that this was a souvenir of that great occasion. Cook, too, may have had his work performed then, and also on previous, and less triumphant, political occasions.[67]

Whether or not these men and their colleagues composed new works for this occasion, there is no doubt that the chapel royal contained not only skilled singers, but composers of the highest class, and that these men accompanied the king even in hazardous enterprises. The chapel royal was not only an aid to the king's spiritual life and piety but was a mobile advertisement of his righteousness, magnificence and his exquisite and adventurous taste. Henry V was not unique in this; his brother Thomas, as we have said, was a notable musical patron, while in the later 1420s another brother, John, duke of Bedford, who was then in France, had in his employ John Dunstable, a composer of European stature. Aristocratic evidence for these years is sparser; apart from John Kyngman's former service to the earl of Salisbury, we know that the college at Arundel castle had a link with Sturgeon, suggesting that the earls of Arundel were in touch with the latest singing styles.[68] Later in the century, as the number of collegiate churches increased and musical style became increasingly elaborate, competition between patrons became increasingly intense, but the king's observance was surely expected to outshine all others, hence the chapel royal's role in impressing members of the domestic nobility as well as distinguished foreign visitors. We get some hints that English music at this time was especially fine; the English nation was considered notable in this regard at the Council of Constance. Much later in his

---

[63] The wills of both survive: Sturgeon's is printed in *The Fifty Earliest English Wills*, ed. F. J. Furnivall, EETS OS 78 (London, 1882), pp. 131–4, and Danet's (in translation) in John Harvey, *Gothic England*, 2nd edn (London, 1948), pp. 181–3. Neither mentions any music.

[64] Bent, 'Sturgeon', in *NGDM*, XXIV, 630.

[65] *GHQ*, pp. 104, 191.

[66] Harvey, *Gothic England*, p. 182.

[67] Bent, 'Cooke, John', in *NGDM*, VI, 288, suggesting that a motet by Cook, *Alma proles regia/Christi miles/Ab inimicis nostris*, would have been especially appropriate for the failed Rogationtide peace negotiations before the Agincourt campaign.

[68] M. Williamson, 'The Will of John Moraston: Musicians within Collegiate and Parochial Communities', in *The Late Medieval English College and its Context*, ed. C. Burgess and M. Heale (York, 2008), pp. 180–98 (pp. 186–7).

career Sturgeon was commissioned by Henry VI's council to select six English singers for the chapel of the Emperor Frederick III, which suggests that England enjoyed an international reputation for musical skill.[69] Music was, of course, only one way in which magnificence was manifested. The accoutrements of the great chapels were also splendid. This physical evidence has almost all been lost, but there remains the superlative Holy Thorn Reliquary,[70] the Erpingham Chasuble[71] and rare survivals of service books to give us a tantalizing glimpse of the liturgy's physical equipment.

Stephen Patrington and the *Gesta Henrici Quinti*

The clergy of the chapel royal were close, in every sense, to Henry V, but even more intimately connected to him were his confessors: Stephen Patrington and his successor Thomas Netter.[72] Both were Carmelite friars – this was a house of Lancaster tradition – and both were highly educated Oxford theologians, pursuers of Lollards and accomplished authors.[73]

It is among this clerical milieu that the author of the *Gesta Henrici Quinti* must surely be sought. Several suggestions have been advanced for the authorship of this anonymous work.[74] One is Jean de Bordin, a Gascon, who was with the English army at Harfleur in 1415. Another is Thomas Elmham, a monk of St Augustine's Canterbury, who became prior of Lenton (1414–27), a Cluniac alien priory outside Nottingham. He was the author of the *Liber Metricus de Henrico Quinto*, which was once thought to have been based upon the *Gesta*. Thomas Rodburne, one of Henry's legatees, was also once considered the author, as was Edmund Lacy, dean of the chapel royal. The author has sometimes been described as 'a royal chaplain',[75] but the description *incerto authore sed capellano in exercitu Regis*, its editors tell us, was added to one of the two surviving manuscripts only during the eighteenth century.[76] Even had it been contemporary, the description 'chaplain' need not necessarily be taken too literally, for its meaning was ecclesiastically imprecise, like 'clerk', for which it was sometimes a synonym. It might also be used as a

---

[69] On 16 October 1442: Emden, *BRUO*, III, 1810.

[70] J. Cherry, *The Holy Thorn Reliquary* (London, 2010).

[71] G. Wraight, 'The Erpingham Chasuble', in *Agincourt 1415: Henry V, Sir Thomas Erpingham and the Triumph of the English Archers*, ed. A. Curry (Stroud, 2000), pp. 104–10.

[72] Allmand, *Henry V*, p. 350 and nn.

[73] The careers of both can be found in Emden, *BRUO*, II, 1343–4 and III, 1435–6; and in *ODNB* (J. Catto, 'Patrington, Stephen'; and A. Hudson, 'Netter, Thomas (*c*.1370–1430)'.

[74] For what follows see the introduction to *GHQ*, pp. xviii–xxiii.

[75] Taylor and Roskell, *GHQ*, p. xviii.

[76] Ibid., p. xv.

self-description by ecclesiastics of very high rank.[77] The author was, however, evidently an ecclesiastic who was well informed about the workings of the king's chapel,[78] and who was in the king's company on a number of occasions, as he noted. He was not necessarily a member of the chapel royal himself, for Henry was also served by such erudite men as the diplomat Richard Hals, and John Stone his secretary. Hals was with the army which sailed to Harfleur in 1415, as, probably, was Stone.[79] This uncertainty applies to others, for, as Professor Curry points out, 'We do not have full information on how many men crossed with the expedition, in addition to those in receipt of military wages.'[80]

This gives us an embarrassment of choice, as Henry V was surrounded by an exceptionally cultured group of servants, both administrators and spiritual or liturgical specialists.[81] The members of the chapel royal and their associates in Henry's armies were a well-educated group: of those who went on the Agincourt campaign about 50 per cent were either certainly or probably graduates. Two features of the text may perhaps give a more precise pointer. The first is the author's choice of biblical quotations. The editors identified forty-five of these, of which thirty-two are from the Old Testament, eight from the New Testament and five from the Apocrypha; four of those are from Maccabees. The preponderance of Old Testament quotations is striking; four times the quotations from the New. Another interesting feature is the final paragraph. Like Philippe de Mézières' 'Letter to King Richard II', the work ends with a prayer for the unity of France and England under one ruler, so that the two powers could speedily turn against 'the unbowed and cruel faces of pagans'.[82] This reminds us that the Turkish menace still existed, and also that the Teutonic Knights were struggling to find enough recruits for their north European endeavours, and had taken their problems to the Church council at Constance.[83] Interest in the Old Testament and the

---

[77] Many heads of religious houses, even the greatest abbots, were apt to describe themselves as the king's chaplains; see *Petitions to the Crown from English Religious Houses c. 1272–c. 1485*, ed. G. Dodd and A. K. McHardy, Canterbury and York Society 100 (2010), *passim*.

[78] *GHQ*, pp. 84 (*alii … sacerdotes*), 88 (*ascripti … clericali milicie*).

[79] On 28 June 1415 Stone took out letters of protection to go aboard, 'Calendar of French Rolls, 1–10 Henry V', in *Forty-Fourth Report of the Deputy Keeper of the Public Records (1883)*, p. 573. Thanks to Maureen Jurkowski for this reference. Stone, a Cambridge graduate, also went abroad in January 1417 and February 1418: ibid., pp. 601, 610. He died intestate in 1419: Emden, *BRUC*, pp. 559–60.

[80] Curry, *Agincourt: A New History*, p. 67.

[81] J. Catto, 'The King's Servants', and 'Religious Change under Henry V', in *Henry V*, ed. Harriss, pp. 75–95, 97–115.

[82] *GHQ*, p. 180.

[83] Philippe de Mézières, *Letter to King Richard II: A Plea made in 1395 for Peace between England and France*, introduced and translated by G. W. Coopland (Liverpool, 1975),

concern for crusading both suggest that the author might be found among the Carmelite Order.[84] As we have seen, both of Henry V's confessors were Carmelite friars.

Though absolute certainty remains elusive, it seems appropriate to offer for the reader's consideration a man with many qualifications for authorship, not as a proven solution to the problem of authorship but as a stimulus to further investigation. Stephen Patrington was a Yorkshireman and was ordained by Archbishop Thoresby between 1366, as an acolyte, and 1370, when he became a priest.[85] Since the canonical age for entering the priesthood was twenty-five, this suggests that he was born in about 1345. Patrington was prior of the Carmelite Order's Oxford house from 1373 until at least 1382, and was prior provincial in England from 1399 to 1413. At Oxford he acquired a theological training, becoming a bachelor of theology in 1382 and a doctor of theology by 1389. It was also in the 1380s that he came to prominence as an opponent of Wycliffite teaching. He was first involved in theological controversy at Oxford, confronting John Wycliffe's followers, an unpopular stance, and later sitting as a member of Archbishop Courtenay's Blackfriars Council in 1382.[86]

Patrington's links with the house of Lancaster were of long-standing. The earliest discernible link is the letter to Gaunt, written by the priors of the four Oxford houses of friars (Augustinian, Carmelite, Dominican, Franciscan), denouncing Wycliffe's follower Nicholas Hereford. It was dated 18 February 1382.[87] On 26 January 1397 Patrington was granted an annuity of £10 by John of Gaunt 'for his good services to the duchess of Lancaster and himself'.[88] A year previously Gaunt had married his long-time mistress, Katherine Swynford, who thus became duchess of Lancaster, and Patrington may well have listened sympathetically to the confessions of the scandalous pair.[89] This grant was made shortly before the parliamentary proceedings which legitimized their four children (given the surname Beaufort) and may have been

---

p. 146; '*quam cicius in indomitas et cruentas facies paganorum*', *GHQ*, p. 180. Cf., 'Shall not thou and I, between Saint Denis and Saint George, compound a boy, half French, half English, that shall go to Constantinople and take the Turk by the beard?' Shakespeare, *Henry V*, Act V, scene II; N. Housley, *The Later Crusades: From Lyons to Alcazar 1274–1580* (Oxford, 1992), pp. 82, 356–61.

[84] A. Jotischky, 'Carmelites and Crusading in the Later Middle Ages', in *The Church on its Past*, ed. P. Clarke and C. Methuen, Studies in Church History 49 (Woodbridge, 2013), pp. 110–20.

[85] Acolyte 19 December 1366; sub-deacon 4 March 1368; deacon 23 September 1368; priest 8 June 1370. The following biography is drawn from *BRUO*, III, 1435–6, and Catto 'Patrington, Stephen', in *ODNB*, unless otherwise indicated.

[86] *Fasciculi Zizaniorum magistri Johanni Wyclif cum tritico*, ed. W. W. Shirley, Rolls Series 5 (1858), pp. 289, 316.

[87] Ibid., pp. 292–5.

[88] *CPR, 1396–9*, p. 535.

[89] Gaunt and Swynford were married in Lincoln cathedral on 13 January 1396.

connected with that event.[90] One of those children, the second son Thomas, by the then earl of Dorset, would later receive a glowing description in the *Gesta*.[91] Patrington continued to enjoy good relations with the next generation of the house of Lancaster; on 24 December 1397 Henry Bolingbroke confirmed his father's annuity,[92] and as Henry IV he heard Patrington preach on Christmas Day 1401.

Stephen Patrington was therefore a man likely to appeal to Henry V as a Carmelite, a long-time friend of the family and an erudite theologian with a record of severity towards heretics. Patrington was Henry V's confessor from early in the reign, and on 24 November 1413 he was granted by letter patent expenses for himself and his household. Its terms deserve scrutiny. He was granted three shillings a day for himself, one colleague (*unius socii suis*), his men (*hominum suorum*) serving devotedly in the king's household (*in hospitio nostro deserventium*) and for four horses and one hackney (*hakenetti*). This was worth £54 12s. a year. He was to employ four stable-boys to care for his horses (*quatuor garcionum, dictos equos custodientium*), each of whom would be paid a penny ha'penny a day for their journeys (*vadiis*), costing another £9 2s. 6d. annually. Patrington himself was granted a further 109s. per annum for lesser expenses (*quibusdam minutis necessarias*). The whole yearly cost was £69 10s. 6d., to be taken at the exchequer at Easter and Michaelmas, until the order was countermanded.[93] From this we may deduce that Patrington, as a valuable servant of the king, was to travel a great deal, probably accompanying the royal household.[94] He must also have been a competent, if not keen, horseman. Alas, this substantial annual income meant that sums for individual journeys or tasks were not recorded on the issue rolls, thus making it impossible to track Patrington's movements with certainty. It does, however, demonstrate that he enjoyed the king's highest esteem.

On Henry Chichele's promotion to the archbishopric of Canterbury in 1414 Stephen Patrington succeeded him as bishop of St David's early in 1415. He was consecrated at Maidstone on 19 June by Archbishop Chichele, assisted by Richard Clifford the bishop of London and Richard Courtenay the bishop of Norwich. Patrington made his profession of obedience to Chichele in the presence of the king and the duke of Bedford, a ceremony which almost certainly

---

[90] This took place on 4 February 1397: *PROME*, VII, 358–9. They had been legitimized by the pope in September 1396.

[91] *ille nobilis capitaneus noster: GHQ*, pp. 114–16.

[92] *CPR, 1396–9*, p. 535.

[93] Rymer, *Foedera*, IX, 72; *CPR, 1413–16*, p. 142.

[94] This is also the conclusion of Catto, 'Patrington, Stephen', *ODNB*, who deduces that his career from June 1415 onwards 'strongly suggests that Patrington generally remained with the king'.

took place in London on 17 June.[95] It is unlikely that Stephen Patrington ever visited his see because, almost at the moment of his consecration, the bishopric of Chichester became vacant by the death of Robert Rede.[96] Steps were at once taken to effect his translation to a see which was much more conveniently placed for a constant courtier, and one, moreover, which had a tradition of mendicant bishops, one of whom had been a king's confessor.[97]

Meanwhile, the king, shortly before the start of his first French expedition, made his will on 24 July 1415. There were forty beneficiaries, and Patrington was named seventh, being preceded only by the Emperor Sigismund, the king's brothers, the archbishop of Canterbury, the king's uncle the bishop of Winchester (Henry Beaufort) and Thomas Langley bishop of Durham. Patrington's legacy was 'the best altar of our closet, along with a chalice, paten, a ewer for holy water, and a gold altar-cloth (*pace*)'.[98]

The deposition of Pope John XXIII by the Council of Constance on 29 May 1415 halted the progress of Patrington's translation, though subsequently, as bishop of St David's and king's confessor, he petitioned to have custody of all the temporalities of Chichester diocese with their appurtenances from Michaelmas 1416 during the vacancy, neither paying a fee for it, nor rendering account at the exchequer. This valuable favour was conceded on 25 August 1416, in a grant which made clear the extent of Henry's generosity.[99] Even after Patrington's death his interests continued to receive royal favour; his successor at St David's, Benedict Nicolls, was ordered to seek no reparation from 'the late bishop', and was not to receive his temporalities until he had given an assurance on this matter. Only after this was given did Henry order the new bishop to receive the temporalities.[100] The calendar hardly gives the flavour of the second letter which tells that the new bishop of St David's 'hath founden seurte in oure Chancellerie that he shal neuer vexe ne inquiete

---

[95] He received papal provision at Constance on 1 February; his consecration took place in All Saints collegiate church Maidstone. The profession of obedience is undated but was made before the consecration, since Patrington was then described as *consecrandus*. He received the spiritualities of his see in London on 17 June 1415: *The Register of Henry Chichele Archbishop of Canterbury 1414–1443*, ed. E. F. Jacob, 4 vols. (Oxford, 1943–7), I, 23–5.

[96] Rede (Reade) died before 21 June 1415.

[97] Rede was a Dominican, as was Thomas Rushook, Richard II's hated confessor (1386– trans. Kilmore 1389): *A Handbook of British Chronology*, ed. E. B. Fryde, D. E. Greenway, S. Porter and I. Roy, 3rd edn (London, 1986), p. 239.

[98] Rymer, *Feodera*, IX, 291; Mortimer, *1415: Henry V's Year of Glory*, pp. 296–7 sets out the beneficiaries very clearly.

[99] *vostre humble oratour Estephen levesque de Seynt David vostre confessour*: TNA, SC 8/230/1474; 'with all liberties, franchises and rights belonging to the bishopric', *CPR, 1416–22*, p. 42.

[100] Signet letters of the king dated 22 March and 15 May 1418: *Calendar of Signet Letters of Henry IV and Henry V*, ed. J. L. Kirby (London, 1978), nos. 822, 829.

thexecutours of the testament of his last predecessor that was our Confessour the which god assoille'.[101]

It is clear, therefore, that Stephen Patrington was very close to the court, and especially to the king himself. He was close enough, we may plausibly think, to have been entrusted with composing this propaganda piece, if the *Gesta* was indeed a royal commission. Alternatively, and more likely, Patrington's close links to, and benefits received from, the royal house over three generations, were surely sufficient to have prompted this well-qualified man to have written on his own initiative. We must now investigate the text itself, asking whether its form and content, as well as what the author tells us about himself, suggests that this theory deserves further consideration.

The Text of the *Gesta Henrici Quinti*

There are several hints that the work is not a truly polished production. The second chapter begins by mentioning, in extremely abbreviated form, Henry's monastic foundations. Their orders are not even specified, each of the three houses being described merely as 'of the order etc., to the honour etc'. It is as though the writer, who was well informed about the three planned foundations, was at that point making a note that he ought to mention them, and planned to return and fill out their story later on.[102] In the final chapter the parliament of October–November 1416 is only sketchily described in two disconnected paragraphs.[103] The *Gesta* was certainly finished by late November 1417, for at the time of writing Sir John Oldcastle, the heretic and failed rebel, was still a fugitive: *latitat a conspectu hominum velut alter Caym vagus et profugus super terram*. Oldcastle was captured in late November 1417, and news of his arrest reached London by 1 December.[104]

The text would accord with what we know of Patrington. Still awaiting the bull of translation which would move him from St David's to Chichester, he seems not to have gone to France with Henry at the start of the campaign which began in July 1417, but he certainly intended to join the king because on 6 November he and six others were licensed by Archbishop Chichele to hear the confessions of those on service in the king's army abroad, and to grant absolution even in specially reserved cases.[105] Two days later he was

---

[101] *An Anthology of Chancery English*, ed. J. H. Fisher, M. Richardson, J. L. Fisher (Knoxville, 1984), no. 24.

[102] *GHQ*, p. 12. The Bridgettine and Carthusian houses were founded, but the Celestine foundation was abandoned, partly through French hostility, but mainly for lack of funds; Beckett, 'Sheen Charterhouse', pp. 36–9.

[103] Ibid., pp. 176–8, 178–80.

[104] Ibid., p. 8; J. A. F. Thomson, 'Oldcastle, John, Baron Cobham (d. 1417)', *ODNB*.

[105] *Reg. Chichele*, IV, 184.

granted letters of protection for one year while overseas with the king.[106] Fate, however, intervened. Stephen Patrington's will is dated 16 November 1417, and was proved by Chichele on 29 December of the same year.[107] Ironically, the bull of Martin V translating the bishop of St David's to Chichester was dated 15 December 1417. Patrington by then was about seventy-two years old, yet his final illness was apparently short and his death unexpected. If he was indeed the author of the *Gesta* this would explain why the text was not thoroughly revised in its entirety.

If the ending of the *Gesta* seems in part rushed or scrappy, the organization of its beginning is surely deliberate. Oldcastle's rising came after the planning to found three religious houses at Sheen, yet it forms the subject of the *Gesta*'s first chapter, while the new religious houses are the subject of chapter 2. How can we explain this reversal? It may be that the writer wished to establish his authority by showing his intimate knowledge of events and closeness to the king, by saying of the encounter between Henry and the Lollard rebels outside London in January 1414: 'I was there.'[108] But it is also true that the pursuit and disciplining of heretics was a major and established policy of the king, who even as a Prince had been keen to suppress them.[109] It was a much longer occupation and interest of Stephen Patrington, who would surely have applauded Archbishop Arundel's pursuit of heretics, especially his strong measures against the University of Oxford where Patrington had earlier been threatened because of his defiance of Wycliffe's followers. This would explain not only his enthusiasm for Arundel as archbishop, but knowledge of that entry in his register which dealt with Oldcastle, in whose trial the king had a strong personal interest.[110] We know that Arundel was a man capable of inspiring affection in others.[111] The author of the *Gesta* seems cooler towards Chichele than towards Arundel, but this would be explained if the author was of an older generation than Chichele, as Patrington certainly was.

At certain points the author writes as an eyewitness, so we must ask what evidence there is for Patrington's movements during the years 1415 and 1416.

---

[106] Rymer, *Foedera*, IX, 509.

[107] *Reg. Chichele*, II, 133–5. Catto, 'Patrington, Stepehen', *ODNB*, following Emden *BRUO*, III, 1435–6, gives his date of death as 22 September, surely unlikely, considering the date of the will, and fails to explain the long pause between 'death' and probation. He also alleges, rather improbably, that the year-long letter of protection was granted 'posthumously'.

[108] 'ego qui scribo …', *GHQ*, p. 10.

[109] Allmand, *Henry V*, pp. 287–8, 290–1.

[110] Lambeth Palace Library, Register of Thomas Arundel II, fols. 142–145v (from microfilm); the glowing tribute to Arundel is in *GHQ*, p. 4.

[111] A. K. McHardy, 'John Scarle: Ambition and Politics in the Late Medieval Church', in *Image, Text and Church, 1380–1600: Essays for Margaret Aston*, ed. L. Clark, M. Jurkowski and C. Richmond (Toronto, 2009), pp. 68–93; *The Chronicle of Adam Usk 1377–1421*, ed. C. Given-Wilson (Oxford, 1997), esp. pp. 246–8.

Following his consecration at Maidstone on 19 June 1415 Patrington returned to London where he began to undertake the administrative tasks which were the bread-and-butter of episcopal life. He performed these duties in London on 22 and 23 June.[112] He then journeyed towards the port of embarkation, for he conducted more diocesan business at Winchester on 1 July.[113] On 24 July he was at Southampton where he witnessed the king's will, and he remained in that neighbourhood because on 11 August 1415 he was at Portchester, again engaged in the business of St David's diocese.[114] At this point his path and the king's diverged; John Claydon, a London skinner, was brought before a tribunal in St Paul's, London, on 17 August, and was examined by the archbishop of Canterbury, the bishops of London, Coventry and Lichfield, and the mayor of London. The bishop of St David's joined the proceedings on Monday, 19 August. Claydon was a long-standing heretic, his trial intended not merely to result in his burning but to serve as a warning to other Londoners. He was burnt on 10 September 1415.[115] Patrington, one of his judges, was still in London on 22 August, transacting diocesan business,[116] but thereafter the trail goes cold.[117]

Patrington, on that evidence, could not have accompanied the king on his journey to Harfleur, but it is entirely possible that he joined him later that month (for shipping continued back and forth across the Channel,[118] though precise documentation of individuals' journeys is impossible[119]) so being able to note the characteristics of the shore where he disembarked, being in time to witness the town's surrender, being on the long march via Agincourt to

---

[112] H. D. Emanuel, 'A Fragment of the Register of Stephen Patryngton, Bishop of St. Davids', *Journal of the Historical Society of the Church in Wales* 2 (1950), 31–45 (esp. pp. 38–9).

[113] Ibid., p. 39.

[114] Rymer, *Foedera*, IX, 293; Emanuel, 'Fragment', p. 39.

[115] For Claydon see A. Hudson, *The Premature Reformation* (Oxford, 1988), pp. 73n., 132, 211–13, 516.

[116] *Reg. Chichele*, IV, 132, 134; Emanuel, 'Fragment', pp. 39–40. Walsingham asserts that the king's imminent departure raised Lollards' spirits, also that Claydon's trial took place before the king set sail: *The St. Albans Chronicle Volume II: 1394–1422*, ed. J. Taylor, W. R. Childs and L. Watkiss (Oxford, 2011), pp. 662–4. On 22 August the mayor of London informed Henry of Claydon's conviction: *Calendar of Letter-Books of the City of London: Letter Book I*, ed. R. R. Sharpe (London, 1909), pp. 140–1.

[117] The loss of the registers of medieval bishops of Wales has been very great, so I could not argue that the ending of Patrington's register at this point was linked to a journey abroad.

[118] Most famously repatriating the sick, see *Chronicle of Adam Usk*, ed. Given-Wilson, pp. 254–6. There is much less precise evidence of traffic going the other way – the issue rolls did not record the names of those travelling to Harfleur after the siege had started. Thanks are due to Anne Curry for help on this point.

[119] The privy seal warrants for issue of 3 Henry V (TNA, E 404/31) contain *c.*600 items for the period March–December 1415, but only two were issued in August and three in September.

Calais, and to have been present at the battle, sitting on a horse among the baggage, at the rear of the fighting (*insedens equum inter evectiones ad dorsum prelii.*).[120] Other pointers may be advanced to suggest that the author of the *Gesta* was not present at the commencement of the siege of Harfleur. Titus Livius, writing under the duke of Gloucester's patronage in the late 1430s, told how, immediately on disembarking in France, Henry fell to his knees in prayer (*tunc ad genua statim procidens deum orat, ut ad ejus divinitatis honorem sibi justitiam ex hostibus faciat*), and that he quickly climbed a steep hill in order that the feast of the Assumption of the Virgin Mary should be suitably celebrated the next day by his men (*ut sollemnitas Assumptionis beatae Marie Virginis postera die honore digno celebraretur a suis*).[121] Given the *Gesta*'s interest in and knowledge of liturgical matters this omission is curious, prompting the question whether its author was there. The *Gesta* is also silent about the taking of booty – in contrast to other chronicle accounts. The chronology of events before Harfleur is unclear despite the existence of several accounts, and the *Gesta* itself gives no dates between 20 August and 10 September.[122]

This would mean that the writer, if this was Patrington, moved swiftly over the Channel to join the king. Quick journeys were certainly possible; the *London Letter-Book I* recorded that the mayor and other Londoners gave thanks for the king's great victory three days after the battle of Agincourt.[123] Evidence from later that year shows that some prelates were remarkably fast travellers. Archbishop Chichele, for example, received the king at Canterbury cathedral on, probably, 17 November 1415, yet was in London to open convocation on the morning of 18 November, according to his register. Stephen Patrington, bishop of St David's, was at the opening of this convocation too.[124] Thus we may ask whether the author of the *Gesta* accompanied the king to France and witnessed the start of the siege of Harfleur, or whether he arrived later and received information about the siege's early days from an eyewitness – the bishop of Bangor, for example.

The king entered London on 24 November 1415, and from then on the *Gesta*'s most detailed descriptions are devoted in the first place to descriptions of pageantry and liturgy, and in the second to accounts of diplomacy, including the visit of the Emperor Sigismund. The two were intertwined; the public celebrations which took place in London and the elaborate liturgy performed during the emperor's visit to Canterbury in August 1416 illustrate vividly the political importance of public and elaborate religious observance. The detailed description of the ceremonies which took place in Canterbury cathedral between 21 and 29 August could only have been provided by

---

120 *GHQ*, p. 84.
121 *Titi Livii Foro-Juliensis Vita Henrici Quini Regis Angliae*, ed. T. Hearne (Oxford, 1716), p. 8.
122 Curry, *Agincourt: A New History*, esp. pp. 77–88.
123 On 28 October: *London Letter-Book I*, p. 144.
124 Allmand, *Henry V*, pp. 96–7; *Reg. Chichele*, III, 3.

someone who was present on those days.[125] It is followed soon after by one of the occasions when the author says he was present, crossing, on 4 and 5 September, from Sandwich to the Calais shore.[126] We may make two points in support of Patrington's authorship at this point. At the end of chapter 22, which described the Canterbury ceremonies, is a paragraph in praise of the king's devoted and fervent performance of his private devotions.[127] Who was better placed than his confessor to know about this very intimate aspect of the king's life? A more public link between the two men comes in the form of the letter patent conferring on Patrington custody of the temporalities of the see of Chichester, with all associated rights. This grant was made on 25 August 1416, at Canterbury.[128] But special pleading is not needed for Patrington's presence in the king's company at this time, for a close rolls memorandum records that on 4 September 1416, when about to embark for France, Henry V conducted business *in quadam camera exteriori infra mansum prioris et fratrum domus ordinis Carmelitarum pro ipso Domino Rege ibidem ordinata*, in the presence of Archbishop Chichele, Thomas (Langley) bishop of Durham, Stephen bishop of St David's, and others.[129]

The loss of most of Patrington's episcopal register means that we cannot construct an itinerary for him, though we have observed him on various dates and precise places in England during the summer of 1415, in London in November 1415 and in the king's presence in Kent in the autumn of 1416. Independent evidence of Stephen Patrington's movements in the period after the autumn of 1415 is sparse, however. He played no active role in any parliament, but all the bishops of Welsh diocese are conspicuous by their absence from lists of triers of parliamentary petitions, and there is no evidence that the bishop of St David's expected to be absent from parliament.[130] He was, though, an assiduous attender at convocation, where his presence was noted on 18 November 1415, and at the long session which lasted from 1 April to 6 June 1416. The bishop of St David's was recorded as present at the gathering's start (1 April) and twice in late May. On the latter occasion he assisted at the consecration of the new bishop of Norwich, John Wakering. His last noted attendance in convocation was in the meeting of 9 to 23 November 1416.[131] On 18 May 1417 he was at Windsor castle assisting in the consecra-

---

[125]   *GHQ*, pp. 150–4.

[126]   Ibid., p. 156.

[127]   Ibid., p. 154.

[128]   *CPR, 1416–22*, p. 42.

[129]   Rymer, *Foedera*, IX, 385–6; and *CCR, 1413–19*, pp. 368–9.

[130]   The only evidence for the appointment of a parliamentary proctor by a Welsh bishop in this reign dates from October 1416 when Robert (Lancaster), bishop of St Asaph, commissioned Benedict (Nicolls) bishop of Bangor and, apparently an afterthought, John (de la Zouch) bishop of Llandaff. Among the five other proctors was Master Adam Usk, canon of St Asaph: TNA, SC 10/46/2660.

[131]   *Reg. Chichele*, III, 10, 15, 21, 30.

tion of Edmund Lacy, former dean of the chapel royal, as bishop of Hereford, when the king was also present.[132] Examination of Patrington's movements in 1415 and 1416 has revealed a number of occasions when he was in the king's presence, though he cannot have sailed to France with Henry in early August 1415. It is possible, however, that he joined the English army later, was on the march to Calais and so was able to observe the battle of Agincourt in person, and a reading of the *Gesta* suggests that its author may not have been present at the start of the siege of Harfleur.

It would be useful if we could compare the prose style of the *Gesta* with other compositions. The hand of its author has been detected in the prologue to the foundation charters for the Charterhouse of Sheen.[133] Stephen Patrington was certainly involved in the king's foundation projects, for in January 1416 he chaired a meeting of monks and theologians which aimed to resolve problems which had arisen over the regulation of the Bridgettine house at Syon.[134] Patrington was said by John Bale, the sixteenth-century antiquary and fellow Carmelite, to have been the author of a number of works (commentaries, lectures and a treatise on the office of priesthood) which have not survived. All that remains of this *corpus* is his *Repertorium Argumentorum*, an early work from his Oxford days, still unprinted, but which was evidently popular, with copies surviving in Cambridge, Dublin, Venice and Florence.[135] One work in which Stephen Patrington's hand can be seen is the collection of anti-Wycliffite material known as *Fasciculi Zizaniorum*.[136] This volume was evidently a Carmelite project which was handed down and added to over several generations. Stephen Patrington is thought to have been the earliest compiler.[137] His name appears at the end of the letter addressed by 'the doctors of Oxford' to John of Gaunt on 18 February 1382 (i.e. *per Patrington*);[138] but he is also thought to be the author of the connecting material which links the assembled documents, and which form the first thirty-two pages in

---

[132]   Ibid., I, 34–5.

[133]   Beckett, 'Sheen Charterhouse', pp. 81–5. The first version was dated 25 September 1414; the second and third on 1 April 1415 (Beckett, 'Sheen Charterhouse', Appendix II, pp. 198–242, transcribes the texts from the charter rolls (TNA, C 53/183, mm. 8–7, C 53/185, mm. 20–19, 8–5)).

[134]   D. Knowles, *The Religious Orders in England, Volume II: The End of the Middle Ages* (Cambridge, 1955), p. 178.

[135]   See J. Catto, 'Wyclife and Wycliffism at Oxford 1356–1430', pp. 175–262 (esp. pp. 198, 200) and M. B. Parkes, 'The Provision of Books', pp. 407–84 (esp. p. 442), in *The History of the University of Oxford*, ed. J. I. Catto and T. A. R. Evans, vol. II (Oxford, 1992). Professor Anne Hudson, who has read this work, tells me that it is 'densely academic, concerned with philosophical and theological issues', and that the only manuscript in England (Cambridge, St John's MS 103) is 'virtually illegible'.

[136]   See n. 86 above.

[137]   J. Crompton, 'Fasciculi Zizaniorum II', *Journal of Ecclesiastical History* 12 (1961), 155–66. This is also the view of Knowles, *Religious Orders in England*, II, 147, n. 1, 148.

[138]   Crompton, 'Fasciculi Zizaniorum II', p. 295.

the Rolls Series edition. None of these works may be helpful in identifying Stephen Patrington as the author of the *Gesta*. Indeed, no definitive answer to the problem of authorship is yet possible. What has been offered here is a further suggestion, the advancement of a name which has not previously been considered.

The *Gesta* and the Clergy

To the puzzling question of the *Gesta*'s authorship we may add that of its readership. Clearly it was not intended for an uneducated public, but for those well versed in Latin. Its language and style indicate that it was aimed at clerics, especially bishops and those in the ranks immediately below them in the hierarchy (i.e. archdeacons, cathedral prebendaries), the abbots of major houses and university scholars, in other words opinion-formers. Clerical support was seen as vital to buttress a regime which was under attack both from theological deviants and aristocratic plotters, and despite the king's triumph at Agincourt, clerical support seemed grudging. On 2 August 1416 Archbishop Chichele complained to his bishops that he understood that his call to say special prayers for peace, Church unity, national prosperity, the harvest, health and for the strenuous peacemaking efforts of Sigismund king of the Romans had been observed with only lukewarm devotion.[139] The English clergy were disgruntled at this time, for they were being taxed not only for the king's wars, but to defray the expenses of the delegation to the Church council at Constance. There is evidence of their reluctance to pay.[140] The clergy, through their leaders, needed to show more enthusiasm for King Henry's policies, both domestic and international. The fact that this readership of higher and promoted clergy was comparatively small does not mean that it was not worth cultivating; 'propaganda did not have to be mass propaganda to be effective'.[141]

Composition of the *Gesta* took place while a general Church council was meeting at Constance, which was attended by a large and prestigious English delegation.[142] The Council of Constance assembled in 1414 to heal the schism

---

[139] *Reg. Chichele*, IV, 158–9. He made similar complaints on 8 May and 22 June 1417: ibid., 167–8, 275–6.

[140] Ibid., III, 3–7, 54, 392–3; *The Register of Bishop Repingdon 1405–19*, ed. M. Archer, 3 vols., Lincoln Record Society 74 (1982), III, nos. 192, 235–6, 270, 301. They had been similarly unenthusiastic about paying expenses for those attending the council of Pisa in 1409: *The Register of Robert Hallum Bishop of Salisbury 1407–17*, ed. J. M. Horn, Canterbury and York Society 72 (1982), nos. 756.

[141] Beckett, 'Sheen Charterhouse', p. 82.

[142] The original clerical delegation was led by Bishops Bubwith of Bath and Wells and Hallam of Salisbury, and included also the abbots of six major monasteries, Rymer,

and reform the Church, and a conciliar readership could explain why the Emperor Sigismund, who was tireless in his efforts to heal the schism, features so prominently in the narrative. More precise diplomatic points were made by the *Gesta*'s author, and noted by its editors.[143] The readership of the *Gesta* may have been essentially domestic, but an international dimension cannot be ruled out.

The council was wrestling with other problems besides the schism; the delegates were also discussing heresy, which was proving a domestic problem for both Sigismund and Henry. On 4 May 1415 it condemned 267 articles in the writings of John Wyclif, and on 6 July 1415 John Huss was burnt.[144] The *Gesta* portrayed Henry as the champion of orthodoxy, not only as the hammer of heretics at home, but also as a positive promoter of traditional, and international, Church values by founding new religious houses. It is possible that the *Gesta* was originally envisaged as equally, or even primarily, a record of Henry V's triumph over Lollardy, but that the author was foiled by Oldcastle's long evasion of capture.

Conclusion

The court and its clerical members whose work we have discussed represented the cultural pinnacle of propaganda designed to impress an elite audience; to reach the wider public Henry V could employ well-established machinery for enlisting support for royal policies. Prayers and processions, organized through the archbishops and bishops, had been used in this way since the thirteenth century, so it is surprising that Henry V's first campaign in France was not preceded by any national call to prayer for its success. Later in the reign the king adopted this traditional practice.[145]

In asking for prayers for military success Henry V was following established tradition, but he added a new element to national liturgical endeavour: he thanked God for his success. Following the celebrations in London to mark his victory at Agincourt (reported at length by the *Gesta* in chapter 15) the convocation of Canterbury province raised the status of the feast of St George in its deliberations on 20 November.[146] Efforts of a similar kind were made in the following year; in January Archbishop Chichele ordered increased obser-

---

Foedera, IX, 162, 167, 169; L. Ropes Loomis, *The Council of Constance: The Unification of the Church* (New York, 1961), p. 481.

[143] *GHQ*, pp. xxv–xxvi.

[144] On Wyclif see A. Hudson and A. Kenny, 'Wyclif, John (*d.* 1384)', *ODNB*.

[145] June 1417 (prayers for the king's expedition); May 1418 (the king and his army); October 1418 (the king going to Normandy); October 1419 (military success); undated 1420 (the king and his army): *Reg. Repingdon*, III, nos. 336, 341, 434, 539; Lincolnshire Archive Office, Register 16 (Richard Fleming), fols. 211–211v.

[146] *Reg. Chichele*, III, 6.

vance of the feasts of Saints George, David, Chad and Winifred, while in May convocation passed an ordinance for observing the feast of St John of Beverley,[147] to make Henry's subjects aware of the favour which these denizens of heaven had granted. The royal progress made in early summer 1421 was intended, in part, to reinforce these measures.[148]

The effectiveness of these propaganda efforts could be described, at best, as mixed. We are accustomed to thinking that the Agincourt victory transformed Henry V's domestic and international standing, yet in 1416, and 1418, as in 1415, there were fears of invasion.[149] We have already seen that mandates to say special prayers for success, issued in 1416 and 1417, were received with little enthusiasm.[150] On the positive side we can point to the celebratory verses composed in the autumn of 1415,[151] and to the fact that Sir Thomas Chaworth of Wiverton (1380–1459), an Agincourt veteran, later commissioned a large and lavish antiphonal which contains the only known source for the chants written in honour of St John of Bridlington, a saint whose shrine Henry visited on his tour in 1421;[152] though Chaworth, a bibliophile and a former Lollard sympathizer, was an unusual member of his class.[153] Even the Agincourt Carol, although it attained popularity, was probably a court, or at least aristocratic production, for this, 'the best known of English carols', mixes English with Latin ('Deo gratias Anglia, redde pro victoria') and calls for singing in two and three parts.[154] One of the ironies of this subject is that those works originally intended for the most restricted audiences now have the widest currency. The music composed for the exclusive and rarefied setting of the chapel royal is now, thanks to modern recordings, available for anyone to hear. The posthumous life of the *Gesta* is even

---

[147] Ibid., pp. 8–10, 14–16.

[148] J. A. Doig, 'Propaganda and Truth: Henry V's Royal Progress in 1421', *Nottingham Medieval Studies* 40 (1996), 167–79.

[149] In May 1416 preparations were made against a French invasion with orders to erect *signa, vocata bekyns*, and to array men at arms, Rymer, *Foedera*, IX, 350–1 and *CPR, 1416–22*, p. 72. For later measures for home defence, including arming the clergy, against possible invasion, see *Reg. Repingdon*, III, nos. 81 (12 June 1415), 468 (6 July 1418), 491 (undated); 1 April 1418, Rymer, *Foedera*, IX, 568–9.

[150] The complaint Archbishop Chichele repeatedly made was that the prayers for national causes were performed 'tepidly', *Reg. Chichele*, IV, 158–9 (1416), 167–8, 175–6 (1417).

[151] *Chronicle of Adam Usk*, ed. Given-Wilson, pp. 258, 262.

[152] This is now available on: *Music for Henry V & the House of Lancaster: The English Cyclic Mass 'Quem Malignus Spiritus' and Ceremonial Motets for Fifteenth-Century Princely Chapels*, The Binchois Consort, Andrew Kirkman, conductor (Hyperion, DISCID: OB 110F12) track two. This disc includes works by Cook, Damet and Sturgeon, also Lionel Power, John Dunstable and 'Roi Henry' himself. The antiphonal belongs to the parish church of St Leonard, Wollaton (Nottingham) and is deposited in the department of manuscripts, University of Nottingham.

[153] *HP*, II, 533–6.

[154] Peter M. Lefferts, 'Agincourt Carol', in *Medieval England: An Encyclopedia*, ed. Szarmach, Tavormina and Rosenthal, p. 11.

more remarkable; its author alleged that Henry, replying to the wish, voiced by one of his commanders[155] on the eve of Agincourt, that their army was larger, replied that he was glad that their numbers were so small. The king's riposte was at best unoriginal,[156] and may have been purely fictional, but this, thanks to Shakespeare, has been but one part of the legacy of this anonymous author, and to a great extent every succeeding generation has been under its spell.

[155] Sir Walter Hungerford, *GHQ*, p. 78. Shakespeare, Act IV, scene iii, put the sentiment into the mouth of (the earl of) Westmoreland, which scans better.
[156] Following I Maccabees 9.

6

'Par le special commandement du roy'. Jewels and Plate Pledged for the Agincourt Expedition

Jenny Stratford

There is no more intriguing example of the use of the English royal treasure as a war chest than the financing of the 1415 expedition which led to the battle of Agincourt. A royal treasure embodied magnificence and served as an arm of diplomacy, but it was also a bank. In times of war and of other pressing need, English kings, like other European rulers, had of course often resorted to raising loans by pledging jewels and plate to corporations, syndicates and wealthy individuals.[1] They would continue to do so until well into the modern period. The arrangements made by Henry V in 1415 seem, however, to be unique. For the first and probably the only time, as well as raising funds by pledging valuables to non-combatants, jewels and plate were pledged directly to the captains indenting for war service to guarantee the second quarters' wages for themselves and their retinues.

A mass of records surrounding the pledging and recovery of these valuables has survived in the National Archives at Kew, in the British Library and elsewhere. The background and administration of the Agincourt campaign, married to a wider political, military and economic context, have been well studied, but the nature and function of the valuables themselves demand closer attention.[2] The surviving documentation is copious, although far from complete. It consists of about 135 so-called jewel indentures, a few being duplicates, as well as the surviving particular accounts of some captains, a single enrolled account and scattered exchequer records surrounding the

---

[1] See, for example, E. B. Fryde, 'Financial Resources of Edward III in the Netherlands, 1337–40', in his *Studies in Medieval Trade and Finance* (London, 1983), pp. 1142–1216; J. Stratford, 'Richard II's Treasure and London', in *London and the Kingdom: Essays in Honour of Caroline M. Barron*, ed. M. Davies and A. Prescott, Harlaxton Medieval Studies 16 (Donington, 2008), pp. 212–29; P. Henwood, 'Administration et vie des collections d'orfèvrerie royales sous le règne de Charles VI (1380–1422)', *Bibliothèque de l'Ecole des Chartes* 138 (1980), 179–215.

[2] Allmand, *Henry V*, esp. chapters 4, 5, 10; A. Curry, *The Battle of Agincourt: Sources and Interpretations* (Woodbridge, 2000); A. Curry, *Agincourt: a New History* (Stroud, 2005).

closure of certain captains' accounts.[3] These documents are also our best and as yet under-exploited source for assessing the contents of Henry V's treasure for which no complete inventory exists.[4] Pioneering work on this aspect of the Agincourt finances was undertaken by Sir Harris Nicolas in the nineteenth century and by J. H. Wylie in the early twentieth century. It was carried forward in the excellent dissertation of E. H. de L. Fagan, completed in 1935, the same year as the jewel indentures were laid down and sewn into their green folders, perhaps no coincidence.[5] Publication of the redis-covered long inventory of Richard II's treasure drawn up at the end of his reign demanded a reinvestigation of these remarkable records, because some of the most conspicuous of Richard's former valuables were pledged for the Agincourt campaign.[6]

The preliminaries to the expedition are well known and it is unnecessary to give more than the sketchiest summary of the financial arrangements.[7] By the early months of 1415 Henry V had decided on war with France. Funds were urgently needed. The first instalment of a double subsidy was due in February, but even if promptly collected this would be insufficient to pay the soldiers. Corporate and individual loans were sought and obtained, headed by 10,000 marks from the citizens of London and nearly £2,000 from Cardinal Beaufort, but the sum collected was still far from enough. These loans, too, were backed up by pledges of valuables.[8]

Indentures drawn up between the king and the captains, most of them dated 29 April, set out the terms and conditions for a year's service. Warrants for the first quarter's wages were issued on the day of sealing and some of the payments for the first quarter can be traced on the one surviving special

---

[3] Most of the jewel indentures are TNA, E 101/45/20 to E 101/45/23. Jewels and plate are also listed in some particular accounts and in the only known enrolled account, TNA, E 358/6, drawn up after 1422. I thank Anne Curry and Maureen Jurkowski for their help with this material.

[4] The valuables delivered to Henry's executors in 1423 (*PROME*, X, 112–62), represent only a fraction of the treasure.

[5] N. H. Nicolas, *History of the Battle of Agincourt*, 2nd edn (London, 1832), Appendix III, pp. 13–18, based on the Rymer transcripts in BL Sloane MS 4600, fols. 251v–254v; Wylie and Waugh, *Henry the Fifth*, I, esp. 468–76. See also J. Barker, *Agincourt, the King, the Campaign, the Battle* (London, 2005); I. Mortimer, *1415. Henry V's Year of Glory* (London, 2009). E. H. de L. Fagan, 'Some Aspects of the King's Household in the Reign of Henry V' (unpublished MA dissertation, University of London, 1935), greatly extends the documentary references.

[6] J. Stratford, *Richard II and the English Royal Treasure* (Woodbridge, 2012). I intend to explore the Agincourt jewel indentures more fully in future.

[7] Curry, *Sources*, pp. 408–57.

[8] *Calendar of Letter-Books of the City of London. Letter-book I*, ed. R. R. Sharpe (London, 1909), pp. 135, 143; *Foedera*, IV (ii), 141; *Memorials of London and London Life in the XIIIth XIVth and XVth centuries*, ed. H. T. Riley (London, 1868), pp. 603–5; Harriss, *Cardinal Beaufort*, Appendix I, no. 5, with references.

issue roll for the Agincourt campaign drawn up for Easter term 1415.[9] The indentures stipulate that the soldiers' wages for the second quarter were to be guaranteed by 'jewels' (meaning jewels and plate). The notional date set for the delivery of the valuables was 1 June. It was envisaged that the men-at-arms and archers promised in the indentures by the individual captains would be mustered on 1 July, but both of these targets proved unrealistic. Special conditions were attached to the pay for the third and fourth quarters.

Many of those serving on the expedition who received valuables as pledges were intimately connected with the king and his household, down to some relatively humble personages, such as the clerk of the Marshalsea. The king's kinsmen, the dukes of Clarence, Gloucester and York and other great magnates brought large retinues. Others indenting were the king's annuitants, his knights and esquires. Others still were probably not fighting men, although indispensable to the expeditionary force. Such were the sergeant tailor, William Tropenell, and the members of the 'medical corps', Nicholas Colnet, Henry's physician, and his two surgeons, Thomas Morstede and William Bradwardine, with their twelve assistants.[10] The services of another non-combatant, John Cliff, the most prominent of the king's minstrels, were secured by a mixed bag of chapel and household plate. These valuables seem not to have been recovered from Cliff's executors until 1434.[11]

How were the pledged valuables brought together and how and where were they parcelled out? Some of the preliminary arrangements are recorded, and once the process was in hand, tight control was kept at the exchequer. At a council in the Tower of London on 27 May, the duke of Bedford, Cardinal Beaufort and Richard Courtenay, bishop of Norwich, treasurer of the chamber and keeper of the jewels, were charged with the delivery and safekeeping of the king's treasure.[12] Some valuables not in current use were stored in the great treasury at Westminster, that is, in the Pyx chapel on the east walk of the abbey cloister.[13] Others may have been in the Jewel Tower within the Palace of Westminster or in the Tower of London. Wherever they were at any particular time (objects went in and out of store and repositories changed), valuables were charged to the respective keepers and safeguarded by their subordinates. Liturgical plate belonging to the peripatetic household chapel was charged to the dean. Objects, whichever department had released them, seem to have been handed over in the treasury and were usually returned at the treasury of receipt.

---

[9] TNA, E 101/45/5.

[10] *Foedera*, IV (ii), 116, 117, 123, 126, 127; Allmand, *Henry V*, p. 214.

[11] *Foedera*, IV (ii), 124, 126; TNA, E 101/46/24; E 101/47/23; E 358/6, rot. 11.

[12] *POPC*, II, 167.

[13] For the Pyx chapel as a treasury, see J. Ashbee, 'The Royal Wardrobe and the Chapter House of Westminster Abbey', in *Westminster Abbey Chapter House*, ed. W. Rodwell and R. Mortimer (London, 2010), pp. 112–23.

On 30 May Courtenay was ordered to deliver jewels and plate to the earl of Arundel as treasurer of England.[14] The indentures with the captains make it clear how many very precious objects were sent from the chamber to serve as pledges, but no inventory or other list of these exists at the time of issue, no doubt because of the traditional exemption of the chamber from accounting at the exchequer. This exemption did not apply to the valuables of the household or the household chapel. On 1 June Edmund Lacy, the dean, indented with Courtenay for well over a hundred gold, silver-gilt and silver chapel goods taken from the vestry.[15] Lacy's indenture contains the resonant but conventional formula, 'by the king's special command', the phrase used in the title of this chapter. Monetary values were given for the chapel goods, but not weights. Values can and do fluctuate, but many of the descriptions are full enough for the objects to be recognized in differently worded earlier and later lists. The gems set in the most precious gold items at the head of the list were carefully enumerated. This sort of detail is essential if the provenance and later history of an object is to be traced.

On 13 June, Roger Leche, the treasurer of the household, responded to the privy seal writ addressed to him five days earlier. He delivered to Courtenay, again by indenture, hundreds of individually less valuable pieces of silver-gilt and silver plate: dozens of salts, candlesticks, cups, pots, spice-plates, dishes large and small, basins, ewers and saucers, a large and heavy alms dish and silver cooking utensils. He gave weights but not values for this enormous quantity of plate, but calculating the value by weight of individual pieces without gems would have been relatively straightforward. Many 'lots' of multiple pieces in Leche's list seem to have been broken up to be pledged to one or another captain. Only those vessels differentiated by one or another prominent feature such as their great size or their heraldry can easily be picked out among the pledges.[16]

For some of the most distinctive pieces among the chapel goods, on the other hand, a whole history can be reconstructed and significant changes in an object can be recognized. Such, for example, is a gold and jewelled reliquary statuette of St Martin on a silver-gilt base weighing 157 ½ oz. The image had been given to Richard II by John, duke of Berry, before 1399, when it was estimated to be worth nearly £460. Much of that value, £340, had been for the gems and pearls set on the pallium, mitre and crozier and on the reliquary capsule containing a bone of the saint. In the intervening years two gems, a sapphire and a balas ruby (the rose-red variety of spinel ruby), and a cluster of pearls seem to have been lost. Lacy's list gives the much lower value of £188. The image was, however, pledged for considerably more, £217 10s., to the young John Holland, who was already styled earl of Huntingdon.

---

[14] *CPR, 1413–16*, p. 329; *Foedera*, IV (ii), 125.
[15] Two copies, TNA, E 101/44/26; E 101/46/6 (incomplete).
[16] TNA, E 101/46/14. The writ is cited in the preamble.

With some other valuables this served to guarantee the wages of a retinue of twenty men-at-arms and sixty archers. After the campaign and recently restored to his title and entailed lands, Huntingdon bought all the pieces pledged to him against the balance owing in his account. In addition to the image of St Martin, these were a cup and ewer in gold and enamel newly made for Henry V by Conus Melver, the king's goldsmith.[17]

An enormous additional administrative burden was imposed by issuing jewels to most of the captains. It has been has estimated that there were at least 250 men bringing companies to the expedition and nearer 300 if those indenting as a group are also included.[18] Some retinues were very large, such as the duke of Clarence's, who indented for 960 men, but others comprised single men-at-arms bringing perhaps two or three archers. Most captains of retinues received valuables as pledges. The speed and efficiency of the clerical bureaucracy was remarkable, even if preparations now concealed from view had begun as early as the end of March or the beginning of April. Each pledge generated besides the indenture itself a mass of subsidiary documentation, warrants, entries on the pell roll and so on. The actual jewel indentures drawn up between Courtenay and the captains followed a standard formula, with provisions for safekeeping of the valuables. The king optimistically undertook at this stage to redeem the valuables by 1 January 1417 or to leave the captains free disposal of them. Each indenture had to include the numbers and composition of the individual captain's intended retinue, the total wages for the full quarter, as well as descriptions, weights and values of the particular items, amounting in all to close control of many hundreds of objects.[19] One part of the indenture sealed by Courtenay remained with the captain and had to be brought in at accounting. The other, with the captain's seal, was delivered for safekeeping at the exchequer by Thomas Chitterne, Courtenay's deputy and eventual successor. In a few instances both parts of an indenture have survived in the National Archives, explaining the existence of the duplicates.

The worth of each piece was estimated by weight of precious metal on a sliding scale of value which took account of workmanship as well as bullion content. Strikingly different metal values were estimated for different objects, but on closer examination there often seems to be a good reason for this variation. The price of gold was normally calculated at 26s. 8d. per Troy ounce, but rose to 30s. for a new cup made for the king, fell to 23s. 4d. for damaged or incomplete pieces, and to as low as 20s. where gold was the subsidiary

---

[17] For this object and for Holland's restoration, TNA, E 101/44/26, rot. 1; E 101/44/6; E 101/45/22, m. 30; E 101/45/7; E 358/6, rot. 9d; *GHQ*, p. 23, n. 2; Stratford, *Richard II*, entry R 909 and pp. 338–9.

[18] Curry, *Sources*, p. 411.

[19] The quarter's wages for an esquire and three archers amounted to £13 11s. 11¼d., for an esquire and two archers £11 6s. 5¼d.

material on a rock crystal object.[20] Silver-gilt and silver were estimated by the Troy pound of 12 ounces. Images and other elaborately worked objects of silver-gilt were routinely valued at 46s. 8d. per pound, whereas plain or damaged silver at the bottom of the range was at 30s. Some silver-gilt was valued more highly at 48s. per pound, such as the silver-gilt vessels pledged to William, Lord Botreaux.[21] To the bullion value was added the worth of any gems or pearls according to their number, size and quality. The status of the recipient may occasionally have influenced the rate at which valuables were appraised. Items pledged to those of lower rank (those less likely to possess objects of similar value of their own), seem sometimes to have been calculated at a higher than expected rate, for example for a damaged piece. Weights and values of many of these objects would no doubt already have existed in lists and inventories now lost to us. Goldsmiths may, however, have been brought in at this stage, as they were later, when certain disputed accounts were closed.[22] Whatever the bullion price estimated, with very few exceptions the matches between the worth of valuables and the anticipated wages for the quarter were calculated to be close, occasionally exact, any difference being in the captain's favour. The total nominal value of the king's treasure pledged was probably nearly equivalent to the cost of an entire quarter's wages for the majority of the expeditionary force, but as we do not have a complete set of indentures or accounts, this cannot be accurately calculated.

The first jewel indentures were dated 5 June and were to important captains.[23] The great majority fall, however, in two blocks, those sealed at Westminster between 13 and 24 June and those sealed at Winchester between 5 and 21 July. Some pledges of valuables for which the indentures are lost can be identified in the particular and enrolled accounts of individual captains. The later fate of some recognizable pieces can be traced among the memoranda of the exchequer published by Palgrave and in proceedings recorded on the unpublished memoranda rolls.[24]

By the time the first jewel indentures were issued, the decision had been taken that the expedition would be to northern France rather than Gascony. Calculations were based on the wage scales for service in the north. Once the sum needed for each captain and his retinue for the second quarter had been calculated down to the last farthing, a package of valuables was approximately matched. Thus an important captain, such as Sir Thomas Erpingham,

---

[20] TNA, E 101/45/21, mm. 9, 12, a rock crystal cup at 20s. and a new hanap (cup) made by Conus, for example.

[21] TNA, E 101/45/22, m. 23.

[22] As in the case of Sir Simon Felbrigg below at n. 40.

[23] TNA, E 101/45/20, m. 37, Edmund, earl of March, with sixty men-at-arms and 180 archers; TNA, E 101/45/21, m. 8, Sir Thomas Dutton with ten men-at-arms and thirty archers.

[24] F. Palgrave, *The Antient Kalendars and Inventories of ... the Exchequer*, 3 vols. (London, 1836), II, 100–253 (hereafter Palgrave, *Kals.*); TNA, E 159 and E 368.

then steward of the king's household, would have several very valuable objects and a relatively insignificant one as a makeweight. An ungilded silver dish valued at 52s. 3d. was matched with two very valuable sets of jewelled cups and ewers, which had been gifts from the dukes of Berry and Burgundy. This made a total of £295 17s. 11d. as security for £294 13s. 10½ d., the wages and regards of twenty men-at-arms and sixty archers, including the higher rates of pay for a banneret and two knights.[25]

Naturally, the greatest captains bringing the largest retinues had the best and therefore the most identifiable objects, those mentioned by most earlier authorities, although the history of some of the most valuable pieces has been poorly understood. A great gold alms dish in the shape of a ship (a nef), known in England as the Tiger because of the miniature tigers in the castles at prow and stern, was pawned to Edward, second duke of York (c.1375–1415). This had been the gift of John, duke of Berry, to his nephew, Charles VI. The muzzled bear supporting the vessel was one of Berry's badges; the tiger was a badge of Charles VI particularly in favour at New Year 1395, when the nef had been presented to him. Less than a year later, in November 1396, it was one of Charles VI's gifts to Richard II during their meeting at Ardres. In Richard's inventory it had been valued at £544, but in 1415 with the gems still intact it was appraised at the lesser sum of £351. The Tiger nef was recovered from York's executors in 1430, before again being pawned to raise money for later campaigns in France, first to Cardinal Beaufort, then to Richard, third duke of York (1411–60). The nef can still be traced among the treasures of the crown in the reign of Edward IV.[26] This was one of several very valuable gold objects given to Richard II by the Valois which were used to finance the 1415 campaign to the tune of at least £2,160.[27]

Lancastrian valuables were also pressed into service. The king's brother, Clarence, was assigned the crown 'Henry', valued at £6,000. Some of the jewelled fleurons and pinnacles were then pawned to the captains in his retinue who had sub-indented with him. The laborious process of recovery can be followed from the first writ in 1416 to around the time of Henry VI's coronation expedition.[28] Henry's 'pusan' of gold, a collar of 'SS' with his badges of crowns and antelopes, had been surety in June for the London citizens for their loan of 10,000 marks.[29] His great gold and jewelled spice-plate adorned with eagles reappears among the limited number of the late

[25] TNA, E 101/45/22, m. 2 (indenture); TNA, E 101/47/20 (particulars of his account).
[26] Stratford, *Richard II*, R 38 and commentary, with citations.
[27] Ibid., R 38, R 39, R 909, R 911, R 912, R 913, R 917, R 970. This total is calculated from the valuations given in 1415, a considerable reduction on those in Richard's inventory.
[28] *Foedera*, IV (ii), 186, 12 July 1415; TNA, E 358/6, rot. 1 dorse; TNA, E 403/696, m. 5, 12 November and 16 November 1430; Palgrave, *Kals.*, II, 131–2, 136; Nicolas, *Agincourt*, Appendix III, pp. 15–16; Wylie and Waugh, *Henry the Fifth*, I, 470–1.
[29] *Memorials*, ed. Riley, p. 613.

king's valuables made available to his executors in 1423. This was one of two precious objects recovered from Richard, earl of Cambridge, after his implication in the Southampton Plot.[30] A second object pledged to Cambridge was a jewelled helmet known as the palet of Spain, which probably had a long history among the valuables of the crown. The palet was pawned to the immensely rich London draper, John Hende.[31]

By late July 1415 at Winchester there are indications that the procedures were more rushed and the pool of suitable objects greatly diminished. Sir Hugh Standish received on 21 July more than forty little objects, many of them damaged and incomplete, ranging from gold beads salvaged from two rosaries and a gold foot from a rock crystal cup to a compass of silver and silver-gilt, an astrolabe, a redundant signet, little silver rings to attach falcons, a fork for green ginger, collars of 'SS', belts and devotional tablets.[32] There are greater discrepancies between the estimated wages and the higher totals for the objects pledged at this late stage, perhaps indicative both of haste and a smaller pool to choose from.

How far was Henry personally implicated in the pledges and how far was his ability to appear in regal state even temporarily diminished? It is likely that on both counts this was only to a very limited extent. Some of the objects in pledge had belonged to Edward III and the Black Prince, to John of Gaunt, to Thomas of Woodstock, to Richard II and to Henry IV. Other vessels had belonged to Henry V himself as Prince of Wales. All these may have been considered out of date and have been relegated to store.[33] Others were certainly damaged, for example by the loss of jewels or the loss of a foot, and were therefore demonstrably not in current use. On the other hand several objects such as the cup and ewer pledged to Huntingdon, newly made by the king's goldsmith, suggest some sacrifice of pieces in actual use in the king's chamber. It is tempting but probably erroneous to regard a very valuable jewel embroidered tunic as a personal possession of Henry's, but this may have been an old garment belonging to one or another of his predecessors. It was pawned in three pieces between 10 and 20 July, the body to Sir Henry Percy for 250 marks, a sleeve each to two other captains for 200 marks.[34] And

---

30 TNA, E 101/45/22, m. 1, valued at £666 13s. 4d.; *PROME*, X, 113, no. 10.

31 Indenture ibid., valued at £166 13s. 4d.; TNA, E 403/675, m. 11, 26 July 1426; E 404/42/266. For the problematic identification of the palet of Spain, cf. Wylie and Waugh, *Henry the Fifth*, I, 471 and Pugh, *Southampton Plot*, pp. 125, 135, n. 6; see now Stratford, *Richard II*, pp. 298–9.

32 TNA, E 101/45/20, m. 28, valuables worth £48 3s. 4d. as security for £45 6s. 9½d.

33 As correctly stated by Wylie and Waugh, *Henry the Fifth*, I, 469, the sword pledged to Sir Thomas Hawley was said to have belonged to Edward, Prince of Wales, not the future Henry V (TNA, E 101/45/22, m. 20; E 358/6, rot. 10), cf. Barker, *Agincourt*, p. 118. TNA, E 101/46/14 includes some table plate with the arms of Henry V as Prince of Wales.

34 Sir Henry Percy, 10 July, TNA, E 101/45/22, m. 37; John Swillington, esq., 15 July, TNA, E 101/45/22, m. 18; Sir Ralph Staveley, 20 July, TNA, E 101/45/21, m. 24.

as for the king's magnificence on campaign, the author of the *Gesta Henrici Quinti* wrote of the king's own treasure seized with his baggage stolen at Maisoncelle. This no doubt included splendid vessels for the table and chapel as well as the crown, True Cross reliquary and state sword, which were, it seems, among the jewels eventually recovered. A list of plate lost from the pantry was printed by Rymer. A search of the final accounts of the officers of the other household departments might reveal more of the plate and other accoutrements taken, as was customary, by the king on campaign.[35]

In many instances the process of accounting with the captains is well documented, but it was complicated because the amounts laid down in the indentures had to be recalculated and this took a long time. The expedition had not lasted for the full second quarter, the numbers of soldiers serving had varied through absences, illness and death, and gains of war had to be factored in. Money had to be found if the jewels were to be redeemed, but the continuing war meant money was in short supply. The process was set in motion in November 1416 when the captains were ordered to account at the exchequer bringing the pledged jewels with them, but captains did not have the freedom promised in their indentures to dispose of the valuables when they had not been paid after nineteen months.

Far more may eventually have been recovered than is sometimes supposed. The concept of 'ancient jewels of the crown' had been invoked in the parliament of 1399 when Richard II was accused of removing crown jewels from the kingdom. This concept was again invoked in 1423 to bar the captains from disposing of certain Agincourt valuables, even if they had not been paid after six months had elapsed between midsummer, the terminal date set for bringing unredeemed valuables to the council, and the following December.[36] In 1427 Humphrey, duke of Gloucester, and Thomas, earl of Salisbury, still unpaid, jointly petitioned in parliament to keep the jewels which had been pledged to them in July 1415 in compensation for their wages of war. They were unsuccessful. Three more years were allowed for the crown to make repayment.[37] As late as 1437 creditors were still blocked from disposing of some unredeemed jewels for a further year. The twists and turns involved in the crown's attempts to recover the valuables pledged in 1415 continued into at least the 1440s.[38]

---

[35] *GHQ*, p. 84 and n. 2 with references; *Foedera*, IV (ii), 163.
[36] *SR*, II, 215, cited in translation, Curry, *Sources*, pp. 452–3.
[37] *PROME*, X, 332, citing TNA, E 175/3/25, pp. 334–7.
[38] General pardon, 27 March 1437, final clause, *PROME*, XI, 222. Stratford, *Richard II*, R 911, a cross given by the duke of Berry pledged to Lord Zouche for £258 (TNA, E 101/45/20. m. 35); in 1446, an attorney defended the Zouche heir in the exchequer court for the non-return of the cross, citing the pardon (TNA, E 159/222, communia Trinity 24 Henry VI, recorda, rot. 1).

The most spectacular of the objects pledged to the earl of Salisbury, a great silver-gilt alms dish in the shape of a ship, can be traced over nearly a century. The nef stood on lion feet, and was engraved with cufic or pseudo-cufic inscriptions. Two men-at-arms stood in the castles at the prow and stern and eight more in turrets along the sides. Pennons and banners displayed the royal and other arms. The nef had belonged to Edward III. It had been in pledge during Richard II's French wars, but had been returned by 1384, and may later have belonged to Thomas of Woodstock. Salisbury no doubt repaired the nef as a great showpiece for his table, because the declared weight increased during the years it was in his possession. In 1431, three years after Salisbury's death, it was returned by one of his executors. The nef was subsequently pledged to Cardinal Beaufort in 1437 and again in 1439, but it was recovered in 1441 and was still in the crown's possession in 1463.[39]

Although the minority council acted to safeguard crown jewels for Henry VI, the way was cleared for some captains who were owed money by the crown to acquire the objects which had been pledged to them. Sir Simon Felbrigg, whose handsome brass survives in Felbrigg church in Norfolk, did so. He had indented for a retinue of twelve men-at-arms and thirty-six archers. The crown owed him nearly £135. The valuables pledged to him were a gold image of St Edward which had been given to Richard II for New Year 1398 by Philip the Bold, duke of Burgundy, and a cup and two ewers of beryl mounted in gold. All these pieces were enriched with gems. They had been Felbrigg's guarantee for £170. Particulars of Felbrigg's account survive in the original pouch of white leather with the long handles used to suspend it in the exchequer. Of his twelve men-at-arms, two had died at Harfleur and six were ill and shipped back to England. He nevertheless had six men-at-arms with him at Agincourt besides thirty-six archers. He had mustered on 8 July at Southampton and accounted for 140 days service, the full official duration of the campaign, but declared no gains of war. In February 1425 the council conceded that these pledged objects should be revalued. This proved greatly to Felbrigg's advantage. Three leading London goldsmiths, John Palyng the younger, John Paddesley and John Wynne, came to the exchequer. Their very detailed valuation of the objects came out at less – by over £24. After several appearances in the exchequer court bringing writs with him, Felbrigg arranged to keep the objects and to pay the difference of nearly £11 between this amount and what the crown owed him.[40]

---

[39] Stratford, *Richard II*, pp. 314–16, commentary to R 571; Oxford, Bodley MS Eng. Hist. C. 775, f. 4; TNA, E 101/400/29; E 159/161, communia, Michaelmas 8 Richard II; E 101/45/21, m. 4. Palgrave, *Kals.*, II, 138–9, 165, no. 27, 185, no. 42, 243, no. 17; Harriss, *Cardinal Beaufort*, pp. 404–5, nos. 31, 40, with references.

[40] TNA, E 101/45/21, m. 25; E 101/45/23, m. 20, 18 June 1415; E 358/6, rot. 5 d.; E 101/45/3; E 368/197, communia, Hilary, m. 12.

The case history of the object documented in the Appendix illustrates what no doubt happened to many valuables during the campaign. It sheds considerable light on how the money to pay the soldiers was actually raised, as well as the accounting procedures and the process of recovering the valuables. This object, like the image of St Martin and the Tiger alms dish, can be traced back to Richard II's reign. It consisted of a jewelled gold cross standing on a gold foot and had been seized from Thomas of Woodstock during the forfeitures of 1397. The Crucifix figure was pinned to the cross with the feet crossed, in the manner typical of late Gothic goldsmiths' work. Three large diamonds represented the nails in the hands and feet of Christ, and a true oriental ruby, rather than the more common balas ruby, the wound in the side. Three smaller diamonds and six large pearls as well as fifty-eight clusters of small pearls ornamented the diadem. On the terminals, probably on the reverse, as on many surviving medieval crosses, were the four evangelists or their symbols. When the cross was listed among Richard II's chapel goods it had weighed 184 ounces Troy and including the gems was valued at £600. It was not among the valuables delivered by Edmund Lacy, the dean, on 1 June, and may have been in use in the chamber or have already have been in store at Westminster or elsewhere.

The cross was by far the most valuable item pledged on the 16 June 1415 to four men closely connected with Henry V's household: Sir Roger Leche, treasurer of the household, Sir Philip Leche, John Stanley and Robert Babthorp, who were then both esquires.[41] Perhaps the large gold foot of the cross was already missing (as it was in 1423), given the considerable drop in value from £600 to £460. Unlike many other captains, Babthorp, who by 1417 had been knighted and was controller of the household, was in a strong position to obtain a rapid settlement. To obtain his discharge he had to produce the cross. The story he told in the exchequer court on 17 May 1417 is instructive.[42] Before setting out for Southampton in 1415, Roger Leche, who had since died, had delivered it to the prominent London goldsmith and capitalist, Drew Barentyn, in a leather case sealed with the seals of all four indentees.[43] No doubt the cross was deposited in London to raise funds, not just for safekeeping. Barentyn had since died and the cross remained with his widow and executrix, Christina. Babthorp obtained a writ ordering her to produce the cross. It was brought to the exchequer the next day and examined by the barons in the presence of Babthorp. Two pearls from one of the clusters on the diadem were found to be missing. Babthorp asserted that Leche had kept these up to the time he died. The cross was handed over for safekeeping to the cofferer, William Kynwolmersh. The account cannot yet have been closed

---

41 Listed among valuables worth £510 15s. pledged as surety for £510 5d., the wages of thirty-six men-at arms and 108 archers.

42 TNA, E 159/193, communia Easter Term 5 Henry V, recorda, rot. 7d.

43 See L. E. M. Walker, 'Barantyn, Drew (c.1350–1415)', *ODNB*.

since the transfer was said to be on behalf of both Henry V and the indentees. After Henry's death, some of the valuables which had been pledged for
Agincourt and had been recovered were transferred to the king's executors
for sale to settle his debts – the valuables inventoried in 1423 on the rolls of
parliament. The cross was among them, but the missing pearls had not been
replaced. Two large pointed diamonds and another cluster of pearls had been
removed for Queen Catherine.

In these few examples of objects pledged, some of the most distinctive
pieces and some of the most valuable have been chosen. Whereas Clarence
had a crown valued at £6,000 and many of the greater captains other really
splendid objects, Nicholas Horton and other esquires of the household were
apportioned a broken cross and kitchen pots.[44] But however old and battered
the objects were, they were all of precious metal and they could be – and
occasionally were – sold for their bullion value.

Further study of the subsidiary records, especially the memoranda rolls,
may clarify to a greater extent the worth of the valuables pledged and the
ratio of those permanently alienated to those recovered by the crown –
relevant to our understanding of the crown's finances during the fifteenth
century. Jewel indentures and accounts have survived for only approximately
50 per cent of the noblemen and knights known to have served as captains
on the campaign. A lesser percentage of such records survive for the esquires,
or for the clerks and craftsmen accompanying the expedition, many of whom
received jewels and plate in pledge. The total value of the known jewels and
plate from these sources is over £25,500, but it would manifestly be wrong
simply to double this figure. Even so it appears that Henry was able to
provide from his treasure for the captains at least the equivalent of a full lay
subsidy of around £33,000 and very likely much more.

Some of the most recognizable pieces had been inherited from Henry's
predecessors, and some of the most imposing had been gifts from Charles VI
and the Valois princes. Others were part of the ordinary stock of the household or were newly made for the king. It is generally assumed that in addition to the sales of jewels to certain captains a great deal was lost, but this
may not have been so, at least during the early successful years of the war
in France to the siege of Orléans in 1429. During Henry V's reign and during
the minority of Henry VI sustained efforts were made to retrieve valuables.
Some were recovered during Henry V's lifetime, while renewed efforts were
made after 1422. By 1423 Henry V's executors had a few of the most magnificent at their disposal. Further recoveries are documented throughout Henry
VI's minority. In the parliament of 1427 when Gloucester and Salisbury petitioned to keep the king's valuables against the money still owing to them, the
jewels were safeguarded for three more years. As late as 1437 the crown was

---

44   TNA, E 101/46/11; E358/6, rot. 6.

assigned yet another year to redeem jewels and plate pledged in 1415. How far this policy was successful in the straightened financial climate of the 1430s and 1440s is uncertain. The incomplete and scattered exchequer sources for tracing the fate of Henry V's treasure document individual cases, but even if fully trawled, may never give a clear-cut answer. Very rich material nevertheless exists, revealing on the one hand more than has ever previously been known of Henry V's treasure, and on the other, the exceptional use he was prepared to make of it in pursuit of his ambitions in France.

APPENDIX

1. Inventory of Thomas of Woodstock's forfeited jewels and plate, 1397 (Stafford, Staffordshire Record Office, D 641/1/3/2, mm. 1–2, no. 9)

[*Marginated*] <Rem' en le Tres' a Westm'>
Un crois d'or large ove iiij evangelistes esteant sur j large pee d'or ove j ymage del crucifix ove j bon ruby [en la] costee du dicte crucifix ove iij grosses dyamandz en les mayns et pees dicell', et sur la dyademe iij meyndres dya[maundes] et vj grosses perles garnessez entour la dicte dyademe ove lviij troches de perles chescun troche de iij perles.

2. Inventory of Richard II's valuables, 1398 or 1399 (TNA, E 101/411/9, m. 33; Stratford, *Richard II*, p. 235)

R 990 Item, un crois large ove iiij ewangelistez esteant sur un large pee d'or ove j crucifix ove j bon rubie en le coste du dit crucifix ove iij grosses diamand' en les mains et pees d'icell', et sur la diademe iij meindres diamantez et vj grosses perlez garnisez entour la dicte diademe ove lviij trochez de perlez chescun troche de iij perlez, pois' xxiij marcz [184 oz. with the foot], et vault outre Cxl li., donnt la somme, DC li.

3. Indenture of Richard Courtenay, bishop of Norwich, treasurer of the chamber, with Sir Roger Leche, treasurer of the household, Sir Philip Leche, Sir John Stanley and Robert Babthorp, 16 June 1415 (TNA, E 101/45/22, m. 7)

Primerement un crois d'or que jadis fuist le duk de Gloucestr' ove un crucefix garniz d'un grand rubie en la playe iij gros diamaundes et iij autres diamaundes et de lviij troches chescun de iij perles et de vj autres perles, prec' de tout, iiij^{cc}lx li. [No weight given].

4. Enrolled account for the 1415 campaign, after 1422
(TNA, E 358/6, rot. 1)
Robert Babthorp et al.
The description and valuation tally with the indenture.

5. Discharge of Babthorp et al. 17 and 18 May 1417
(TNA, E 159/193, communia Easter Term 5 Henry V, recorda, rot. 7d.)

6. Henry V's inventory, 1423
(*PROME*, X, 118, 135, nos. 105, 530, 531)

105 Item, j crois d'or, qe jadis estoit a Thomas duke de Gloucestr', ovec j crucifix garniz en la plaie a coste d'un rubie pris CC li., en la mayn senestre d'un diamande poynte, pris xx li., en la diademe garniz de iij diamandes pris de toutz xx li. et vj perles pris vj li. et lvij troches par tout, chescun troche de iij perles, pris le troche xxxs., pois en tout x libres viij unces [128 oz.], pris l'unce xxiijs. iiijd; en tout, iiij^{cc}iiij^{xx} li. xvjs. viijd.

(*In custodia officiorum domine regine*)
530 Item, ij diamand' parteignent a le crois qe jadis fuist au Thomas, duk de Gloucestr', pris le pece, xx li.
531 Item, j troche de perle, qe partient audit crois, pris, xxxs.

7

Henry V and the Cheshire Tax Revolt of 1416[1]

Michael Bennett

After his triumphal return to England in November 1415, Henry V wasted no time resting on his laurels. He was eager to consolidate his achievements in France, most especially his capture of Harfleur, and to seek opportunities to build on them. His victory at Agincourt provided favourable circumstances for securing the necessary resources. The parliament of November 1415 brought forward the collection of the next instalment of the double subsidy granted in 1414. Early in 1416 he summoned another parliament to meet in March to enable him to secure the necessary resources for a further expedition. As Anne Curry has shown, the mobilization of men and resources in 1416 was on a scale comparable to the Agincourt campaign of 1415 and the expedition of 1417.[2] Though Henry was generally successful in winning support for the war in France, he rapidly became aware of the limits to the nation's capacity and readiness to underwrite his ambitions. All the parliament in March was prepared to concede was another acceleration in the payment of the subsidy already granted in November.[3] Earlier in the month, however, he had made a special effort to secure a subsidy from the palatinate of Chester. With its traditions of soldiering, the county had some investment in the prosecution of the war in France. As earl of Chester since 1399, Henry established close relations with leading knights and squires in Cheshire and in 1415 recruited some 700 Cheshire men for service in France.[4] Though the county notables acceded to the king's request for a grant of 3,000 marks in March 1416, the collection of

---

[1] I would like to acknowledge the encouragement and assistance of the editor, the anonymous readers and the other contributors, especially Professors Anne Curry and Mark Ormrod.

[2] Anne Curry, 'After Agincourt, What Next? Henry V and the Campaign of 1416', in *The Fifteenth Century VII: Conflicts, Consequences and the Crown in the Late Middle Ages*, ed. L. Clark (Woodbridge 2007), pp. 23–51 (at p. 41).

[3] Allmand, *Henry V*, p. 392.

[4] H. Nicolas, *History of the Battle of Agincourt, and of the Expedition of Henry the Fifth into France, in 1415*, 2nd edn (London, 1832), p. 385. It is not clear that this number was actually raised. See A. Curry, *Agincourt. A New History* (Stroud, 2005), pp. 76–7 and discussion below.

the first instalment provoked considerable resistance. By the end of the year the king found himself accepting the need to scale back his expectations.

The Cheshire tax revolt, if that is not too grand a title, was noted forty years ago but has not been examined in any detail.[5] The indictment rolls provide the only direct evidence of the unrest. Their testimony, though revelatory, is necessarily partial and incomplete.[6] Other records of the palatinate provide useful contextual information. Happily, too, there is extant a subsidy or mise book from this time. Previously assigned to 1405–6, it was actually drawn up in 1416 and annotated during the collection process.[7] Needless to say, the disturbances arose in the context of a set of social and institutional arrangements that were highly particular. The palatinate of Chester was administratively distinct from the rest of the kingdom. The county had a distinct political structure, shaped by its close relations to the king or his eldest son and its palatinate institutions. Politically and socially it was dominated by a clannish oligarchy of knightly and gentry families.[8] It had a reputation for lawlessness and political restiveness. There were 'loyalist' risings in Cheshire in 1387, 1393, 1400 and 1403.[9] Still, a study of the revolt in 1416 can perhaps provide some insight on the relations between crown and community in the

5   M. Bennett, 'Late Medieval Society in Northwest England' (unpublished Ph.D. thesis, University of Lancaster, 1975), pp. 107–8; A. Curry, 'The Demesne of the County Palatine of Chester in the Early Fifteenth Century' (unpublished MA thesis, University of Manchester, 1977), pp. 275–7; M. Bennett, *Community, Class and Careerism: Cheshire and Lancashire Society in the Age of* Sir Gawain and the Green Knight (Cambridge, 1983), pp. 51–2; I. M. W. Harvey, 'Was there Popular Politics in Fifteenth-Century England?' in *The McFarlane Legacy: Studies in Late Medieval Politics and Society*, ed. R. H. Britnell and A. J. Pollard (Stroud, 1995), pp. 155–74; T. Thornton, 'Taxing the King's Dominions: The Subject Territories of the English Crown in the Late Middle Ages', in *Crises, Revolutions and Self-Sustained Growth: Essays in European Fiscal History, 1130–1830*, ed. W. M. Ormrod, M. Bonney and R. Bonney (Stamford, 1999), pp. 97–109 (at p. 108).

6   TNA, CHES 25/11, mm. 9–11d. A section of the indictment has been transcribed, translated and published in *Records of Early English Drama: Cheshire, including Chester*, ed. E. Baldwin, L. M. Clopper and D. Mills, 2 vols. (London, 2007), I, 716–19, 966–9.

7   The John Rylands University Library [hereafter JRUL], Manchester, Tatton of Wythenshawe Muniments, TW/345. The dating of '1405' appears in pencil on the back cover of the book. The date is derived from the heading to the list of assessments in Eddisbury hundred which identifies it as the subsidy raised in the term of the Nativity St John the Baptist, 7 Henry IV (June 1406). Though all subsequent scholarship has attributed the codex to 1405–6, it is clear that the part relating to Eddisbury and Macclesfield hundreds is a relic. In the other five hundreds the names of the collectors are those of the men appointed in April 1416 and the information refers to the collection of the first instalment.

8   M. J. Bennett, 'A County Community: Social Cohesion amongst the Cheshire Gentry, 1400–1425', *Northern History* 8 (1973), 24–44.

9   J. G. Bellamy, 'The Northern Rebellions in the Later Years of Richard II', *BJRL* 47 (1965), 254–74; P. NcNiven, 'The Men of Cheshire and the Rebellion of 1403', *Transactions of the Historic Society of Lancashire and Cheshire* 129 (1980 for 1979), 1–29; P. Morgan, *War and Society in Medieval Cheshire, 1277–1403* (Manchester, 1987), chapter 5.

reign of Henry V, especially the practical political realities that the king faced
in his attempt to mobilize the resources of the realm. The evidence relating
to the disturbances in Cheshire is the more valuable in that it provides some
evidence of the political capacity of yeomen and other members of the lower
orders.

After celebrating Christmas 1415 at Eltham, Henry moved to the Tower of
London, signalling his determination to get back to business. On 21 January
writs were dispatched for elections for a parliament to meet on 16 March. Two
days later he sent letters to members of his retinue to come to Westminster to
discuss arrangements for a new expedition. According to a London chronicle,
he remained in the Tower until 26 February and then, on 28 February, 'rood
northewarde'.[10] Though J. H. Wylie noted this statement, he did not consider
the significance of the king's departure from the capital.[11] Given his priori-
ties at this time, a reasonable supposition would be that he was intending to
meet up with leading lords and knights in the midlands prior to parliament.
A detail in the Chester indictment rolls supports this surmise. It reports that
on Ash Wednesday, 'at his last coming towards Chester', Henry was granted
a subsidy of 3,000 marks by the leading men of the county. Implicitly, it attests
a specific event, a meeting on 4 March between the king and the unnamed
Cheshire magnates. The wording suggests that the king did not come all
the way to Chester. Perhaps he came no further north than Coventry, the
assembly-point for his allies and retainers, including Cheshire men, in June
1412.[12] Still, the phraseology suggests that he did most of the travelling. He
may have visited Hugh Stafford, Lord Bourchier, at Madeley in Staffordshire, close to the border with Cheshire. The supposition that Henry actually
entered Cheshire finds some support in the accounts of William Troutbeck,
chamberlain of Chester, a key player in organizing the subsidy. Though he
habitually claimed reimbursement for travel outside the county, he sought no
travel allowance for this time.[13] The likeliest place for a meeting in the county
was Nantwich. On the road between London and Chester, it was a place of
some concourse. In June 1415 the keeper of the bears of the duke of Bedford,
if not the king's brother himself, had had a memorable stay in the town.[14]

---

[10] BL Cotton MS Cleopatra C IV, fol. 28r. The date of departure is mistranscribed by
Kingsford as 27 February: *Chronicles of London*, ed. C. L. Kingsford (Oxford, 1905), p. 123.

[11] Wylie and Waugh, *Henry the Fifth*, II, 206n. The lack of documentation regarding Henry's
movements helps to explain the lack of an itinerary in Allmand, *Henry V*. An itinerary
is a feature of almost all the other medieval volumes in the Methuen/Yale English
Monarchs series.

[12] P. McNiven, 'Prince Henry and the English Political Crisis of 1412', *History* 65 (1980),
1–16 (at pp. 7–8).

[13] TNA, SC 6/776/3, m. 2d.

[14] A number of townsmen were indicted for an assault on 'Hugh the Berward, keeper of
the bears of the duke of Bedford': TNA, CHES 29/119, m. 12.

In riding northwards in late winter, Henry showed his readiness to sacrifice his own comfort in his drive to mobilize the resources of his kingdom. Though he may have conducted other useful business, he had his sights set on the palatinate of Chester. Lacking representation in parliament and exempt from the subsidies voted there, Cheshire had not as yet made a direct financial contribution to Henry V's war effort. Earlier kings and earls of Chester, of course, had not entirely neglected the resources of the palatinate. In the 1340s Edward III and Edward Prince of Wales raised large sums by reference to their feudal rights and by exploiting the profits of justice. In 1346 a subsidy was sought, seemingly to mark the knighting of the prince, and the tenants in chief 'freely' granted an aid of £1,000. During a visit to Chester in September 1353 the Black Prince met county notables in a quasi-parliamentary assembly. In return for confirming the palatinate's privileges and promising not to subject the county to a general eyre for thirty years, he received a common fine of 5,000 marks.[15] The levies or 'mises' required some justification, a process of negotiation and the semblance of consent. By this time a system was established by which each township paid a set sum to a mise of 1,000 marks, with the lord of the manor paying a set proportion of the township's assessment.[16] In the last quarter of the fourteenth century, however, Cheshire largely managed to avoid all taxation. It was explicitly acknowledged that it was exempt from the parliamentary lay subsidies. Richard II's cultivation of the palatinate as a power-base led him to be generous to Cheshire men. In 1389 the sheriff of Chester agreed, on behalf of the county community, to a mise of 3,000 marks, but for some reason it was never raised.[17] In 1398, in an even more remarkable move, Richard actually granted the men of Cheshire 3,000 marks as compensation for their losses in his service at the battle of Radcot Bridge. This sum was apportioned to the seven hundreds, seemingly in proportion to their contributions to the mise.[18] The Lancastrian revolution of 1399 brought a harsher regime. In 1401 a mise of 1,000 marks was raised in honour of the new earl of Chester, the future Henry V, and in 1403 a fine of 3,000 marks was imposed on Cheshire following its involvement in Hotspur's rebellion.[19] Traditions of consent to taxation were a relatively distant memory in Cheshire by 1416.

---

[15] P. Booth, *The Financial Administration of the Lordship and County of Chester, 1272–1377* (Manchester, 1981), pp. 118–22. For a list of grants of the Cheshire mise in the late Middle Ages and a discussion of the system, see Thornton, 'Taxing the King's Dominions', pp. 101–5.

[16] The earliest mise book, probably dating back to the reign of Edward III, is extant as TNA, CHES 38/25/2.

[17] Bennett, *Community, Class and Careerism*, pp. 219–22.

[18] TNA, CHES 2/70, m. 7d; CHES 2/73, m. 6; 'Calendar of Recognizance Rolls of the Palatinate of Chester', Part I in *Thirty-Sixth Report of the Deputy Keeper of Public Records* (1875), Appendix 2, p. 99.

[19] Morgan, *War and Society in Medieval Cheshire*, pp. 207–18.

Even if a meeting in Chester would have been more appropriate, Henry showed sensitivity in coming so far from the capital to treat with the leaders of the county community. There is no record of the names of the knights and gentlemen involved in the negotiation. It is not even clear whether Sir Gilbert Talbot, justiciar of Chester, was in the county at this time or involved in the process.[20] William Troutbeck, the chamberlain of Chester, was the king's chief agent in the business. He had been responsible for raising the county contingent for service in France in 1415 and was asked to clarify the king's will in relation to the tax in autumn 1416.[21] Another key figure was perhaps Sir John Stanley, the son and namesake of the knight who had served as steward of the household to Henry as Prince of Wales and brokered the settlement in Cheshire after the rebellion of 1403. Recently knighted, he was soon to emerge as the most powerful magnate in the north-west.[22] His presence in the king's entourage at this time is suggested by the reward on 24 March for his 'labour and trouble' in discovering the king's right to the wardship of the manor of Withington, Lancashire.[23] Though organized in haste, the meeting was presumably well attended. Four years earlier no fewer than sixty-three knights and squires from all parts of Cheshire had met in Macclesfield to witness the settlement of a dispute between Sir Thomas Grosvenor and Robert Legh of Adlington.[24] It can be assumed that John Legh of Booths, the sheriff of Cheshire, and most of the knights and gentlemen who were subsequently appointed as collectors of the mise, were in attendance.

The men who were involved in the grant and collection of the mise included a significant number who had served in France. It is not clear whether William Troutbeck, the leader of the county contingent, actually crossed the Channel. It may be that he only led them as far as Southampton. It is not entirely certain that Sir John Stanley, who appears as a knight for the first time in 1416, can be identified with the squire of this name on the Agincourt campaign. There can be little doubt, however, that there was significant mobilization in Cheshire. The chamberlain was required to raise fifty men-at-arms and 650 archers in the palatinate. In 1416 his accounts record the payment of wages in respect of twenty men-at-arms and 252 archers who had served at Harf-

---

[20] Sir Gilbert Talbot, justiciar of Chester, had wider interests and responsibilities, especially in the lordship of Ireland.

[21] Nicolas, *Battle of Agincourt*, p. 385; TNA, CHES 25/11, m. 10.

[22] Bennett, *Community, Class and Careerism*, pp. 215–23.

[23] Sir Nicholas Longford, who as sheriff of Lancaster had led a contingent of Lancashire archers at Agincourt, had died shortly after his return seised of the manor of Withington, which he held of the king as duke of Lancaster, a point that had been concealed by his heirs: J. Booker, *A History of the Ancient Chapels of Didsbury and Chorlton, in Manchester Parish* (Manchester, 1857), pp. 110–11.

[24] Bennett, 'A County Community', esp. pp. 25–7, 43–4.

leur and Agincourt.[25] The names of the local captains, in whose company the men served, constitute the bulk of the information available regarding the service of Cheshire knights and squires in France in 1415. It is telling, then, that they show that no fewer than seven of the collectors of the mise, namely Sir John Savage, Sir Ralph Bostock, John Honford, John Manley, John Kingsley and John Pigot, had been the king's comrades in arms the previous year. There is some reason to believe, moreover, that the payments do not adequately reflect the scale of Cheshire's participation.[26] Specifically authorized by the king in December 1415, they have something of the character of payments left outstanding.[27] Since the county contingent had obviously been broken into smaller units at some stage, it is probable that the Cheshire men had been reassigned not only to local captains but also to a range of retinue-leaders who needed to make up shortfalls in their companies. For the king and the chamberlain there would have been advantage in this arrangement. In addition, some retinue-leaders would have recruited independently in Cheshire, making the county's contribution potentially larger than the 700 men proposed for the county contingent.

There were clearly more Cheshire knights and squires who served in France in 1415 than appear in the records of the time.[28] An especially intriguing case is John Bromley of Baddington, who played an active role in collecting the mise in 1416. According to family tradition, he distinguished himself by recovering the standard of Guienne after its loss by Hugh Stafford, Lord Bourchier, in a skirmish near Corbie, shortly before Agincourt.[29] The action is documented in a charter of March 1417, transcribed in Holinshed's *Chronicles*, in which Bourchier granted Bromley, his kinsman, an annuity of £40 as a reward for this signal service.[30] As Anne Curry has shown, the role of the two men in this engagement finds no support in other records: since the king had left Bourchier in command at Harfleur, it seems unlikely that he was at Corbie.[31] Still, the charter should not be dismissed too summarily as a forgery.

[25] TNA, SC 6/776/4, mm. 4–4d; Curry, *Agincourt: A New History*, pp. 76–7, where she gives the total as 247.

[26] In October 1415 over thirty Cheshire men, including several squires, were indicted for desertion from Portsmouth and Harfleur: TNA, CHES 25/11, m. 5d.

[27] TNA, SC 6/776/4, m. 4d.

[28] The search for service records of Cheshire men in 1415 has been greatly facilitated by the AHRC Project on 'The Soldier in Later Medieval England' and its database at http://www.icmacentre.ac.uk/soldier/database/search.php

[29] There was a military engagement near Corbie on 17 October during which a powerful French sortie from the town was driven back by English archers. According to Curry, it was 'recorded only in English chronicles, suggesting that it was regarded as a moment of success worthy of record': Curry, *Agincourt: A New History*, p. 129.

[30] R Holinshed, *Chronicles of England, Scotland, and Ireland*, ed. H. Ellis, 6 vols. (London, 1808), III, 75–6. I. Bromley, *Bromley: A Midlands Family History and the Search for the Leicestershire Origins* (Leicester, 2007), p. 40, mistakenly gives the date March 1416.

[31] Curry, *Agincourt: A New History*, p. 140.

It does not stand alone: it appears among other Bromley muniments transcribed in the late sixteenth or early seventeenth century.[32] There are many details that make it creditworthy. Lord Bourchier, who died without issue in 1420, was scarcely a household name in Tudor times. The charter is dated at Madeley, Staffordshire, with which Bourchier was only briefly associated. John Bromley, who was knighted in France later in 1417 and died in harness in 1419, is correctly described as a squire. If Bromley's feat of arms at Corbie cannot be credited, the most likely explanation is that an authentic grant of an annuity had been glossed. Even in this scenario, however, the likelihood is that Bromley had served in France in 1415. His appointment as a collector of the mise in 1416 is his first and only appearance in country administration. The generosity of Bourchier's grant, at a time when he was seeking men for service in France, suggests that he valued Bromley's military credentials. It is clear from other sources that Bromley was a dedicated soldier. He was knighted in 1417 and was subsequently appointed captain of Domfront.[33] His receipt of a handsome annuity from Bourchier helps explain his own generosity in the grant of annuity to a Cheshire squire in 1418. Bromley's military service cost him his wife, who during his absence eloped with a neighbour, and his life, after being severely wounded at Caudebec in 1419.[34]

Henry chose his moment well. Ash Wednesday, the first day of Lent, was a time for sacrifice and belt-tightening. The terms of the subsidy were announced with the appointment of the tax collectors on 5 April. It referred to a grant freely made, with the assent of all, by the prelates, magnates and *proceres*, that is, the leading gentry, on behalf of the county community. The sum was to be paid in three instalments, the first on the feast of the Invention of the Holy Cross, that is 3 May, the second on the feast of St Martin's in Winter, that is 10 November 1416, and the third on the feast of the Nativity of St John the Baptist following, that is 24 June 1417.[35] The men appointed as collectors in the seven hundreds were prominent members of landed society, including eight knights. They were required to collect the sums of money specified for the townships in an appended list. The mise book in the John Rylands University Library is based on this template. The bulk of the codex relates to the subsidy of 1416, with the lists of townships in five of the seven hundreds appearing under the names of the newly appointed collectors. The last two folios, listing the sums collected in the hundreds of Wirral and Eddis-

---

[32] Bodleian Library, Oxford, MS Ashmole 804, p. 4.

[33] Bodleian Library, Oxford, MS Ashmole 804, p. 6.

[34] 'Calendar of Deeds, Inquisitions, and Writs, enrolled on the Plea Rolls of the County of Chester – Ric. 2 to Hen. 7', in *Twenty-Ninth Report of the Deputy Keeper of Public Records* (1869), Appendix 6, p. 75; Bromley, *Bromley*, p. 41.

[35] TNA, CHES 2/89, m. 6.

bury, however, seem not to have been updated and relate to the collection of
1407.[36]

The collection should have proceeded in an orderly fashion. In his capacity
as earl of Chester, Henry was well known, well respected and probably well
liked in the palatinate. His success in France can only have added to his
prestige in a county community more martially inclined than most. Unlike
England as a whole, which had granted a double subsidy to fund the expedition of 1415, the palatinate had not hitherto made a direct financial contribution to the war effort. Mark Ormrod has drawn attention to the production
of a book detailing the tax contributions of townships across the kingdom
that may have been designed to inculcate local pride in making possible the
English triumph in arms.[37] The men of Cheshire, of course, could claim to
have made a disproportionately large contribution in kind. This consideration, though, added some urgency and edge to the process of collection.
Henry had not paid all the wages of his soldiers. One of the first calls on the
levy of 1416 was the payment of outstanding wages to 272 Cheshire men
for their service at Harfleur and Agincourt.[38] It seems most unlikely that the
collection began on schedule. If some lords paid their share of the assessment
promptly in May, many of them assuredly did not. Few townships seem to
have paid their contributions in a timely manner.

In July some of the knights and squires appointed as tax collectors took
steps to raise the outstanding dues. On Monday, 6 July Sir William Brereton,
a collector in Northwich hundred, came to Sandbach, in the heart of Cheshire.
Unable to secure the township's substantial contribution of £3 10*d.*, he seized
animals by way of distraint. A group of husbandmen and servants from the
township forcefully took them back. Within a fortnight the men of Sandbach,
however, made amends by paying their tax in full.[39] In the north of Cheshire,
the commissioners making a circuit of the townships of Bucklow hundred
seem to have found it even harder to exert their authority. On 16 July Sir
George Carrington met with armed resistance at Baguley, led by the village
constables, and at Timperley, led by John Chadderton, described as *armiger*,
and possibly a former soldier.[40] In early August three other commissioners,
namely Sir Peter Dutton, Richard Warburton and William Danyell, were likewise frustrated in their attempts to distrain cattle by the men of Runcorn and
other townships in the lordship of Halton, an estate of the duchy of Lancaster.
Later in the month Thomas Mascy of Tatton, a colleague in the Bucklow
commission, had a similar experience in Knutsford, Tatton and other town-

---

[36] The John Rylands University Library, Manchester, Tatton of Wythenshawe Muniments,
TW/345.
[37] W. M Ormrod, 'Henry V and the English Taxpayer', p. 215 in this volume.
[38] TNA, SC 6/776/4, mm. 4–4d.
[39] TNA, PRO, CHES 25/11, mm. 9–9d.
[40] TNA, PRO, CHES 25/11, m. 11d.

ships that might have been expected to show deference to the head of the house of Mascy of Tatton.[41]

By this time there were disturbances in south Cheshire. An early flash-point was Tiverton, half way between Chester and Nantwich. On 1 August Henry Spurstow, a collector in the hundred of Eddisbury, took two oxen to the value of 22*s.* 4*d.* A group of husbandmen from Tiverton promptly took them back. Spurstow had a similar experience in the neighbouring town-ship of Beeston.[42] In the hundred of Broxton, in the south-west, matters were likewise getting out of hand. Richard Cholmondeley, who in his prime had been one of the captains of Richard II's bodyguard, met with a humiliating rebuff near his own seat at Cholmondeley. In response to his distraint of cattle in Tushingham and Bickley, some men from Tushingham made hue and cry and blew horns. After gathering a large force in the neighbourhood they pursued the former royal favourite as far as Hatton Heath.[43] On 4 September, when Cholmondeley's colleagues rounded up six oxen and eight cows from three other villages and drove them to Malpas, a disgruntled husbandman hurried to the parish church and rang the bell to gather a crowd to disrupt the tax collection. The dissidents, including Menrick the Welshman, keeper of the mill at Edge, and several other men of Welsh background, drove away the collectors and rescued the cattle.[44] Ten days later there was trouble for Roger Bruyn, subsequently knighted in France, at Barrow, a manor of Sir John Savage, a retinue-leader at Agincourt.[45] There were disturbances at this time, too, in the hundred of Nantwich. John Bromley, who reputedly put the French to flight at Corbie, experienced stiff opposition at Audlem, though he seems to have been able to secure payment a few days later. A week later the resistance in Wybunbury proved more stubborn. Thomas Keffes of Hough, yeoman, and men from neighbouring villages in the parish threatened the collectors with violence and rang the church bell to call for reinforcements. On 16 September, when Bromley sent his brother to collect the tax in Nant-wich, a crowd gathered, allegedly armed with swords and staves, and the church bell was rung to call out other townsmen, successfully preventing any levy or distraint of animals.[46]

In the middle of October the unrest became more general. In the north-east corner of Cheshire there was open defiance of the tax collectors. On 14 October, Sir John Savage and Sir Lawrence Fitton, collectors in the hundred

---

[41] TNA, PRO, CHES 25/11, m. 10d.

[42] TNA, PRO, CHES 25/11, m. 9.

[43] TNA, PRO, CHES 25/11, m. 9d.

[44] TNA, CHES 25/11, m. 9d. For the large number of men of Welsh background in Tushingham and Cholmondeley, see P. Morgan, 'Cheshire and Wales', in *Power and Identity in the Middle Ages: Essays in Memory of Rees Davies*, ed. H. Pryce and J. Watts (Oxford, 2007), pp. 195–210 (pp. 204–5).

[45] TNA, CHES 25/11, m. 9.

[46] TNA, CHES 25/11, m. 10.

of Macclesfield, were challenged by a large body of men armed with swords, staves and bows and arrows. The indictment names forty-six of them, all identified as yeomen from sixteen townships, including Northenden, Staveley, Hollingworth, Stockport, Hyde, Romiley, Marple, Bredbury, Bramhall and Poynton.[47] In the meantime matters were getting out of hand in the hundred of Nantwich. The arrest of Roger Pollard, a smith, in Nantwich led a comrade to hasten to Wybunbury for support. On 20 October Thomas Keffes, who had played a leading role in the disturbances in Wybunbury in September, came with a band of followers to Nantwich, rang the church bells and gathered an angry crowd to release Pollard from prison. In a confrontation with the collectors of the mise, they wounded one of them, John Wettenhall, deputy-sheriff of Chester, with bowshot. The insurgents then withdrew to Wybunbury and over the next day gathered support from neighbouring parishes.[48] On 22 October Keffes led some 300 men into the hundred of Broxton, found supporters in and around Malpas, and set about preparing to make a stand in *montes de Broxon*, the Broxton Hills.[49] It is not clear how events played out. However, soon afterwards Thomas Keffes was taken prisoner and his comrades were seeking to negotiate a settlement with the chamberlain of Chester.

It is evident that there was resistance to the collection of the mise in many parts of Cheshire in 1416. Though only a minor revolt, there was some escalation in the range, scale and organization of the opposition. In the early episodes the resistance took a somewhat ritualized and indirect form. The collectors, clearly failing to secure compliance, distrained the animals of the village. Groups of men gathered to rescue them, calling on their neighbours by making hue and cry, blowing horns and ringing church bells. The pattern was repeated in village after village, suggesting a degree of planning and coordination. The unrest was surprisingly widespread. There were documented disturbances in six out of seven hundreds. Furthermore, it is unlikely that the indictment rolls include all the acts of evasion and defiance. Though the tax collectors were leaders of county society, including knights and squires who had recently served in France, they seem not to have been keen to force the matter. They may have shared some of the concerns about the subsidy and the liberties of the palatinate. In some cases, at least, they were able to secure payment when tempers cooled. By October, however, the

---

47   TNA, CHES 25/11, m. 9d.

48   TNA, CHES 25/11, m. 10.

49   Around ten miles south of Chester, the Broxton Hills mark the south-eastern boundary of the Cheshire Plain. Emerging from woodland cover they have commanding views of the surrounding countryside. In 1656 Daniel King referred to them as 'those mountains, called the Broxton Hills ... the antient [sic] breeding place of a great family in this county, the Dodds': D. King, *The Vale Royal of England, or, The County Palatine of Chester Illustrated*, ed. T. Hughes (London, 1852), p. 52.

situation was becoming serious. The likelihood is that a large proportion of the townships had still not paid the sums that had supposedly been due in June. The armed standoff in the hundred of Macclesfield and the violence and insurrection in the hundreds of Nantwich and Broxton required sterner measures. Henry V, who was by this stage seeking supply from a new parliament for an expedition in the New Year, cannot have been impressed by reports from the palatinate. A decision was taken to lay before the county court in January 1417 a series of indictments relating to the disturbances. The leaders of Cheshire society attended this session in force. Most of the leading tax commissions served in the juries of presentment. Rather remarkably, the first named members of the juries in the hundreds of Broxton and Macclesfield were Sir John Osbaldeston and Sir John Keighley, who were not Cheshire men at all. They were successful career soldiers from Lancashire, both recently knighted, Osbaldeston in Picardy.[50] Their presence suggested that the authorities meant business.

The disturbances in 1416 reflect social division as much as local solidarity. The contributions set down for the townships, which varied quite markedly, may never have been equitable. A distinctive feature of the mise was that for each township the lord was required to pay a share, usually a quarter or a third. It might be assumed that this sum was paid separately and, especially in 1416, more promptly. Annotations in the mise book do attest, in respect of a few townships, discrete payments corresponding to the shares of the lords and communities. The indictments, however, often contain details of the amounts demanded by the commissioners and clearly show, in all cases where they include the information, that the collectors were seeking to raise the full amounts, inclusive of the lord's share. The collectors in the hundred of Bucklow, for example, sought 40s. in Knutsford, 66s. 8d. in Audlem, 23s. 4d. in Tatton and 28s. in Rostherne, the exact sums specified in the mise book.[51] The inequity of the process is especially apparent at Tatton, where the lord of the manor was assessed to pay a third. The man responsible for the collection was none other than Thomas Mascy, the lord of Tatton. Mascy had not only failed to pay his own share but was making it a general charge on the village. In regard to apportioning the tax within the community, it can perhaps be fairly assumed, by analogy with practice elsewhere in England, that the more substantial householders shouldered the main burden. Some of the men involved in the early disturbances, however, were husbandmen and servants who cannot be supposed to have been the major taxpayers. The explanation may be that the township's failure to pay the assessment led the collectors to distrain animals on the common land, some of which belonged to

---

[50] The knighting of Sir John Osbaldeston at Pont-Sainte-Maxence is recorded in a chronicle compiled for Sir John Fastolf: Curry, *Agincourt: Sources and Interpretations*, p. 88; *The Victoria History of the County of Lancaster* (1911), VI, 319–25.

[51] TNA, CHES 25/11, m. 10d.

smallholders. More generally, however, men of more substance led the oppo-sition. In Bucklow hundred, for example, most the men retrieving animals were described as *valetti* or yeomen. In the disturbances in October yeomen were even more to the fore. In Macclesfield hundred, yeomen from a dozen villages gathered together in arms to drive away the tax collectors before they had a chance to impound animals. In south Cheshire Thomas Keffes of Hough, yeoman, emerged as a leader and briefly defied the authorities, with some 300 men, in the 'mountains' of Broxton.[52]

Furthermore, there were issues relating to the nature of the taxation. The official line, as spelled out in the indictment, was that the levy was a subsidy made *per tam majores quam minores totius comitatus Cestrie*, that is, by both the greater and lesser men of the entire county community.[53] The state-ment acknowledged the principle, well established in England, that taxation required consent. The problem was that many people, most especially the yeomanry, who were required to contribute to the subsidy felt that they had not been party to the agreement. Such a sentiment did not necessarily imply any expectation to be directly consulted or indeed any notion that consent could be withheld. In the English parliament the convention was that elected members would consider the king's case for a subsidy and, after discussion and perhaps negotiation, agree to it on behalf of their communities. Even at the national level, as Ormrod has observed, the legal fiction persisted that the subsidies had actually been granted in the county courts, notionally at the sessions in which the business of parliament had been announced and knights of the shire elected.[54] Though the county notables presumably settled most important matters behind closed doors, it cannot be assumed that the yeomen and others were mere ciphers. They had some opportunity to inform themselves about public affairs and make their concerns known. In the palati-nate of Chester, perhaps even more than elsewhere in England, the county court assumed some of the character of a parliamentary assembly. In practice, of course, the mise of Chester had been more often imposed as a fine than granted as a subsidy. The men of Cheshire would have been especially sensi-tive on this point. In 1416 they had to take on trust the nature of the king's request and the terms of the grant made. The men of the hundred of Maccles-field firmly believed that the tax should not have been levied on them as it

---

[52] It would be interesting to know more about Thomas Keffes and his fate. The surname is very unusual and seemingly unique to Cheshire. His name cannot be found in 'The Soldier in Later Medieval England' database. There were others of that name in the area in the late fifteenth century, including Nicholas Keffes and Richard Keffes, rector of Barthomley: D. J. Clayton, *The Administration of the County Palatine of Chester, 1442–1485* (Manchester, 1990), p. 260; E. Hinchcliffe, *Barthomley in Letters from a Former Rector to his Eldest Son* (London, 1856), p. 350.

[53] TNA, CHES 25/11, m. 9d.

[54] Ormrod, 'Henry V and the English Taxpayer', p. 192 in this volume.

had not been granted with the assent of the *entire* county community.[55] There may have been some suspicion that the king had requested financial support from the county notables but had not sought a general subsidy.[56]

The flow of events over the summer may have added to uncertainty about the justification for the mise. In March the king was planning a further expedition to France.[57] A fortnight after his meeting with the Cheshire men, he sought from parliament the means 'for the due and appropriate continuation' of the war, 'so honourably begun'. He obtained no more than an agreement to bring forward to May the collection of a subsidy that was scheduled for November. By April, however, Henry had lost the initiative to the French, and the Emperor Sigismund's arrival in England on a peace mission made a truce likely.[58] This easing of pressure may have inclined the collectors in Cheshire to delay the collection. Though Henry was assembling troops in Southampton to reinforce Harfleur, including levies from Cheshire, there was no real urgency until the middle of July when intelligence arrived that the French had broken off negotiations and were bent on recapturing the town.[59] Even then, the king settled for a naval expedition under his brother, the duke of Bedford. Setting out in early August, the expedition won an important victory in the mouth of the Seine.[60] By this stage, it was all too clear that there would be no royal expedition until 1417. In October the king was able to secure from parliament a double subsidy for a major campaign in the New Year. The alarms and excursions of summer and autumn perhaps explain the somewhat fitful attempts to raise the subsidy in Cheshire. The chamberlain of Chester was in London from late April to early June, in Southampton for three weeks in July and then in Westminster for a month around October.[61] The insurgents consistently sought clarification of the king's will and, ultimately, a meeting with the chamberlain. It may well be that they were being deliberately obtuse, but there were grounds for genuine uncertainty and confusion in respect of the original grant and the king's specific demands.

The events of 1416 show that Cheshire politics were not exclusively the concern of the magnates and the gentry elite. The importance of the middling ranks of rural society in national life is increasingly well recognized. The more substantial freeholders, the yeomanry, bore a lot of the weight of taxation. They also played vital roles in local administration and law enforcement. As I. M. W. Harvey has argued, they were becoming more and more

---

[55] ... *summa predicta super eos fieri et levari non deberet eo quod summa illa ex assensu totius communitatis comitatus predicti concessa non fuit*: TNA, CHES 25/11, m. 9d.

[56] TNA, CHES 25/11, m. 9d.

[57] For the king's plans in spring 1416, see Curry, 'After Agincourt', pp. 30–2.

[58] Ibid., pp. 32–5.

[59] Wylie and Waugh, *Reign of Henry the Fifth*, III, 16–18.

[60] Curry, 'After Agincourt', pp. 35–40.

[61] TNA, SC 6/776/3, m. 2d.

sure of themselves in their dealings with their social betters and indeed with the crown in the fifteenth century.[62] The raising of taxes, of course, was often the catalyst for action. There is nothing especially unusual about stalling over taxation and in recovering cattle distrained by the collectors. Still, the impression is that the disturbances in Cheshire in 1416 involved a broader and better informed intransigence: a general tax strike, in the face of which county notables had to withdraw. There was a measure of coordination within and between parishes and hundreds. The men in one village reportedly dispatched one of their number to the nearest parish church to ring the bell to summon men from neighbouring villages; men from different villages and parishes acted together to thwart the tax collectors; resistance to the tax collection in one hundred seems to have inspired similar action elsewhere. It is as well to remember that, in addition to being taxpayers and local officials, many of the yeomen and husbandmen presumably had military experience. It is probable that as many as 800 Cheshire men served in France in 1415, perhaps as many as one in twenty of the adult male population.[63] The groups of men who faced down the gentry in Longdendale on the edge of the Pennines or in the 'mountains' of Broxton almost certainly included archers who had held their ground, less than a year earlier, against the French cavalry at Agincourt.

The indictments themselves document only some of the acts of resistance and certainly do not provide a full account of the concerns at play. They do reveal, however, elements of political consciousness. Especially interesting is the degree to which they show some familiarity with ideas of representation and consent. Anthony Pollard has recently argued the need to take seriously the degree to which the broader community felt involved in parliamentary politics, pointing to their role in the election process and their familiarity with the processes of petitioning.[64] The fact that the yeomen of Cheshire, who lacked the experience of electing knights of the shire to serve in the national parliament and were less directly concerned with its business, showed a lively awareness of ideas of representation and consent, is some testimony to the broad diffusion of such notions. There is other evidence of political consciousness. The men who resisted the taxation had some capacity for organization. They may have set forward their demands in writing. The men in south Cheshire who had gathered under the leadership of Thomas Keffes set forward three articles for negotiation with William Troutbeck, chamberlain

---

[62] Harvey, 'Was there Popular Politics in Fifteenth-Century England?'

[63] J. C. Russell estimated the total population of Cheshire in 1377 at around 24,000. A total of around 48,000 would make more sense: Bennett, *Community, Class and Careerism*, pp. 53–60. Even this larger figure would translate only to around 16,000 adult males.

[64] A. J. Pollard, 'The People and Parliament in Fifteenth-Century England', in *The Fifteenth Century X: Parliament, Personalities and Power: Papers Presented to Linda S. Clark*, ed. H. Kleineke (Woodbridge, 2011), pp. 1–16.

of Chester. The first article was that no further collection was to take place until the king's will was made known. The second and third articles were that no action should be taken against the rebels and that Thomas Keffes, in prison in Chester castle, should be released.[65]

From the archival traces, it is not clear how the story ended. There was obviously significant delay in raising the first instalment. The impression is that a large number of townships still had not paid their contributions to the mise by autumn. The indictments themselves presumably served to add to the pressure. The annotations to the mise book suggest that the final payments in Bucklow hundred were not made until March 1417. The men of the township of Preston had defied the commissioners in early August 1416. It was not until 1 March in the following year that Sir Peter Dutton put his initials to attest Preston's payment of the tax.[66] At some stage, presumably over the winter of 1416–17, there was some rescheduling of the further instalments. A second instalment of 1,000 marks had originally been scheduled for November and the third and final instalment of 1,000 marks for June 1417. It seems to have been accepted that, given the difficulties and delays with the first instalment, no more than an additional half instalment of 500 marks could be raised in time for the king's expedition. The collection of the other half of the subsidy of 3,000 marks was postponed until 1418. On the national stage Henry V had adopted the device of seeking to accelerate the collection of subsidies, at least until parliament made clear its dissatisfaction with this approach.[67] In Cheshire, however, the king appears to have so far conceded the point as to allow deceleration. The palatinate of Chester was certainly treated relatively leniently, especially when it is borne in mind that the funds raised went directly to cover the wages of the soldiers recruited in the county.[68] The success of its resistance in 1416 probably served to inspire Cheshire's stubborn defence of its rights in later decades.[69]

The tax revolt in 1416 offers rare insight into plebeian politics in the small towns and villages of Cheshire. The indictments, though brief and formulaic, show some degree of independence and agency among yeomen and men of lesser rank. They also suggest a capacity for political action and thinking that was more complex and subtle than might be imagined. Especially striking is the availability to men who were outside the national parliamentary system of the language of representation and consent. The impression, too,

---

[65] TNA, PRO, CHES 25/11, m. 10.

[66] JRUL, Tatton of Wythenshawe Muniments, TW/345.

[67] Allmand, *Henry V*, p. 392.

[68] The second instalment was assigned to Sir John Savage and his company for the defence of Calais: Curry, 'The Demesne of the County Palatine of Chester', pp. 268, 279, citing TNA, SC 6/1303/2, m. 2d.

[69] For assertions by the county community in the 1430s and 1440s of its right to be consulted and negotiate in respect to taxation, see Thornton, 'Taxing the King's Dominions', pp. 101–4.

is that they acted with some knowledge of national affairs. A point to bear in mind, of course, is that many of the insurgents may have seen service with Henry, both before and after he became king. Mobilization for war involved the politicization of broad sections of the population. In May 1416 the king sought a levy of 400 men in Cheshire, and in June and July William Troutbeck led companies of local men to Southampton for service in France.[70] Cheshire was presumably awash with reports and rumours about the king's plans, his financial needs and the politics of taxation. Equally, of course, the events throw some light on Henry and his relations with his subjects. His setting out from London to meet with Cheshire notables on 4 March, a bare ten days before the opening of parliament in Westminster, underlines his energy and commitment to the tasks of kingship. It shows some respect for the knights and squires who had served under him in France and the privileges of the palatinate. The episode, too, attests his political realism, his preparedness to acknowledge the burdens he was imposing and to moderate his demands. The king's pardon of a man who had killed a collector in a confrontation over tax in Lancashire in 1417 suggests that he might have been merciful to Keffes and his cohorts.[71] He needed men of their sort in France. In 1417, as in 1415, he was looking to Cheshire more for manpower than money.

---

[70] Curry, 'After Agincourt?', pp. 36–7.
[71] Ormrod, 'Henry V and the English Taxpayer', p. 202 in this volume.

8

Henry V and the English Taxpayer

W. Mark Ormrod

Henry V's reputation as manager of the crown's resources stands higher in the current generation of historians than perhaps ever before, and the king's strengths in this area are now routinely regarded as an essential element, alongside the more sensational achievements in war, of the second Lancastrian king's claims to greatness. A strong tradition of scholarship from Ramsay and Steele to McFarlane and Harriss has engaged in detail with two aspects of Henry's gift for finance: his management of parliaments and convocations to effect one of the most intense bouts of taxation experienced in England over the course of the Hundred Years War; and his equally impressive control of the expenditure of those taxes, which ensured, almost uniquely in the Middle Ages, a successful balance between income and expenditure.[1] But a good deal less attention has been given to two other important aspects of the tax history of Henry's reign. How was taxation experienced on the ground by the tens of thousands of ordinary taxpayers who were called upon regularly to open their purses? And how sustainable was the tax system on which Henry built his conquest of Normandy and his ambitions for the settlement of France? By addressing the fiscal history of Henry's reign from the perspective of the taxpayer, we may usefully test the current powerful orthodoxy about the functionality of the Lancastrian fiscal state.

Over the course of his reign of nine and a half years, Henry V was granted a total of ten and one-third parliamentary subsidies of fifteenths and tenths, eight of which were collected in the period of most intensive military action between November 1414 and November 1419.[2] The convocation of Canter-

---

[1] J. H. Ramsay, *A History of the Revenues of the Kings of England*, 2 vols. (Oxford, 1925); A. Steel, *The Receipt of the Exchequer, 1377–1485* (Cambridge, 1954); K. B. McFarlane, *Lancastrian Kings and Lollard Knights* (Oxford, 1972); G. L. Harriss, 'The Management of Parliament' and 'Financial Policy', in *Henry V*, ed. Harriss, pp. 137–58, 159–79; Harriss, *Cardinal Beaufort*. I am very grateful to Alex Brayson for stimulating discussion about fiscal theory and practice in the fifteenth century, which has helped profoundly to illuminate this study.

[2] M. Jurkowski, C. L. Smith and D. Crook, *Lay Taxes in England and Wales, 1188–1688* (Kew, 1998), pp. 79–84.

bury granted ten and a half tenths, and that of York seven and a half; the most significant burden was borne between November 1414 and May 1420, when six and a half tenths fell due for collection in the southern province and five and a half in the northern. (The final moiety of the last tenth granted by the province of York fell due only after Henry's death.) Following precedents established under Henry IV, the two convocations also granted several subsidies on benefices normally exempt from taxation (four and a half tenths in Canterbury province, and one in York) and one poll tax on non-beneficed clergy (in Canterbury province in 1419).[3] The principal indirect tax controlled by parliament, the wool subsidy, was collected continuously through the reign; the rates inherited from Henry IV and renewed in 1413 were £2 3s. 4d. per sack for denizen merchants and £2 10s. for aliens, but the life grant of the subsidy in November 1415 raised the alien rate to £3 per sack; with the exception of a very short period at the very beginning of the Hundred Years War, these were the highest rates at which the *maltolt* had been collected in its entire history.[4] Finally, the other indirect subsidy over which parliament had formal control, tunnage and poundage, was collected at rates that had been standard since 1402 (3s. per tun of wine and 1s. in the pound value of general merchandise); the king receiving a life grant of this subsidy, along with the *maltolt*, as signal reward for his great victory at Agincourt in 1415.[5]

The full meaning of these data will become evident towards the end of this chapter, where they are analysed in such a way as to compare the fiscal burden under Henry V with that under other high-taxing kings of the later Middle Ages. To begin with, though, we need to acknowledge what Henry did *not* accomplish within the tax system. Whereas every English ruler since Henry II had tried to introduce new forms of extraordinary taxation, Henry V's reign was almost entirely devoid of experimentation. The first and most obvious point in this respect relates to the absence of any attempts to challenge the privileged status of the two ancient palatinates of Durham and Cheshire. (Lancashire, raised to a palatinate only in 1351, never enjoyed such status and remained part of the regular tax system.) No evidence has as yet come to light to suggest that Henry's administration followed the practice, observable under Edward III and Henry VI, whereby the bishop of Durham was persuaded to impose his own taxes that were then handed over as a

---

3   A. McHardy, 'Clerical Taxation in Fifteenth-Century England: The Clergy as Agents of the Crown', in *The Church, Politics and Patronage in the Fifteenth Century*, ed. R. B. Dobson (Gloucester, 1984), pp. 160–92, supplemented by details of clerical tax grants recorded in the online TNA E 179 Database, www.nationalarchives.gov.uk/e179

4   Data derived from *PROME* and *CFR, passim*; the rates presented in graphic form in E. M. Carus-Wilson and O. Coleman, *England's Export Trade, 1275–1547* (Oxford, 1963), p. 196, are not accurate.

5   W. M. Ormrod, 'The Origins of Tunnage and Poundage: Parliament and the Estate of Merchants in the Fourteenth Century', *Parliamentary History* 28 (2009), 209–27.

free gift to the royal exchequer.[6] In Cheshire, Henry certainly asserted his right – as earl of Chester rather than as king – to collect direct taxes. But as Michael Bennett's contribution to this volume shows, the strong tradition of fiscal particularism in the county meant a much greater questioning of the obligation to pay than was the case in other parts of the realm. Consequently, the mise of 1416 sparked organized resistance of a nature and scale that (as we shall see) were entirely exceptional in the kingdom at large, not least in terms of the way that the government negotiated a pragmatic compromise involving a significant reduction in the amounts charged.[7]

A similar apparent passivity may be detected in relation to parliamentary taxes, both direct and indirect, imposed on the kingdom at large. Henry V certainly accepted and used some relatively new taxes developed under his two immediate predecessors. Tunnage and poundage was one such, initiated under Edward III and Richard II but collected permanently only since 1401; another was the extension of clerical taxation, first attempted in 1371 and then applied more systematically under Henry IV, to include benefices not normally subject to clerical tenths and flat-rate charges on unbeneficed clergy.[8] On the other hand, Henry V seems never to have contemplated a repetition of the unusual income taxes to which parliament had resorted, as a matter of exception, in 1404 and 1411.[9] Nor did the king consider any significant reform of the system for assessing and collecting clerical tenths and lay fifteenths and tenths, even though the valuations set by these taxes had been fixed as far back as 1291 (for the clergy) and 1334 (for the laity). And the interesting proposal of the Commons in 1420 for a standing tax on all foreigners entering and leaving the realm in order to pay for the defence of the coasts was simply shelved and forgotten.[10]

The one occasion when Henry V seems genuinely to have pushed at the boundaries of the fiscal constitution was in May 1421 when, as argued by Harriss, he may have tried to persuade parliament to authorize peacetime direct taxation. If so, then his failure in this regard was decisive: despite the grant of a further subsidy in the December parliament of the same year, the history of both direct and indirect taxation in the early reign of Henry VI was to witness a firm return to the principle that the Lancastrian settlement of France, under the treaty of Troyes, ought not to be paid for out of the king's

---

[6]   W. M. Ormrod, 'An Experiment in Taxation: The English Parish Subsidy of 1371', *Speculum* 63 (1988), 58–82 (pp. 77–9); C. D. Liddy, 'The Politics of Privilege: Thomas Hatfield and the Palatinate of Durham, 1345–81', in *Fourteenth Century England IV*, ed. J. S. Hamilton (Woodbridge, 2006), pp. 61–79 (pp. 71–5); C. D. Liddy, *The Bishopric of Durham in the Late Middle Ages: Lordship, Community and the Cult of St Cuthbert* (Woodbridge, 2008), pp. 27–8, 206–8.

[7]   M. Bennett, 'Henry V and the Cheshire Tax Revolt of 1416', in this volume, pp. 171–86.

[8]   Ormrod, 'Experiment in Taxation', pp. 58–82; McHardy, 'Clerical Taxation', p. 174.

[9]   Jurkowski, Smith and Crook, *Lay Taxes*, pp. 74–5, 78–9.

[10]   *PROME*, IX, 256.

revenues from England.[11] Finally, Henry V seems never to have felt the need to explore the two most obvious missing elements of the tax system inherited from his predecessors: an internal sales tax of the kind much exploited by many of his contemporaries in continental Europe and contemplated by the English parliament on at least one occasion in the late fourteenth century;[12] and an increase in the duties on the export of cloth, perhaps in the form of a parliamentary subsidy akin to the *maltolt*, and which might then go some way to addressing the chronic problem of a system of indirect taxation that relied so heavily on one declining export commodity, raw wool. In considering the political acceptability and economic sustainability of the Henrician fiscal state, we therefore need to be properly mindful of the significant limitation within which the second Lancastrian king chose, or was required, to operate.

The discussion that follows aims to address Henry V's record as tax-gatherer on three fronts. First, I review the available evidence for the mechanisms by which tax grants were communicated to the localities and the nature of the political dynamic thus set up between the crown and the taxpayer. Secondly, I consider the evidence for the way in which taxation was applied on the ground, its strong reliance on a sense of active participation in the system and its implications for the effectiveness of the Lancastrian fiscal state. Thirdly, I present data to establish the real burden of taxation under Henry V and compare it with other peaks of fiscal activity between the 1290s and the 1540s. Because the *maltolt* had become a permanent levy in peacetime as well as in war since the time of Edward III, the dynamics of the customs system were very different from those of lay fifteenths and tenths and clerical tenths, and the first two sections concentrate exclusively on the experience of direct taxation. In the third section, however, the taxes on exports and imports are considered alongside direct subsidies in order to assess the wider economic implications of Henry's tax policies. What emerges is not only a very strong sense of compliance with the demands of the crown but also a notable balance between the tax base and fiscal extraction that made this arguably one of the most sustainable fiscal regimes of the later Middle Ages.

*

In thinking about how Henry V's taxes were perceived from below, we can usefully begin with some discussion of the ways in which the crown and the political establishment publicly articulated their justifications for extraordinary war finance. The debates in parliaments and convocations that produced the long series of taxes enumerated above have been very thoroughly analysed, and need not detain us in any detail here. As is well known,

---

11 Harriss, 'Management of Parliament', pp. 149–51.
12 *PROME*, IV, 190–1.

the high-level negotiation of taxation took place within a well-defined set of philosophical and political maxims: that there should be a clear demonstration of need, often articulated in the language of 'urgent necessity' and specifically directed to the defence of Church and realm; that the burden of taxation should be in general proportion to the ability of the kingdom to support the cost; and that the concession and collection of one subsidy ought normally to guarantee a moratorium on any demands for further levies.[13] Henry V's ability to manipulate these limitations upon taxation in a manner that was at once advantageous to the crown and acceptable to the polity has been frequently remarked: one might comment particularly on the intricate negotiations towards the speeding up of terms set for payment of direct taxes and the securing of new subsidies before the expiration of old ones, both of which practices significantly eroded the normal restrictions on concurrent levies.[14] The issue that remains much less understood, and which forms the focus of this and the next section, relates to the practicalities of taxation *after* the grants in parliament and convocation. How did Henry V's regime use the mechanisms of information exchange to disseminate the circumstances and terms of tax grants to its subjects in the provinces, and thus to guide public opinion about taxation? And to what extent did the crown involve itself in the operations of tax assessment and collection such as to uphold both its own fiscal interests and its acknowledged responsibilities to the economic welfare of its subjects?

Considering Henry V's reputation as the great communicator, it is remarkable just how little written information about taxation was routinely made available in the localities. Since taxes granted in parliament were not issued as statutes in this period, the tax schedules submitted by the Commons (which occasionally included the kind of extended comment on the diplomatic and military context that might have been thought useful to the propa-

---

13 For the scholastic principles, see E. Isenmann, 'Medieval and Renaissance Theories of State Finance', in *Economic Systems and State Finance*, ed. R. Bonney (Oxford, 1995), pp. 21–52. Their application in England is developed in detail by G. L. Harriss, *King, Parliament and Public Finance in Medieval England to 1369* (Oxford, 1975).

14 *HP*, I, 134. For full details, see the descriptions of lay and clerical tax grants in www.nationalarchives.gov.uk/e179. Notwithstanding his erosion of the principle that taxes should not overlap, Henry was clearly sensitive particularly to issues of clerical privilege around tax grants. In the winter of 1414–15 he overrode the chancery and exchequer's attempt to have the bishops certify immediately the names of the collectors of the two tenths recently conceded and thus effectively upheld the clergy's concern that the crown would attempt to collect both simultaneously: *CCR, 1413–19*, p. 167, with background in *CFR, 1413–22*, pp. 90–1, 133–4. As a result, the clergy were able to hold firm to core principles even when there was some obvious compromise over timing: in June 1416 the convocation of Canterbury, in drawing forward the payment date for the first of the two tenths conceded in November 1415 from November 1416 to June 1416, announced that its concession had been made *in defensionem ecclesiae et regnum anglicane aliasque necessarias et graves expensas*: TNA, C 270/13, no. 21.

ganda machine) were not sent down to the sheriffs as part of the system for the proclamation of new legislation.[15] Rather, the crown seems to have relied in this as in previous generations on two other channels: the oral reports made in the county and urban courts when elected members of the Commons returned to their constituencies; and the Latin letters patent of appointment of collectors of taxes, which may have been summarized in the vernacular in those same assemblies as part of the formal inception of the tax in the relevant area of jurisdiction.

On the whole, the text of the tax commissions altered little from one subsidy to the next. Since Henry V (so unlike his father in this respect) enjoyed his tax grants almost entirely free of any conditions over their administration and expenditure, he clearly felt under no particular obligation to inform his subjects of the few strings that were attached. The long-held conventions surrounding the *plena postestas* of parliamentary representatives, and their right to bind their constituents in the taxes they authorized, also made it strictly unnecessary to provide further detailed justification of the subsidies for dissemination in the localities. Nevertheless, the sense of a contract with the county communities remained an essential part of the discourse of lay taxation. The exchequer continued routinely to record a comfortable fiction, unchanged since the early fourteenth century, that fifteenths and tenths were paid in each county by the 'earls, barons, knights and other men of the community of the shire'.[16] And the clause regularly inserted by the chancery into tax commissions ordering 'dukes, earls, barons, knights, lords of towns, freemen and the whole community of the shire' to be intendant upon the assessors strongly suggests that grants of lay subsidies were indeed adumbrated with some degree of formality, via the letters of commission, in the localities.[17] Consequently, while the crown was usually content to let its record speak for itself and allow the local reception of tax grants to take its own course, it was alive at least to the need to arm its agents with the context, and core principles, under which the relevant tax had been granted and should be collected:

---

[15] The tax schedules of Henry V's reign (encompassing both direct and indirect taxation), as recorded on the parliament rolls, are: *PROME*, IX, 11–12, 39, 68–9, 116–18, 137, 179–80, 209, 233, 314–15. In spite of some interesting precedents for the issuing of tax grants by statute under Edward III (e.g. *SR*, I, 289–90), the inclusion of verbatim transcriptions of the Commons' schedules of taxation in the formal text of parliamentary statutes did not become a matter of course until the very end of the fifteenth century: *SR*, II, 555–6, 642–3, citing *PROME*, XVI, 97–100, 297–300. The case of Robert Geffe, MP for New Romney, who paid to have a copy of the parliament roll for 1406 made for the benefit of his constituency, raises the interesting possibility that members of the Commons acted as conduits for the transmission of written texts of tax schedules and other formal proceedings to the localities. But the example is as unique as the parliament to which it relates. See *HP*, II, 173.

[16] See the wording of the formal accounts of the county collectors contained in TNA, E 359/19, *passim*.

[17] E.g., *CFR, 1413–22*, pp. 84–5.

that is, that it had been authorized for 'the defence of the realm and the safe-guard of the sea', that it should be collected from all lay persons 'both great and small' and that the clergy should be made to contribute on the basis of moveable property held on lands acquired by the Church since 1291 and thus not liable to clerical tenths.[18]

There are also some signs, towards the end of Henry V's reign, of a more instrumental approach to this system designed to influence opinion among local political elites and encourage those now perhaps becoming weary of the king's apparently endless fiscal demands. In May 1421, while the crown was putting significant pressure on the convocation of Canterbury to grant what parliament would not tolerate – a peacetime direct tax – various heads of religious houses complained collectively to the crown that they were often called upon to act as collectors of tenths in areas far beyond their normal place of residence, with resulting costs and associated troubles. It is perhaps a measure of the crown's nervousness over the way in which this new subsidy would be received that the chancery allowed the temporary concession on this matter to be issued as a fully fledged statute for proclamation in the localities.[19] More strikingly, the commissions to the collectors of the lay subsidy granted in December 1421 included, very unusually, the verbatim text of the parliamentary ordinance acknowledging the difficulties arising from the recent major re-coinage and allowing that gold coins of earlier issue be accepted at full face value in payments towards the first instalment of the tax. The official text of this ordinance on the parliament roll was in English, and the Latin tax of the commissions thus incorporated, for the first time in the reign, a piece of extended vernacular prose that was suitable for oral dissemination *in extenso* in the county and civic courts.[20] Henry V is tradition-ally acknowledged to have used written English as a means of expressing a special relationship with certain privileged individuals and communities, above all with the city and guilds of London, though recent work by Gwilym Dodd has argued strongly against the idea of a conscious 'language policy'

---

18   *CFR, 1413–22*, pp. 25, 84, 119, 149, 170, 219, 298, 413. For the principles involved in the taxation of the clergy under lay subsidies, see J. F. Willard, *Parliamentary Taxes on Personal Property, 1290 to 1334* (Cambridge MA, 1934), pp. 93–109.

19   *Records of Convocation*, ed. G. Bray, 20 vols. (Woodbridge, 2005–6), V, 108–11; TNA, SC 8/24/1159, printed in *Petitions to the Crown from English Religious Houses, c. 1275 to c. 1485*, ed. G. Dodd and A. K. McHardy, Canterbury and York Society 100 (2010), no. 173; *PROME*, IX, 270; *SR*, II, 208; Harriss, 'Management of Parliament', p. 151. More generally the crown was quick throughout the reign to protect the heads of religious houses by granting and upholding charters of exemption allowing them immunity from appointment as collectors of tenths: see e.g. *CPR, 1413–16*, p. 172; *The Register of Henry Chichele, Archbishop of Canterbury, 1414–1443*, ed. E. F. Jacob, 4 vols., Canterbury and York Society 42, 45–7 (1938–47), III, 395–7.

20   *CFR, 1413–22*, pp. 414–15, citing *PROME*, IX, 316. The right to pay taxes in gold had been acknowledged ever since the first introduction of the gold coinage under Edward III: see, e.g., *PROME*, IV, 393.

on the part of the Lancastrian government.[21] It was only in 1420, for example, with the promulgation of the treaty of Troyes, that Henry's government actually bothered to prepare texts of key documents in English for *viva voce* proclamation throughout the realm.[22] The example of the tax ordinance of 1421 thus stands as a striking but ultimately still rather isolated piece of evidence of the way that English could sometimes be used to serve the wider public relations machine of the Lancastrian state.

A similar point applies to official communications concerning the taxation of the Church. It was the convention for the archbishops of Canterbury and York to submit formal schedules of tax grants to the crown, on receipt of which the chancery would issue writs to each bishop requesting the appointment of tax collectors who would then be accountable to the exchequer for the proceeds of the relevant subsidy. Since the start of Henry IV's reign, the writs for the appointment of collectors had begun to repeat verbatim the archbishops' certificates in such a way as effectively to confirm the crown's commitment to three very important governing principles: that certain named and specially privileged ecclesiastical institutions were exempt from the subsidy; that the ecclesiastical ordinaries might be empowered to certify cases of serious poverty in order to allow appropriate alleviation within the administration of the tax; and that (as we have noted above, and a particular insistence of the clergy) no other taxes would be raised for the duration of the current subsidy.[23] In the later years of Henry V's reign, however, the chancery went noticeably further, and began also to incorporate into these writs more of the contextual concerns that had been articulated by the two convocations in respect of the relevant tax grants. Thus in 1418 and 1420 the writs

---

[21] For a summary of the traditional approach, see Allmand, *Henry V*, pp. 421–5. For revisionism, see G. Dodd, 'The Spread of English in the Records of Central Government, 1400–1430', in *Vernacularity in England and Wales, c. 1300–1550*, ed. E. Salter and H. Wicker (Turnhout, 2011), pp. 225–66; G. Dodd, 'Trilingualism in the Medieval English Bureaucracy: The Use - and Disuse - of Languages in the Fifteenth-Century Privy Seal Office', *Journal of British Studies* 51 (2012), 253–83.

[22] *CCR, 1419–22*, pp. 118–20; J. Doig, 'Political Propaganda and Royal Proclamations in Late Medieval England', *Historical Research* 71 (1998), 253–80 (pp. 264–5). This, too, was a very rare occurrence, and it was not until Edward IV's time that the central government routinely sent out written texts in English for proclamation: W. M. Ormrod, 'The Use of English: Language, Law, and Political Culture in Fourteenth-Century England', *Speculum* 78 (2003), 750–87 (pp. 785–7).

[23] *CFR, 1399–1405*, pp. 123, 134–5, 160–1, 197, 225, 293; *CFR, 1405–13*, pp. 35, 94–5, 140–1, 209–10, 242–4; *CFR, 1413–22*, pp. 31–2, 51–2, 98–9. The certificates of tax grants surviving in episcopal registers may be readily compared with the follow-up royal writs for the reign of Henry V in *Records of Convocation*, IV, 397–8, 398–9; V, 12–13, 18–19, 28–9, 34–5, 43–5, 56–9, 83–7, 108–11; XIII, 335–7, 348–9, 357–8, 362–3, 366–7, 370–2. Some of the original certificates also survive in TNA, C 270/13, 14. For an example of a return of impoverished benefices certified by the ecclesiastical ordinary see TNA, E 179/52/234, from the diocese of Salisbury in 1417.

for the appointment of collectors in the province of York acknowledged that taxes had been granted notwithstanding the 'notorious poverty' into which churchmen had been driven by scarcity of coin and Scottish incursions. And in 1420 and 1421 the king expressed strong sympathy with the hapless plight of the northern clergy as a result of recent murrains of beasts and the 'grievous floods and violence of continuous rains and tempests, whereby the grain and hay have been irrecoverably beaten down'.[24] Just as the commissions to assessors of lay taxes were used as a means of convincing the secular polity of the crown's good faith, so at times were the writs for the appointment of collectors of clerical subsidies quite powerful tools in the fiscal-political dialogue between the king and the bishops.

The other way in which Henry V sought to use written communication as a means of influencing opinion among the elite in the provinces was through the many letters despatched under the secret seal and signet requesting major figures to make payments of their taxes in advance of the dates fixed in the formal grants, and thus to ease the chronic problem of cash-flow. An instance from June 1417 may suffice as indicative of the kinds of rhetoric employed in this correspondence. Henry addressed letters of privy seal, in French, to various members of the ecclesiastical hierarchy of the southern province. The current tax, he reminded them, had been explicitly granted on the basis of the 'great necessity that we have for money, in order to undertake our voyage upon the sea … for the rescue of our town of Harfleur [which is] besieged by our French enemies and others'.[25] Now 'our voyage requires great haste, [but] the men of our retinue cannot go with us unless they have their wages paid in hand'. Notwithstanding that the convocation of November 1416 had deferred the payment date for an earlier tenth from November 1417 to June 1418 and made this a condition for the grant of a further double tenth, Henry now requested that the leaders of the Church might hand over their contributions to the deferred tax a whole year in advance, at the upcoming feast of the Trinity. Neither in rhetorical form nor in substance was this device at all new.[26] Nevertheless, the letter of 1417 provides a good example of Henry V's well-known persuasion techniques and his considerable ability to call his greater subjects to stand by their public obligations to the military state.

*

To assess how readily and happily Henry V's England settled into an extended regime of heavy taxation, we may now examine the evidence for tax exemp-

---

[24] *CFR, 1413–22*, pp. 235–6, 324, 410–11; *Records of Convocation*, XIII, 363, 366, 71.

[25] TNA, E 207/12/13.

[26] For a good comparator from the period of the siege of Calais in 1347, see *Registrum Johannes de Trillek episcopi Herefordensis*, ed. J. H. Parry, Canterbury and York Society 8 (1912), pp. 267–8.

tion, tax avoidance and tax evasion over the course of the reign. The only major permanent exemptions that Henry allowed by his personal fiat were to ecclesiastical institutions. In line with his identity as upholder of the true religion, the king was quick to confirm and extend the standing exemptions allowed on both clerical and lay taxes to favoured orders and enterprises. Among those securing enhanced protection under Henry V were the Carthusians of Mount Grace Priory; a wide variety of impoverished female houses such as the minoresses of Aldgate, London and the sisters of the hospital of St James, Canterbury; the benefices appropriate to major construction projects such as the fabric fund of York Minster; and, predictably enough, the king's own personal foundations of Syon and Sheen.[27] Henry also intervened when the clerical subsidies were extended to benefices not included in the 1291 *Taxatio* in order to confirm that earlier royal charters to institutions such as St Stephen's Chapel, Westminster, and New College, Oxford, should be taken to extend tax exemption to all those institutions' dependent churches.[28] And the king continued the habit of his predecessors in allowing extraordinary exemptions from taxation to major ecclesiastics in recognition of their arduous commitment to affairs of state: the remission allowed to Archbishop Arundel of Canterbury at the time of the latter's involvement in the suppression of Oldcastle's rebellion in January 1414 is a striking case of this convention.[29]

Most exemptions to major clerics and ecclesiastical corporations were, then, markers of privilege rather than indicators of poverty. But the crown was also properly accommodating in cases of obvious hardship. Four of the parish churches of the city of Norwich were allowed temporary exemption from taxation in 1413 on account of the recent severe fire in the city; and Henry V regularly extended to Meaux Abbey the exoneration allowed by his father in recognition of the abbey's chronic difficulties with flooding.[30] Over the winter of 1419–20, those caught up in the still novel process of taxing stipendiary priests were quick to argue for exemptions on the grounds that they were already taxed for clerical and/or lay subsidies, that they were below the threshold for assessment or – as in no fewer than forty-four cases in

---

27 TNA, SC 8/294/14700, 295/14701, 332/15735A–15735B; *CChR, 1341–1417*, pp. 469–70, 483; *CPR, 1413–16*, pp. 276–7; *CCR, 1413–19*, pp. 172, 211; *CFR, 1413–22*, pp. 31–2, 51–2, 98–9. For the alleviation of the clerical tenth upon Torksey Priory in 1417 see TNA, SC 8/180/8982; *CPR, 1416–22*, pp. 114–15.

28 *CCR, 1413–19*, pp. 163, 252–3, 258. The crown assiduously followed up on the confirmation of New College's exemption by ordering the collectors of the lay subsidy in Oxford to return any moneys that might have been collected from the society: TNA, E 179/161/82.

29 *CPR, 1413–16*, p. 157.

30 *CFR, 1413–22*, pp. 31–2, 51–2; TNA, E 359/17, rot. 12; etc. For further discussion of this and other cases of ecclesiastical exemptions in the next reign see R. C. E. Hayes, '"For the State and Necessity of the Realm": Clerical Taxation in the Reign of Henry VI', in *Clergy, Church and Society in England and Wales, c.1200–1800*, ed. W. J. Sheils and R. C. E. Hayes (forthcoming).

the diocese of Norwich – that they fell into the category defined as 'decrepit from age or other notable infirmity'.[31] While there could be occasional minor squabbles over the accuracy of information, the chancery and exchequer were more or less required to accept without further investigation the evidences of impoverishment provided by the ecclesiastical ordinaries.[32] In the diocese of Lincoln, Bishop Repingdon regularly issued instructions to tax collectors to remit charges upon impoverished religious houses, especially nunneries, for which the collectors then made petition for release at the exchequer.[33] In similar vein, the collectors of the two clerical tenths of 1414 in the diocese of London were allowed a deduction of £4 after swearing (without recorded explanation) that they had been unable to collect the sum.[34] On the margins of the realm at least, leniency seems to have been almost the norm. Early in the reign the abbot of Vale Royal was remitted nearly £72 on which he and his predecessor had previously been distrained for the clerical tenth in the archdeaconry of Cardigan in 1400–1, but which the crown now acknowledged as having been uncollectable as a result of the revolt of Owain Glyndŵr.[35] And in 1421 Bishop Zouch of Llandaff reported that, since nothing could be raised from the clergy in his diocese, he had not bothered to appoint collectors; the

---

[31] TNA, E 179/45/74, 50/34, 50/35; *Records of Convocation*, V, 83–7. A list of clerical defaulters compiled in the diocese of Worcester in 1419 included, alongside a number of religious houses and larger churches, the names of four humble chaplains refusing to contribute to their concurrent special subsidy: TNA, E 179/58/80.

[32] Such information was often supplied in the episcopal letters to the exchequer returning the names of collectors appointed in the relevant diocese: see, for example, *The Register of Edmund Lacy, Bishop of Exeter (A.D.1420–1455)*, ed. F. C. Hingeston-Randolph and O. J. Reichel, 2 vols. (Exeter and London, 1909–15), I, 86–7, 138; *Registrum Thome Poltone episcopi Herefordensis, 1420–1422*, ed. W. W. Capes, Canterbury and York Society 22 (1918), pp. 6–8. In 1416 the keeper of the spiritualities of the bishopric of Norwich wrote to the treasurer and barons of the exchequer to apologize for having omitted some names from the list of impoverished houses previously supplied, and added five more for good measure: TNA, E 179/45/52F. For a dispute over the values attached to exempt benefices in the archdeaconry of Derby, see TNA, E 368/193, rot. 176.

[33] TNA, E 179/35/166B-166Q; 35/201D–201F; 36/210A; 36/213; 58/59B. For an example of a *constat* or transcript supplied by the exchequer to certify future exemption of religious houses, see that issued to the nuns of St Michael, Stamford in 1422: TNA, E 179/279/74. For further examples of petitions submitted by collectors at the time of account requesting remission of the charges on impoverished houses see TNA, E 179/15/107, 109, 112; etc.

[34] TNA, E 179/42/89G; TNA, E 359/18, rot. 35. In 1415 the abbot and convent of Lavenden (Bucks.) were pardoned £20 on the abbot's account as collector of the final clerical tenth of Henry IV's reign because of the impoverishment of their own house: *CPR, 1413–16*, p. 287.

[35] *CPR, 1413–16*, p. 201. That this was a matter of grace rather than of evidence is suggested by a simultaneous deal struck over the arrears of Vale Royal's own tax charges: *CPR, 1413–22*, p. 197. The bishop of Hereford's report on impoverished churches in Wales and the Marches in 1415 resulted in a temporary reduction of £40 on the total charged upon his diocese: TNA, E 359/18, rot. 41.

diocese's contribution to the king's forthcoming expedition would instead be by way of that other potent currency, prayer.[36]

The question of exemption was very different in the case of the taxation of the laity. Since 1334 the crown had given up the task of re-assessing lay wealth every time a new tax was granted, and had simply devolved to each vill and town the responsibility to raise a set quota towards the king's taxes. The taxes were still known as fifteenths and tenths, to reflect the fact that they ought to be levied on the value of moveable property at a rate of a fifteenth in the countryside and a tenth on the royal domain and in urban areas. However, local practice could vary significantly. In the towns, the comparative ease of assessing household goods and/or stock in trade meant that civic officials were able significantly to extend the number of householders paying taxes over the century after 1334.[37] In the countryside, assessment of moveables – chiefly, by the fifteenth century, livestock – remained an important criterion, but in many areas liability to taxation was based either entirely on the holding of particular tenements whose heads of household had been taxed in 1334 or on a combination of tenure and moveable wealth.

Most of the evidence so far accumulated for tax redistribution in the countryside tends to come from later in the fifteenth century. But there are at least a few references that allow us to conclude that the position was well established in the time of Henry V. A complaint by the parliamentary Commons in 1407 about people who removed their livestock from their places of residence in order to evade assessment provides an important indicator that the assessment of moveables, however crudely operated, was still observed in many areas.[38] And conversely, an inquiry in 1417–18 into the amount that the small community of North Nibley ought to provide towards the quota for the tax district of Uley and Woodmancote (Gloucestershire) confirmed that practice was based on tenure; the local jury provided a powerful sense of the sanctity of custom by asserting explicitly that this had been the case continuously from 1334 to 1415.[39] For all these reasons, then, formal, perpetual exemp-

36 TNA, E 179/279/68.

37 C. Dyer, 'Taxation and Communities in Late Medieval England', in *Progress and Problems in Medieval England: Essays in Honour of Edward Miller*, ed. R. H. Britnell and J. Hatcher (Cambridge, 1996), pp. 168–90 (pp. 175–7), and C. Dyer, 'Costs and Benefits of English Direct Taxation, 1275–1525', in *La fiscalità nell'economia europea secc. XIII–XVIII*, ed. S. Cavaciocchi, 2 vols. (Florence, 2008), II, 909–24 (pp. 916–18), summarize a large literature on the topic. See also R. H. Britnell, 'Tax-Collecting in Colchester, 1487–1502', *Historical Research* 79 (2006), 477–87; R. Willcock, 'A Fifteenth-Century Tax List from the Wapentake of Claro, West Riding of Yorkshire', *Northern History* 45 (2008), 173–83; M. Forrest, 'The Distribution of Medieval Taxation in Southern England: New Evidence from Surrey, Middlesex, and Dorset', *Southern History* 31 (2010), 27–47.

38 *PROME*, VIII, 444–5.

39 TNA, E 179/113/158. North Nibley was confirmed as owing 16s. towards the district's overall quota of £3 14s. 7d., for which see *The Lay Subsidy of 1334*, ed. R. E. Glasscock (London, 1975), p. 96. For another similar dispute between the vills of Easington and

tion of individual laypeople from taxation did not normally fall within the purview of the crown. Certain privileged groups, such as the king's moneyers and the inhabitants of the Cinque Ports and the Stannaries, enjoyed release from liability in a tradition stretching back beyond 1334.[40] At the time of Oldcastle's rebellion in January 1414 Henry V seemed about to create a new class of privileged exempt by announcing that any individual or commonalty responsible for delivering up the heretical leader would henceforth be duly discharged from 'all taxes, tallages, tolls, fifteenths and other quotas hereafter granted to the king or his heirs'; identical incentives were also offered in the campaign leading up to Oldcastle's eventual capture and execution in 1417.[41] In the event, however, the triumph of orthodoxy yielded no tax holiday. The marked reluctance of the crown to extend special-interest exemptions was entirely of a piece with the important tradition that all heads of lay households were potentially subject to taxation: or, as the collectors' commissions in this period put it, that 'no one be spared'.[42]

When tax exemptions were added anew to the fifteenths and tenths in the fifteenth century, they were therefore almost always made in the interests not of privileged individuals but of impoverished communities. The northernmost counties of Cumberland, Westmorland and Northumberland were routinely exempted from fifteenths and tenths through the reign of Henry V on the basis that repeated Scottish raids and general dearth had left them too poor to pay.[43] In the English counties bordering on the marches of Wales, too, there was some acknowledgement of inability to pay as a consequence of the rebellions of the previous reign.[44] The crown held faith with certain adjustments of tax quotas made in previous reigns on the basis of poverty, such as those allowed to the town of Oakham and several surrounding villages in Rutland since 1344 and to the dwindling settlement of Ravenser Odd in the East Riding of Yorkshire since 1373.[45] The best documented case of such alleviation in our period is that of the port of Melcombe, which campaigned

---

Chilton (Bucks.) from early in the reign of Henry V, and which again cites very self-consciously the tax history of the area, see TNA, SC 8/306/15253.

[40] Willard, *Parliamentary Taxes*, pp. 110–37. For the routine exemption of the king's moneyers in the London tax accounts of Henry V's reign, see TNA, E 179/141/48; 141/50.

[41] *CCR, 1413–19*, pp. 106–7, 379; *CPR, 1416–22*, p. 83.

[42] *CFR, 1399–1405*, pp. 113, 186–7, 282; *CFR, 1405–13*, pp. 61, 90, 179.

[43] *Northern Petitions Illustrative of Life in Berwick, Cumbria and Durham in the Fourteenth Century*, ed. C. M. Fraser, Surtees Society 194 (1982), pp. 155–7; *CPR, 1413–16*, pp. 28, 57, 275, 371, 381; *CPR, 1416–22*, p. 53.

[44] The collectors of the two fifteenths and tenths of 1415 in Shropshire were remitted a total of £159 6s. 2d. (for the two taxes) because various enumerated vills 'lie waste, destroyed and burned' after the Glyndŵr revolt: TNA, E 179/166/55. For further discussion see H. Watt, '"On Account of the Frequent Attacks and Invasions of the Welsh": The Effect of the Glyn Dŵr Rebellion on Tax Collection in England', in *Reign of Henry IV*, ed. Dodd and Biggs, pp. 48–81.

[45] TNA, E 359/19, rots 16, 20, 21. For the decline of Ravenser Odd, which had already

actively and vocally in parliament and the exchequer over the late fourteenth and fifteenth centuries for reduction of its tax quota and other fiscal impositions, and under Henry V was regularly remitted 13s. 4d. of its total tax burden of £18 6s. 8d.[46] But other towns and villages also benefited from relief. The burgesses of Truro, who had long complained of their impoverishment from plague and war, had secured partial remission of their tax burden by royal letters patent of Richard II and Henry IV covering more or less the entire period from 1378 to 1420; although a request in the parliament of May 1421 for a further period of exoneration was not agreed, the tax records make it clear that the governments of Henry V and Henry VI observed what was now effectively a permanent reduction in the town's tax quota.[47] Very occasionally, too, the clerical and lay evidence comes together to reveal the economic effect of more recent national emergencies. John Roland, the incumbent of Portland church, was exempted from the clerical tenth because his benefice had been 'burned, plundered and excessively diminished' in the French attack on the island in May 1416; and a year later nearly £12 was written off the lay tax quota for Portland in recognition of the real damage to the local economic infrastructure from this notorious event.[48]

The major question that arises over the distribution of taxation among the laity under Henry V is not, then, about who enjoyed formal exemption but instead about the degree to which taxation reflected the ability of different social groups to pay. What few fragments of evidence remain suggest that by the early fifteenth century the landed elite had successfully minimized the amounts it paid towards direct taxation. The tendency from the middle of the fourteenth century to lease out demesne lands and rely not on direct farming but on rents meant that, at village level, most lords of manors were no longer directly holding either the lands or the moveables that were the basis for direct liability. The resort to alternative taxes on income targeted at the greater men of the realm, as employed under Henry IV and again under Henry VI, was itself a tacit admission that the fifteenths and tenths now hardly touched the nobility and greater gentry. Before 1334, and in the first generations after the tax reform of that year, it had been common for members of the peerage to claim the right to make their own arrangements with the exchequer for

set in by the mid-fourteenth century, see *A History of the County of York, East Riding, V: Holderness Wapentake, Southern Part*, ed. K. J. Allison (Oxford, 1984), p. 68.
[46] TNA, SC 8/19/922–924; SC 8/125/6206, 6227, 6246; SC 8/126/6256, 6267; SC 8/128/6371, 6388; SC 8/171/8504; SC 8/185/9214; SC 8/236/11784; TNA, E 359/19, rots 16d, 22; *A History of the County of Dorset II*, ed. W. Page (London, 1908), pp. 187–8.
[47] TNA, SC 8/23/1119–1120, 23/1121, 76/3767; *CCR, 1377–81*, pp. 54–5, 129; *CPR, 1408–13*, p. 215; TNA, E 359/19, rots 19, 21.
[48] TNA, SC 8/230/11473; TNA, C 270/13, no. 19; *Records of Convocation*, V, 43–5; *CFR, 1413–22*, pp. 185–6; TNA, E 359/19, rot. 22; *History of the County of Dorset II*, p. 191; Allmand, *Henry V*, p. 224. Roland also successfully secured pardon of the tenth in 1418: *CPR, 1416–22*, p. 179.

their tax contributions; the notes in the enrolled tax accounts of the with-drawal of the relevant sums from the collectors' accounts provide important and neglected evidence for the continuing involvement of the magnates in tax payments in the era of the Black Death.[49] Under Henry V, however, the enrolled accounts are almost entirely devoid of such detail. While this does not prove that lords did not make some contribution,[50] it also tends to suggest that the amounts were now sufficiently trifling as to make the fuss of personal accounting unnecessary and allowed for immediate settlement with the local tax collectors. In acknowledging that the English nobility and gentry were unusual in fifteenth-century Europe in having no formal exemption from taxation, we should never forget that they had a strong vested interest in upholding a system that so signally underrated their own capacity to pay.

Very occasionally over the reign, too, we encounter cases where members of the upper orders of society regarded it as appropriate to evade or even actively resist the clutches of royal tax-gatherers. Michael Bennett's study of the Cheshire mise of 1416 yields valuable indicative evidence of the prob-lems that arose when gentlemen tax collectors won themselves a tax holiday by deliberating neglecting to make their own contributions and forcing their manorial tenants to make up the difference.[51] In theory, members of the social and political elite who defaulted on their tax payments were, like all taxpayers, liable to the rigours of distraint of goods and, if necessary, imprisonment for non-compliance.[52] In cases of less powerful people, simply the threat of such sanctions seems to have been enough to make most come to their senses and pay up; and since local assessors could themselves be liable to private litigation if those charged with non-payment chose to challenge distraint, it was strongly in the interests of communities to find informal mechanisms by which liabilities could be resolved and the tax quota met.[53] In those rare cases where force was applied against members of the social elite, however, it could often prove counter-productive. The men commissioned to collect the first lay subsidy of Henry V's reign in Shropshire subsequently complained that the county's representatives at the parliament of 1413, Robert Corbett

---

[49] K. Fildes, 'The Baronage in the Reign of Richard II' (unpublished Ph.D. thesis, University of Sheffield, 2009), p. 47.

[50] In 1386, Michael de la Pole, earl of Suffolk, was said to pay 50 per cent of the taxation of South Wheatley (Notts.) from the profits of his demesne manor there: *CIM, 1219–1485*, no. 91. For other arguments relating to the continued liability of the nobility, see G. Dodd, 'The Lords, Taxation and the Community of Parliament in the 1370s and Early 1380s', *Parliamentary History* 20 (2001), 287–310.

[51] Bennett, 'Henry V and the Cheshire Tax Revolt', pp. 171–86.

[52] e.g. *CFR, 1413–22*, p. 85. The county-level collectors could also be subject to distraint for non-settlement of accounts. See, e.g., the case of the collectors of the fifteenth and tenth of 1415 in Bucks: TNA, E 199/2/7.

[53] For the threat of prosecution for unlawful distraint against the local assessors in Southam (Glocs.) in *c.*1417, see TNA, SC 8/168/8365.

and Richard Lacon, had nominated them to the commission deliberately in order to stir up ill will against them and to confound the collection of the tax. When the collectors had appeared at Corbett's manors to distrain him for non-payment, the latter's servants had set upon them with swords; and subsequently Corbett and his brother had orchestrated a full-scale attack on the commissioners at Oldbury, in which several of the latter's followers had been left for dead. It was these dramatic altercations over taxation that actually prompted Henry V to announce his personal presidency of the Shropshire visitation of the king's bench. But while the crown eventually found in the collectors' favour – to the extent that it pardoned them the sum of £19 left uncollected from the tax – it never punished Corbett and Lacon, who continued uninterrupted up the *cursus honorum* of local office-holding.[54]

Another case of the effective condoning of non-payment of taxes by a member of the establishment occurs at the end of the reign, when Henry V authorized an inquiry to establish whether John Travers, gentleman, might be given a pardon for the accidental homicide in December 1417 of John Barenbon, one of the collectors of the fifteenth and tenth in Lancashire. It was revealed in the resulting inquisition that Barenbon had been killed while he attempted to distrain Travers for non-payment of taxation. The county worthies who attested that the death had been an unfortunate accident were much influenced by what they saw as the tax collector's over-zealous use of armed force in proceeding against Travers; and in confirming the defendant's good intentions and securing him his pardon, they effectively condoned his original act of resistance.[55]

Finally, senior members of the clergy might also be involved in acts of non-compliance, especially in respect of their liability to lay subsidies.[56] In 1417 John Gloucester, the collector of the lay tenth in the city of Oxford, was attacked by the abbot of Osney and his men as he attended divine service in the city church of St Mary Magdalen. Gloucester was dragged bleeding from the church and locked up until he promised not to proceed further with the distraint on the abbot for a contribution of £2 5s. towards the subsidy. On this occasion the crown was less inclined to indulge the act of defiance and ordered a special commission of oyer and terminer to investigate the matter.[57] Nevertheless, this clutch of cases is highly revealing of the landed and ecclesiastical elite's determination to control their own fiscal destinies and, in tax disputes as in so many other things, to regard themselves as entitled to meet legitimate force with equal or greater acts of violence.

---

[54] TNA, SC 8/23/1130; TNA, C 49/14, no. 3; TNA, C 1/69/168; TNA, SC 8/23/1146–1148; TNA, SC 8/141/7023; *CPR, 1416–22*, p. 28; *HP*, II, 653–4; III, 541–3.

[55] *CPR, 1422–9*, p. 7.

[56] In 1402 parliament had complained that members of the clergy often sued out writs exempting them from fifteenths and tenths: *PROME*, VIII, 199–200.

[57] *CPR, 1416–22*, p. 208.

*

The major question that remains about the redistribution of the tax burden upon the laity is the degree to which it bore upon the poor. After 1334 the crown had ceased to require the observation of a threshold of assessment below which individuals would not be taxed. (This threshold had varied in earlier taxes, but in 1332 the fifteenth and tenth had been set at 10s. of move-able property in the countryside and 6s. in the towns, thus fixing the lowest tax payments at 8d. and 7d. respectively.)[58] In Kent, where (uniquely) the commissioners had continued after 1334 to enumerate individual taxpayers in the county-level accounts submitted at the exchequer, the result had been a significant increase in the number of persons paying small amounts in tax contributions, to the direct benefit of the wealthier sort.[59] And in the imme-diate aftermath of the Black Death large numbers of landless wage-earners had also been drawn indirectly into the tax net through the temporary expe-dient of allocating the money penalties taken under the new labour laws in relief of tax quotas.[60]

However, the idea that post-plague England witnessed a deliberate conspiracy on the part of the elite to transfer the burden of taxation on to the shoulders of the lower peasantry cannot be taken too far. The most regressive forms of direct subsidy, the poll taxes of 1377 and 1380–1, were completely discredited after the Peasants' Revolt, and flat-rate levies on persons with insufficient assessable wealth were only introduced again in the tax reforms of the early Tudors. As Fenwick has pointed out, dramatic changes in the population and prosperity of individual communities during the second half of the fourteenth century could sometimes lead to an increase, rather than a decrease, in the amounts that the gentry and the upper peasantry had to pay in order to meet the quota.[61] A dramatic example of the phenomenon comes in the claim lodged at Henry V's last parliament by the inhabitants of New Shoreham (Sussex) that their tax quota of £12, once borne by a town of over 500 people, was now levied on a mere thirty-six doughty souls – who, it was pointed out, might well leave the place entirely deserted if they did not get the relief they so urgently deserved.[62]

The Kent material again offers at least some perspective on the system as it was operating in the early fifteenth century. Unfortunately for the modern

---

[58] Willard, *Parliamentary Taxes*, p. 88.
[59] 'The Kent Lay Subsidy of 1334–5', ed. C. W. Chalkin and H. A. Hanley, in *Documents Illustrative of Medieval Kentish Society*, ed. F. R. H. Du Boulay, Kent Archaeological Society Records Publications 18 (1964), pp. 58–172.
[60] B. H. Putnam, *The Enforcement of the Statute of Labourers* (New York, 1908), pp. 98–138.
[61] C. C. Fenwick, 'The English Poll Taxes of 1377, 1379, and 1381: A Critical Examination of the Returns' (unpublished Ph.D. thesis, University of London, 1983), pp. 19–20.
[62] TNA, SC 8/24/1169. For the parallel campaign by the inhabitants of Rottingdean, see TNA, SC 8/24/1170.

researcher, the form of the tax records from this county changed after the events of 1381: the collectors continued to return the names of all those house-holders who claimed exemption under the privileges of the Cinque Ports but, probably in direct response to the sensitivities around self-determination raised in village communities in Kent during the Peasants' Revolt, now began to follow the practice already adopted with regard to the Ports of Sussex and simply provided sum totals for the amounts liable in each tax district, without any indication of the identities and valuations of individual taxpayers.[63] The lists of exempt persons holding in the Cinque Ports that continued to be sent in to the exchequer from Kent and Sussex in the early fifteenth century have a certain obsessive quality, with the amounts claimed given to the last farthing and with single claims sometimes running as low as a halfpenny.[64] Neverthe-less, this should not be taken to suggest that the persons thus released were necessarily poor. Exemption was attached to tenure rather than to capacity; and the repetition across two or more tax districts of the names of persons claiming the privileges of the Ports is sufficiently frequent as to hint that the relevant householders were often rather more prosperous than their single exemptions might suggest.[65] Nor can we assume that the local tax assessors in these areas took the same comprehensive approach when it came to assessing and levying subsidies from those still liable. From 1334 to the 1370s, when the tendency to regressive taxation was probably at its strongest, only about half the households in Kent had fallen within the tax net, and an informal threshold of 5s. (yielding a payment of 4d. for a whole fifteenth and tenth) seems to have been widely observed.[66] There is nothing to suggest that such a system did not also operate in this county (and perhaps, by extension, in others) during the reign of Henry V.

Despite the undoubted downward shift in the burden of taxation since 1334 and the very crude determinants of liability operated by urban and rural communities, then, what little evidence there is tends to indicate that, at a local level, tax liability continued in the early fifteenth century to be linked in

---

[63] The change can be demonstrated readily by a comparison of TNA, E 179/123/29 (1372) and TNA, E 179/123/49 (1383). For Sussex practice, see, e.g., TNA, E 179/189/67; 225/38; 225/39.

[64] See, for example, TNA, E 179/124/83 (account of the two fifteenths and tenths of 1415); TNA, E 179/124/88 (account of the two fifteenths and tenths of 1416); and TNA, E 179/124/89 (account of the first of the two fifteenths and tenths of 1417).

[65] See, for example, the case of Joanna Feld, skinner, who appears twice (seemingly as the same person) in the tax district of Faversham in 1415, exempted once for 6d. and secondly for 1d.: TNA, E 164/7, fols. lxxxvii, lxxxviii. In the same account, the name Walter Boner appears in Faversham district exempt of 2¼d., but in Larkfield district exempt the much more substantial assessment of 1s.: TNA, E 164/7, fols. lxxxviii, xcii.

[66] Dyer, 'Taxation and Communities', pp. 173–4; Fenwick, 'English Poll Taxes', pp. 19–20; W. M. Ormrod, 'Poverty and Privilege: The Fiscal Burden in England (XIIIth–XVth Centuries)', in La fiscalità, ed. Cavaciocchi, II, 637–56 (pp. 642–3).

some basic manner to the ability to pay. The logical conclusion for the realm at large is that the real burden of taxation tended to be borne chiefly by the more substantial tenants of the manor (whether holding in free or servile tenure, since royal taxation was blind to that distinction),[67] supplemented by lesser charges on the middling sort of smallholders and, where local conditions made it absolutely necessary, on cottagers and wage-labourers.

The evidence for exemption, evasion and liability to taxation in the early fifteenth century thus tends towards a strongly functionalist model of compromise, in which the crown devolved responsibility for both liability and exemption to ecclesiastical and secular officials in the provinces and was rewarded with a high-level of compliance among the tax-paying population. We need to acknowledge that this put severe constraints on central government's ability to counter demands for the relief of communities and the exoneration of unpaid debts. When it attempted to double-check such claims, it was forced over and over again to rely on sources of information that had a strong vested interest in maintaining the status quo. Thus in 1419 when the exchequer had suspicions about the list of impoverished churches in the diocese of Hereford, its only available recourse was to go back to the bishop who had supplied the schedule in the first place.[68] The certificates provided by the local bailiffs of the Cinque Ports were normally accepted without challenge as proof of the exemptions claimed by those holding in privileged tenure in Sussex and Kent.[69] But when the exchequer decided to run controls on the lists of exempt persons, it was restricted to referring the information up through the hierarchy of officeholders within the Ports, who were either obstructive of the process or simply content, for obvious reasons, to confirm the information already supplied.[70] The investment of significant time and resource into such investigations also did little to address the resulting anom-

---

[67] See an interesting case from the early fifteenth century in which the free tenants of Cobham (Surrey) claimed that the abbot of Chertsey had withdrawn the portion of the fifteenth due from his servile tenants in the vill and that he ought now to pay that amount rather than it being assessed on the free: TNA, SC 8/271/13533.

[68] *Registrum Edmundi Laci episcopi Herefordensis, 1417–1420*, ed. A. T. Bannister, Canterbury and York Society 22 (1918), pp. 67–81. In 1421, after Bishop Lacy had been promoted from Hereford to the see of Exeter, the exchequer issued him with a writ of *certiorari* to provide information on the incumbents of Kenton, Poltimore, Whitestone, Wembworthy and St Mary Steps, Exeter, in order to establish whether their claims to exemption on taxes raised in 1415–19 were valid: *Register of Edmund Lacy, Bishop of Exeter*, I, 68–9.

[69] See, for example, the system in operation in Sussex in 1421: TNA, E 179/225/42. Sometimes, indeed, the county assessors in Sussex seem to have felt it sufficient to return the bailiffs' certificates to the exchequer and to provide global totals of the amounts exempt in each tax district, rather than making their own consolidated lists of exempt persons and of the amounts to be deducted: see, for example, TNA, E 179/189/67.

[70] TNA, E 368/193, rots 185d–186; and see the extant list of claimed exemptions for the lay subsidy of 1416 sent back for ratification by the warden of the Ports in 1422: TNA, E 179/225/38. The original certificates of exemption in Sussex for the 1416 subsidy

alies; and shortfalls in tax receipts as a result of error or collusion simply had to be written off.[71] In this respect Henry V's regime was very much the victim of a hidebound bureaucratic system that notoriously placed more emphasis on accountability than it did on productivity.

All these shortcomings and limitations only serve, however, to emphasize the remarkable resilience of the system of direct taxation in early fifteenth century England and the sound sense of judgement exercised by the government of Henry V in the management of it. For all the exemptions and allowances enumerated above, Henry probably allowed significantly fewer reductions to the tax base than had Edward III, Richard II and Henry IV. And at a best guess, the net yield of a fifteenth and tenth had been eroded by around £2,000 since 1334, and was still running in the 1410s at about £36,000, while a clerical tenth levied in both provinces had dropped since the 1320s from around £18,000 to some £16,000 in the 1410s.[72] It was only in the very different political and economic circumstances of the reign of Henry VI that parliament began to insist, after 1433, that the overall value of a fifteenth and tenth be much more significantly and systematically reduced, first by £4,000 and then, from 1446, by £6,000.[73] And finally, of course, the greatest testimony to the resilience of the tax system as operated under Henry V (the example of Cheshire in 1416 notwithstanding) is the striking absence of concerted opposition. In every other period of intense taxation between the twelfth and the sixteenth century, rulers faced the stark reality of resistance and revolt – either from the lay and clerical elite, as under John, Henry III, Edward I and Henry IV, or from the popular element, as under Richard II, Henry VI, Henry VII and Henry VIII.[74] Even the great extractor Edward III had faced widespread opposition, and the open rumour of uprising, during the controversial opening stages of the Hundred Years War.[75] No doubt Henry V's notable success at the outset of the reign in suppressing the Southampton Plot and

---

also survive in E 179/225/39, with strays in E 179/234/1 and E 179/364/172. Similar processes are recorded in E 179/225/36 and E 179/225/42.

[71] See a telling case from the early 1440s in which an elaborate investigation of an erroneous assessment upon the hospital of St John the Baptist, Oxford, for contribution of £4 10s. to the lay fifteenth and tenth led not to the reassessment of the town but simply to the condoning of the outstanding debt: TNA, E 368/214, *Status et visus compotorum*, Mich., rot. xii; TNA, E 199/37/14.

[72] See the detailed calculations of I. R. Abbott, 'Taxation of Personal Property and of Clerical Income, 1399 to 1402', *Speculum* 17 (1942), 471–98 (pp. 479, 492).

[73] For a comprehensive contemporary schedule of the resulting changes to the tax burden across the shires, see TNA, E 163/28/3/1.

[74] M. L. Bush, 'The Risings of the Commons in England, 1381–1549', in *Orders and Hierarchies in Late Medieval and Renaissance Europe*, ed. J. H. Denton (Basingstoke, 1999), pp. 109–25; C. Valente, *The Theory and Practice of Revolt in Medieval England* (Aldershot, 2003).

[75] J. R. Maddicott, 'The English Peasantry and the Demands of the Crown, 1294–1341', in *Landlords, Peasants and Politics in Medieval England*, ed. T. H. Aston (Cambridge, 1987), pp. 285–359 (pp. 348–9).

Oldcastle's rebellion reminded his subjects, in timely fashion, of the risks of further resistance to their public obligations: it is significant that the poem 'The Crowned King', written *c.*1415, while implicitly critical of regressive taxation, was also very clear about the king's undeniable right to demand 'a soleyn subsidie to susteyne his werres'.[76] In the end, however, it was persuasion rather than coercion that surely determined the fate of the Lancastrian fiscal machine. Just as Edward III had managed successfully to operate the tax system through the extraordinary emergency of the Black Death of 1348–9 on the back of his recent victories at Crécy and Calais, so must Henry V's successful record of sustained extraction in the 1410s be accounted for in large measure by the public confidence and commitment inspired by his feats at Harfleur and Agincourt. The overwhelming sense of compliance with the fiscal demands of the crown in the latter period suggests more than merely a reluctant resignation to the inevitability of taxes. As the tense fiscal politics of the reigns of Richard II and Henry IV gave way to a sense of common purpose and public responsibility, the very act of paying taxes was coming to be seen, by its contributors among civic and rural society, as a badge of honour and status.[77]

*

We now move to the macro-economic level and attempt to make some overall assessment of the real burden of taxation in England under Henry V. Table 1 estimates the net revenue due from direct taxes on the laity and clergy and the customs and subsidies collected at the ports for each financial year from 1412–13 to 1421–2, arranging the portions of direct taxes according to the various dates at which they fell due (and incorporating any revisions to those dates made subsequent to the original grants). By no means all the sums eventually accounted for were paid by the collection dates, and we need to remember that the accounting for stray payments to Henry V's taxes ground on for many years through the minority of Henry VI. But the scheme employed here provides the most straightforward means of representing the pressure of taxation year on year across the reign. Thus Table 1 helps to substantiate two important shifts of gear at the beginning and end of the reign, with taxes increasing significantly from the point of commitment to the French war in 1414 and dropping again markedly after the treaty of Troyes of 1420. Equally striking is the continuous and significantly high pressure of taxation over the six consecutive years from Michaelmas 1414 to Michaelmas 1420. Between those dates, direct taxation ran every year at over £50,000, and

---

[76] 'The Crowned King', in *The Piers Plowman Tradition*, ed. H. Barr (London, 1993), p. 206.
[77] W. M. Ormrod, 'The Politics of Pestilence: Government in England after the Black Death', in *The Black Death in England*, ed. W. M. Ormrod and P. G. Lindley (Stamford, 1996), pp. 173–6.

in 1416–17 reached just short of £100,000; the average annual burden of direct taxation was some £69,600. And with indirect taxation raising approximately £50,000 a year, the combined total of tax revenue for the six years ran to £710,700, or £118,500 a year.

Table 1 Revenue from direct and indirect taxation, 1412–22

Financial year (Sept.–Sept.)	Direct taxation (laity & clergy) (£)	Indirect taxation (all customs & subsidies) (annual average) (£)	Total tax revenue (£)
1412–13	25,500	53,200	78,700
1413–14	52,000	46,800	98,800
1414–15	52,000	48,600	100,600
1415–16	88,000	47,800	135,800
1416–17	97,100	48,400	145,500
1417–18	69,200	53,800	123,000
1418–19	51,200	51,400	102,600
1419–20	60,300	43,000	103,300
1420–1	0	43,400	43,400
1421–2	25,500	45,800	71,300

Source. W. M. Ormrod, 'Revenues to the English Crown from Direct and Indirect Taxation 1168–1547', European State Finance Database, http://esfdb.websites.bta.com

Such figures mean comparatively little, however, without some systematic contextualization. Table 2 therefore compares the face value of the taxes collected in 1414–20 with those for the three other most intense periods of taxation across the later Middle Ages: Edward I's simultaneous wars in France, Scotland and Wales in the mid-1290s; Edward III's opening forays of the Hundred Years War during the late 1330s; and the major emergency around the loss of overseas possessions and the security of the realm of England during the minority of Richard II in the late 1370s.[78]

The first point to be remarked in respect of Table 2 is that Henry V's sustained activity was more prolonged than any of the other three periods identified. This makes all the more remarkable the general point made in the previous section: namely, that Henry V successfully avoided the major confrontations over taxation encountered by Edward I in 1297, by Edward III in 1340–1 and by Richard II in 1381 – all of which, very tellingly, had required the crown to withdraw controversial new experimental taxes and thus, in the short term, significantly to reduce the overall level of fiscal extraction.

[78] For the peaks and troughs of taxation across the period from the 1290s to the 1450s see W. M. Ormrod, 'The Domestic Response to the Hundred Years War', in *Arms, Armies and Fortifications in the Hundred Years War*, ed. A. Curry and M. Hughes (Woodbridge, 1994), pp. 87–94.

Table 2 Direct and indirect taxation at peaks of fiscal activity
between 1290 and 1420

Financial years (Sept.–Sept.)	Direct taxation (laity & clergy) (annual average) (£)	Indirect taxation (all customs & subsidies) (annual average) (£)	Total tax revenue (annual average) (£)
1294/5–1296/7	90,900	35,200	126,100
1336/7–1340/1	95,200	31,300	126,500
1377/8–1380/1	62,000	57,300	119,300
1414/15–1419/20	69,600	48,800	118,500

Source. See Table 1.

The other preliminary observation that we can make from these figures is about the balance between indirect and indirect taxation. Down to the early fourteenth century the crown's extraordinary expenditure was supported very largely by direct taxation of the laity and clergy. But the establishment of the wool subsidy as a permanent element in the customs system from the 1340s onwards meant that, for the rest of the Hundred Years War, the norm was for revenues from indirect taxation to exceed those from direct subsidies – as occurred, indeed, at the beginning and the end of Henry V's reign. The profits of indirect taxation were in long-term decline from the late fourteenth century, but kept a generally steady state between the reigns of Henry IV and Henry V and only fell away significantly after the reduction in the rate of the wool subsidy from 1422 and the disruptions to overseas trade consequent upon the bullion ordinances of 1429–30. In spite of the comparatively high yield of the customs system, however, direct taxation always exceeded indirect taxation in the six fiscal years that encompassed the great sequence of military activity from the siege of Harfleur to the treaty of Troyes, and on average ran over £20,000 in excess of the profits of the ports. Across the century after the Black Death, there is in fact no other period in which direct taxation proved so large a proportion of royal income and thus so crucial a resource in the crown's fiscal armoury.[79]

The latter point raises further questions about the real burden of taxation in Henry V's England and the ability of the contemporary economy to sustain the costs of war. Table 3 takes the data on direct taxation and expresses it in relation to three economic indicators: the volume of the currency; Gross Domestic Product (GDP); and the size of the population. It goes almost without saying that there are huge uncertainties underpinning some of the calculations represented here. Keen debate continues, for example, on the volume of the currency and the calculation of GDP, and in taking the esti-

[79] W. M. Ormrod, 'England in the Middle Ages', in *The Rise of the Fiscal State in Europe, c. 1200–1815*, ed. R. Bonney (Oxford, 1999), p. 42.

mates respectively of Martin Allen and Nicholas Mayhew for these two items, we need to acknowledge the quite significant discrepancies (both in methodology and in results) between their findings and those of Spufford, Britnell, Snooks, Campbell and others.[80] To reflect these uncertainties, the population figures accept a calculation of 2.75 million for the late 1370s, as extrapolated from the poll tax returns of that era; but the figures given for other periods attempt to incorporate what are currently regarded as the ranges of plausible estimates.[81]

For all the uncertainties, and in spite of the wide margin of error that has to be allowed, the data set out in Table 3 appear to tell a quite consistent and revealing story. On all three bases, the cost of taxation seems to have been as high, and often very significantly higher, under Henry V than under Edward I, Edward III and Richard II. The data in relation to the currency are striking, for they accentuate the enormous challenges faced by taxpayers and tax collectors in bullion-starved late medieval England. The resulting logistical strain, which was a major political issue in the 1330s, is generally absent from the public discourses of the 1410s. But it shows up in rather striking fashion in 1419 when, in response to continuing concern about the outflow of specie from the realm, the crown agreed (at least in principle) that money raised in lay and clerical taxes should not be sent over to France but instead re-circulated within the English economy through the purchase of clothing, equipment and provisions for the king's armies.[82]

To the extent that we can rely on what are necessarily very impressionistic measures, however, it is the calculations based on GDP that are probably more immediately revealing, indicating as they do that the overall value of government extraction tended to stick in the post-plague economy at about 2 per cent of GDP for direct taxation alone and up to 3.5 per cent for direct and indirect taxation combined. Here at least the comparison can also be extended into the early modern period. Even after the major reforms under the early

---

[80] On the money supply, in addition to the sources cited under Table 3, see P. Spufford, *Money and its Use in Medieval Europe* (Cambridge, 1989), p. 420; Britnell, *Commercialisation*, p. 180; J. H. Munro, 'Before and after the Black Death: Money, Prices and Wages in Fourteenth-Century England', in *New Approaches to the History of Late Medieval and Early Modern Europe*, ed. T. Dahlerup and P. Ingesman (Copenhagen, 2009), pp. 335–64. The debate on GDP centres on the year 1300, for which there are widely divergent calculations: see G. D. Snooks, 'The Dynamic Role of the Market in the Anglo-Norman Economy and Beyond', in *A Commercialising Economy: England 1086 to c. 1300*, ed. R. H. Britnell and B. M. S. Campbell (Manchester, 1995), pp. 27–54; N. Mayhew, 'Modelling Medieval Monetisation', in *A Commercialising Economy*, ed. Britnell and Campbell, pp. 55–77.

[81] For a critical survey of the recent debates on the population, see S. H. Rigby, 'Introduction', in *A Social History of England, 1200–1500*, ed. R. Horrox and W. M. Ormrod (Cambridge, 2006), pp. 1–30.

[82] PROME, IX, 235; J. H. A. Munro, *Wool, Cloth and Gold: The Struggle for Bullion in Anglo-Burgundian Trade, 1340–1478* (Toronto, 1972), 72 and n. 21.

Table 3 Economic indicators of the burden of taxation at peaks
of fiscal activity between 1290 and 1420

	Financial years (Sept.–Sept.)	1294/5– 1297/8	1336/7– 1340/1	1377/8– 1380/1	1414/15– 1419/20
	CURRENCY				
A	Estimated face value of coinage (silver+gold) = total (£m)	(2.0+0.0) = 2.0	(1.5+0.0) = 1.5	(0.8+0.2) = 1.0	(0.2+0.8) = 1.0
B	Direct taxation (money of account) as % of coinage	4.56%	6.45%	6.20%	6.96%
C	Direct + indirect taxation (money of account) as % of total coinage	6.31%	8.43%	11.93%	11.85%
	GDP				
D	Estimated GDP (£m)	4.66–5.00	4.00	3.5	3.5
E	Direct taxation (money of account) as % of GDP	1.82%– 1.95%	2.38%	1.77%	1.99%
F	Direct + indirect taxation (money of account) as % of GDP	2.52%– 2.70%	3.16%	3.40%	3.36%
	POPULATION				
G	Estimated population (m)	4.5–6.0	4.0–5.5	2.75	2.0–2.5
H	Direct taxation: per capita, per annum (money of account)	3½d.–5d.	4½d.–5½d.	5½d.	7d.–8½d.
J	Direct and indirect taxation: per capita, per annum (money of account)	5½d.–7d.	6d.–7½d.	10½d.	11d.–14d.

Sources. Row A: M. R. Allen, 'The Volume of the English Currency, 1158–1470', *EcHR*, 2nd ser. 54 (2001), 595–611. Row D: N. Mayhew, 'Population, Money Supply and the Velocity of Circulation in England, 1300–1700', *EcHR*, 2nd ser. 48 (1995), 238–57. Row G: J. Hatcher, *Plague, Population and the English Economy, 1348–1530* (London, 1977), pp. 68–73; M. Overton and B. M. S. Campbell, 'Production et productivité dans l'agriculture anglaise, 1086–1871', *Histoire & mesure* 10 (1996), 255–97; B. M. S. Campbell, *English Seigniorial Agriculture, 1250–1450* (Cambridge, 2000), pp. 37–40, 399–406; P. J. P. Goldberg, *Medieval England: A Social History, 1250–1550* (London, 2004), pp. 71–87.

Tudors, the weight of direct taxation in the 1520s and the 1540s represented only something in the region of 1.6 per cent and 1.8 per cent respectively of current GDP.[83] In fact, it was not until the eighteenth century that the English state was able to move decisively beyond the effective ceiling set during the reigns of Richard II and Henry V.[84]

Before we proceed to refine these figures further, we may also usefully consider the real economic burden of the indirect taxes collected as customs and subsidies on exports and imports. Expressing indirect taxation in per capita terms can obviously be misleading, since the customs and subsidies were paid only by those involved in overseas trade. On the other hand, a proportion of the tax burden was clearly passed on to the denizen population at large in the form of lower market prices for goods intended for export and higher ones for imported commodities. Row J of Table 3, which combines the totals for direct and indirect taxation and expresses them in notional charges 'per capita, per annum', therefore tells a story of late medieval fiscal structures from the point of view of the taxpayer-cum-consumer, with an apparently inexorable rise in the burden of taxation – amounting to anything between 100 per cent and 150 per cent of face value – between the 1290s and the 1410s.

Another and rather more meaningful way of expressing indirect taxation is as a proportion of the overall value of exports and imports. The high rates of duty maintained on wool exports under Henry V, coupled with a modest increase over the previous reign in the volume of exports and imports, meant that indirect taxation represented a relatively high proportion – at least 14.5 per cent – of the total value of exports and imports in the 1410s. This figure may have been lower than the exceptional 18.5 per cent achieved by Edward III's government in the boom years of the 1350s, but it is still impressive in comparison with the 3.5–5 per cent achieved in the early fourteenth century and the 9–12 per cent to which the rate dropped again between the 1430s to the 1480s.[85] As with direct taxation, then, so with indirect, Henry V's

---

[83] R. H. Britnell, 'The English Economy and the Government, 1450–1500', in *The End of the Middle Ages? England in the Fifteenth and Sixteenth Centuries*, ed. J. L. Watts (Stroud, 1998), pp. 89–116 (pp. 101–2), employing data from R. Hoyle, 'War and Public Finance', in *The Reign of Henry VIII: Politics, Policy and Piety*, ed. D. MacCulloch (Basingstoke, 1995), pp. 75–99 (p. 93).

[84] P. K. O'Brien and P. A. Hunt, 'The Rise of a Fiscal State in England, 1485–1815', *Historical Research* 66 (1993), 129–76 (pp. 160–1). For further discussion see W. M. Ormrod, 'Government Records: Fiscality, Archives and the Economic Historian', in *Where is Economic History Going? Methods and Prospects from the 13th to the 18th Centuries*, ed. F. Ammannati (Florence, 2011), pp. 197–224 (pp. 217–18).

[85] Calculations based on the estimates of the value of overseas trade made by Lloyd, 'Overseas Trade', pp. 96–124, and J. L. Bolton, *The Medieval English Economy, 1150–1500* (London, 1980), p. 307, set against the data for revenue from the customs and subsidies cited in Table 1. For further comment see W. M. Ormrod, 'Finance and Trade under

record seems to have represented something close to a peak of resource extraction in post-plague England.

To understand how it was possible to move the great tax machine of the English crown into the new overdrive of the 1410s and achieve such remarkable levels of fiscal activity, however, we need to appreciate rather more fully the complex and shifting relationship between taxation, economy and population. The dramatic increases in the per capita burden of taxation between the 1290s and the 1410s set out in rows H and J of Table 3 provide a stark reminder of the demographic revolution that had intervened. But to express these figures only in money of account is obviously to ignore the huge changes that had also occurred through the later fourteenth century in the distribution of wealth and the real value of money. It is only when the figures are further adjusted according to the price and real wage indices, in Table 4, that we begin to see a real comparison of the relative burden of taxation across the later Middle Ages.

Table 4 The real burden of direct taxation: per capita, per annum
contributions adjusted according to price and wage indices
(constant values of 1450–75)

Financial years (Sept.–Sept.)	1294/5– 1297/8	1336/7– 1340/1	1377/8– 1380/1	1414/15– 1419/20
Direct taxation: per capita, per annum (money of account)	3½d.–5d.	4½d.–5½d.	5½d.	7d.–8½d.
Direct taxation; per capita, per annum (deflated by price index)	3d.–5d.	5d.–6d.	5½d.	6d.–7½d.
Direct taxation: per capita, per annum (deflated by real wage index)	7½d.–10½d.	9d.–10½d.	7d.	7d.–9d.

Sources. Data from Table 2 expressed according to price and real wage indices from E. H. Phelps Brown and S. V. Hopkins, *A Perspective on Wages and Prices* (London, 1981), pp. 13–59.

The staple goods used to create the Phelps Brown–Hopkins price index employed in Table 4 were still running relatively high in the early fifteenth century, and the conversion of the per capita burden by price index therefore leaves the 1410s still out ahead in terms of the real burden of taxation, even if the range is now slightly narrowed. But the truly revealing data are those

Richard II', in *Richard II: The Art of Kingship*, ed. A. Goodman and J. L. Gillespie (Oxford, 1999), pp. 155–86.

yielded by the conversion to real incomes: that is, the notional per capita tax burden expressed in relation to the purchasing capacity of contemporary wages (Phelps Brown and Hopkins's index for the cost of a 'basket of consumables'). This calculation reveals, in truly dramatic fashion, the positive impact upon fiscality under Henry V of the wage revolution experienced in England between the 1370s and the 1410s. Under Edward I and Edward III, in the pre-plague economies, with prices generally high and wages low, the per capita burden converted in relation to the purchasing capacity of the later fifteenth century rises dramatically. After the Black Death, however, the major economic redistribution arising from a new shortage of labour and the consequent escalation of wage rates means that, in spite of the huge reduction in the population, the per capita figure during peaks of fiscal activity tends to stick at the very bottom end of the pre-plague range, around 7d., and even under Henry V reaches no higher than the mid-range for the 1290s and 1330s.

In assessing the significance of these findings, it is obviously necessary to stress that the experience of wage-earners was not that of the population as a whole. We have already remarked that landless labourers were still comparatively rarely assessed for taxation in this period; as Dyer has concluded, the group that probably felt the pinch during high levels of fiscal extraction in the fifteenth century were the smallholders, for whom a tax demand of between 4d. and 8d. could still represent a significant burden.[86] Nevertheless, the increase in the purchasing capacity of wage-labourers was part of a wider restructuring of the economy in which many tenant farmers also felt a real benefit in the form of a withering of seigniorial dues and a gradual decline in rent charges.[87] Suddenly, then, it begins to become apparent why there was so little recorded outcry or organized resistance to taxation in the 1410s. The high-level of compliance with Henry V's tax policies was not simply about the king's charisma and credibility. It also had a great deal to do with the fact that an increasing number of those who bore the brunt of direct taxation could more easily afford to do so.

None of this is necessarily to suggest that the system operated in the 1410s was economically sustainable in the long term or that, by extension, the evolving and ambitious war aims of Henry V were at all realizable: here we really do enter into the realms of the speculative and the counter-factual. But these attempts to quantify the real burden of taxation in this reign give some further, firm justification to the view that the determined efforts of English parliaments and convocations significantly to reduce the burden of taxation in the period after the treaty of Troyes were based just as much in political and constitutional arguments as they were in the perception or reality of national poverty. And if Henry V pushed the English fiscal machine to the

---

[86] Dyer, 'Taxation and Communities', pp. 189–90.
[87] C. Dyer, *Standards of Living in the Later Middle Ages: Social Change in England, c. 1200–1500* (Cambridge, 1989), pp. 109–50.

very peaks of its post-plague productivity, the practical limits of resource extraction were ultimately determined not by economic capacity but by deep political structures that set strict limits on the crown's exploitation of the real tax base.

*

Among the more unlikely memorabilia of the battle of Agincourt is a remarkable bound manuscript, compiled and kept at the exchequer in the fifteenth and sixteenth centuries, containing the 'parcels of the fifteenth and tenth of the third year of the reign of our sovereign lord King Henry V'. Over some 350 rubricated folios and in a fair book hand, an unidentified clerk painstakingly copied out all the extant particulars of account rendered by the collectors of this tax, enumerating every town and vill assessed for the subsidy on moveables and the quota that each contributed to the great enterprise of 1415.[88] The compilation may have been no more than the self-indulgence of a statistically minded bureaucrat. It may also have been intended to act as a book of precedents against which future claims for remissions and exonerations might be usefully checked during audits at Westminster. But the particular choice of the tax granted in the year of Henry V's most astonishing military achievement surely also suggests something by way of wider celebration. As Michael Postan remarked in his penetrating analysis of the costs of the Hundred Years War, military victories abroad were not merely the work of the happy few, but the result of a deep engagement, by many thousands of non-combatant English men and women, in the countless economic enterprises that serviced the war effort.[89] Chief among those enterprises, and the one that involved by far the largest proportion of the population across almost the entire country, was the payment of taxes. The extension of tax liability to a larger proportion of the population may have compounded certain of the systemic inequities in the system. But it also gave a larger proportion of people than ever before a sense of personal connection both with the war and with the accompanying business of the state. In this sense the exchequer's book of fifteenths and tenths commemorates the collective endeavour of the English state and the English taxpayer: the closest approximation that the fifteenth century could make to a kind of Domesday of Agincourt.

In 1995, I berated Henry V for his failure to exploit the political goodwill of his reign and carry out a root-and-branch reform of the fiscal system.[90] The analysis undertaken here leads me to revise that stance. There remains

---

88 TNA, E 164/7.
89 M. M. Postan, 'The Costs of the Hundred Years' War', *Past & Present* 27i (1964), 34–53.
90 W. M. Ormrod, *Political Life in Medieval England, 1300–1450* (Basingstoke, 1995), pp. 136–7. For critical comment on this approach, see C. Carpenter, *The Wars of the Roses: Politics and the Constitution in England, c. 1437–1509* (Cambridge, 1997), p. 272.

serious doubt as to whether, had he lived, Henry could have overcome the fundamental problems created when parliament made it clear that the treaty of Troyes had effectively ended England's obligation to pay for the ongoing war in France. On the other hand, this dilemma was fundamentally about the constitutional status of England's new acquisitions across the Channel, and only secondarily about concerns over the sustainability of the war state. Henry V's very real achievement was to run the existing system at as high a capacity as any monarch between the early thirteenth and the mid-sixteenth centuries, and yet to avoid the political controversies and popular revolts that beset every other high-taxing king from Henry III to Henry VIII. It would be ironic indeed to represent the 1410s as a golden age of the English taxpayer. And yet it would be hard to identify any other period in later medieval England in which the crown was apparently so successful in aligning its own fiscal needs with the political, administrative, social and economic expectations of its subjects.

9

Henry V, Flower of Chivalry[1]

Craig Taylor

Introduction

On 6 November 1422, the coffin of Henry V was carried to a funeral carriage by eight chamber knights, with four earls holding each of the corners of a cloth of gold on top of it, and four knights supporting a canopy above the coffin. Two of the horses that drew the carriage were decorated with the arms of England, and the other three horses wore the arms of St Edmund, St Edward and St George. As the procession moved towards Westminster, the coffin was followed by knights and pages on horseback, carrying the king's helmet and the shields of England and France. After the Requiem Mass at Westminster Abbey the following day, three knights rode their horses up to the high altar where they removed their armour, symbolically representing Henry V's laying down of his knightly responsibilities in death.[2]

As these elaborate rituals demonstrated, Henry V was celebrated not merely as a monarch but also as a great knight. Kingship and chivalry were not separate constructs in late medieval didactic works, chronicles and biographies which praised ideal qualities like loyalty, largesse, honour and above all prudence that were essential for both kings and knights. Both were founded upon the cardinal virtues of justice, temperance, prudence and fortitude that were so important not just for kings and knights but for all Christians. Contemporary authors constantly emphasized the obligations of a king to fight, but also of a knight to be wise and prudent, especially when serving

---

[1] I would like to dedicate this chapter to Maurice Keen, who sadly passed away while I was completing the final draft.

[2] W. H. St John Hope, 'The Funeral, Monument and Chantry Chapel of Henry V', *Archaeologia* 65 (1913–14), 129–86 (pp. 133–5), and Thomas Walsingham, *The St. Albans Chronicle, Volume II 1394–1422*, ed. J. Taylor, W. R. Childs and L. Watkiss (Oxford, 2011), pp. 776–8, together with Allmand, *Henry V*, p. 178 and L. Monnas, 'Textiles from the Funerary Achievement of Henry V', in *The Lancastrian Court: Proceedings of the 2001 Harlaxton Symposium*, ed. J. Stratford (Donington, 2003), pp. 125–46.

as a lord or a military commander.[3] Before the king's death, John Page had written an eyewitness account of the siege of Rouen during the winter of 1418, in which the French negotiators declared that Henry V was the foremost prince on earth, praising his discretion, manhood and mercifulness, and identifying him above all as a 'conquerowre'.[4] After the king had died, Michel Pintouin, chronicler of Saint-Denis, was almost as effusive, declaring that Henry had demonstrated a range of qualities including magnanimity, prudence and wisdom, and as a result had been more equipped to conquer a region or country than any other prince of the age.[5] In 1420, John Lydgate had concluded the *Troy Book* by declaring that Henry V ought to be 'registred worthi as of name / In the highest place of the hous of fame.'[6] In his verses on the *Kings of England* written around 1426, Lydgate described Henry as a lodestar of knighthood because he was wise, manly and successful in both peace and war, and expert in martial discipline. He concluded that Henry was now 'Able to stonde among the Worthi Nyne', that is to say the Nine Worthies such as Judas Maccabeus, Hector, Alexander the Great, Arthur and Roland who formed the highest pantheon of chivalric culture.[7]

As Page, Pintouin and Lydgate all attested, Henry V's chivalric fame was based first and foremost upon his martial exploits. Henry V 'displayed notably the qualities of chivalrous leadership'.[8] In particular he had secured great military successes in northern France, including the victory at Agincourt in 1415, the conquest of Normandy and the establishment of the Dual Monarchy through the treaty of Troyes and his marriage to the Valois princess Katharine. This resulted in a fundamentally different chivalric reputation, for example, from that of his father. Before seizing the English throne in 1399,

---

3 M. H. Keen, 'Chivalry and English Kingship in the Later Middle Ages', in *War, Government and Aristocracy in the British Isles, c.1150–1500: Essays in Honour of Michael Prestwich*, ed. C. Given-Wilson, A. Kettle and L. Scales (Woodbridge, 2008), pp. 250–66. Also see G. L. Harriss, 'Introduction: the Exemplar of Kingship', in *Henry V*, ed. Harriss, pp. 1–29 (p. 26): 'Perfect kingship indeed embraced perfect knighthood.'

4 *The Historical Collection of a Citizen of London in the Fifteenth Century*, ed. Gairdner, Camden Society n.s. 17 (London, 1876), p. 33.

5 *Chronique du Religieux de Saint-Denis contenant le règne de Charles VI, de 1380 à 1422*, ed. L. Bellaguet, 6 vols. (Paris, 1839–52), VI, 480–2, and also see 162–4 and pages 224–5 below.

6 John Lydgate, *Lydgate's Troy Book*, ed. H. Bergen, 4 vols., EETS ES 97, 103, 106 and 126 (1906–35), III, 876.

7 John Lydgate, *The Minor Poems of John Lydgate*, ed. H. N. MacCracken, 2 vols., EETS OS 192 (London, 1934), II, 716. Lydgate echoed these comments in his translation of Laurence Calot's pedigree for Henry VI, declaring that there would never be a manlier man, either in terms of his worthiness of governance or prowess, given his worthy conquest of France. Moreover, in a ballad dedicated to Henry VI, Lydgate presented the Nine Worthies, and other 'noble worty conquerrors' as examples, along with his father, 'a myrrour of manhede' and a model of 'knyghthode'. Ibid., pp. 619 and 628–9.

8 Keen, 'Chivalry and English Kingship in the Later Middle Ages', p. 255.

Henry Bolingbroke had travelled far and wide performing deeds of arms in tournaments and on crusade. Given the scarcity of opportunities to fight in France during a lull in the Hundred Years War, and his own freedom from the responsibilities that he would bear as king after the usurpation of 1399, he had lived the life of individual errantry that was often celebrated in chivalric literature.[9] In contrast, Henry V had little opportunity for such knightly adventures because he was so heavily involved in wars in Wales and France. Indeed, various chroniclers claimed that as he lay on his deathbed, Henry V expressed his sadness that he had not had the chance to fulfil his desire to go on crusade because there had been no peace with France.[10]

On the other hand Henry V had little time for tournaments and other courtly games that were as commonplace as crusading in the chivalric imagination.[11] His marriage to the Valois princess Katharine was above all a diplomatic match intended to secure his claims in France, and few contemporary writers attempted to imbue it with the romance of courtly literature. A rare exception was John Audelay who argued in a carol written for Henry VI in 1429 that one major reason for the war in France was his father's 'loue of Mayd Kateryn'; the fact that Audelay was addressing Henry VI may explain the desire to play up the idea of a love match between the husband and wife.[12] Henry V certainly did not favour the chivalric games that were so popular at other late medieval courts. Thomas Walsingham had famously criticized Ricardian knights for valuing courtly behaviour above war. Such charges could hardly have been laid against Henry V and his courtiers.[13] Following his marriage on 22 May 1420, for example, Henry V did not even take the time to watch a traditional celebratory tournament, instead setting

---

[9] L. Staley, 'Gower, Richard II, Henry of Derby, and the Business of Making Culture', *Speculum* 75 (2000), 68–96 (pp. 83–7), and A. Tuck, 'Henry IV and Chivalry', in *Henry IV: the Establishment of the Regime, 1399–1406*, ed. G. Dodd and D. Biggs (York, 2003), pp. 55–71 (pp. 56–7). Also see pages 245–6 below.

[10] *The Brut, or the Chronicles of England*, ed. F. W. D. Brie, 2 vols., EETS OS 131 and 136 (London, 1906–8), II, 493, and see note 48 below.

[11] Henry V did grant robes to 'Dames de la Fraternite de Saint George' on the occasion of the feast of St George in 1413, but only one more lady was given this honour during his reign, his wife Katharine in 1421: J. L. Gillespie, 'Ladies of the Fraternity of Saint George and of the Society of the Garter', *Albion* 17 (1985), 259–78 (pp. 264 and 270–1).

[12] *Historical Poems of the XIVth and XVth Centuries*, ed. R. H. Robbins (New York, 1959), p. 109.

[13] Thomas Walsingham, *The St. Albans Chronicle, Volume I, 1376–1394*, ed. J. Taylor, W. R. Childs and L. Watkiss (Oxford, 2003), p. 814 and Walsingham, *St. Albans Chronicle, 1394–1422*, pp. 382 and 686–8, together with W. M. Ormrod, 'Knights of Venus', *Medium Aevum* 73 (2004), 290–305. Monstrelet did complain about the pomp at the French court under the regency of Henry V: Enguerran[d] de Monstrelet, *La chronique d'Enguerran de Monstrelet en deux livres avec pièces justicatives (1400–44)*, ed. L. Douët d'Arcq, 6 vols. (Paris, 1857–62), IV, 98–101.

off to lay siege to Sens.[14] Indeed, English commentators took great pains to demonstrate that Henry had abandoned the rashness and irresponsibility of youth when he acceded to the throne in 1413. The *Brut* famously reported that Henry dismissed his old friends, and replaced them with those who had dared to criticize his behaviour. This claim was repeated in the *First English Life of Henry V*, written in 1513, which also suggested that Henry V had undergone a moral and spiritual transformation as he acceded to the throne.[15] Such comments echoed a constant theme in medieval literature, which contrasted the folly of inexperienced and misdirected youth, exactly the kind to indulge in games of love, tournaments and knightly adventures, with the prudence, wisdom and leadership of their elders.[16]

Indeed, the example of Henry V demonstrates the problems caused by romantic notions of chivalry that have come to dominate the modern imagination. Today, the word conjures up images of a past in which knights fought for honour, spent their lives trying to impress and to romance ladies especially by taking on quests and adventures, and treated battle and warfare as a game in which it was more important to play by the rules than to seek victory at any cost. In the Middle Ages, the ideals of knighthood were much more complicated.[17] There was no simple, fixed set of rules or standards for how such men should behave, and certainly no sense that to be chivalrous was a black or white proposition. Princes, noblemen and knights were expected to demonstrate prowess, courage and loyalty, as well as other important qualities such as largesse, mercy and prudence, in the pursuit of honour, fame and glory. Yet the precise meaning and practical relevance of such ideals was far from fixed. The ideal qualities and actions of kings, knights and men in general were in constant debate across a wide range of genres throughout

---

[14] Allmand, *Henry V*, p. 151. Later that summer, Henry V did famously fight with lances against the defenders in the siege tunnels under the walls of Melun. Jean de Waurin, *Recueil des croniques et anchiennes istories de la Grant Bretaigne, a present nommé Engleterre par Jehan de Waurin, seigneur du Forestel*, ed. W. Hardy and E. L. C. P. Hardy, 5 vols. (London, 1864–91), II, 328.

[15] *The Brut*, II, 594–5, and *The First English Life of King Henry the Fifth, Written in 1513*, ed. C. L. Kingsford (Oxford, 1911), pp. 17–19. Also see Allmand, *Henry V*, pp. 63–4, together with the careful refutation by Gwilym Dodd of the *Brut*'s claim that Henry replaced his old friends in 1413, pp. 000–000 above.

[16] The same notion was alluded to in the famous story of the tennis balls, discussed on pp. 000–000 below.

[17] It is important to recognize that when medieval authors used the term 'chivalry', it was most commonly as a collective noun to describe the knights, rather than in a more abstract sense as their values or ideals. Thus the Agincourt Carol reported that Henry V invaded Normandy 'With grace & myght of chyualry', and Hoccleve praised Henry and his fellow knights of the Order of the Garter as the 'flour of chivalrie': W. G. Müller, 'The Battle of Agincourt in Carol and Ballad', *Fifteenth-Century Studies* 8 (1984), 159–78 (p. 160), and Thomas Hoccleve, *Hoccleve's Works: the Minor Poems*, ed. F. J. Furnival and I. Gollancz, rev. J. Mitchell and A. I. Doyle, EETS ES 61 and 73 (London, 1970), p. 41.

the high and late Middles Ages. For example, if knights were to prove their honour in battle, was it more worthy to fight in tournaments, local wars or on crusade? Were there practical, legal or moral limits on when knights could resort to violence? Was it more important to be a brave leader in battle, or to be prudent and cunning in order to secure victory? Underpinning these difficult questions was the fact that knightly values were first and foremost concerned with ethical behaviour, and hence drew upon extremely complex debates that had driven Christian moral philosophy throughout the Middle Ages.[18]

Thus rather than attempting to measure and to judge the actions of Henry V against some imagined, idealized vision of chivalric ideals, it is more important to recognize that the way in which Henry V's life and career were framed by contemporary writers offered an important contribution to English cultural debates about knighthood. In the *Troy Book*, John Lydgate emphasized the importance of chivalric narratives both as witnesses and judges of the achievements, honour and fame of great men, but also as sources of ethical and moral advice on how knights and princes ought to behave.[19] The same may be said of the accounts of Henry V's life, such as the anonymous *Gesta Henrici Quinti* (c.1417), the *Liber Metricus* (c.1418) by Thomas Elmham, the *Vita et Gesta Henrici Quinti* (mid-1430s) by an anonymous author known as the Pseudo-Elmham and the *Vita Henrici Quinti* (c.1438) by Tito Livio Frulovisi.[20] These accounts have traditionally been viewed as works of political propaganda, intended to support the continuation of Henry's wars in France, both during his lifetime and after his death when his political legacy was defended by his closest supporters.[21] Yet the posthumous biographies were also works of commemoration that sought to transform the deeds of arms and reputation of a great knight into more eternal fame and glory, a central element of chivalric culture.[22] The *Vita et Gesta Henrici Quinti* and the *Vita Henrici Quinti*, for example, may be seen as adjuncts to the work to build a chantry chapel for Henry V that began in 1437.[23] Moreover, all of the accounts of Henry V

---

[18] I discuss these questions in detail in my forthcoming book, *Chivalry and the ideals of Knighthood in France During the Hundred Years War* (Cambridge, 2013).

[19] N. Perkins, 'Representing Advice in Lydgate', in *The Lancastrian Court. Proceedings of the 2001 Harlaxton Symposium*, ed. J. Stratford (Donington, 2003), pp. 173–91 (pp. 174–8).

[20] C. L. Kingsford, *English Historical Literature in the Fifteenth Century* (Oxford, 1913), pp. 45–69; A. Gransden, *Historical Writing in England II: c.1307 to the Early Sixteenth Century* (London, 1982), pp. 194–219; J. S. Roskell and F. Taylor, 'The Authorship and Purpose of the Gesta Henrici Quinti', *BJRL* 53 (1970–1), 428–64, and 54 (1971–2), 223–40; D. Rundle, 'The Unoriginality of Tito Livio Frulovisi's Vita Henrici Quinti', *EHR* 123 (2008), 1109–31.

[21] Gransden, *Historical Writing in England II*, p. 197.

[22] S. K. Gertz, *Visual Power and Fame in René d'Anjou, Geoffrey Chaucer and the Black Prince* (New York, 2010), pp. 13–32.

[23] Rundle, 'Unoriginality of Tito Livio Frulovisi's Vita Henrici Quinti', pp. 1127–8, and Hope, 'The Funeral, Monument and Chantry Chapel of Henry V', pp. 129–86. The following year, Archbishop Chichele began the construction of All Souls College, dedicated in

made very deliberate choices about the way in which they represented him, and hence presented Henry as a very specific model of kingship, knighthood and masculinity, championing not just war in France and dynamic military leadership, but also ideas of justice, selflessness, discipline and service to God that echoed and supported centuries of clerical sermons addressed to the aristocracy.[24]

A Mighty and Puissant Conqueror

Jean Fusoris, canon of Notre-Dame in Paris, claimed to have met Henry V at Winchester just before the Agincourt expedition in 1415. The Frenchman reported that the king had a priestly air, and that it was his brother, Clarence, who seemed more like a soldier.[25] Yet there is no doubt that Henry V repeatedly displayed great personal bravery and skill in battle throughout his long military career. For example, he was reportedly wounded in the face by an arrow during the battle of Shrewsbury on 21 July 1403, but still continued to fight.[26] After the battle of Grosmont in 1405, he was praised in parliament as a man of 'bone coer et corage'.[27] Henry's greatest personal triumph was at Agincourt, where he not only 'had bothe the felde and the victory', but also 'faught manly'.[28] One anonymous verse account of the Agincourt campaign praised Henry for both his leadership in the battle but also for his personal prowess and bravery:

part to prayer for the souls of Henry V, Clarence and the soldiers who had died in the French wars: J. Catto, 'The World of Henry Chichele and the Foundation of All Souls', in *Unarmed Soldiery. Studies in the Early History of All Souls College* (Oxford, 1996), pp. 1–13.

24 There is a parallel here to recent debates about John Lydgate, who is increasingly regarded as a complex author who did not merely serve as a Lancastrian propagandist, but also raised ethical and practical questions about war, knighthood and models of kingship and masculinity. See, for example, L. Patterson, 'Making Identities in Fifteenth-Century England: Henry V and John Lydgate', in *New Historical Literary Study: Essays on Reproducing Texts, Representing History*, ed. J. N. Cox and L. J. Reynolds (Princeton, 1993), pp. 69–107, and P. Strohm, 'Hoccleve, Lydgate and the Lancastrian Court', in *The Cambridge History of Medieval English Literature*, ed. D. Wallace (Cambridge, 1999), pp. 640–61, together with the more recent comments of D. A. Pearsall, '*Crowned King*: War and Peace in 1415', in *The Lancastrian Court*, ed. Stratford, pp. 163–72 (pp. 169–70), and C. Nall, *Reading and War in Fifteenth-Century England from Lydgate to Malory* (Cambridge, 2012), pp. 75–113.

25 L. Mirot, 'Le procès de Maître Jean Fusoris, chanoine de Notre-Dame de Paris (1415–1416). Épisode des négociations franco-anglaises durant la guerre de Cent Ans', *Mémoires de la Société de l'histoire de Paris et de l'Ile de France* 27 (1900), 137–287 (p. 175).

26 Walsingham, *St. Albans Chronicle, 1394–1422*, p. 370.

27 *PROME*, VIII, 341.

28 Müller, 'The Battle of Agincourt in Carol and Ballad', p. 161. Also see Walsingham, *St. Albans Chronicle, 1394–1422*, p. 678.

That day he faught with his owne hond,
He sparyed nother heigh no lowe
There was no man his dynt myght stond.[29]

The English king may have deliberately challenged the French to focus their attack upon him by wearing a crown above his basinet in order to identify himself clearly. Chroniclers reported that eighteen French men-at-arms led by the lord of Croy accepted the bait, and attempted unsuccessfully to knock the crown from Henry's head.[30] Moreover, during the mêlée, Henry V reportedly fought off the attackers who threatened his wounded brother, Humphrey, duke of Gloucester.[31]

Yet it was less Henry's personal skill and courage than his military leadership that was the foundation of his chivalric reputation. He learned the art of war in the suppression of the Welsh rebellion led by Owain Glyndŵr.[32] Then his short reign witnessed a remarkable series of victories in France, from the famous battle at Agincourt to the attack on Pontoise on 30 July 1419, where two groups of men led by the earl of Huntingdon and Gaston de Foix scaled the walls of the town immediately after the truce had come to an end.[33] Modern historians have carefully debated Henry's skill as a strategist, questioning, for example, his plan in leading his army out from Harfleur on the expedition that culminated in the battle of Agincourt. Did Henry make a deliberate miscalculation that was only rescued by his tactical success on the battlefield, or had he always planned to fight the French army in order to secure such a pivotal victory?[34] Less controversy surrounds his programme of conquest of northern France, clearly inspired by the lessons that he learned during the Welsh wars, where English success had been built upon securing

---

[29] *Chronicle of London from 1089 to 1483*, ed. N. H. Nicolas and E. Tyrrell (London, 1827), p. 228. Also see the comments on this poem in V. J. Scattergood, *Politics and Poetry in the Fifteenth Century* (London, 1971), p. 55: 'No hero of romance could have acquitted himself better.'

[30] Wavrin, *Recueil des croniques*, II, 207–8, and Lefèvre de Saint-Rémy, *Chronique de Jean Le Févre, seigneur de Saint-Remy*, ed. F. Morand, 2 vols. (Paris, 1866–81), I, 249–50. Allmand argues that this demonstrated the king's 'sense of chivalry': *Henry V*, pp. 88–9.

[31] Tito Livio dei Frulovisi, *Titi Livii Foro-Juliensis Vita Henrici Quinti, regis Angliæ: accedit, sylloge epistolarum, a variis Angliæ principibus scriptarum*, ed. T. Hearne (Oxford, 1716), p. 20.

[32] Allmand, *Henry V*, pp. 16–38 and R. R. Davies, *The Revolt of Owain Glyndŵr* (Oxford, 1995).

[33] Walsingham, *St. Albans Chronicle, 1394–1422*, pp. 740–2, and J. Taylor, 'The Chronicle of John Strecche for the Reign of Henry V', *BJRL* 16 (1932), 137–87 (pp. 143, 179–80), as well as Allmand, *Henry V*, pp. 133–4.

[34] See, for example, Curry, *Agincourt: A New History*, pp. 133–69; C. J. Rogers, 'Henry V's Military Strategy in 1415', in *The Hundred Years War: A Wider Focus*, ed. L. J. A. Villalon and D. J. Kagay (Leiden, 2005), pp. 399–428, and J. W. Honig, 'Reappraising Late Medieval Strategy: The Example of the 1415 Agincourt Campaign', *War in History* 19 (2012), 123–51.

coastal strongholds like Beaumaris, Caernarfon, Conwy and Harlech through which men and provisions could be channelled to the war, and inland castles that could ensure control over territory.[35] Yet the essential point is that for medieval audiences, results mattered far more than the planning that went into achieving them, and thus the sheer scale of Henry V's military victories established him as one of the greatest military leaders in medieval English history.

As a result, the model of kingship and chivalry that Henry V represented was characterized first and foremost by conquest.[36] Following the sealing of the treaty of Troyes in 1420, Thomas Hoccleve delighted in the king's great victories in France, describing him as the 'Swerd of knyghthode' and celebrating him as a 'worthy Conqueror'.[37] In the carol dedicated to Henry VI by John Audelay in *c*.1429, Henry V was described as 'a conqueroure' who 'wan his moder with gret onoure'.[38] Henry's tomb at Westminster Abbey was completed by 1431, and though no trace of the epitaph survives today, a contemporary French author reported that the inscription read 'Henricus Quintus, dux Normanorum verusque conquestor eorum, heres Francorum decessit et rector eorum'.[39] In the *Boke of Noblesse*, written immediately after the loss of Normandy and completed in 1475, William Worcester offered nostalgic praise for Henry V as a mighty and powerful conqueror.[40] When the palace of Richmond was rebuilt between 1499 and 1501, the walls of the hall were adorned with pictures of individuals like Brutus, Arthur and Henry V who had been 'noble waryours and kinges of this rial realme with their fachons and swordes in their handes'.[41]

Chivalric literature was full of stories of conquerors, such as Alexander the Great and King Arthur who had led an expedition against the Romans. These narratives did not merely celebrate aggression and military victory, but also posed difficult questions about the justification for wars of conquest, the damage that they inflicted upon civilians and the consequences of such

---

[35] R. A. Newhall, *The English Conquest of Normandy, 1416–1424: A Study in Fifteenth-Century Warfare* (New Haven, 1924); and Allmand, *Henry V*, pp. 24 and 36–8.

[36] Keen, 'Chivalry and English Kingship in the Later Middle Ages', pp. 262–6.

[37] *Hoccleve's Works: the Minor Poems*, pp. 308–9. Also see *Lydgate's Troy Book*, ed. Bergen, III, 875.

[38] *Historical Poems*, ed. Robbins, p. 110.

[39] *Debating the Hundred Years War: Pour ce que plusieurs (La Loy Salicque) and a Declaration of the Trew and Dewe Title of Henri VIII*, ed. C. Taylor, Camden 5th s. 29 (Cambridge, 2006), p. 80.

[40] William Worcester, *The Boke of Noblesse Addressed to King Edward the Fourth on his Invasion of France in 1475*, ed. J. G. Nichols (London, 1860), pp. 15–17. For similar comments, see *The Libelle of Englyshe Polyce: A Poem on the Use of Sea-Power*, ed. G. Warner (London, 1926), pp. 51–3; *The Brut*, II, 373; W. O'Sullivan, 'John Manyngham: An Early Oxford Humanist', *Bodleian Library Record* 7 (1962), 28–39 (pp. 37–9).

[41] *The Receyt of the Ladie Kateryne*, ed. G. Kipling, EETS OS 296 (Oxford, 1990), p. 72.

external engagements for unity and peace at home.[42] Such questions were inevitably relevant for Henry V's great wars of conquest, and were most clearly highlighted by French commentators. For example, the chronicle attributed to Jean Juvénal des Ursins reported that the citizens of Meaux complained to Henry V about the behaviour of English soldiers during the siege of the city from October 1421 to May 1422, and in response the king declared that war without fire was as worthless as sausages without mustard.[43] The same chronicler questioned the entire legal basis for the war through the story of Sir John Cornwall, whose son was killed by a shot from a cannon during the siege of Meaux. According to the chronicle, Cornwall reacted to this tragedy by denouncing the entire war as an escalation from the original mission to seize Normandy into an attempt to usurp the crown of France from its rightful heir, the Dauphin.[44] Robert Blondel went further in presenting the sudden death of Henry V shortly after the siege of Meaux as divine punishment for his brutality and impiety.[45]

Similar concerns were raised by Burgundian chroniclers, albeit in a more careful manner given the shifting allegiances of their dukes during the fifteenth century.[46] Enguerrand de Monstrelet delicately raised questions about Henry's excessive ambition for power, for example by the evocative story of how Henry as Prince had taken up his father's crown, thinking that Henry IV had died, only for the king to wake up and observe him.[47] Monstrelet also described how, on his deathbed, Henry V declared his great regret that

---

[42] L. Patterson, 'Making Identities in Fifteenth-Century England: Henry V and John Lydgate', in *New Historical Literary Study: Essays on Reproducing Texts, Representing History*, ed. J. N. Cox and L. J. Reynolds (Princeton, 1993), pp. 69–107 (p. 97), and also see, for example, F. J. Riddy, 'Contextualizing *Le Morte Darthur*: Empire and Civil War', in *A Companion to Malory*, ed. A. S. G. Edwards and E. Archibald (Cambridge, 1996), pp. 55–73. Some modern scholars have viewed Lydgate's *Siege of Thebes* as a work that warned about the practical danger of aggressive foreign war, regardless of the merits of the legal case. See, for example, R. W. Ayers, 'Medieval History, Moral Purpose, and the Structure of Lydgate's *Siege of Thebes*', *PMLA* 73 (1958), 463–74 (p. 467), and J. Simpson, *Reform and Cultural Revolution* (Oxford, 2002), pp. 65, 105–6.

[43] *Choix de chroniques et mémoires relatifs à l'histoire de France avecs notices biographiques*, ed. J. A. C. Buchon (Paris, 1875), p. 565. It is important to note that the veracity of this report must be in doubt given that the chronicler could not have been present at the meeting.

[44] Ibid., p. 566. Also see, for example, the *Chronique du Religieux de Saint-Denis*, ed. Bellaguet, VI, 448.

[45] R. Blondel, *Oeuvres de Robert Blondel*, ed. A. Héron, 2 vols. (Rouen, 1891–3), I, 198–9 and 364–5, and N. Pons and M. Goullet, 'Robert Blondel, *Desolatio regni Francie*. Un poème politique de soutien au futur Charles VII en 1420', *Archives d'Histoire Doctrinale et Littéraire du Moyen Age* 68 (2001), 297–374.

[46] The chroniclers themselves alluded to the divisions amongst the Burgundian party during the course of alliance with Henry V. See, for example, Monstrelet, *La chronique*, IV, 78–9, echoed in Georges Chastellain, *Œuvres de Georges Chastellain*, ed. K. de Lettenhove, 8 vols. (Brussels, 1863–8), I, 292.

[47] Monstrelet, *La chronique*, II, 328–9, and also see *First English Life*, ed. Kingsford, pp. 13–16.

in dying so young, he had not had the chance to bring peace to France and then to go to recover Jerusalem. This was an entirely commonplace claim, but one that did serve to highlight the fact that his wars of conquest lacked the true nobility of the crusade.[48] Georges Chastellain was even more abrupt, portraying Henry V as a tyrant driven by a vainglorious desire for power, in contrast to Philip the Good, duke of Burgundy, who had merely sought revenge for his murdered father and eventually put aside that blood feud for the greater good.[49]

For the defenders and publicists of Henry V, the wars of conquest were given moral validity by his legal claims both to the duchy of Normandy and other lands, as well as to the throne itself, as the rightful heir and hence saviour of France. English lawyers and diplomats carefully developed dossiers that set out Henry's legal rights such as the *Liber Recordorum* cited by the author of the *Gesta Henrici Quinti*, a position paper prepared for Henry V before the negotiations at Alençon in 1418, and transcripts of Anglo-French treaties relating to the duchy of Guyenne.[50] Yet these were extremely complex legal questions that did not need to be explained in details to a more general audience outside of the orbit of diplomats and lawyers.[51] More important was the fact that Henry V prosecuted his legal claims in a formal manner, and in particular that he could claim to have exhausted efforts to find a peaceful solution before resorting to warfare to defend his rights.[52] The importance of exploring diplomatic solutions before taking up arms as a last resort was not only underlined by medieval just war theory, but also played out in chivalric literature such as Lydgate's *Troy Book*, in which both the Greeks and the Trojans at least offered each other the opportunity to secure a peaceful solution before the outbreak of war.[53] Thus Henry's chancellors repeatedly emphasized to parliament the refusal of the French to negotiate in good faith, and thus placed responsibility for the war upon the Valois monarchy rather than on the English king who was ultimately a true man of peace.[54] In early

---

48 Monstrelet, *La chronique*, IV, 112, and Chastellain, *Œuvres*, I, 334. Also see p. 219 above.

49 Chastellain, *Œuvres*, I, 321–2, and also see 180, 220–2 and 312.

50 *GHQ*, pp. xxxix–xl, 14, 18 56, 95, 130 and 138; *English Medieval Diplomatic Practice, Part I*, ed. P. Chaplais, 2 vols. (London, 1982), I, 207–23; M. G. A. Vale, *English Gascony, 1399–1453* (Oxford, 1970), pp. 78–9. Also note the compilations produced during the reign of Henry VI by Thomas Bekington, bishop of Bath and Wells, which must have built upon an existing dossier developed earlier in the war: BL MSS Cotton Tiberius B xii, Harley 861, and Harley 4763, together with Oxford, Bodleian Library, MS Bodley 885.

51 C. D. Taylor, 'War, Propaganda and Diplomacy in Fifteenth Century France and England', in *War, Government and Power in Late Medieval France*, ed. C. T. Allmand (Liverpool, 2000), pp. 70–91.

52 This requirement is an essential context for understanding the norms and rituals that Henry and his armies performed in war, as reported in the narrative sources and discussed in Honig, 'Reappraising Late Medieval Strategy', pp. 123–51.

53 Nall, *Reading and War*, pp. 78–93.

54 For example, *PROME*, IX, 66, 114–15 and 177. Also see *GHQ*, pp. 134–6, 176–8.

August 1419, Henry sent letters to Pope Martin V, the college of cardinals, Louis III, duke of Bavaria, and Charles I, duke of Lorraine, arguing that his repeated efforts to make peace had been scuppered by the French, forcing him to resort once again to warfare.[55]

The charge that the Valois were proud, arrogant and deceitful was hardly new in the fifteenth century. Medieval English writers repeatedly characterized the French as treacherous and deceitful, which served to justify military action and also provided a powerful commentary on the importance of honesty and truth on the part of princes and noblemen. Just before the Agincourt campaign, the anonymous poem *Dede is Worchyng* warned that the French could not be trusted and therefore advised Henry V to give up attempts to negotiate with them.[56] These traditional themes were given powerful form in the story that French ambassadors who met with Henry V at Kenilworth in 1414 presented him with tennis balls and cushions for him to lie upon, thereby suggesting that he was more inclined towards courtly games and pastimes than warfare.[57] Such arrogance on the part of the French may seem somewhat implausible given the threat that Henry represented and their obvious desire to prevent an invasion, as seen in the major concessions offered by the last-minute mission to England led by the archbishop of Bourges in June 1415.[58] Yet whether the story of the tennis balls was true or not, it certainly served to legitimize Henry's martial response towards the French who had not merely refused to meet his rightful demands but also treated him with derision and scorn. It deliberately and self-consciously echoed the story of another great conqueror of chivalric legend, Alexander the Great, who was also mocked by his enemy, Darius king of Persia, through a gift of a children's ball game.[59] The *Brut* chronicle proudly reported that Henry returned the gift of the tennis balls to the French as stones thrown from catapults during the siege of Harfleur in 1415.[60]

Henry V's wars of conquest were also justified by the argument that God had supported the invasion, as proved by the extraordinary victories that continued a pattern of success dating back to the reign of Edward III.[61] After he had defeated a much larger Welsh army near Grosmont on 11 March 1405, a young Prince Henry had written to his father describing the battle and

---

[55] *English Medieval Diplomatic Practice Part I*, ed. Chaplais, II, 452–62.

[56] *The Digby Poems: A New Edition of the Lyrics*, ed. H. Barr (Exeter, 2009), pp. 212–13.

[57] Taylor, 'The Chronicle of John Strecche', pp. 149–50; *Memorials of Henry the Fifth, King of England*, ed. C. A. Cole (London, 1858), p. 101; *Historical Poems*, ed. Robbins, p. 109.

[58] *English Medieval Diplomatic Practice, Part I*, ed. Chaplais, I, 129–35. Allmand has suggested that the story of the tennis balls may represent a chance remark overheard by one of the English ambassadors to France: *Henry V*, pp. 71–2.

[59] R. F. Green, *Poets and Princepleasers: Literature and the English Court in the Late Middle Ages* (Toronto, 1980), pp. 186–7.

[60] *The Brut*, II, 374–6.

[61] *GHQ*, pp. 122–4.

attributing his victory over these rebels to the hand of God.[62] This was a central theme of the rhetoric presented to parliament during Henry's French wars. For example, on 4 November 1415, the chancellor, Henry Beaufort, emphasized the fact that Henry V had received divine support for his fight to recover his rights in France. He celebrated the victory at Agincourt by comparing Henry V to Judas Maccabeus, and carefully attributed the victory to the hand of God.[63] Similarly, the *Gesta Henrici Quinti* championed the image of Henry V as a devoted servant of God and the Church, who had not fought for selfish reasons, but rather for justice. In the account of the start of the expedition from Harfleur, the king echoed I Maccabees 3. 8 in emphasizing the ability of their smaller force to defeat a larger enemy with God's support.[64] Just before the battle of Agincourt, the narrator reported, Henry dismissed Sir Walter Hungerford's concerns by announcing that God would protect them against the arrogant French, just as he had supported Judas Maccabeus before he had lost faith.[65] After the English victory, the anonymous author of the *Gesta* underlined the contrast in size between the two armies as proof of God's support for Henry V.[66] These themes were emphasized in the *Gesta*'s account of Henry's return to England, notably in the pageant held in London to celebrate his victory.[67] Similarly, the Agincourt Carol offered a repeated refrain or burden, 'Deo gracias', calling upon the singers to give thanks to God; these same words were displayed on a tower in Cheapside during the celebrations in London after the battle.[68] The *Gesta Henrici Quinti* also reported on Beaufort's speech before parliament in March 1416, in which he again invoked divine support for Henry V who had attempted to negotiate with the French in order to secure his legitimate claims, but had been forced

---

62 *POPC*, I, 249: 'Mes il est bien voirs que la victoire nest pas en la multitude de poeple ... mes en la puissance de Dieu.'

63 *PROME*, IX, 114–15. Also see *A Macaronic Sermon Collection from Late Medieval England. Oxford, MS Bodley 649*, ed. P. J. Horner (Toronto, 2006), p. 416.

64 *GHQ*, p. 60. Nall draws attention to the discussion of larger groups of soldiers being defeated because of their falsehood and lack of just cause in Lydgate's *Siege of Thebes*, in her *Reading and War*, pp. 97–9.

65 *GHQ*, p. 78, and for a further allusion to Maccabeus, see p. 146. As the editors note, the notion of Judas Maccabeus meeting with disaster because of a final lapse of faith does not tally with his heroic death in I Maccabees 9.

66 Ibid., p. 94.

67 Ibid., p. 104, and also see the poem once ascribed by Lydgate, describing these events, in ibid., p. 191, together with Allmand, *Henry V*, pp. 97–9 and S. Tolmie, 'Quia hic homo multa signa facit: Henry V's Royal Entry Into London, November 23, 1415', in *The Propagation of Power in the Medieval West: Selected Proceedings of the International Conference, Groningen 20–23 November 1996*, ed. M. Gosman, A. Vanderjagt and J. Veenstra (Groningen, 1997), pp. 363–79.

68 Müller, 'The Battle of Agincourt in Carol and Ballad', 160–3, and *GHQ*, pp. 110–12.

to go to war because of their pride and obstruction: the victory at Agincourt proved that God supported the English.[69]

Later biographies of Henry V underlined these themes in other ways. For example, the *First English Life of Henry V* recounted a dramatic story of a meeting between Henry V and St Vincent Ferrier, who died in 1419 and was canonized in 1455. Ferrier supposedly came to Henry V during the siege of Rouen in order to persuade the king to give up the war. In response, Henry declared that he was the 'scourge of God, sent to punish the people of God for there synns' and then spoke with Ferrier in private for two or three hours. At the end, Ferrier declared that he had initially believed Henry to be a tyrant, but was convinced that his war was just.[70] This story had not appeared in earlier narratives. For example, Thomas Walsingham had merely reported that Henry V summoned Ferrier to preach before him at Caen on Monday, 16 May 1418 and was deeply impressed by the Dominican's intelligence, spirit and fervour.[71]

In short, as Catto has argued, Henry's 'project for founding an English empire in France ... sometimes seemed to assume the moral force of a crusade'.[72] Yet there are a number of important points to make about the significance of this vision for English debates about chivalry and knighthood. First and foremost, it marked a clear movement away from a very traditional and long-standing vision of knightly identity that was bound up with real crusading in the Holy Land. The stories of great heroes like Godfrey de Bouillon remained popular, as demonstrated by the fact that Henry V himself borrowed such a book from the countess of Westmorland, but also the continued invocation of the Swan Knight by other Englishmen such as Richard Beauchamp.[73] Yet in practice, the example of Henry V amplified a tendency within English chivalric culture to pull back from the celebration of traditional Crusades to the Holy Land as the zenith of knightly activity.

---

69 Ibid., p. 122, and also see *PROME*, IX, 114–15.
70 *First English Life*, ed. Kingsford, pp. 130–2. Peyronnet has connected this meeting with the effort by Jean duke of Brittany to mediate between the English and the French, though the evidence is extremely fragile. G. Peyronnet, 'L'étrange rencontre d'un conquérant dévot et d'un prédicateur messager de paix: Henri V d'Angleterre et saint Vincent Ferrier (1418)', *Revue d'histoire écclesiastique* 150 (1992), 663–81.
71 Walsingham, *St. Albans Chronicle, 1394–1422*, pp. 732–4.
72 J. Catto, 'The Burden and Conscience of Government in the Fifteenth Century', *TRHS* 17 (2007), 83–99 (p. 98). Also see the wider context for these notions in N. Housley, '*Pro deo et patria mori*: Sanctified Patriotism in Europe, 1400–1600', in *War and Competition Between States*, ed. P. Contamine (Oxford, 2000), pp. 221–48, and N. Housley, *Religious Warfare in Europe, 1400–1536* (Oxford, 2002).
73 J. E. Krochalis, 'The Books and Reading of Henry V and his Circle', *Chaucer Review* 23 (1988), 50–77 (p. 65), together with A. R. Wagner, 'The Swan Badge and the Swan Knight', *Archaeologia* 97 (1959), 127–38; S. Crane, *The Performance of Self: Ritual, Clothing and Identity During the Hundred Years War* (Philadelphia, 2002), pp. 113–16, and Y. Liu, 'Richard Beauchamp and the Uses of Romance', *Medieval Aevum* 74 (2005), 271–87 (p. 271).

Moreover, the emphasis upon divine support for Henry V's wars meant that many narratives played down the importance of individual knightly prowess and deeds of arms in the wars in France. Ballads and poems celebrating the victory at Agincourt or the siege of Rouen did identify individual knights, including Henry V himself, who had performed great deeds of arms.[74] In contrast, the *Gesta Henrici Quinti* made no attempt to glorify the prowess and courage of individuals in the manner of traditional chivalric narratives and especially biographies.[75] Indeed, the anonymous chaplain carefully reported Henry V's humility and lack of pride after his great triumphs. During the public celebrations in London, for example, he described Henry V as wearing a simple gown and riding with just a small number of men from his house-hold rather than a large escort of men-at-arms, thereby demonstrating his concern to thank God rather than indulge in personal glorification.[76] In short, an emphasis upon God's support for Henry V and the English went hand in hand with a discouragement of individual honour and glory, echoing the traditional clerical warnings against the temptations of pride, vainglory and boasting which were the characteristic sins of the conqueror.[77]

English narratives often had little to say about the precise importance of Henry V as a leader on the battlefield. In 1436, the French constable Arthur de Richemont took members of his retinue to the battlefield of Agincourt in order to discuss the tactics and deployments in their original terrain, praising

---

[74] See, for example, *The Battle of Agincourt*, written around 1443, which identified leading English soldiers including the dukes of Gloucester and York, the earls of Huntingdon, Oxford and Suffolk, and knights such as Sir Thomas Erpingham: *Historical Poems*, ed. Robbins, pp. 76–7, together with another verse account written perhaps in the 1440s, in *Chronicle of London*, ed. Nicolas and Tyrrell, pp. 216–33. Also see *Agincourt: Sources and Interpretations*, ed. Curry, pp. 288–98.

[75] C. T. Allmand, 'Some Writers and the Theme of War in the Fourteenth and Fifteenth Centuries', in *Krieg im Mittelalter*, ed. H.-H. Kortüm (Berlin, 2001), p. 169, and C. D. Taylor, 'English Writings on Chivalry and Warfare During the Hundred Years War', in *Soldiers, Nobles and Gentlemen: Essays in Honour of Maurice Keen*, ed. P. Coss and C. Tyerman (Woodbridge, 2009), pp. 65–6.

[76] *GHQ*, p. 112, and also see Walsingham, *St. Albans Chronicle, 1394–1422*, p. 682. The anonymous author of the *Vita et Gesta Henrici Quinti* even claimed that Henry V was so concerned about the danger of pride and vainglory that his nobles were reluctant to talk to Elmham about the king and his achievements: *Thomae de Elmham, Vita et Gesta Henrici Quinti, Anglorum Regis*, ed. T. Hearne (Oxford, 1727), p. 80.

[77] *Letters of Queen Margaret of Anjou and Bishop Beckington and Others, Written in the Reigns of Henry V and Henry VI*, ed. C. Monro, Camden Society 86 (London, 1863), pp. 4–5, and *Agincourt: Sources and Intepretations*, ed. Curry, p. 273. Thomas Bradwardine had deliv-ered a powerful sermon in the aftermath of victory at Crécy in 1346, warning about the dangers of pride and vainglory, and emphasizing the importance of God in determining victory or defeat: H. A. Oberman and J. A. Weisheipl, 'The *Sermo Epinicius* Ascribed to Thomas Bradwardine (1346)', *Archives d'histoire doctrinale et littéraire du moyen âge* 25 (1958), 295–329.

the English tactical success.[78] In contrast, the *Gesta Henrici Quinti* did not even report that the English king had given a great speech before the battle, often the most effective means for narrators and chroniclers to highlight the importance of the commander. Instead, the anonymous chaplain recounted the story of Henry V's exchange with Hungerford, which highlighted God's great role in the victory at Agincourt but inevitably played down the importance of Henry V as an inspirational leader.[79] The *Liber Metricus* of Thomas Elmham did give Henry V a speech, citing past victories won by the English, warning that he should never be taken prisoner or ransomed, and calling upon St George and the Virgin Mary to support them.[80] The reference to the danger of a king being captured on the battlefield at least acknowledged a counter-argument to the English celebration of royal leadership in battle. In France, the capture of King Jean II at the battle of Poitiers had triggered a powerful public reconsideration of the wisdom of the monarch taking such a direct role in warfare. For example, Christine de Pizan recognized that a king could give heart to an army, as seen with Alexander the Great, Clovis and Charlemagne, but warned that a ruler should avoid battle except against rebellious subjects, lest he be captured, dishonouring him, his blood and his subjects, and also causing great harm to his country.[81] Such ideas gained little traction in fifteenth-century England, despite the fact that Henry V's heir presumptive, the duke of Clarence, was defeated and killed at the battle of Baugé on 22 March 1421.[82]

Finally, the emphasis upon divine support for Henry V's aggressive wars inevitably went hand in hand with the commonplace notion that their ulti-

---

[78] Guillaume Gruel, *Chronique d'Arthur de Richemont, connétable de France, duc de Bretagne (1393–1458)*, ed. A. Le Vavasseur (Paris, 1890), p. 126.

[79] *GHQ*, p. 78. That Henry did speak before the battle was attested by French chroniclers, such as Wavrin, *Recueil des croniques*, II, 203–4, Lefèvre de Saint-Rémy, *Chronique*, I, 245–6, and the *Chronique du Religieux de Saint-Denis*, V, 554–6. Also see A. Curry, 'The Battle Speeches of Henry V', *Reading Medieval Studies* 34 (2008), 77–98.

[80] *Memorials of Henry the Fifth*, ed. Cole, p. 119. Also see Walsingham, *St. Albans Chronicle, 1394–1422*, pp. 676–8, as well as *Historical Poems*, ed. Robbins, pp. 74–5, together with *Agincourt: Sources and Interpretations*, ed. Curry, p. 290. Thomas Hoccleve had recounted the story of King Codrus of Athens who preferred to die in battle rather than witness his men being defeated: Thomas Hoccleve, *The Regiment of Princes*, ed. C. R. Blyth (Kalamazoo, 1999), pp. 155–6.

[81] Christine de Pisan, *Le livre des fais et bonnes meurs du sage roy Charles V*, ed. S. Solente, 2 vols. (Paris, 1936–40), I, 131–2, 163–4 and 242–4, and C. M. Laennec, 'Christine "Antygrafe": authorship and self in prose works of Christine de Pizan with an edition of BN fr. ms 603, *Le livre des fais d'armes et de chevallerie*' (unpublished Ph.D. dissertation, 2 vols., Yale University, 1988), II, 33–5.

[82] J. D. Milner, 'The Battle of Baugé, March 1421: Impact and Memory', *History* 91 (2006), 484–507 (pp. 489–90). The importance of this disaster for the royal succession was implicitly recognized in the account in the *First English Life*, ed. Kingsford, pp. 173–4, which quickly moved from the death of Clarence to the news of the conception and birth of the new heir to the throne, the future Henry VI.

mate goal was to win peace. In the epilogue to the *Troy Book*, John Lydgate celebrated Henry V's successes in Normandy and in securing his place in the French royal succession thanks to the treaty of Troyes. He also emphasized that this now promised to bring an end to war between the two countries, and therefore called Henry V 'the prince of pes'.[83] This notion was repeated by Lydgate in the epilogue to the *Siege of Thebes*, which again emphasized the prospect of peace and concord after the wars described in that work, echoing the hope offered by the treaty of Troyes in 1420.[84] Pearsall has wisely warned against seeing this as an attempt to curb the martial zeal of the king, but rather as an attempt to echo royal policy and a celebration of Henry's moment of triumph.[85] Nevertheless, such claims must have seemed increasingly hollow in the context of a never-ending war in France that became increasingly unpopular and unsustainable.[86] Even before the end of the reign of Henry V, there were mounting problems with recruitment and financing, reflecting both the long-standing burden placed upon his English subjects, but also a mounting hope that the treaty of Troyes had brought an end to the war to secure Henry's rights in France.[87] Adam Usk concluded his chronicle by reporting public complaints at the demands for financial support for the earl of Salisbury's efforts to avenge the disaster at Baugé and to maintain the Dual Monarchy. Thus Usk concluded with a prayer that Henry V would not find the sword of God turned against him, as had happened for other great heroes of chivalry like Julius Caesar, Alexander the Great, Hector of Troy, king of Persia and even Judas Maccabeus.[88] In short, there were challenges in Lancastrian England to what Morgan has defined as 'an ethos of public life defined as the realization of king-led war-enterprise'.[89]

---

[83] *Lydgate's Troy Book*, ed. Bergen, III, 869–71.

[84] John Lydgate, *Lydgate's Siege of Thebes*, ed. A. Erdmann and E. Ekwall, 2 vols., EETS ES 108 and 125 (London, 1911–30), II, 192.

[85] D. A. Pearsall, 'Lydgate as Innovator', *Modern Language Quarterly* 53 (1992), 5–22 (pp. 14–15).

[86] M. H. Keen, 'The End of the Hundred Years War: Lancastrian France and Lancastrian England', in *England and her Neighbours, 1066–1453: Essays in Honour of Pierre Chaplais*, ed. M. C. E. Jones and M. G. A. Vale (London, 1989), pp. 297–311.

[87] A. Goodman, 'Responses to Requests in Yorkshire for Military Service Under Henry V', *Northern History* 17 (1981), 240–52 (pp. 240–5), and J. A. Doig, 'Propaganda and Truth: Henry V's Royal Progress in 1421', *Nottingham Medieval Studies* 40 (1996), 167–79.

[88] Adam Usk, *The Chronicle of Adam Usk, 1377–1421*, ed. and trans. C. Given-Wilson (Oxford, 1997), pp. 268–70.

[89] D. A. L. Morgan, 'The Household Retinue of Henry V and the Ethos of English Public Life', in *Concepts and Patterns of Service in the Later Middle Ages*, ed. A. Curry and E. Matthew (Woodbridge, 2000), pp. 64–79 (p. 68).

Expert in Martial Discipline

Alongside his great reputation as a warrior and a conqueror, Henry V was also celebrated as a man who was 'Gretly expert in marcial disciplyne'.[90] Jean de Wavrin and Jean Le Fèvre praised Henry V for his strict punishment of those who disobeyed his orders, arguing that the English king had maintained the discipline of knighthood ('discipline de chevalerie') just like the ancient Romans.[91] English narrative sources also underlined the great efforts that Henry V took to ensure that his soldiers behaved in a controlled manner.[92] For example, the *Gesta Henrici Quinti* reported that upon landing at Harfleur in August 1415, Henry issued ordinances against arson, attacks upon churches and their property, and violence against clerics and women.[93] The biographers famously reported that Henry V hanged a soldier for stealing a gilded pyx from a church during the Agincourt campaign.[94] Thomas Walsingham also reported that in 1417 the king reacted to an attack upon a monk by issuing special ordinances protecting all members of the church and their property, and this protection was so effective that Norman peasants were said to have donned clerical disguise whenever English soldiers were in their area, and even to have tonsured themselves.[95] All of these reports served as clear evidence of Henry V's just and disciplined views of warfare and violence, while also championing the traditional concerns of clerical commentators for protection from the danger posed by knights and soldiers.

This praise of Henry V as a disciplined and merciful leader may seem odd to modern commentators given the king's treatment of the French prisoners taken during Agincourt on 24 October 1415.[96] Having thrown back initial waves of attackers, the beleaguered English army faced the threat of a new French assault led by the counts of Marle and Fauquembergue, together with an assault from the rear on the baggage train. It was at this moment that

---

[90] Lydgate, *Minor Poems*, II, 716.

[91] Wavrin, *Recueil des croniques*, II, 429, and Lefèvre de Saint-Rémy, *Chronique*, I, 67–8. Also see Monstrelet, *La chronique*, IV, 116.

[92] R. A. Newhall, 'Discipline in an English Army of the Fifteenth Century', *The Military Historian and Economist* 2 (1917), 141–51, and A. Curry, 'The Military Ordinances of Henry V: Texts and Contexts', in *War, Government and Aristocracy in the British Isles, c.1150–1500: Essays in Honour of Michael Prestwich*, ed. C. Given-Wilson, A. Kettle and L. Scales (Woodbridge, 2008), pp. 214–49.

[93] Then, when leaving the town en route to Calais, the king prohibited burning, lay wasting or taking more food than was needed for the march: *GHQ*, pp. 26 and 60.

[94] *GHQ*, p. 68; *Vita et Gesta Henrici Quinti*, ed. Hearne, p. 53 (and also see pp. 318–19); Tito Livio dei Frulovisi, *Titi Livii*, p. 13; and *First English Life*, ed. Kingsford, pp. 44–5.

[95] Walsingham, *St. Albans Chronicle, 1394–1422*, pp. 712–14.

[96] Discussions of this are legion, but see, for example, Curry, *Agincourt: A New History*, pp. 212–21, and C. J. Rogers, 'The Battle of Agincourt', in *The Hundred Years War (Part II): Different Vistas*, ed. L. J. A. Villalon and D. J. Kagay (Leiden, 2008), pp. 37–132 (pp. 99–103).

Henry V ordered his men to execute their prisoners in order to prevent these captives from taking advantage of the attack, and to allow their guards to join the fight. According to Jean de Wavrin, the English soldiers were reluctant to obey, and so he instructed a squire and 200 archers to carry out his order.[97] It is impossible to know how many Frenchmen were killed as a result of Henry's command.[98] To execute a significant number of prisoners would have been difficult under those circumstances, and it may well be that the command was merely an attempt to frighten them and thereby make them more compliant.[99] Certainly a large number of prisoners did survive the battle. Contemporary chroniclers estimated the number of French prisoners taken at Agincourt as anything between 700 and 2,200.[100] The most famous prisoner was Charles, duke of Orléans, who was held in captivity in England until 1440.[101] On the evening after the battle, Henry V dined with the duke and other leading prisoners in the village of Maisoncelle, observing the chivalric niceties.

It is certainly true that if even one prisoner was executed on the order of Henry V, then he failed to meet modern standards of behaviour in warfare. Yet in the late Middle Ages, the laws governing the conduct of warfare were still developing, largely through custom and practice, though lawyers and intellectuals were increasingly attempting to impose greater discipline and clarity. Thus Honorat Bovet in the *Arbre des batailles* (*c*.1389) and Christine de Pizan in *Le livre des fais d'armes et de chevalerie* (*c*.1410) tried to distinguish carefully between violence committed during the heat of battle, and the abuse of a prisoner after a formal surrender. They argued that those taken in battle could be killed, but once a man had been formally accepted as a prisoner, he should be treated with pity and mercy. Both writers emphasized that the only possible justification for killing an enemy away from the battlefield was that he might escape and thereby prolong or escalate the war.[102] It was precisely

---

97 Wavrin, *Recueil des croniques*, II, 216–17. The *Gesta* did not suggest that Henry V gave an order to kill the prisoners, instead presenting this as a response to the French attack upon the English rearguard: *GHQ*, pp. 90–2, and also see Curry, *Agincourt: A New History*, pp. 216–18 and 220–1.

98 One of them was probably Antoine de Bourgogne, duke of Brabant, who had supposedly been trying to conceal his identity, presumably to avoid paying too high a ransom. S. Boffa, 'Antoine de Bourgogne et le contingent brabançon à la bataille d'Azincourt, 1415', *Revue belge de philologie et d'histoire* 72 (1994), 255–84 (pp. 275–8).

99 Allmand, *Henry V*, p. 95.

100 R. Ambühl, 'Le sort des prisonniers d'Azincourt (1415)', *Revue du Nord* 89 (2007), 755–88 (p. 756).

101 W. Askins, 'The Brothers Orléans and their Keepers', in *Charles d'Orléans in England, 1415–1440*, ed. M.-J. Arn (Cambridge, 2000), pp. 27–45.

102 H. Biu, 'L'*Arbre des batailles* d'Honorat Bovet: étude de l'oeuvre et édition critique des textes français et occitan' (unpublished PhD dissertation, 3 vols., Université Paris IV Sorbonne, 2004), II, 756–7 and 783 (c. 80 and 113); Christine de Pizan, *Le livre du corps de policie*, ed. A. J. Kennedy (Paris, 1998), pp. 27 and 77 (I, c. 15 and II, c. 13); Laennec,

this distinction that made the killing of the Christian prisoners following the battle of Nicopolis in 1396 so shocking, when just 300 out of 6,000 Christian soldiers were ransomed, after the majority had been executed.[103]

Yet the situation at Agincourt was very different from Nicopolis, because the battle was still raging when Henry V gave his command. Holding prisoners under such circumstances created obvious practical problems. Long before the battle, Henry V had released the prisoners taken during the siege of Harfleur, recognizing the difficulty of guarding them during the battle.[104] The author of the *Gesta Henrici Quinti* reported that during the main stage of the battle of Agincourt, the English did not have time to accept the surrender of soldiers in the French vanguard because of the sheer pressure of the mêlée, and therefore had to kill them without regard for their status.[105] Indeed, the duke of Alençon reportedly tried to surrender to Henry V in person but was killed by one of his bodyguards.[106] It was only after the failure of the main French attack that the English soldiers, and in particular the archers, began to pull survivors like Arthur de Richemont from the piles of bodies in front of them, not so much out of a sense of human kindness than because of the prospect of financial reward in the form of ransoms.[107] But the prospect of a new French attack meant that such opportunities had to be sacrificed to the greater importance of securing the victory. Indeed, eight years later, a combined army of English and Burgundians were explicitly ordered not to take prisoners during the battle of Cravant until after the victory was clearly secured, and warned that any captives taken before that point would be put to death.[108]

Thus the order to kill the prisoners was neither unlawful nor unchivalric, contrary to the modern presumption that chivalry was synonymous with treating enemies with mercy and respect. After all, the French had fought under the oriflamme banner, which promised no quarter in battle.[109] Thomas Walsingham reported that the English soldiers were only too aware that the French would not spare anyone other than the king and perhaps the greatest

'Christine "Antygrafe"', II, 219–21. It is important to emphasize the potential gap between the moralizing position of the intellectuals and the reality of war. Edward III, for example, killed all the prisoners the day after the battle of Halidon Hill, presumably because he had forbidden his men from taking them in the first place. C. J. Rogers, *War Cruel and Sharp: English Strategy Under Edward III, 1327–1360* (Woodbridge, 2000), p. 74.

[103] J. Richard, 'Les prisonniers de Nicopolis', *Annales de Bourgogne* 68 (1996), 75–83.

[104] They were instructed to surrender themselves at Calais: *GHQ*, pp. 54–6.

[105] Ibid., pp. 90–2.

[106] Monstrelet, *La chronique*, III, 119–20.

[107] Gruel, *Chronique d'Arthur de Richemont*, pp. 17–18, and R. Ambühl, 'A Fair Share of the Profits? The Captors of Agincourt', *Nottingham Medieval Studies* 50 (2006), 129–50, and R. Ambühl, 'Le sort des prisonniers d'Azincourt (1415)', pp. 755–88.

[108] Monstrelet, *La chronique*, IV, 160.

[109] Allmand, *Henry V*, p. 94.

lords.[110] Jean de Wavrin famously said that Henry V had enflamed his troops by claiming that the French would cut off three fingers from the bowhand of any archer who was captured.[111] Crucially, medieval commentators on the battle of Agincourt, even from the French side, did not attack Henry V for his action.[112] There were important precedents, such as the battle of Aljubarrota on 14 August 1385. According to the account offered by the famous chivalric chronicler, Jean Froissart, the Portuguese and English forces had defeated the vanguard of the Franco-Castilian army, but were then faced by a second great wave of attackers. Realizing the danger that their prisoners might break free during the attack, the king of Portugal gave the order to kill all the prisoners. Froissart described this as a great pity, but accepted that it was better to slay than to be slain (*il vault mieulx occhirre que estre occhis*), and declared that there could be no trust in one's enemy (*nul ne doit avoir fiance en son ennemi*).[113]

Henry V also demonstrated a ruthless brutality in the numerous sieges through which he conquered Normandy, that again may be incompatible with modern romantic notions of chivalry but accorded with medieval views of the laws of war. For example, the English king was responsible for a great deal of suffering on the part of the Rouennais during the siege of the city over the winter of 1418. Rather than damage the city and its defences, Henry chose to starve it into surrender, and in a moving poem John Page described the pitiful condition of the inhabitants who were forced to eat horses, dogs, cats, mice and rats.[114] Particularly tragic was the fate of those poor unfortunates who were left to die outside of the walls of the city, trapped between the two armies. Page claimed that Guy le Boutellier and the garrison of Rouen had pushed these *bouches inutiles* out of the city, expecting the English to feed them. Henry V did indeed provide them with some food at Christmas, but in Page's account the king was also careful to underline that he had not put them there and was therefore not responsible for casualties of war.[115]

Brutality during sieges did serve an important military purpose, offering a stark warning to future defenders of the dangers of attempting to resist

---

110 Walsingham, *St. Albans Chronicle, 1394–1422*, pp. 674, 678.
111 Wavrin, *Recueil des croniques*, II, 204. Also see Monstrelet, *La chronique*, III, 105.
112 *Chronique du Religieux de Saint-Denis*, ed. Bellaguet, V, 564; Wavrin, *Recueil des croniques*, II, 216–17; Monstrelet, *La chronique*, III, 108–9; Lefèvre de Saint-Rémy, *Chronique*, I, 258–9.
113 Jean Froissart, *Chroniques de Jean Froissart*, ed. S. Luce, G. Raynaud, L. Mirot and A. Mirot, 15 vols. (Paris, 1869–1975), XII, 161–2, and also see J. G. Monteiro, 'The Battle of Aljubarrota (1385): A Reassessment', *Journal of Medieval Military History* 7 (2009), 75–103.
114 *Historical Collection of a Citizen of London*, ed. Gairdner, pp. 18–19. I am grateful to Joanna Bellis for allowing me to see her excellent and stimulating discussion of the *Siege of Rouen* in a draft of her forthcoming monograph, *The Word in the Sword: Writing the Hundred Years War 1337–1600*, chapter 3.
115 *Historical Collection of a Citizen of London*, ed. Gairdner, pp. 20–2, 29–30 and 35–6. Also see Monstrelet, *La chronique*, III, 299–301, and Wavrin, *Recueil des croniques*, II, 255–63.

Henry V and his armies. The challenge of capturing strongholds like Caen and Rouen had dramatically increased because of the improvements to urban defences in the face of English attacks dating back to the reign of Edward III.[116] Thus the siege of Falaise lasted from late 1417 until the middle of February 1418, and that of Rouen from the end of July 1418 until January 1419. The threat of dire treatment for resisting an English army was an essential weapon in encouraging at least some strongholds to surrender without extended sieges. After the capture of Harfleur in 1415, for example, Henry was able to secure provisions from towns like Arques and Eu without any military action, simply as a payment to secure protection from the English army.[117] Monstrelet claimed that after the capture of Rouen in January 1419, there was widespread fear of Henry: when the town of Sens surrendered on 10 June 1420, many of the inhabitants wore red crosses in order to indicate their loyalty to Henry V.[118]

Moreover, Henry V's actions were carefully characterized as harsh measures towards those who rebelled or resisted his authority, and this was balanced by fair treatment of anyone who was willing to accept his authority.[119] As Contamine has remarked, 'no town was in a position to close its gates to the King, his representatives and his troops without being considered disobedient and rebellious'.[120] Michel Pintouin, author of the chronicle of the monk of Saint-Denis, reported that the Frenchmen taken prisoner at Agincourt had reported that Henry V initially appeared to be proud and vindictive, but in fact behaved worthily and was a king who showed no mercy towards rebels but did ensure that those who obeyed him were treated well.[121] In a letter written to Charles VI on 28 July 1415, Henry V recalled the authority of Deuteronomy 20, which required those attacking a city to make a final offer of peace, but then authorized powerful retribution against those who persisted in their resistance.[122] The *Gesta Henrici Quinti* claimed that the same law inspired the English king in his negotiations and treatment of the city of Harfleur in 1415. He called upon the garrison to open the gates and to surrender to him as the rightful duke of Normandy, citing

---

[116] Allmand, *Henry V*, p. 115.

[117] Ibid., p. 85.

[118] Monstrelet, *La chronique*, III, 307–8; and Chastellain, *Œuvres*, I, 140–1.

[119] For more detailed discussion of this point, see the chapter by Neil Murphy in this volume.

[120] P. Contamine, 'The Soldiery in Late Medieval Urban Society', *French History* 8 (1994), 1–13 (p. 12).

[121] Pintouin also said that Henry V abused the royal right to punish disobedience when he treated those who had refused to surrender to him at the siege of Caen in 1417 as traitors. This was not only cruel but also unjust because these people were not his subjects: *Chronique du Religieux de Saint-Denis*, VI, ed. Bellaguet, 162–4.

[122] Ibid., V, 526–30; Monstrelet, *La chronique*, III, 78–81; Lefèvre de Saint-Rémy, *Chronique*, I, 218–21.

Deuteronomy 20 which also stated that if defenders persisted in their rebellion against rightful authority, then all males should be put to the sword and the women, children and all the property would become spoils of war to be shared amongst the attacking soldiers.[123] When Harfleur did finally surrender on 22 September 1415, Raoul de Gaucourt and the leading men were required to walk out wearing ropes around their necks, and to surrender ceremonially to the English king who was sitting upon a dais.[124] As Allmand notes, 'Here was the reception of the rebels by their rightful lord.'[125] Yet having secured the town, Henry exercised restraint towards the inhabitants, allowing those who were willing to swear allegiance to him to remain alongside colonists brought from England, free from the fear that he would allow his soldiers to treat them as if they were the enemy.[126] Similarly, the defenders of Rouen agreed with Henry on 13 January 1419 that they would surrender within six days if no relief arrived: the English were to receive eighty hostages including twenty knights and esquires, a fine of 300,000 crowns, the garrison was to be imprisoned and the citizens would build a new ducal palace. In return, those who paid homage to Henry as duke were allowed to keep their possessions.[127]

After the treaty of Troyes, Henry V was regent and heir to the French throne, which only reinforced his ruthless treatment of those who resisted his authority. For example, Thomas Walsingham reported that when Meaux surrendered on 2 May 1422, Henry V offered mercy towards the inhabitants, except for Scotsmen, Irish and English deserters, and those who had violated their oaths of allegiance to him.[128] By the treaty of surrender agreed in late April, Henry V had explicitly demanded that the leaders of the defence, including the captain, the bastard of Vaurus, and his brother Denis, as well as

123 *GHQ*, pp. 34–6, and also see pp. 48, 154.

124 Usk, *Chronicle of Adam Usk*, p. 254, and *Chronicles of London*, ed. C. L. Kingsford (Oxford, 1905), pp. 118–19. Also see *GHQ*, p. 52.

125 Allmand, *Henry V*, p. 81.

126 In an anonymous verse account of the Agincourt campaign written perhaps in the 1440s, Henry V was portrayed as merciful for his treatment of the defenders of Harfleur, in being willing to negotiate despite his anger at them for trying to prevent him from controlling a stronghold that was rightfully his: *Chronicle of London*, ed. Nicolas and Tyrrell, pp. 219–23.

127 BL MS Harley 4763, fols. 123r–123v, cited in Allmand, *Henry V*, p. 126. Also see the long account by John Page of the negotiations, during which the English king allowed the citizens of Rouen to inform Charles VI and the duke of Burgundy that they were under attack because this was 'a poynt of chevalrye': *Historical Collection of a Citizen of London*, ed. Gairdner, p. 40.

128 Walsingham, *St. Albans Chronicle, 1394–1422*, p. 770. Similarly, when Compiègne surrendered on 16 May 1422, Henry V gave a safe conduct to supporters of the Dauphin, but demanded that Gascon, Irish and Welsh deserters be handed over, along with anyone who had broken an oath to support the treaty of Troyes. Paris, Bibliothèque National de la France, MS français 1278, fol. 113r.

the *bailli* Louis Gast and his lieutenant Jean de Rouves, should stand trial. In addition, he called for the surrender of an individual named Orace who had sounded his horn in mockery of the English king during the siege. Apparently the defenders had taunted Henry V by bringing a donkey up to the walls and braying with a trumpet, calling upon the attackers to come and rescue their 'king'. When he finally secured these prisoners, Henry quickly ordered the beheading of the captain without a formal trial, and the body and head were then publicly displayed outside of the town. Vaurus's brother, Louis Gast, Jean de Rouves and Orace were taken to Paris and executed there.[129]

It is important to remember that rightful vengeance was just as powerful a theme in chivalric culture as mercy. When Sir John Oldcastle was captured and brought before parliament on 14 December 1417, he reportedly declared that the true Christian ought to show mercy because vengeance was God's alone.[130] But kings also had a duty to be vengeful against those who disobeyed their royal authority, entrusted to monarchs by God. The anonymous author of the *Gesta Henrici Quinti* emphasized the importance of the law of Deuteronomy in the education and mindset of Henry V, who implicitly served God like Moses and punished those who disobeyed God's law.[131] The harsh and severe treatment of rebels was a hallmark of Henry V's reign.[132] Oldcastle had been a friend of the king, and had served under the Prince's command in Wales. Yet thirty-eight men were executed for treason for their role in the uprising that he led in January 1414, and Oldcastle himself was burnt as a heretic and a traitor on 15 December 1417.[133] At the end of July 1415, Edmund Mortimer earl of March betrayed the so-called Southampton Plot against the king, led by Richard earl of Cambridge, Henry Lord Scrope

---

[129] Paris, Bibliothèque National de la France, MS français 1278, fol. 87v, and also see Monstrelet, IV, pp. 93–6 and Lefèvre de Saint-Rémy, II, pp. 51–5. Many chroniclers suggested that the bastard of Vaurus was punished for his cruelty towards English, Burgundian and even French, and he was also accused of acts of extraordinary cruelty to local peasants. *Journal d'un Bourgeois de Paris, 1405 a 1449, publié d'après les manuscrits de Rome et de Paris*, ed. A. Tuetey (Paris, 1881), pp. 170–2, and also see B. Bove, 'Deconstructing the Chronicles: Rumours and Extreme Violence During the Siege of Meaux (1421–1422)', *French History* 24 (2010), 501–23.

[130] Walsingham, *St. Albans Chronicle, 1394–1422*, p. 728.

[131] *GHQ*, p. 154, and also see Catto, 'The Burden and Conscience of Government in the Fifteenth Century', p. 97.

[132] Throughout his father's reign, there had been rebellions and acts of disloyalty in support of the deposed king, Richard II, not to mention Owain Glyndŵr's resistance to the authority of Henry as Prince of Wales from 1400 until his death in perhaps 1416: S. Walker, 'Rumour, Sedition and Popular Protest in the Reign of Henry IV', *Past and Present* 166 (2000), 31–65; A. Dunn, 'Henry IV and the Politics of Resistance in Early Lancastrian England, 1399–1413', in *The Fifteenth Century III. Authority and Subversion*, ed. L. Clark (Woodbridge, 2003), pp. 5–23; Allmand, *Henry V*, pp. 16–38; Davies, *The Revolt of Owain Glyndŵr*.

[133] Allmand, *Henry V*, pp. 294–305; and the essay by Jurkowski in this volume (pp. 103–29).

of Masham and Sir Thomas Grey of Heton.[134] Again, the king was quick
to punish the main conspirators for their role in conspiring to kill him and
for fomenting revolt. Scrope received particularly harsh treatment because
he had committed treason not only in plotting against the king, but also in
breaking his oath as a Knight of the Garter. His head was publicly displayed
on Micklegate Bar in York, and his lands quickly confiscated.[135]

There is no doubt that Henry V had little time for those who broke their
word of honour, perhaps the most important foundation of chivalric society.[136]
Thomas Hoccleve had offered a very typical discussion of the importance of
keeping one's word in the *Regiment of Princes*, citing the famous example of
Marcus Regulus and concluding that 'Amonges alle thynges in a knyght, /
Trouthe is a thyng that he ne lakke may.'[137] As Prince of Wales, Henry publicly
attacked the Armagnacs who had reneged on the treaty of Bourges agreed
with Henry IV in 1412.[138] At the end of September 1418, Nicolas de Gennes
negotiated the surrender of Cherbourg to the English after a siege that had
lasted five months, and was given a safe-conduct to go to Rouen. When that
city fell to Henry V in January 1419, Gennes was captured, tried and executed
for treason on the grounds that he had surrendered Cherbourg for money,
and thereby betrayed his lord, King Charles VI, even though Henry V had
himself benefited from this treachery.[139]

Similarly, Henry V showed little mercy to those responsible for the murder
of John the Fearless at Montereau in September 1419, breaking the oaths
that the Dauphin and his supporters had taken to keep the peace during a

---

134 T. B. Pugh, 'The Southampton Plot of 1415', in *Kings and Nobles in the Later Middle Ages*,
ed. R. A. Griffiths and J. Sherborne (Gloucester, 1986), pp. 62–89, and T. B. Pugh, *Southampton Plot*.

135 Ibid., pp. 62–3; Allmand, *Henry V*, pp. 77–8, and H. Collins, 'The Order of the Garter,
1348–1461: Chivalry and Politics in Later Medieval England', in *Courts, Counties and
Capitals in the Later Middle Ages*, ed. D. Dunn (Stroud, 1996), pp. 155–80 (pp. 177–8),
and H. Collins, *The Order of the Garter 1348–1461: Chivalry and Politics in Late Medieval England* (Oxford, 2000), p. 125. Also see the careful note of Scrope's treason in the
context of the Order of the Garter, in *GHQ*, p. 132.

136 It has been suggested that Henry V staged the reburial of Richard II in part because
of a sense of obligation to the king who had dubbed him as a knight: J. L. Gillespie,
'Richard II: Chivalry and Kingship', in *The Age of Richard II*, ed. J. L. Gillespie (Stroud,
1997), pp. 115–38 (pp. 128–9).

137 Hoccleve, *Regiment of Princes*, pp. 103–11. Lydgate's *The Siege of Thebes* also explored the
importance of truth and keeping one's word, and demonstrated that duplicity, falsity
and treason at the highest levels could lead to division or warfare. Patterson, 'Making
Identities in Fifteenth-Century England', pp. 74–5. For the wider context, see Taylor,
Chivalry, Honour and Knighthood, chapter 2.

138 Walsingham, *St. Albans Chronicle, 1394–1422*, pp. 610–14, and P. McNiven, 'Prince
Henry and the English political crisis of 1412', *History* 65 (1980), 1–16.

139 Wavrin, *Recueil des croniques*, II, 244–5, and Monstrelet, *La chronique*, III, 242–3, together
with M. H. Keen, *The Laws of War in the Late Middle Ages* (London, 1965), p. 46.

parley.[140] In the summer of 1420, the captain of Melun, Arnaud Guilhelm, lord of Barbazan was captured during the siege after personally fighting with Henry V in a mine under the walls. Barbazan was a councillor and chamberlain to the Dauphin and would have been executed for his part in the treasonous murder of Jean sans Peur at Montereau but for the fact that one of the officers of arms was his brother-in-law. Instead, Barbazan was held in Château-Gaillard for seven years.[141] But Chastellain reported that Henry V was less lenient towards another defender at Melun, Bertrand de Caumont; in this case, the English king declared that he would have executed even his own brother Clarence if he were guilty of treason, because he would not have any traitors ('traistres') around him.[142]

It is certainly true that a lifetime in military service meant that Henry valued the service of his loyal supporters, and he took great pains to ensure that this was rewarded through appropriate largesse.[143] For example, the king made careful use of property confiscated in France to reward his servants and provide them with the resources to support the defence of the English foothold.[144] He also dubbed fifty new knights through the ceremony of the Bath on 8 April 1413, the day before his own coronation.[145] For many, the dubbing must have represented a public acknowledgement of their loyal service to the Prince of Wales, and a mark of honour.[146] On 23 April 1418, Henry V dubbed five new knights during the feast of St George at Caen.[147] One was the Hainaulter Louis Robessart, who had fought alongside Prince Henry against Owain Glyndŵr in Wales, and would become the king's standard-bearer on 30 August 1421. Robessart later earned a famous reputation after he died on 27 November 1430 when he and his fellow Burgundians encountered a Valois

---

[140] M. G. A. Vale, *Charles VII* (Berkeley, 1974), pp. 27–30.

[141] Keen, *The Laws of War*, pp. 48–9. Also see *First English Life*, ed. Kingsford, pp. 167–71.

[142] Chastellain, *Œuvres*, I, 184–5.

[143] Note Dodd's emphasis upon the importance for Henry V of 'the loyalty and friendship of individuals he was counting on most to help him rule his kingdom' (p. 66 above).

[144] R. A. Massey, 'The Land Settlement in Lancastrian Normandy', in *Property and Politics: Essays in Later Medieval English History*, ed. A. J. Pollard (Gloucester, 1984), pp. 76–96, and R. A. Massey 'The Lancastrian Land Settlement in Normandy and Northern France, 1417–1450' (unpublished Ph.D. dissertation, University of Liverpool, 1987), together with Allmand, *Henry V*, pp. 198–204.

[145] Nine knights of the bath had been created in the same way in 1377 at the coronation of Richard II, and either forty-two or forty-six in 1399: Allmand, *Henry V*, pp. 64–5, and F. Pilbrow, 'The Knights of the Bath: Dubbing to Knighthood in Lancastrian and Yorkist England', in *Heraldry, Pageantry, and Social Display in Medieval England*, ed. P. Coss and M. H. Keen (Woodbridge, 2002), pp. 195–218 (pp. 208–9 and 216n.).

[146] It is important to note that, as Pilbrow himself admits, this article was based upon a partial study of the surviving records: Pilbrow, 'The Knights of the Bath', pp. 199–200 and 208–9.

[147] Walsingham, *St. Albans Chronicle, 1394–1422*, pp. 730–2.

force including Frenchmen and Scots near Amiens; Robessart preferred to face death rather than take shelter in a castle, though he did order his men to withdraw when the battle was lost.[148]

Henry V also made extensive use of the Order of the Garter.[149] He had himself been elected to the Order in September 1399, along with his brothers Thomas, John and Humphrey.[150] As king, he did not enjoy the same opportunities to create new members of the Order as his father had after the usurpation of 1399, but when he did exercise this power, he preferred soldiers with proven military experience, and often with a history of service to him as Prince of Wales.[151] At the same time, he was not shy about using the Order of the Garter as political patronage, for example electing such men as Thomas Montagu, earl of Salisbury and John Holland, later earl of Huntingdon, in 1414 and 1415, as public acknowledgement of their recovery of status after their fathers had taken part in the failed Earls' Rising of 1400.[152] Most famously, Henry V's diplomatic efforts to win the support of the Emperor Sigismund culminated in the emperor's admission to the Order of the Garter on 24 May 1416 at a delayed service in honour of St George at Windsor castle.[153] When the English delegation to the Council of Constance met the emperor on 29 January 1417, Sigismund was wearing a Lancastrian collar, and two days later he wore the robes of the Order of the Garter at High Mass.[154]

Conclusion

Henry V was celebrated during his lifetime and after his death as an exemplar of kingship and chivalry. In particular, he was praised for his great success as a military leader and conqueror, as well as for the importance that he placed upon martial discipline, loyalty and the ruthless treatment of those who betrayed him or their own word. Less attention was given to those qualities

---

148 Lefèvre de Saint-Rémy, *Chronique*, II, 194–5 and Chastellain, *Œuvres*, II, 133–5, together with D. A. L. Morgan, 'From a Death to a View: Louis Robessart, Johan Huizinga and the Political Significance of Chivalry', in *Chivalry and the Renaissance*, ed. S. Anglo (Woodbridge, 1990), pp. 93–106 (pp. 93–5).

149 Collins, *Order of the Garter*.

150 Collins, 'The Order of the Garter, 1348–1461', pp. 166–7.

151 Collins, *Order of the Garter*, pp. 47–8, 119–20, and also see Collins, 'Order of the Garter, 1348–1461', pp. 169–70: this was a 'long-term policy to cultivate a body of tried and trusted soldiers who were to be the mainstay of his military ambitions'.

152 Collins, 'Order of the Garter, 1348–1461', p. 177, and Collins, *Order of the Garter*, pp. 123–4.

153 Henry V also gave the emperor the SS collar of the Lancastrians: *GHQ*, p. 132, and Collins, *Order of the Garter*, pp. 168–70. Also see *The Beauchamp Pageant*, ed. A. Sinclair (Donington, 2003), pp. 120–1.

154 *Foedera*, IV, ii, 192–3.

that are more synonymous with chivalry in the modern imagination, such as courtly love, crusading, tourneying or treating war as if it were some noble game. This in turn demonstrates the problems with anachronistic assumptions about medieval chivalry and simplistic readings of medieval chivalric writings that offered more complex debates about how the ideal king, knight or man should behave.

Henry V certainly had the opportunity to read and study a great deal of chivalric writing during the course of his life.[155] As a youth, he spent time in the household of Richard II, who owned French romances, the *Roman de la Rose*, a collection of poetry by Jean Froissart and perhaps also the Chandos Herald's verse biography of the Black Prince.[156] In 1403, Richard Ullerston, fellow of Queen's College Oxford, dedicated a Latin treatise on the duties of knighthood, *De Officio Militari*, to Henry as Prince of Wales.[157] Seven years later, Thomas Hoccleve addressed the vernacular *Regiment of Princes* to Henry, a work that drew heavily upon three main sources, the *De Regimine Principum* of Giles of Rome, the apocryphal letter of Aristotle to Alexander the Great known as the *Secreta Secretorum*, and Jacques de Cessoles' *Le livre du jeu d'échecs*.[158] During the same period, Prince Henry acquired one of the earliest copies of *Troilus and Criseyde*, the only manuscript of a work by Geoffrey Chaucer that was certainly owned by an English medieval king.[159] Henry also commissioned John Lydgate's *Troy Book* on 31 October 1412, just six months before his accession to the throne, and this work was completed in 1420.[160] On

155 K. B. McFarlane, *Lancastrian Kings and Lollard Knights* (Oxford, 1972), pp. 116–17 and 233–8, and Krochalis, 'The Books and Reading of Henry V and his Circle', pp. 50–77. Also see A. I. Doyle, 'English Books In and Out of Court from Edward III to Henry VII', in *English Court Culture in the Later Middle Ages*, ed. V. J. Scattergood and J. W. Sherborne (London, 1983), pp. 163–81; J. Stratford, 'The Early Royal Collections and the Royal Library to 1461', in *The Cambridge History of the Book in Britain, Vol. 3: 1400–1557*, ed. L. Hellinga and J. B. Trapp (Cambridge, 1999), pp. 255–66.

156 E. Rickert, 'King Richard's Books', *The Library* 4th s. 13 (1933), 144–7; R. F. Green, 'King Richard II's Books Revisited', *The Library* 5th s. 31 (1976), 235–9; P. J. Eberle, 'Richard II and the Literary Arts', in *Richard II: the Art of Kingship*, ed. A. Goodman and J. L. Gillespie (Oxford, 1999), pp. 231–53; A. Taylor, '"Moult bien parloit et lisoit le Franchois", or did Richard II Read with a Picard Accent?' in *The Vulgar Tongue: Medieval and Postmedieval Vernacularity*, ed. F. Somerset and N. Watson (Philadelphia, 2003), pp. 132–44. Also see *La Vie du Prince Noir [The life of the Black Prince], by Chandos Herald. Edited from the Manuscript in the University of London Library*, ed. D. B. Tyson (Tübingen, 1975).

157 Cambridge, Trinity College, MS B. 15. 23, fols. 16v–22r, and Corpus Christi College, MS 177, art. 26, fols. 179r–84r.

158 Hoccleve, *The Regiment of Princes*.

159 New York, Pierpont Morgan Library, MS M. 817, and also see Krochalis, 'The Books and Reading of Henry V and his Circle', p. 50.

160 *Lydgate's Troy Book*, ed. Bergen, I, 3–4 and III, 869. *The Siege of Thebes* may have also been written in the final two years of the reign of Henry V, though the evidence for this is not

28 April 1419, Charles de Beaumont, constable of Navarre, promised to send Henry V his book of *Guiron le Courtois*, an Arthurian romance, and Henry V also borrowed a narrative of Godfrey de Bouillon from the countess of Westmorland.[161] Henry V also commissioned from the Burgundian Ghillebert de Lannoy a narrative of his journey to Jerusalem.[162]

It is impossible to establish whether any of these works actually influenced and shaped Henry's values and behaviour. According to an inventory of the hangings in his tent while he was fighting in France, his tapestries celebrated St George and heroes of romances such as Perceval, Octavian and Bevis of Hamptoun, which might give some indication as to his personal taste.[163] Yet it is important to note that in public he was more commonly associated with saints rather than figures from chivalric romance. The *Gesta Henrici Quinti* for example reported that during the siege of Harfleur in 1415, the English prayed to the Virgin and to St George as protectors of the crown of England, and banners of St George were placed on the town after it was taken.[164] Thomas Elmham reported that Henry V prayed to the Virgin Mary, St George and St Edward the Confessor before the battle of Agincourt, and it is perhaps not surprising that these figures were also prominent in the celebrations after the battle, as well as at Henry's funeral seven years later.[165] Indeed, the feast of St George was promoted from a 'lesser double' to 'greater double' festival in November 1415, after Convocation had proposed the change two years earlier.[166]

Contemporary writers naturally claimed that Henry V was inspired by the reading of books.[167] For example, in the *Regiment of Princes*, Hoccleve had no doubt that Prince Henry would read his book, just as Henry had already read the three major sources for the *Regiment*, including Giles of Rome's *De Regimine Principum*.[168] Lydgate also claimed that Prince Henry loved to read ancient books that offered models of virtue and which encouraged both manliness and virtue, citing as an example Vegetius's *Epitoma Rei Militaris*.[169] The *Gesta Henrici Quinti* cited military advice from Giles of Rome's *De Regimine Prin-*

conclusive and there is certainly no indication of a patron for this work. D. A. Pearsall, *John Lydgate (1371–1449): A Bio-Bibliography* (Victoria, 1997), p. 22.

161 Krochalis, 'The Books and Reading of Henry V and his Circle', pp. 64–5.
162 Ibid., p. 65.
163 Ibid., p. 63.
164 *GHQ*, pp. 54 and 66.
165 *Memorials of Henry the Fifth*, ed. Cole, p. 121; *GHQ*, p. 106, and Hope, 'The Funeral, Monument and Chantry Chapel of Henry V', pp. 129–86.
166 Walsingham claimed that it was Henry V himself who had originally proposed the idea. Walsingham, *St. Albans Chronicle, 1394–1422*, p. 620.
167 Taylor, *Chivalry, Honour and Knighthood*, chapter 6.
168 Hoccleve, *Regiment of Princes*, pp. 97–102.
169 *Lydgate's Troy Book*, ed. Bergen, I, 3.

cipum during his account of the siege of Harfleur,[170] and during a disputation in Oxford in 1420 the king was commended for having waged war in France according to the advice given in Giles's *De Regimine Principum*.[171] Hoccleve later declared in his *Dialogue with a friend* that he had decided not to prepare an English translation of Vegetius's *Epitoma Rei Militaris* for Humphrey, duke of Gloucester because the duke already knew so much about warfare that it would be unnecessary.[172] Such flattering testimony was designed not just to underline the prudence and capability of Henry V and Gloucester, but also to persuade future audiences of the utility of these texts, and of course of the intellectuals who interpreted them.

In the real world chivalry and knighthood were not learned merely through books. During the first thirteen years of Henry's life, until the Lancastrian usurpation and Henry's elevation to Prince of Wales on 15 October 1399, there was no expectation that he would ever become king and, as such, his education must have followed the typical pattern for the high aristocracy, as he learned horsemanship, martial skills, hunting and the like.[173] During those formative years, his father Henry Bolingbroke must have offered a powerful role model of chivalric enterprise, as he took part in the tournament at St-Inglevert in 1390, and joined two expeditions against the Lithuanians between 1390 and 1393.[174] Perhaps even more powerful would have been the way that Bolingbroke was willing to stand by his word in 1398, offering to

---

[170] Contrary to the opinion of C. F. Briggs, *Giles of Rome's 'De Regimine Principum': Reading and Writing Politics at Court and University, c.1275–c.1525* (Cambridge, 1999), pp. 2, 64, the text does not explicitly state that Henry V drew upon this advice, but rather validates the guidance that it provided by reference to the narrative of the siege: *GHQ*, pp. 28, 40–2.

[171] Oxford, Magdalen College, MS 38, fol. 17v.

[172] Thomas Hoccleve, *Thomas Hoccleve's 'Complaint' and 'Dialogue'*, ed. J.A. Burrow. EETS OS 313 (Oxford, 1999), p. 101. Gloucester owned Vegetius's work in Latin, as well as a French translation by Jean de Vignay (Cambridge, Cambridge University Library, MS Ee. 2. 17). A. Sammut, *Unfredo duca di Gloucester e gli umanisti italiani* (Padua, 1980), pp. 38, 45, 80, 95 and 100–1.

[173] Henry also learned, for example, grammar and the harp: McFarlane, *Lancastrian Kings and Lollard Knights*, p. 115 and N. Orme, *From Childhood to Chivalry: The Education of the English Kings and Aristocracy, 1066–1530* (London, 1984), pp. 146, 166 and 183. He also had access to books on hunting, such as Edward, duke of York, *The Master of Game by Edward, Second Duke of York: the Oldest English Book on Hunting*, ed. W. A. and F. Baillie-Grohman (London, 1904).

[174] Tuck, 'Henry IV and Chivalry', pp. 55–71, together with E. Gaucher, 'Les joutes de Saint-Inglevert: perception et écriture d'un événement historique pendant la guerre de Cent Ans', *Le moyen âge* 102 (1996), 229–43, and F. R. H. Du Boulay, 'Henry of Derby's Expedition to Prussia', in *The Reign of Richard II*, ed. F. R. H. Du Boulay and C. M. Barron (London, 1971), pp. 153–72, together with *Expeditions to Prussia and the Holy Land Made by Henry Earl of Derby (afterwards King Henry IV) in the Years 1390–1 and 1392–3*, ed. L. Toulmin-Smith, Camden Society n.s. 52 (London, 1884).

take part in a trial of battle to prove his accusation before the court of chivalry that Thomas Mowbray, duke of Norfolk, had spoken treasonable words against Richard II.[175] After 1399, Prince Henry had the opportunity to learn about military leadership in the field, during the Welsh wars.

Yet whether Henry was genuinely inspired by chivalric writings, or was even a man of honour in the modern romantic sense, is ultimately less important than the fact that he cultivated a reputation not just as a king but also as model of chivalry, which in turn had tremendous practical importance for his success and power.[176] During his lifetime, Henry V and his supporters took great care to shape his reputation through public events such as the victory parade in London on 23 November 1415 after Agincourt, or his recounting of the further successes in France during a royal progress in 1421.[177] At the same time, accounts of his life, from brief references by John Lydgate to the great chronicles and biographies written by Thomas Walsingham and the anonymous author of the *Gesta Henrici Quinti* helped to establish the long-standing fame of Henry V as a great military leader and conqueror, inspired and supported by God, striving for justice rather than self-aggrandisement, and always pursuing justice.

The importance of reputation was most obvious in military terms, where Henry V's actions and fame inspired his own troops but also challenged and frightened his enemies. For example, on 27 September 1415, Henry V sent a personal challenge to the Dauphin to settle their dispute in single combat. After no word was received within the eight days that Henry had offered, the English expedition left Harfleur.[178] This traditional, legal challenge undoubtedly helped to rally his own host and put heavy pressure on the French forces to respond to his *chevauchée* through the Norman countryside.[179] The victory at Agincourt not only increased English support for his war in France, but also made the Valois monarchy extremely reluctant to risk another battle with Henry V, which in turn enabled the English king to conquer Normandy without significant interference or external challenge to any of his sieges.[180] Monstrelet even suggested that Henry came to regret this situation when he wished to avenge the death of his brother Clarence at the battle of Baugé

---

[175] Walsingham, *St. Albans Chronicle, 1394–1422*, p. 108, and Allmand, *Henry V*, pp. 11–12.

[176] For the importance of Henry Bolingbroke's 'European-wide reputation' in influencing English and international reactions to his usurpation of the English throne in 1399, and building a circle of loyal supporters that would serve him throughout his reign, see Tuck, 'Henry IV and Chivalry', pp. 55, 68 and 70–1, as well as the important ideas of Staley, 'Gower, Richard II, Henry of Derby', pp. 85–7.

[177] GHQ, pp. 100–12, and Monstrelet, *La chronique*, IV, 25–6.

[178] GHQ, pp. 54–6.

[179] Rogers, 'Henry V's Military Strategy in 1415', pp. 407–10.

[180] Ibid., p. 399. Also see, for example, Newhall, *The English Conquest of Normandy*, pp. 104–15, 121.

in March 1421.[181] Whether the Burgundian chronicler was right or not, it is clear that Henry's reputation had already played a decisive role in allowing him to take advantage of the chaos that followed the murder of Jean, duke of Burgundy in September 1419.[182]

181 Monstrelet, *La chronique*, IV, 70.
182 Allmand, *Henry V*, p. 136.

10

War, Government and Commerce:
The Towns of Lancastrian France under
Henry V's Rule, 1417–22

Neil Murphy

The reign of Henry V saw the greatest expansion of English power in France since the conquests of Edward III. In contrast to the *chevauchées* of the fourteenth century, which were raids intended to destroy crops and demoralize the population, the type of warfare prosecuted by Henry V was designed to lead to a lasting territorial settlement. As administrative, economic and military centres, the possession of towns was fundamental to Henry's strategy in France. While relations between Lancastrian rulers and their urban subjects in France have attracted the attention of historians such as Christopher Allmand, Anne Curry and Guy Thompson, for the most part these studies look broadly at the entire period of Lancastrian rule and tend to concentrate on the Dual Monarchy, rather than Henry V's period of rule in France.[1] Amongst the most important of these works is Anne Curry's study of the

---

[1] A notable exception to this is Anne Curry's study of Harfleur from 1415 to 1422: A. Curry, 'Harfleur et les Anglais, 1415–1422', in *La Normandie et l'Angleterre au Moyen Age*, ed. P. Bouet and V. Gazeau (Caen, 2003), pp. 249–63. For towns in Lancastrian Normandy see: C. Allmand, *Lancastrian Normandy 1415–1450: The History of a Medieval Occupation* (Oxford, 1983); C. Allmand, 'Local Reaction to the French Reconquest of Normandy: The Case of Rouen', in *The Crown and Local Communities in England and France in the Fifteenth Century*, ed. J. R. L. Highfield and R. Jeffs (Gloucester, 1981), pp. 146–61; A. Curry, 'Bourgeois et soldats dans la ville de Mantes pendant l'occupation anglaise de 1419 à 1449', in *Guerre, pouvoir et noblesse au Moyen Âge: mélange en l'honneur de Philippe Contamine*, ed. J. Paviot and J. Verger (Paris, 2000), pp. 175–84; A. Curry, 'L'occupation anglaise du XVe siècle: la discipline militaire et le problème des gens "vivans sur le pais"', in *La Normandie dans la guerre de Cent Ans 1346–1450*, ed. J.-Y. Marin (Milan, 1999), pp. 47–9; A. Curry, 'Pour ou contre le roi d'Angleterre? La discipline militaire et la contestation du pouvoir en Normandie au XVe siècle', in *Images de la contestation du pouvoir dans le monde normand (Xe–XVIIIe siècle)*, ed. C. Bougy and S. Poirey (Caen, 2007), pp. 147–62; A. Curry, 'The Impact of War and Occupation on Urban Life in Normandy, 1417–1450', *French History* 1 (1987), 157–81; A. Curry, 'Les villes normandes et l'occupation anglaise: l'importance du siège de Rouen (1418–19)', in *Les villes normandes au Moyen Age: renaissance, essor, crise: actes du colloque international de Cerisy-la-Salle, 8–12 octobre 2003*,

military role performed by the towns of Lancastrian Normandy.[2] Rather than focusing on the urban military sphere, this chapter looks broadly at the Lancastrian monarchy's urban policy in France and considers the interplay between municipal administration, commerce and conflict. Instead of looking across the entire period of Lancastrian rule in France, the discussion will provide focused examination of the five years from Henry V's second invasion of Normandy in August 1417 to his death in August 1422. It will be argued that this was a crucial period when the Lancastrian monarchy developed a coherent policy towards its urban subjects in France.

Most studies of Lancastrian France focus on Normandy. With the exception of Paris, those territories which came under Lancastrian domination following the treaty of Troyes have not received the same attention from historians.[3] In contrast, this chapter will look at Lancastrian rule across the north of the kingdom, focusing especially on Henry's relations with municipal elites across the urban belt that ran from the borders of Brittany in the west to Flanders in the east, while also seeking to draw comparisons with England's relations with Gascon towns. A close examination of Henry's treatment of French towns is possible due to the survival of an abundance of administrative sources detailing his period of rule in France. Foremost amongst these documents are the records kept by the Lancastrian administration, including the French, Gascon and Norman rolls, which are complemented by a range of civic documents, especially the registers of municipal deliberations and financial accounts for towns such as Abbeville, Amiens, Beauvais, Bordeaux, Mantes and Senlis.[4] The chapter will begin with an examination of Henry's treatment of the urban population of Normandy, before moving on to look at

---

ed. P. Bouet and F. Neveux (Caen, 2006), pp. 109–23; F.-X. Lemercier, 'Falaise pendant l'occupation anglaise', in *Villes normandes*, ed. Bouet and Neveux, pp. 125–38.

2   A. Curry, 'Towns at War: Norman Towns under English Rule, 1417–1450', in *Towns and Townspeople in the Fifteenth Century*, ed. J. A. F. Thomson (Gloucester, 1986), pp. 148–72. Although this study is principally focused on the period of the Dual Monarchy, Professor Curry also makes some important observations on Henry V's rule in the duchy (pp. 157–60).

3   For Paris, see J. Favier, 'Occupation ou connivence? Les anglais à Paris (1420–1436)', in *Guerre, pouvoir et noblesse*, ed. Paviot and Verger, pp. 239–60; G. L. Thompson, *Paris and its People under English Rule: The Anglo-Burgundian Regime 1420–1436* (Oxford, 1991).

4   The most extensive of these are the Norman rolls, which were begun again with Henry's invasion of France in August 1417 and following with his death in August 1422 (TNA, series C 64). Calendars for this series of documents have been printed both in the Deputy Keeper's Reports and by Bréquigny, who also provided some transcriptions. Where possible, I have consulted the original documents, as not all the key information is given in the calendars, though I have also included the calendar references. See Bréquigny, 'Roles normands et français et autres pièces tirées des archives de Londres par Bréquigny en 1764, 1765 et 1766', ed. L. Pusieux, *Mémoires de la Société des Antiquaires de Normandie*, 23 (1858); *Annual Reports of the Deputy Keeper of the Public Records* [DKR], XLI, XLII, XLIV (London, 1880–3).

his actions in Picardy, Champagne and the Ile-de-France following the sealing of the treaty of Troyes in May 1420.

The Administration of Norman Towns

When Henry landed at Touques in Normandy on 1 August 1417, he already held the strategically important town of Harfleur. He expelled a large number of the native population and replaced them with English settlers.[5] The scale of English immigration into Harfleur between its capitulation and the commencement of the Norman rolls in August 1417 is difficult to judge. The French rolls record only one grant of a house to an English settler at Harfleur before 1417, though English settlement in the town was certainly more extensive than this.[6] As well as placing a garrison in Harfleur, the crown made grants of property to English merchants and tradesmen to encourage them to settle in England's most recent territorial acquisition.[7] When Henry returned to Normandy in August 1417 to begin his systematic conquest of the duchy, Caen, the principal town in Lower Normandy, closed its gates on him. After a two-week siege, Henry took the town by force and permitted his soldiers to pillage it.[8] Henry claimed to be the legitimate duke of Normandy and used Caen to give a demonstration to the other towns of Normandy of the consequences of resisting his rule.

The expulsions at Harfleur and the pillaging of Caen were, however, uncharacteristic of Henry's actions in Normandy, and his subsequent treatment of Norman towns was marked by conciliation and clemency. Henry presented himself to the native population as the legitimate duke of Normandy who was returning to restore the traditional liberties of the duchy.[9] For Henry, the possession of the capital of Normandy, Rouen, was of great significance and, as Anne Curry has observed, Henry starved the town into submission rather than taking it by assault. He wanted to maintain Rouen's fortifica-

---

5   Curry, 'Impact of War', p. 160; Curry, 'Harfleur', p. 250.
6   *DKR*, XLIV, 576–7.
7   *POPC*, II, 184–5, 196–7. This was the same size as the wartime garrison at Calais: J. L. Kirby, 'Financing of Calais under Henry V', *BIHR* 23 (1950), 165–77 (p. 166); S. Rose, *Calais: An English Town in France, 1347–1558* (Woodbridge, 2008), p. 27. For proclamations made at London to encourage immigration into Harfleur see: *Calendar of the Letter-Books. City of London. Letter-Book I, 1400–1422*, ed. R. G. Sharpe (London, 1909), p. 161.
8   P. Carel, *Etude sur la Commune de Caen* (Caen, 1888), p. 152.
9   A. Curry, 'Lancastrian Normandy: The Jewel in the Crown', in *England and Normandy in the Middle Ages*, ed. D. Bates and A. Curry (London, 1994), pp. 239–52 (pp. 248–9). By the end of 1418, Henry had re-established the Norman *Chambre des Comptes* at Caen and the office of *grand sénéchal de Normandie*, which had been abolished in 1204: Allmand, *Lancastrian Normandy*, p. 83; A. Bossuat, 'Le Parlement de Paris pendant l'occupation anglaise', *Revue Historique* 229 (1963), 19–40 (p. 21).

tions as intact as possible, as he planned to make the city his administrative base in France.[10] Henry ordered the building of a new palace in Rouen soon after entering the city, and appeared in public dressed in the arms of the duchy of Normandy.[11] If he wanted the local population to recognize him as the legitimate duke of Normandy rather than as a foreign conqueror, he had to turn his attention to ruling the population of the duchy. This he did by inviting urban populations across the duchy to petition him to have their liberties and franchises confirmed. The confirmation of urban charters was crucial for townspeople, as these liberties underpinned their political and economic rights. Rather than seek to destroy or curtail the extent of urban freedoms, Henry confirmed the charters of all Norman towns, including those which had offered resistance. In addition to Caen, Harfleur and Rouen, these included Argentan, Bayeux, Carentan, Coutances, Dieppe, Eu, Évreux, Falaise, Gournay, Honfleur, Louviers and Montivilliers. Although Henry tended to confirm the rights and liberties of bishops and monastic communities as they had stood before the loss of Normandy in 1204, he confirmed the liberties of many Norman towns as they stood in the reign of Philip VI.[12] This is because Norman towns had obtained a mass of liberties and franchises between the loss of Normandy in 1204 and Henry's conquest of 1417–19. As such, Henry could not revert to the pre-Valois era without eroding the bulk of the rights that underpinned urban prosperity in the duchy.

The administration of Normandy was an issue of immediate concern to Henry. The captain and the *bailli* were the two principal royal officials in French towns during the later Middle Ages. The captain oversaw the military affairs of his town, particularly the organization of the garrison, while the *bailli* acted as the king's principal judicial and administrative representative in the locality. Once a Norman town came into his possession, one of Henry's first actions was to fill both positions with Englishmen. For example, Walter Hungerford was made captain of Cherbourg, Walter Beauchamp became *bailli* of Rouen, while William Bourchier received the captaincy of Dieppe.[13] Once we look beyond the top rung of royal officials, however, we find a remarkable degree of continuity in the administration of the duchy. Indeed, the bulk of Norman officials retained the positions which they had held prior to Henry's invasion. Although John Radeclyf was appointed as the new *bailli* of Evreux on 2 May 1418, Odart Tanquere was confirmed in his position as advocate

---

10 Curry, 'Siege of Rouen', pp. 243–6.
11 TNA, C 64/11, 53d, 34d (*DKR*, XLII, 318, 357); *Chronique normande de Pierre Cochon*, ed. C. de Robillard de Beaurepaire (Rouen, 1870), p. 281; *Les croniques de Normandie, 1223–1453*, ed. A. Hellot (Rouen, 1883), p. xii.
12 See, for example, the confirmation of liberties made to the town of Pontoise: TNA, C 64/15 (*DKR*, XLII, 402). The bishop of Lisieux had his rights confirmed as they stood in a charter issued by King John in 1199: TNA, C 64/17 (*DKR*, LXII, 445).
13 TNA, C 64/9, 15 (*DKR*, XLI, 696); C 64/10, 32 (*DKR*, XLI, 730).

and counsellor for the *bailli*.[14] Even in cases where positions fell vacant due to the death or exile of the previous occupier, they were largely refilled with Norman appointees. For example, on 23 August 1419 John Caselier, a native citizen of Rouen, was given the position of royal sergeant of the waters and forests in the duchy of Normandy in the place of John Bassor.[15] As Henry's captains and *baillis* were constantly on the move in 1417–19 and could not permanently reside in their areas of jurisdiction, these French officials were crucial to the effective working of the royal administration in towns across the duchy. The capability of these individuals to ensure the continued day-to-day running of the administration can be seen when we turn our attention to the land settlement that accompanied Henry's conquest of Normandy. Almost every grant of land or property recorded on the Norman rolls includes specific details of who held land in advance of Henry's landing on 1 August 1417 and how the land was held.[16] The smooth transfer of land in the aftermath of the conquest of Normandy is testament both to the effectiveness of the organs of local government which Henry retained and the forward planning and detailed local knowledge displayed by the Lancastrian administration in France.

As well as keeping the staff of the original Norman administration largely intact, Henry did not interfere in the composition of municipal governments and confirmed the authority of civic administrations, once they had taken oaths of loyalty to him.[17] The Lancastrian administration also took measures to prevent English *baillis* and captains from encroaching on the rights of Norman municipal councils. They were forbidden from collecting illegal tolls on goods or restricting the efforts of town councils to collect taxes.[18] Municipal councils were responsible for the issuing of trading licences and the appointment of a range of urban officials. Although Henry did not seek to curtail these powers, he did confirm all the licences and appointments made by civic administrations, an action which enabled him to demonstrate that municipal authority was ultimately derived from him. He also confirmed a wide range of urban grants and positions, especially in the weeks following the fall of Rouen in January 1419, when he was able to turn his attention towards governing the duchy. He confirmed all the sergeants appointed by Rouen's municipal council in February 1419, and he made similar confirmations each time a new sergeant was appointed.[19] Municipal positions were ratified by

---

14 TNA, C 64/9, 25d (*DKR*, XLI, 713).
15 TNA, C 64/12, 26d (*DKR*, XLII, 324). I have preserved the anglicized versions of French forenames used in the records.
16 The records of Caen and Harfleur, which were to become the two centres of English immigration, were amongst those burned by Henry.
17 For example, see his confirmation of the rights of the jurisdiction and authority of the municipal council of Dieppe: *CPR, 1416–22*, p. 333.
18 TNA, C 64/11, 14d (*DKR*, XLII, 328). See also Curry, 'Towns at War', pp. 159–60.
19 TNA, C 64/10, 32, 29, 19 (*DKR*, XLI, 751, 753, 755).

the Lancastrian crown, and no appointment was too small to escape its attention. On 18 June 1418 Henry confirmed Simon de la Rivière's appointment as carrier of corn to the corn market at Évreux, and on 24 February 1419 he confirmed Stephen de Baudribosc and John de Cauville as sellers of salt fish in Rouen.[20] The confirming of these grants was a mark of sovereignty, and Henry used them as method to enforce his authority in Normandy, while the continuity of office-holding also encouraged the smooth running of the duchy's administration.

As well as keeping the royal and civic administrations of Normandy largely intact, the Lancastrian leadership permitted townspeople who took an oath of loyalty to retain their goods and property.[21] The oaths tended to be taken communally at the time of the town's capitulation. When Evreux surrendered to Thomas, duke of Exeter, for example, the inhabitants were accorded a general grant confirming the inhabitants in the possession of all the goods and properties.[22] Merchants who were absent from their town of residence at the time of its capitulation were given a period of grace in which to take the oath.[23] Lancastrian rule was not universally accepted, and some chose to emigrate rather than swear an oath of loyalty to a ruler whom they regarded as a foreign invader. This trend is especially apparent in the early stages of Henry's conquest, when the population could hope that the English king's presence in the duchy was a temporary aberration and that Valois rule would soon be restored. When Caen fell in September 1417, many of the native inhabitants chose to leave for Brittany, Flanders and the Ile-de-France rather than live under Lancastrian rule.[24] With the fall of Rouen in January 1419, it became apparent that the Valois monarchy was incapable of offering adequate protection to its people. As Lancastrian rule began to appear permanent, many former inhabitants of Normandy, such as the parents of Thomas Basin, future bishop of Lisieux, returned to the duchy and swore an oath of loyalty to Henry, so that they could take up residence in their home towns again.[25]

20 TNA, C 64/9, 22d (*DKR*, XLI, 714); C 64/10, 35d (*DKR*, XLI, 750).
21 For the Lancastrian land settlement in Normandy see: C. Allmand, 'The Collection of Dom Lenoir and the English Occupation of Normandy in the Fifteenth Century', *Archives* 6 (1964), 202–10; C. Allmand, 'The Lancastrian Land Settlement in Normandy, 1417–50', *Economic History Review* 21 (1968), 461–79; Allmand, *Lancastrian Normandy*, especially chapter 3; R. Massey, 'The Land Settlement in Lancastrian Normandy', in *Property and Politics: Essays in Later Medieval English History*, ed. A. J. Pollard (Gloucester, 1984), pp. 76–96; R. Massey, 'The Lancastrian Land Settlement in Normandy and Northern France, 1417–1450' (unpublished Ph.D. thesis, University of Liverpool, 1987).
22 TNA, C 64/9, 17 (*DKR*, XLI, 695).
23 TNA, C 64/9, 24 (*DKR*, XLI, 684).
24 Allmand, *Lancastrian Normandy*, pp. 84–5; Curry, 'Siege of Rouen', pp. 238–9; L. Pusieux, *Siège et prise de Caen par les Anglais en 1417* (Caen, 1856), pp. 65–6.
25 L. Rioult de Neuville, 'Résistance à l'occupation anglaise dans le pays de Lisieux de 1424 à 1444', *Bulletin de la société des antiquaires de Normandie* 16 (1892), 329. For surrenders

Henry attached great importance to the swearing of oaths, as they underlined the legitimacy of his rule. Indeed, he even dispatched Philip Repingdon, bishop of Lincoln, and Thomas Polton, dean of York Minster, to Rome to receive oaths of loyalty from any Norman clergy present at the papal curia.[26] He instructed his Norman *baillis* to issue proclamations stating that all those who returned to swear fealty would have their full rights restored.[27] A large population meant more people to tax, and the Lancastrian administration devised a number of policies to increase the number of inhabitants of Normandy, which was suffering from depopulation in the early fifteenth century due to the combined effects of war, plague and famine.[28] It granted letters of safe conduct to all those who wished to come and take the oath of loyalty, and acted to prevent English soldiers from molesting or falsely imprisoning those coming to Henry.[29] The Lancastrian crown also declared that all who returned to take the oath would have their goods and property restored to them, no matter what crimes they had committed.[30] The policy was successful, and in 1419–20 people returned to Normandy from towns across the kingdom of France, including Abbeville, Boulogne, Orléans, Paris, Poitiers, Tournai and Tours, which lay at the very centre of Valois power in the fifteenth century.[31]

As part of its efforts to minimize population loss, the Lancastrian crown also granted out the lands and properties of those who had fled Normandy and were declared to be rebels. After the fall of Caen in September 1417, royal proclamations were made in London offering grants of property in the town to English merchants.[32] The Lancastrian administration targeted English urban immigration into Harfleur and Caen and both of these towns were marked out as distinct from the others that came into Henry's possession during his conquest of 1417–19. They were declared to be *villam regis* in

---

made to Henry following the fall of Rouen see: TNA, C 64/10, (*DKR*, XLI, 741–3); C 64/11, (*DKR*, XLI, 761–7).

[26] TNA, C 64/12, 18d (*DKR*, XLII, 358).

[27] TNA, C 64/12, 21d (*DKR*, XLII, 326).

[28] See especially: G. Bois, *The Crisis of Feudalism: Economy and Society in Eastern Normandy c. 1300–1550* (Cambridge, 1984), pp. 316–27.

[29] TNA, C 64/13, 28d (*DKR*, XLII, 372); C 64/9, 40d (*DKR*, XLI, 708); C 64/10, 27d (*DKR*, XLI, 754); C 64/11, 21d (*DKR*, XLII, 326). One Guiot Aubert was accorded a pardon by Henry as he had been prevented from coming to swear loyalty by English soldiers who had imprisoned him: TNA, C 64/16, 20 (*DKR*, XLII, 442).

[30] TNA, C 64/10, 27d (*DKR*, XLI, 754).

[31] TNA, C 64/10, 31, 30, 27, 26, 19–17; C 64/12, 16; C 64/13, 15 (*DKR*, XLI, 731–5, 741–2; *DKR*, XLII, 347, 367). People continued to return to Normandy well into the reign of Henry VI. For pardons issued in the name of Henry VI to those returning see: *Actes de la chancellerie d'Henri VI concernant la Normandie sous la domination anglaise (1422–35)*, ed. P. Le Cacheux, 2 vols. (Rouen, 1907–8), II, 337, 355.

[32] *Collection générale des documents français qui se trouvent en Angleterre recueillis et publiés par Jules Delpit* (Paris, 1847), pp. 220–1.

the Norman rolls, in contrast to other towns of the duchy which were called *villam nostorum*, though the exact nature of the difference between these two designations is unclear from the surviving sources.[33] An examination of the Norman rolls reveals that 419 grants of property in Norman towns were made between his invasion of the duchy in August 1417 and his death in August 1422. As the graph below shows, the overwhelming majority of these grants were made in Harfleur (217), followed by Caen (132).

Number of grants of urban properties and land made by Henry V, August 1417 to August 1422 (Norman Rolls, TNA, C 64/8–17)

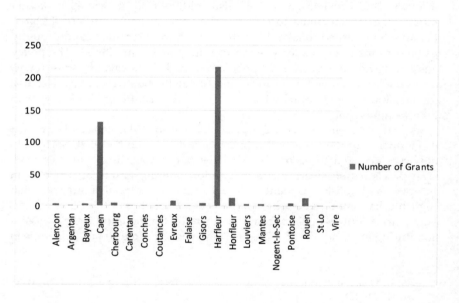

Grants of one or two properties in places such as Argentan and Carentan arose from the need to provide houses for the new captains and *bailli*, and these towns were not targeted for English settlement. Perhaps more surprising is the low number of property grants in Rouen, which Henry was then developing as the centre of his administration in France. When we turn to the registers of the *tabellionnage* for Rouen, which record property rentals in the town, a different picture emerges and we find evidence for the presence of a significant body of English merchants resident in the Norman capital.[34] Indeed,

---

[33] See, for example: C 64/13, 16 (Bréquigny, 148); C 64/14, 6 (Bréquigny, 157).
[34] The *tabellionage* registers for Rouen are held at the Archives départementales de la Seine-Maritime, 2E1/168 to 2E1/184. For an analysis of these registers see: P. Cailleux,

between 1 October 1419 and 22 March 1421 the *tabellionnage* registers for Rouen list 189 property contracts involving the English.[35] The London merchant, Thomas le Clerc, for example, was renting nine shops in the St-Maclou parish of the city by 1421.[36] The disparity of the evidence provided by the Norman rolls and the *tabellionnage* registers for Rouen can in part be explained by the primacy of Rouen's position in Lancastrian France. The Lancastrian crown did not need to offer grants of land and property to encourage immigration into the economic and administrative centre of the duchy. In contrast, we can see the high provision of grants of property at Caen and Harfleur as an attempt to encourage English immigration into problem towns. Part of the population of Harfleur (possibly up to 2,000 people) was expelled from the town following its surrender, and it was developed on a colonial model, similar to Edward I's actions in Wales and Edward III's actions at Calais.[37] Caen was already in decline by the early fifteenth century and the population loss that followed Henry V's siege (estimates vary from between 500 to 2,000 people) only exacerbated existing problems.[38] The grants of property offered by the Lancastrian administration at Harfleur and Caen acted as an incentive to encourage English migrants to come and settle in these under-populated towns and restore some degree of economic growth. There were also simply fewer vacant properties available in Rouen to grant to English settlers, as, in contrast to Caen and Harfleur, there were few exiles from the Norman capital. We should also be careful about exaggerating the extent of English immigration into Norman towns. Although Caen had the second largest number of English urban settlers in the duchy, they were generally contained in the

---

'La présence anglaise dans la capitale normande: quelques aspects des relations entre Anglais et Rouennais', in *Normandie et l'Angleterre*, ed. Bouet and Gazeau, pp. 265–76.

[35] Cailleux, 'Présence anglaise', p. 267. It may also be the case that English settlement in towns was more extensive, but remains hidden due to a lack of surviving similar series of records for other towns across the duchy during its early period of Lancastrian rule. However, as with Rouen, such immigration lay beyond the government-sponsored programme of targeting English settlement into Caen and Harfleur.

[36] Massey, 'Land Settlement', pp. 83–4; Massey, 'Lancastrian Rouen: Military Service and Property Holding, 1419–49', in *England and Normandy*, ed. Bates and Curry, pp. 270–3. See also A. Dubuc, 'Le tabellionage rouennais durant l'occupation anglaise (1418–1445)', *Bulletin philologique et historique (jusqu'à 1610), année 1967* (1969), 797–808; A. Barabé, *Recherches historiques sur le tabellionage royal, principalement en Normandie* (Rouen, 1863), pp. 132–5; P. Le Cacheux, *Rouen au temps de Jeanne d'Arc et pendant l'occupation anglaise (1419–1449)* (Rouen, 1931).

[37] Allmand, *Lancastrian Normandy*, pp. 84, 86; R. R. Davies, 'Colonial Wales', *Past and Present* 65 (1974), 3–23 (especially pp. 20–3).

[38] Many of these workers moved to Breton towns, such as Rennes, where they developed the cloth industry of the duchy: Pusieux, *Siège de Caen*, pp. 65–6. For estimates of the population loss at Caen see: Allmand, *Lancastrian Normandy*, p. 84.

St Pierre parish and they had little, if any, representation on the municipal council during Henry's period of rule.[39]

As well as rewarding his English supporters with land and property, Henry also made similar grants to his Norman urban subjects. This was part of an early manifestation of a trend more strongly associated with the late fifteenth century, whereby urban elites sought to increase their power and status by investing their profits in land-holding.[40] The land settlement orchestrated in Lancastrian Normandy allowed merchants from across the duchy and beyond, who had displayed their loyalty to Henry, to gain power in the countryside. Henry sanctioned the marriage of townsmen to Norman heiresses and even pardoned the abduction of widows by Parisian merchants.[41] This move bound these merchants closer to Henry, as they were often required to perform a service for holding the land. For example, William Sebire, a citizen of Rouen, was granted the lands of Guy de Pitre (who had been declared a rebel) in tail male on 12 July 1421, in return for providing yearly homage and a spear tip, the typical feudal render of a tenant-in-chief.[42] The Lancastrian crown also provided grants of urban property to its loyal Norman subjects. This permitted Henry to increase his body of support in towns such as Louviers and Bayeux, which had not suffered a major population loss and where he did not wish to encourage English settlement.[43] The Lancastrian administration also took measures to encourage the Norman population to remain in their home towns. In September 1419, the inhabitants of Rouen were exempted from the rents that they were due to pay to the king, while the rent which the poor paid on their houses at Caen was frozen.[44]

In spite of the range of measures taken by the Lancastrian crown to appeal to the urban population of Normandy, Henry's rule was not universally accepted in the duchy. Although many disgruntled urban inhabitants relocated to Valois areas of the kingdom, there were disturbances amongst some of those who chose to remain in Normandy. A commission was formed by William Talbot on 26 June 1418 with instructions to arrest and imprison those persons who had attended recent seditious meetings in Caen.[45] At Dieppe, the captain of the town, William Bourchier, was given the power to arrest

---

[39]   Curry, 'Impact of War', p. 168.
[40]   See B. Chevalier, *Les bonnes villes de France du XIVe au XVIe siècle* (Paris, 1982), pp. 141–3; G. Huppert, *Les Bourgeois Gentilshommes: An Essay on the Definition of Elites in Renaissance France* (Chicago, 1977).
[41]   On 22 June 1422, the Parisian Richard Aoust was pardoned by Henry for the abduction of Isabel de Hellande, widow of one John Dechère: TNA, C 64/17 (*DKR*, XLI, 444).
[42]   TNA, C 64/16, 32 (*DKR*, XLII, 413).
[43]   TNA, C 64/9, 15, 14 (*DKR*, XLI, 696–7).
[44]   TNA, C 64/11, 20, 25d (*DKR*, XLI, 798, XLII, 325).
[45]   TNA, C 64/9, 20d (*DKR*, XLI, 714).

all those suspected of betraying the town into enemy hands.[46] Rather than initiating or supporting anti-Lancastrian actions, French municipal councils worked with Henry's administration to quell acts of sedition, and it was partly due to the efforts of the municipal elite that the trouble at Dieppe in 1419 was quickly contained. Urban elites distanced themselves from civic disturbances and worked to maintain good relations with Henry. When trouble broke out at Mantes in December 1421 following unlawful assemblies of towns-people, the municipal council was quick to separate itself from the events and seek a pardon from Henry.[47] Henry made an example of those people he had executed for participation in acts of sedition. On 27 August 1418 John Lorenden was executed for treason and his body quartered. The captains of Harfleur, Pont de l'Arche, Louviers and Évreux all received a quarter, with the instructions that it was to be displayed in a prominent part of the town and thus act as an example of the consequences of treason.[48] On the whole, such executions were rare in Henry V's Normandy, especially after the fall of Rouen, when the native population tended to accept his rule. This gave the Lancastrian crown the stability required to restore the urban economy and expand its rule into other parts of the kingdom.

Picardy, Champagne and the Ile-de-France

The terms of the treaty sealed at Troyes on 21 May 1420 made Henry V heir to the throne of France. While Charles VI was permitted to retain his position as king for the rest of his lifetime, Henry was made regent.[49] The treaty was followed by a *lit de justice* held at the Parlement of Paris on 23 December 1420 at which the 'soi-disant' Dauphin was formally disinherited from the succession.[50] This legitimized Henry's claims to the throne of France and led to numerous towns across northern France coming under his rule.[51] Although

---

46 TNA, C 64/11, 23d (*DKR*, XLII, 325). This inquest resulted in a number of convictions, with one of the guilty, Cardot Divers, receiving a royal pardon for having turned king's evidence: TNA, C 64/12, 31 (*DKR*, XLII, 341).

47 Curry, 'Towns at War', p. 158.

48 TNA, C 64/9, 15d (*DKR*, XLI, 716).

49 The full text of the treaty is given in: A. Curry, 'Two Kingdoms, One King: The Treaty of Troyes (1420) and the Creation of a Double Monarchy of England and France', in *The Contending Kingdoms: France and England 1420–1700*, ed. G. Richardson (Aldershot, 2008), pp. 23–42 (pp. 39–41).

50 He was then banished from the kingdom on 6 January 1421: A. Leguai, 'La "France bourguignonne" dans le conflit entre la "France française" et la "France anglaise" (1420–1435)', in *La 'France Anglaise' au Moyen Age* (Paris, 1988), pp. 41–52 (p. 45).

51 Some townspeople who had fled Normandy in 1417–19 now found themselves living under Lancastrian rule, including the migrants from Gournay and Gisors who were permitted to reside permanently at Beauvais in 1419 'pour eschever qu'ils ne fussent

the municipal council of Senlis had refused to give fealty to Henry V in 1419, it recognized him as regent and heir to the French throne following the treaty of Troyes.[52] The influence of the duke of Burgundy was instrumental in persuading many northern towns to accept Lancastrian rule in France. In the aftermath of the murder of John the Fearless at the bridge of Montereau, the Dauphin was strongly identified with the Armagnac party and many northern towns were more inclined to accept the rule of the duke's ally, Henry V, rather than the Valois claimant to the throne.[53]

Those towns which came under Henry's rule in May 1420 did so by treaty rather than surrender, and Henry's attitude towards the royal officials in these areas stood in contrast to his policy of appointing English *baillis* in Normandy. All five *baillis* appointed by Henry in November and December 1420 were French (Melun, Vermandois, Amiens, Meaux and Chartres) and many of them were to prove to be as loyal to him as his own English supporters were in Normandy, especially Robert Le Jeune. Originally from Arras, Le Jeune had moved to Amiens where he served as a lawyer in the employ of the civic administration. He was one of the delegation sent to the Estates-General held at Paris in December 1420, where he was appointed *bailli* of Amiens in the place of Denis de Brimeu, a loyal Dauphinist.[54] It is likely that Le Jeune's appointment to the position of *bailli* was due to the influence of Philip the Good. Under John the Fearless, Le Jeune had proved himself to be a devoted supporter of the Burgundian cause. He had accompanied John to Beauvais in 1417, where he was instrumental in persuading the townspeople to open their gates to the duke and his men.[55] The appointment of French *baillis* suited Henry who wanted to avoid being seen as a foreign invader imposing foreign officials in the wake of the treaty of Troyes. Le Jeune distinguished himself in his loyalty to the Lancastrian regime and set about rigorously collecting the town's portion of the *taille* of 400,000 *écus* levied by the Estates-General of December 1420. Although these actions won Le Jeune the animosity of the townspeople, they endeared the new *bailli* to Henry V who opted not to stay at the episcopal palace (the customary residence for visiting kings) but at the house of Le Jeune when he came to Amiens in January 1421.[56]

Englès': R. Rose, *Ville de Beauvais. Inventaire sommaire des archives communales antérieures à 1790* (Beauvais, 1997), p. 9.

52 TNA, C 64/12, (*DKR*, XLII, 360).

53 F. Autrand, *Charles VI* (Paris, 1986), p. 591.

54 For the *baillis* of Amiens see: E. Maugis, *Essai sur les recruitment et les attributions des principaux offices du siège du bailliage d'Amiens de 1300 à 1600* (Paris, 1906).

55 *Mémoires de Pierre de Fenin*, ed. E. Dupont (Paris, 1837), p. 76.

56 L. M. A. Calonne d'Avesne, *Histoire de la ville d'Amiens*, 3 vols. (Amiens, 1899–1906), I, 375; *Pierre de Fenin*, ed. Dupont, p. 150; *Journal de Clément de Fauquembergue Greffier du Parlement de Paris 1417–1435*, ed. A. Tuetey, 3 vols. (Paris, 1903–15), III, 178; E. Maugis, *Essai sur le régime financier de la ville d'Amiens du XIVe à la fin du XVIe siècle, 1356–1558* (Amiens, 1838), p. 18.

Paris was foremost amongst those northern towns which accepted Henry as regent and heir to the throne of France after May 1420. As the administrative centre of the kingdom, Henry needed control of Paris if he hoped to make his rule in France permanent. Good relations developed between Henry and the capital following the capitulation of Rouen, with the Parisians making their own separate peace with Henry in November 1419. As part of his bid to encourage the support of the capital, Henry worked to provide the stability and security necessary for commerce along the Seine, and on 24 January 1420 he reassured the Parisian municipal council that he would confirm its liberties when he became king of France.[57]

Although the Burgundian entry into Paris in 1418 had led to Chartres throwing off Armagnac rule, a number of other towns to the south of Paris remained under Armagnac control.[58] Two days after his marriage to Catherine of France at Troyes, Henry set out to bring these towns under his rule. After taking Sens (10 June 1420) and Montereau (1 July 1420), Henry made for the Armagnac stronghold of Melun. When the town finally capitulated in November after a long and gruelling siege, Henry allowed those inhabitants who took the oath to him to retain their goods and property. Although he permitted the general populations of Armagnac towns to continue to live unhindered, Henry's treatment of their ruling elites was more severe than it had been in Normandy. According to Monstrelet, between 500 and 600 of the leading citizens of Melun were taken hostage and imprisoned in Paris, and when Meaux fell in May 1422 between 600 and 700 of the wealthiest inhabitants were taken as prisoner to England and the *bailli*, Loys Gast, executed in Paris.[59] Not only had Armagnac towns continued to resist Lancastrian rule after the treaty of Troyes, members of their populations (such as Arnauld Guilhem, lord of Barbazan, the governor of Melun) were also implicated in the murder of John the Fearless. By the terms of the treaties of surrender made with Armagnac-held towns, those inhabitants suspected of involvement in the murder of the late duke of Burgundy were exempt from receiving pardon and had to be handed over to Anglo-Burgundian forces.[60] The shift of power to the Lancastrian crown in the region offered some towns the opportunity to throw off Armagnac rule. Although Compiègne had a population that was broadly pro-Burgundian, the surrender of its hated Armagnac

[57] TNA, C 64/11 (*DKR*, XLI, 808); C 64/12 (*DKR*, XLII, 338).

[58] A. Chédeville, *Histoire de Chartres et du pays chartrain* (Toulouse, 1983), p. 134.

[59] *La Chronique d'Enguerran de Monstrelet*, ed. L. Douet-d'Arcq, 6 vols. (Paris, 1857–62), III, 14–15; IV, 93–6.

[60] See, for example, the treaties of submissions for Compiègne and Melun: L. Carolus-Barré, 'Compiègne et la guerre, 1414–1430', in *La 'France Anglaise'*, pp. 383–92 (p. 388); M. H. G. Nicollet, *Histoire de Melun* (Melun, 1845), pp. 238–9.

garrison (imposed on the town in 1418) to the duke of Bedford in June 1422 was a moment of relief for the townspeople.[61]

Not all pro-Burgundian towns initially welcomed Lancastrian rule, especially when they feared that the treaty of Troyes would cause them to be separated from the kingdom of France and subject to English laws and customs. This concern was especially apparent in Abbeville, the capital of the county of Ponthieu, which had been brought to Edward I in 1299 by his wife, Margaret of France. By the terms of the treaty of Brétigny (1360), the English king was to hold Ponthieu in full sovereignty, and when Abbeville's municipal council received a letter from Philip the Good stating that the county was to pass to Henry V, they feared that they were to become part of Henry's English crown.[62] In response to this letter, the municipal council dispatched deputies to both Henry and the Parlement of Paris to voice their protests against this move. In order to allay the fears of the municipal council – and in a move consistent with his attempts to be seen as the legitimate ruler of France by the native population, rather than as a foreign conqueror – Henry sent letters to Abbeville declaring that they were not to be made part of his English crown and that he had reunited the county of Ponthieu with the throne of France.[63]

We find evidence of some factional conflicts and disturbances in towns which had accepted the treaty of Troyes. When the *échevins* of Amiens learned that members of the English delegation returning from Troyes in April 1420 intended to pass through Amiens, they paid the knight guiding the delegation 40 *écus* to lead them away from the town.[64] In spite of taking such precautions, the English embassy entered Amiens, where their presence posed a threat to the town's stability, as elements of the wider population held Armagnac–Dauphinist sympathies. Although no attacks were launched on the English during their brief stay in Amiens, shortly after their departure – and possibly in response to their presence in the town – Dauphinist elements in the population caused disturbances. The town council identified one Guillaume Ledoulx, a Franciscan, and Guillaume Pertrisel, a tavern keeper, as the ringleaders and took measures to put a swift end to the 'plusieurs delis et maléfices'.[65] The municipal council sent messengers to Paris on 17 May

---

[61] For the text of the treaty of surrender, see Carolus-Barré, 'Compiègne et la guerre', pp. 387–92.

[62] For Ponthieu see: S. B. Challenger, *L'Administration anglaise du Ponthieu après le traité de Brétigny, 1361–1369* (Abbeville, 1975).

[63] A. Ledieu, *Ville d'Abbeville. Inventaire sommaire des archives communales antérieures à 1790* (Abbeville, 1902), p. 9.

[64] Following the knight's failure to keep the English way from Amiens, the municipal council wrote to him demanding the return of its money: A[rchives] M[unicipales] A[miens], BB 2, fol. 149v.

[65] AMA, BB 2, fol. 150r; E. Maugis, *Recherches sur les transformations du régime politique et social de la ville d'Amiens des origines de la commune à la fin du XVIe siècle* (Paris, 1906), pp. 21–2.

to assure the Parlement that Amiens had not gone into rebellion and were taking efforts to quell the disturbances.[66] As with the elites ruling Norman towns, who acted to report and contain any acts of sedition against their Lancastrian masters, municipal councils in the north-east of the kingdom took similar measures in order to maintain favourable relations with Henry. Although we find some examples of the presence of clergy in disturbances against Lancastrian rule in French towns, a study of towns in the north-east of the kingdom extends Christopher Allmand's finding for Norman clergy that 'there is precious little evidence of a considered and hostile attitude ... to the reality of English rule'.[67] In spite of the declaration made by Gerard of Montagu, bishop of Paris, to the population of the capital, that the English were 'ennemis de ce royaume', this sentiment was not shared by the canons of the cathedral chapter of Notre-Dame of Paris.[68] Indeed, they played an important role in Henry's joint entry into Paris with Charles VI on Advent Sunday (1 December) 1420, along with many other members of the city's clergy.[69] This entry provided the population of Paris with an opportunity to consolidate its good relations with the expected future king of France, while Henry used the event as a means of promoting the political settlement created by the treaty of Troyes.[70]

The years 1420–2 saw the Lancastrian monarch lead a number of progresses across northern France as part of his attempts to establish good relations with those towns which had accepted the treaty of Troyes. When Henry and Catherine visited Amiens in January 1421, they were ceremonially received by the townspeople who offered the royal couple the expensive gifts of silverware customarily presented at the inaugural entry of a new ruler.[71] The municipal deliberations state that this was done for the good of the town and that such gifts were designed to win the affection of the recipient, who it was hoped would act in the future interests of the town. The municipal council went on to provide further gifts to members of the households of both Henry and Catherine in the similar expectations of future assistance.[72] This propaganda

---

66   AMA, BB 2, fols. 150r, 153r.
67   C. Allmand, 'The English and the Church in Lancastrian Normandy', in *England and Normandy*, ed. Bates and Curry, pp. 287–97 (p. 289).
68   E. Déprez, 'Un essai d'union nationale à la veille du traité de Troyes (1419)', *Bibliothèque de l'Ecole des Chartes* 99 (1938), 343–53 (p. 352).
69   G. Grassoreille, 'Histoire politique du chapitre de Notre-Dame de Paris pendant la domination anglaise 1420–1437', *Mémoires de la société de l'histoire de Paris et de l'Ile-de-France* 9 (1882), 109–92 (pp. 115–16).
70   *Journal de Fauquembergue*, ed. Tuetey, III, 388–9; *Choix de pièces inédites relatives au règne de Charles VI*, ed. L. Douët d'Arcq, 2 vols. (Paris, 1863–4), II, 408; *Parisian Journal*, ed. Shirley, pp. 153–4; *Chronique de Jean Le Févre*, ed. Morand, I, 21; *Chronique de Monstrelet*, ed. Douet-d'Arcq, IV, 15–17.
71   *Chronique de Jean Le Févre*, ed. Morand, I, 29.
72   *Chronique de Monstrelet*, ed. Douet-d'Arcq, IV, 24.

drive by the Lancastrian monarchy appears to have hit its mark, and it is interesting to note that when Charles VI and Henry V made a joint entry into Senlis in 1422, it was Henry rather than Charles who was given the most expensive gifts from the townspeople, with financial accounts of the town stating that it was done in consideration of the fact that Henry was regent and heir to the throne of France.[73]

Urban Military Responsibilities

Towns were military centres and played an important role in Henry's strategy in France. While the major operations of Henry V's armies in France were confined to the north of the kingdom, it is worth remembering that English rule continued to be maintained in Gascony. Bordeaux's *Jurade* was crucial to Lancastrian rule here.[74] Bordeaux had obtained a remarkable degree of self-autonomy during the early years of the fifteenth century, in return for which it exercised a crucial military role in the region.[75] The city's *Jurade* raised its own armies and developed a military policy which was influenced by economic concerns and access to resources. Indeed, the military actions directed by the city against Valois forces in 1420–2 were in part motivated by its attempts to restore control over the important wine-producing region of the *Haute-Pays*, from which much of its wealth derived.[76]

If Bordeaux came to play a vital role in the offensive capabilities of the Lancastrian monarchy in Gascony, Henry's conception of the military role performed by the towns of Normandy was essentially defensive. The state of urban fortifications was of great concern to the Lancastrian crown. Therefore, Henry continued the Valois monarchy's policy of permitting municipal councils to keep the revenue raised on the taxes of certain goods brought into the town for sale, such as wine, with the condition that the money was put into the defence of the town.[77] This was a concession that he had previously

---

[73] Paris, Bibliothèque nationale de France, Collection de Picardie 5, fol. 116r.

[74] For Bordeaux's role against the French offensive of 1405–7 in Gascony see *Registres de la Jurade. Déliberations de 1406 à 1409*, ed. J. N. Dast Le Vacher de Boisville (Bordeaux, 1873), p. 145; G. Pépin, 'The French Offensives of 1404–1407 against Anglo-Gascon Aquitaine', *Journal of Medieval Military History. Volume IX: Soldiers, Weapons and Armies in the Fifteenth Century*, ed. A. Curry and A. R. Bell (Woodbridge, 2011), pp. 1–40 (pp. 13–15); Y. Renouard, *Bordeaux sous les rois d'Angleterre* (Bordeaux, 1965), pp. 415–16.

[75] This mass of franchises and liberties obtained by the city are recorded in its *Livre des Bouillons*: *Archives de Bordeaux, Vol. 1: Livre des Bouillons*, ed. J. N. Dast Le Vacher de Boisville (Bordeaux, 1867). See also Renouard, *Bordeaux*, pp. 425–6, 456.

[76] *Registres de la Jurade. Déliberations de 1414 à 1416 et de 1420 à 1422*, ed. J. N. Dast Le Vacher de Boisville (Bordeaux, 1883), pp. 396, 398, 401, 422, 434, 447, 449, 505, 507, 512, 519–25, 550, 553, 577, 597, 609. See also: R. Boutruche, *La crise d'une société: seigneurs et paysans du Bordelais pendant la guerre de cent ans* (Strasbourg, 1963), pp. 222–3.

[77] In Normandy Henry made grants to fortify Falaise, Vire, Carentan, Bayeux, Dieppe,

granted to Bordeaux in June 1416, in preparation for his second invasion of France.[78] Towns whose fortifications had been especially badly damaged could receive additional grants of revenue beyond the right to collect such taxes on goods. On 20 May 1418 the municipal council of Falaise received the sum of 800 crowns from Henry in order to rebuild the town's fortifications which had been badly damaged during its siege.[79] Although the Lancastrian crown worked to prevent the French population from being molested by English soldiers, lingering suspicions of the fidelity of some urban populations in Normandy led it to restrict the control exerted by municipal councils in providing for their own defence. Under normal conditions, French town councils were responsible for organizing the *guet*, which was the rota of townsmen obliged to stand guard on the walls of the town. However, concerns over the loyalty of urban populations led Henry to retain control over the *guet* in some Norman towns, and in May 1418 he exempted a number of the inhabitants of Caen from serving guard on the town walls.[80]

Henry also imposed garrisons of English soldiers on Norman towns following his conquest of the duchy. Although townspeople resisted the imposition of garrisons by any ruler, they especially resented the imposition of a garrison composed of foreign soldiers.[81] While some of the men who served in these garrisons came to be integrated into local society during the course of the Dual Monarchy, Henry V preferred to keep garrisons separate from the civilian population. He sent letters to the captains of Caen, Falaise and Cherbourg on 23 August 1419 instructing them not to allow soldiers of the garrison to take quarters in the town.[82] The size of garrisons was a concern for local populations, as the presence of large numbers of frequently idle soldiers caused severe disruption to urban life. The Lancastrian administration acted to curb the size of urban garrisons, and in October 1419 it ruled that the only

Rouen, Gisors, Mantes, Vernon, Montevilliers, Chaumont, Caen, Argentan, Neufchâtel, Coutances, Honfleur, Harfleur, Evreux and Louviers: TNA, C 64/9, 20; C 64/10, 11; C 64/11, 14d; C 64/12, 9d, 44d, 50; C 64/13, 29; C 64/14, 17d; C 64/15, 13, 23d, 24, 28d, 29; C 64/16, 6d, 7, 36d; C 64/17, 21d, 26d, 27d (*DKR*, XLI, 682, 711, 754, 760–1, 788, 806; *DKR*, XLII, 317, 328, 334, 356, 359, 363, 391, 398, 402, 405–7, 423, 427, 438, 447, 449).

[78] TNA, C 61/117, 18; T. Carte, J.-P. de Bougainville and J. Barois, *Catalogue des rolles Gascons, Normans et François, conservés dans les archives de la Tour de Londres* (London, 1743), p. 200. For the wider military preparations in Gascony during this period see: M. G. A. Vale, *English Gascony, 1399–1453* (Oxford, 1970), pp. 68–75.

[79] TNA, C 64/9, 32 (*DKR*, XLI, 686). This was in addition to the grant that he had made to the municipal council two months earlier to allow them to collect the tolls on wine, beer and salt brought into the town for sale: TNA, C 64/9, 37 (*DKR*, XLI, 682).

[80] TNA, C 64/9, 23 (*DKR*, XLI, 690).

[81] B. G. H. Ditcham, '"Mutton Guzzlers and Wine Bags": Foreign Soldiers and Native Reactions in Fifteenth-Century France', in *Power, Culture, and Religion in France c.1350–c.1550*, ed. C. Allmand (Woodbridge, 1989), pp. 1–13 (pp. 10–11); Massey, 'Lancastrian Rouen', p. 276.

[82] TNA, C 64/11, 25d (*DKR*, XLII, 325).

soldiers permitted within town walls were those strictly necessary for the defence of the town.[83] In contrast to his actions in Normandy, Henry did not impose English garrisons on those towns in Picardy, Champagne and the Ile-de-France which had acknowledged his rule following the treaty of Troyes. Towns such as Amiens and Senlis were not taken by conquest and Henry respected their privileges not to have troops garrisoned within their walls.[84] Although garrisons were still imposed on Norman towns after the treaty of Troyes, there were few English soldiers present in Paris during this period and Clément de Fauquembergue, *greffier* of the Parlement of Paris, notes that only a small group of soldiers accompanied Henry when he visited the capital in 1421.[85] Henry wanted to avoid being seen as a conqueror imposing an army of occupation on a city which had come to him by treaty rather than conquest, and these soldiers are likely to have been his personal bodyguard.

Henry V was fighting on multiple fronts in France, and while Normandy was largely pacified by 1420, he had to maintain his position in the north-east of the kingdom. This region was overrun with soldiers loyal to the Dauphin, who were the cause of serious disturbances in Artois and Picardy during the summer of 1421.[86] English forces were stretched and Henry came to rely on his ally Philip the Good, who agreed to undertake the campaign against the Dauphinists in the region.[87] Towns in the north-east were expected to contribute to the duke's campaign and Amiens' town council received a letter in July that year requesting that they send troops and equipment to Philip the Good, who was then laying siege to St Riquier.[88] Although the financial situation of Amiens was perilous in 1421, it was essential that order be restored to the region as quickly as possible if the town were to prosper in the future. The town council adopted a range of money-raising schemes to send crossbowmen to the sieges of the nearby Dauphinist strongholds of Gamanches, Araines, Le Quesnoy and St Riquier.[89] This permitted the municipal council to demonstrate its loyalty to the new regime and reduce the threat that the Dauphinist forces posed to the security of the town.[90] By the time of Henry's

---

[83] TNA, C 64/11, 16d (*DKR*, XLII, 328).

[84] J. Favier, *Paris au XVe siècle, 1380–1500* (Paris, 1974), p. 186; J. Favier, 'Occupation ou connivence? Les Anglais à Paris (1420–1436)', in *Guerre, pouvoir et noblesse au Moyen Age*, ed. J. Paviot and J. Verger (Paris, 2000), pp. 239–60 (pp. 250–1).

[85] *Journal de Fauquembergue*, ed Tuetey, II, 20.

[86] Allmand, *Henry V*, p. 162.

[87] R. Vaughan, *Philip the Good: The Apogee of Burgundy* (Harlow, 1970), p. 12.

[88] AMA, CC 18, fol. 19r.

[89] The town council was still paying for the costs of the wages of the crossbowmen sent to St Riquier on this occasion in 1424: AMA, CC 19, fol. 40v. This is in contrast to Normandy where the costs of urban crossbowmen were paid for by the Lancastrian crown: Curry, 'War and Occupation', p. 166.

[90] By the end of 1421, however, Amiens was financially exhausted and the town council asked Richard, earl of Warwick, to be excused from sending troops to his siege of St

death in August 1422, the Lancastrian administration expected French towns to provide troops and equipment for the prosecution of their wars and he developed a range of economic measures to encourage their prosperity.

The Urban Economy of Lancastrian France

Between 1417 and 1422 almost the entire urban economic network of northern France fell under Lancastrian rule. Before Henry could fully draw on the economic resources of these towns, he had to alleviate the damage caused by years of war. Although Rouen was the commercial centre of the duchy of Normandy and one of the largest towns in France, its prosperity was severely damaged by the siege of 1418–19. Henry encouraged merchants to travel to the town and sell food to the starving population, and on 15 January 1419, four days before its planned surrender, he instructed his officials across Normandy to issue proclamations stating that all dealers of provisions were to go to Rouen.[91] In the aftermath of the surrender, Henry also issued merchants from the town with letters of protection permitting them to buy provisions in the surrounding area and bring them back to sell.[92] During his conquest of Normandy, merchants from neighbouring territories applied to Henry for letters of safe conduct to trade in the duchy. In theory, these letters guaranteed that the bearers would not be molested by soldiers and royal officials as they transported their goods across the duchy. The principal destination for merchants trading in Normandy was Rouen, which the Lancastrian administration was then working to return to its prominent position in the economy of northern France.[93]

In the months following the capitulation of the town, Henry adopted a pro-active economic policy designed to stimulate trade. He encouraged merchants from across the kingdom to trade with the town; letters of safe conduct were issued to merchants from the French towns of Avranches, Carpentras, Paris, as well as the papal enclave of Avignon; the regions of Brittany, Flanders and Navarre; and the Italian city of Lucca. The majority were issued to Breton merchants, who were benefiting from a period of extended truce between Henry V and John V, duke of Brittany.[94] In Table 1 we can see a sharp rise in the number of safe conducts granted from 1419, following the reopening of Rouen's markets and the development of a period of relative peace in the

Valéry due to the costs 'soustenus pour le fait des guerres' in the previous year: AMA, CC 18, fol. 79v.
[91] TNA, C 64/10, 38d (*DKR*, XLI, 748).
[92] TNA, C 64/10, 40, 38 (*DKR*, XLI, 723–5).
[93] For the efforts taken by the Lancastrian crown towards Rouen during this period see: TNA, C 64/11, 10–77 (*DKR*, XLII, 315–29).
[94] See G. A. Knowlson, *Jean V, duc de Bretagne et l'Angleterre (1399–1442)* (Cambridge, 1964), pp. 103–25.

duchy. Applications for letters of safe conduct went into sharp decline from May 1420, when the treaty of Troyes made the need for such letters redundant. Safe conducts issued after this date went to Breton merchants who wanted to ship goods by sea between England and Normandy: these were designed to protect them from attack by English ships. Henry deliberately concentrated these measures on Normandy in order to restore the commercial activity of the duchy's towns. Breton merchants who attempted to use safe conducts to trade in Bordeaux in October 1421 were arrested and imprisoned.[95] This underlined a policy of separating Gascony from France, for the Gascon towns of Bordeaux, Bayonne and Dax were not considered to be a part of the French kingdom but part of the patrimony of the English crown.

Table 1 Number of letters of safe conduct granted
by Henry V to Breton merchants

Regnal Year (21 March to 20 March)	Number
1418–19	41
1419–20	134
1420–1	23
1421–2	4
1422 (up to 31 August)	4

There was some initial disruption to the economic network following the separation of France into those areas which recognized the treaty of Troyes and those territories that remained loyal to the Dauphin. Chartres lay close to the Dauphin's heartland of support, and its trading links with the Loire towns, especially Orléans, collapsed after 1420. However, its merchants soon redirected their trading networks to the north, and focused on the markets at Paris and Rouen instead.[96] Henry V prohibited trade with Dauphinist France and any of his subjects who received letters of safe conduct from rival political authorities were to be subject to punishment.[97] Henry had treated Normandy as distinct from France prior to the sealing of the treaty of Troyes, which caused complications for the urban economy, as French merchants who wanted to trade in the duchy were subject to the same tolls as foreign merchants.[98] This action was detrimental to the activities of those Parisian

---

95 *Registres de la Jurade*, ed. Dast Le Vacher de Boisville, pp. 569, 590, 591.
96 Chédeville, *Histoire de Chartres*, pp. 134–6. For the extent of the trading network of the town's merchants see: C. Billot, *Chartres à la fin du Moyen Age* (Paris, 1987), pp. 237–43.
97 One William Allart received a pardon on 8 May 1422 for having accepted a letter of safe conduct from the Dauphin: TNA, C 64/17, 20 (*DKR*, XLII, 442).
98 In early May 1420, for example, a number of Italian merchants were given a safe conduct by Henry to permit them to trade in both Normandy and France TNA, C 64/13, 20 (*DKR*, XLII, 365).

merchants who began to trade with Normandy following the peace treaty made between Henry and Paris in November 1419. In order to encourage these merchants to trade in Normandy, on 1 February 1420 Henry V promised to abolish the tolls they were liable to pay.[99] This led to an immediate sharp increase in the extent of trade between Rouen and Paris, as shown in Table 2 below.

Table 2 Number of safe conducts issued to Parisian merchants trading with Rouen[100]

Month/Year	Amount
November 1419	1
December 1419	11
January 1420	1
February 1420	29
March 1420	14
April 1420	13
May 1420	6

Although there was often fierce rivalry between the merchants of Paris and Rouen during the later Middle Ages, they were mutually reliant on each other for trade.[101] As the largest city in western Europe and with an estimated population of 100,000, Paris depended on the import of food from towns across northern France, and the capital was suffering a time of great scarcity in early 1419. Conflict across the north of the kingdom had cut off trade with coastal areas, and fresh salt-water fish was scarce in Paris.[102] When trade reopened with Normandy, Parisian merchants travelled to the markets at Rouen and Dieppe to buy fresh salt-water fish and transport them to the capital. In addition to fish, both cheese and firewood were also expensive in the capital, and from 1419 Henry granted licences to Parisian merchants to transport both commodities from Rouen and to Paris.[103] These licences permitted those Parisian merchants who were prepared to travel to a zone of recent conflict with the opportunity to make large profits on the goods which they brought to sell in the capital. While the commercial importance of Paris had declined in the early fifteenth century as a result of civil war, foreign invasion and the

---

[99] TNA, C 64/12, 30 (*DKR*, XLII, 341).
[100] This information is taken from TNA, C 64/11–12.
[101] For the rivalry between Paris and Rouen, see R. Cazelles, 'La rivalité commerciale de Paris et de Rouen au Moyen Age: compagnie française et compagnie normande', *Bulletin de la Société de l'histoire de Paris et de Ile-de-France* 96 (1969), 99–112.
[102] *Parisian Journal*, ed. Shirley, pp. 138, 155.
[103] TNA, C 64/12 (*DKR*, XLII, 334, 341, 366).

relocation of prominent Italian merchants and bankers to Bruges, the city's position on the road and river networks of northern France and its role as a centre of distribution for luxury goods ensured that it remained economically important, and both Henry and the Parisian municipal authorities took actions to encourage the restoration of its fortunes from 1419 to 1420.[104]

Foreign merchants also traded in Normandy, and traders from Milan and Lombardy were amongst those who submitted to Henry at the capitulation of Louviers.[105] Henry worked to maintain Normandy's trading links with the Italian cities, and by 1420 merchants from Lucca were once again trading in the duchy.[106] Amongst the provisions of the treaty of Canterbury (1416), which created an alliance between Henry and the Emperor Sigismund, was the right for the subjects of both monarchs to have access to the lands of the other.[107] One of the economic consequences of this treaty was the appearance of a number of merchants from the Holy Roman Empire in post-conquest Normandy. Although there is evidence of some limited urban trading between northern French towns and England prior to his invasion of 1415, the extent of this trading increased after 1420.[108] French merchants were quick to capitalize on opportunities for trade with England, especially in supplying provisions to Normandy.[109] Following the peace made at Troyes, the markets of Calais were reopened to French merchants. While Henry had taken measures to reinforce Calais' status as an English town in the early years of his reign, his policy was more ambiguous after the treaty of Troyes 1420, when merchants from northern French towns began redeveloping a presence in the town.[110] For these merchants, Calais was a French town, and while merchants from Amiens had been trading in the staple at Calais from 1420, it was not until 1426 that they were told by royal officials that they had to pay border tolls as Calais was 'dehors des mettes de cest royaume [of France]'.[111]

Henry acted swiftly and decisively to stop attacks on French merchants by his English subjects.[112] In May and June 1420 he ordered that goods taken from French merchants trading with Bruges by ship, which had been seized at sea and brought to Guernsey, were to be returned immediately with full

---

[104] See J. Favier, 'Une ville entre deux vocations: la place d'affaires de Paris au XVe siècle', *Annales ESC* 28 (1973), 1245–79 (pp. 1245–50).

[105] TNA, C 64/9, 15 (*DKR*, XLI, 696).

[106] TNA, C 64/12, 15 (*DKR*, XLII, 367).

[107] Allmand, *Henry V*, pp. 108–9.

[108] *DKR*, XLIV, 554, 558.

[109] On 19 May 1421 one William Bargier, a merchant from Dieppe, was granted a licence by Henry to transport grain from Yarmouth to Dieppe: *DKR*, XLIV, 628.

[110] *CPR, 1416–22*, p. 231; *DKR*, XLIV, 543

[111] AMA, BB 3, fol. 67r. See also, N. Murphy, 'Between France, England and Burgundy: Amiens under the Lancastrian Dual Monarchy, 1422–35', *French History* 26 (2012), 143–63 (pp. 151–2).

[112] TNA, C 64/11 (*DKR*, XLII, 312).

compensation for any losses.[113] As well as seeking to protect trade at sea, Henry also moved to restore peace quickly to the roads. With the breakdown in central authority in 1417–19, roads across the north of the kingdom had become dangerous and commerce all but ceased. In response to these perils, Henry took measures to halt attacks on French merchants engaged in regional trade and restore order to the roads and rivers.[114] The towns of the north-east were dependent on the Seine, Yonne and Oise rivers for trade, and measures were taken to ensure the safety of fluvial traffic by putting a halt to attacks on merchants by Dauphinist forces. The coherent economic policy introduced by the Lancastrian administration was successful and had restored a strong degree of peace and stability to northern France by the time of Henry's death in August 1422.

Conclusion

Henry V's successes in France were defined by his possession of towns: he began his conquest of France by laying siege to the town of Harfleur, and he died from a bout of dysentery contracted while he was camped outside the walls of Meaux. During the period of Henry's rule in France the Lancastrian administration developed a number of measures designed to alleviate the effects of warfare on the north and to return prosperity to the region. The records of the Lancastrian government show that municipal concerns were at the forefront of its attention in France from 1417 to 1422. Although Henry had taken vast swathes of countryside during his conquest of Normandy, he was obliged to grant most of this land to his supporters and the Lancastrian crown was unable to raise significant revenues from these rural lands.[115] As one of the principal sources of revenue for the crown to draw on, it was essential for Henry to redevelop the urban economy of northern France. Once the sealing of the treaty of Troyes in May 1420 had technically established peace between England and France, there was no legal obligation for the English parliament to provide finance for the king's conflicts in his French lands.[116] This was a French civil war and the English population expected that it would be funded by French taxes. While the crown still had access to important taxes such as the wool subsidy, the costs of fighting a foreign war were high and Henry's conquests in France led to the widespread imposition of taxes in December 1420 and January 1421 in order to restore the debased

---

[113] TNA, C 64/9, 23d, 34d (*DKR*, XLI, 709, 713).

[114] TNA, C 64/12, 27, 33d (*DKR*, XLII, 357, 363); C 64/15, 10d (*DKR*, XLII, 409).

[115] Allmand, *Lancastrian Normandy*, p. 71; A. R. Bridbury, 'The Hundred Years' War: Costs and Profits', in *Trade, Government and Economy in Pre-Industrial England: Essays Presented to F. J. Fisher*, ed. D. C. Coleman and A. H. John (London, 1976), pp. 80–95 (p. 91).

[116] Allmand, *Henry V*, p. 376.

currency, with further direct taxes being levied on the townspeople to meet the costs of war.[117]

The resurgence of trade was a key factor in this economic drive, and under Henry's rule merchants from French towns engaged in both regional and national trade. Henry was also careful to present himself as a French ruler to the townspeople of France, and demonstrate that they would not be ruled as a conquered population. The Lancastrian administration protected the interests of French merchants against exactions from the English. Henry maintained native urban administrations in their position and worked to prevent encroachments on their authority from English royal officials. The legacy Henry left was crucial to the establishment of the Dual Monarchy, and his son ruled over a kingdom which extended across much of the northern half of the kingdom. The small town of Nevers, for example, which lay only 60 kilometres from Bourges, the heartland of Charles VII's kingdom, had its rights and liberties confirmed by Henry VI.[118] An examination of Henry V's policy towards the towns of France shows the remarkable degree of success that the Lancastrian crown could achieve when it took a determined effort to appeal to its French subjects. While Henry died before he could be crowned king of France, the crucial measures taken by his administration to restore prosperity to the towns of northern France laid the groundwork for the period of peace and prosperity achieved by the duke of Bedford by the mid-1420s, which marked the highpoint of Lancastrian rule in France.

---

[117] *Recueil des monuments inédits de l'histoire du tiers état*, ed. A. Thierry, 2 vols. (Paris, 1853), I, 88.
[118] F. Boutillier, *Ville de Nevers. Inventaire sommaire des archives communales antérieures à 1790* (Nevers, 1876), p. 132.

11

Writing History in the Eighteenth Century: Thomas Goodwin's
The History of the Reign of Henry the Fifth (1704)

Christopher Allmand

Few will know of Thomas Goodwin, author of *The History of the Reign of Henry the Fifth, King of England, &c.*, whose 'Nine Books' or chapters, each broadly covering a regnal year, was published in London in 1704. He was the son of another Thomas Goodwin, a leading divine of his day, regarded as one of the founding fathers of Congregationalism, who was president of Magdalen College, Oxford (before resigning at the restoration of the monarchy in 1660) and, as chaplain to Oliver Cromwell, had been in attendance at the Protector's deathbed. Thomas (the younger), born about 1650, received part of his education in the Low Countries, and later became a non-conformist minister whose main contribution was the foundation of a school at Pinner, in Middlesex, where future ministers received their training. He was also responsible for editing his father's writings, which appeared in a number of volumes. In 1695 he published *A Discourse on the True Nature of the Gospel*, and nine years later, ironically perhaps since it was the work of a man whose father had been associated with the abolition of monarchy, came the book on Henry V.[1]

Short as it was, an earlier article on the younger Goodwin published in the original *Dictionary of National Biography* in 1890 had made reference to the book.[2] Regrettably, it does not feature in either the longer entry or its appended list of 'sources' published in the more recent *Oxford Dictionary of National Biography*, a curious omission which denies Goodwin his right to be considered an early contributor to the historical reputation of the Lancastrian king.

The text was dedicated to John, Lord Cutts (1661–1707), a leading soldier of his day who fought on King Billy's side at the Boyne, and later enhanced his

---

[1] For the Goodwins, father and son, see two articles by T. M. Lawrence: 'Goodwin, Thomas (1600–1680)', and 'Goodwin, Thomas (c.1650–1708?)', *ODNB*.

[2] *Dictionary of National Biography*, ed. L. Stephen and S. Lee, 63 vols. (London, 1885–1901), XXII, 150.

reputation while serving in a senior position under the duke of Marlborough at Blenheim. His reward had been the gift of an Irish barony and an honorary degree from the University of Cambridge.[3] In his enthusiasm, and spurred on by the idea that 'a faithful Recital of Noble Actions erects a Monument to the Hero more lasting than Statues' and 'delivers down the great Example to the Wonder and Imitation of succeeding Ages', Goodwin came perilously close to making comparisons between Cutts and Henry V (and even the Black Prince). Cutts's military career, the author wrote, 'happily reviv'd the antient Martial Genius and Vigor of the *English* People; especially since Your Sword is drawn against the same Enemy [the French] ... whom our Ancestors fought and conquer'd ... Our *Black Prince*'s and Fifth *Henry*'s Wars are now no longer acted only in our Theaters.' Goodwin expressed admiration at Cutts's courageous actions which, he claimed, had contributed 'not only the Liberties of our own Country, but those of all *Europe* ...'[4]

In the heavily didactic Preface which follows, Goodwin set out the benefits to be gained from the reading of history. On the one hand 'Mankind being of the same Make and Complexion in all Ages, we may read our own Follies in the Miscarriages of others who have liv'd before us', while 'the Reigns of such Kings [as Henry V] are truly a Blessing, not only to their happy Subjects, but to Mankind in all times'. More significantly, Goodwin reminded his readers that history teaches rulers how 'to promote the publick Good' and, not insignificantly, how to defend their subjects' 'Liberties and Estates against the Invasions of ambitious Neighbours'. There is here a strong sense that contemporary issues and ideas influenced the way that Goodwin presented his royal subject to his readers.[5]

We may wonder whether this kind of history, written some three centuries ago, is likely to be of value or interest to a more objective, twenty-first-century approach to the subject. Few of those (including myself) who have studied Henry V in past years have paid much attention to Goodwin's work, although Benjamin Williams, first editor of the *Gesta Henrici Quinti*, regretted the lack of appreciation accorded by historians to his 'laborious research',[6] while in 1919 J. H. Wylie commented, in a manner which recalls the pot calling the kettle black, on Goodwin's 'minutely detailed account of the reign', giving him credit, in particular, for using unprinted sources.[7] In the same year R. B. Mowat described the work as 'valuable because of its copious references to

---

[3]   H. M. Chichester, 'Cutts, John, Baron Cutts of Gowran (1660/61–1707)', rev. John B. Hattendorf, *ODNB*.

[4]   T. Goodwin, *The History of the Reign of Henry the Fifth, King of England, &c* (London, 1704), pp. iii–iv.

[5]   Ibid., pp. v–vi.

[6]   *Henrici Quinti, Angliae Regis, Gesta*, ed. B. Williams (London, 1850), p. xiii.

[7]   Wylie and Waugh, *Henry the Fifth*, II, 87.

chronicles and State papers',[8] while, more recently, Keith Dockray referred to the work as the first major secondary study of the reign, although he considered Goodwin to have used English and French chronicle sources in a rather uncritical fashion.[9] Most recently of all, Anne Curry has drawn attention to Goodwin's work in her book on the sources and interpretations for the study of the battle of Agincourt.[10]

The traditional view of the king, largely the creation of fifteenth-century writers, was to be taken up by their counterparts in the sixteenth century, before forming the basis of Shakespeare's well-known dramatic representation of events. Such a view placed much emphasis upon the king, a man of strong, patriotic character and almost heroic personality, whose actions were directed towards overcoming the obstinacy of the French who refused to do justice by granting him his rights. Moral pressure having failed, the king was driven to use force. The victory at Agincourt, which saw a small 'band of brothers' bring down a larger but uncoordinated army, sealed Henry's reputation as a soldier and battlefield leader who could inspire his people to greatness.

The way of seeing the history of a country through the life and actions of the king was traditional. From his own time Henry had been regarded as the person who would decide the course which his country was to follow; whether it did so successfully depended largely on him. In the case of Henry, the conflict with France was made to dominate all other issues. The king's leadership in every aspect of this conflict constituted the core of the story as both contemporary and later writers, following in their footsteps, were to tell it. In such accounts the king assumed (or was given) centre stage; for better or worse, he decided policies and determined reactions to moves by foreign leaders, particularly by those in France. It was Henry's consistency of purpose, his forbearance when faced by French intransigence and refusal to satisfy his just demands that determined what happened before he led his army on the first of his expeditions to France in 1415.

At Agincourt, on 25 October of that year, God pronounced in favour of the English. The outcome of the battle became part of legend and, as such, was to earn the plaudits of those who, in 1599, were the first to see Shakespeare's dramatic reconstruction of certain episodes in the history of the reign.[11] Agincourt had been no ordinary encounter, and the victor was no ordinary man. For better or worse, Henry's reputation was founded on military success based on king and army having confidence in each other. Before long, he would be back in France, and a two-year-long process of conquest would lead

---

[8]   R. B. Mowat, *Henry V* (London, 1919), p. 329.
[9]   K. Dockray, *Henry V* (Stroud, 2004), p. 60.
[10]   Curry, *Agincourt: Sources and Interpretations*, pp. 371–4.
[11]   See J. Shapiro, *1599. A Year in the Life of William Shakespeare* (London, 2005), especially pp. 81–3, 98–103.

to the overrunning and occupation of much of northern France. This, in turn, would lead to the political settlement of the treaty of Troyes (1420) which yielded Henry the title of 'heir to the kingdom of France'. He was now only one heart beat from achieving his ambition, the crown of France. However, it was his heart which failed to beat long enough and, consequently, it was his son who would claim the prize. However, none would deny that it was the military achievement of the reign which won Henry the respect in which his people (and others) were to hold him.

As the title made clear, however, Goodwin's *History* was intended as a history of Henry's reign as a whole, a considerable advance on earlier approaches. Yet, unlike a modern history, it would take little or no account of the state or 'mood' of England, the country's political, social and economic situation, as it stood when the new king ascended the throne. With nothing said about the previous reign, and in the absence of a sense of continuity with the past, the reader was denied the opportunity to consider the reign, and Henry's kingship, in terms of their relationship with that past and, perhaps, the future, too. Questions such as where the reign stood in relation to the resolution of both short- and long-term problems were not asked; nor was there any consideration of what Henry made of his inheritance, or what he bequeathed to his successor. The outcome of events implied that, when all was said and done, as a successful soldier-king who had defeated the French enemy, Henry would be judged as having fulfilled the hopes of the most demanding of Englishmen.

It is not surprising, however, that in creating the image of the king Goodwin should have looked to the chroniclers and others whose names are cited in the margins of his book as having provided him with the basic building blocks upon which to develop his story. Yet, in doing so, Goodwin was seeking to do more than simply restate facts and positions long since available to those who might have taken the trouble to read them. Much had occurred during the intervening years, not least the growth in appreciation of the value of a variety of historical sources, which propitious times now made it possible to use.

Consider what sources were available to Goodwin, and what use he made of them. The reader will immediately be struck by the fact that, as noted, the author provided a bibliography, if not an altogether complete one, of his printed sources. The 'CATALOGUE of AUTHORS cited in this History' (a list of 'historians of known repute' whose works reoccur time and again in the marginal notes) included some seventy-five items, in English, Latin and French, Italian and Castilian, drawn from a number of European printing presses.[12] For English events and concerns we find him using the chronicles of Thomas Walsingham, John Hardyng and John Capgrave, all of whom

---

[12] Goodwin, *History*, pp. vii–viii.

had lived through the years described. Polydore Vergil, Ralph Holinshed and John Stow were among the sixteenth-century authors upon whose work he also drew. French and Burgundian chroniclers cited included (among others) the Monk of Saint-Denis, Pierre Fenin, Jean le Fèvre and Enguerrand de Monstrelet, a list which would not disgrace a modern bibliography. It is evident that Goodwin was able to use, to good effect, the chronicles in their sixteenth- and seventeenth-century editions which were the product of the growth of historical studies characteristic of these times in England, France and other continental states.

That development had witnessed the publication of much history of the European Middle Ages. Closely associated with this had been the search for, and the publication of, medieval records by scholars in France, England, Germany and elsewhere. Not surprisingly, the works of these antiquarian scholars featured large in Goodwin's text. The great collections of John Leland (d.1552), John Bale (d.1563), Matthew Parker (d.1575), Henry Spelman (d.1641) and William Dugdale (d.1673) provided material incorporated by Goodwin into his work. His knowledge of the published researches of continental collector-editors, such as those of Melchior Goldast (d.1635), testifies to both the seriousness of his intent and his ability to seek material collected by foreign scholars which might add both breadth and depth to the life and work of his subject. Consideration of Goodwin's bibliography underlines the fact that he was no insular scholar, but one very much aware of continental scholarship and what it might contribute towards putting Henry V's achievement within a context broader both historically and geographically.

Printed texts alone did not satisfy Goodwin. There was another important source of information to be tapped, 'the greater Authority of the Records of the Nation, and Manuscripts of the Cotton, and other Librarys', which he described as 'the chief Ornaments of my History'.[13] These could be used to take the story beyond the parameters within which it had, until now, largely been written. Letters, memoranda and diplomatic instructions contemporary with the events with which they were associated could be used to describe the processes of government and policy formation, the exchanges between the king's representatives and those of other rulers and the correspondence between rulers, secular and spiritual.

The work of the early seventeenth century antiquarian, Sir George Buck, whose *History of the Life and Reigne of Richard the Third*, written in 1619 but not published until 1646, had been an attempt to rehabilitate that king's reputation through the critical use of surviving manuscript evidence, set a path which Goodwin would follow.[14] Both made use of the historical record in putting their cases before the reading public, although Goodwin was not

---

[13] Ibid., p. vi.
[14] A further edition would be published in 1706.

required to do so in the same polemical way as Buck had been. In Goodwin's case the marginal notes found on most pages emphasized the use he made of manuscript sources; in many cases he even identified the very folio or membrane from which he was quoting.[15] It was his wish that his statements should be verifiable; references to texts were given so that 'the Reader may see what Edition I made use of'. Now involved, the reader could then consider critically statements made by Goodwin who claimed to write 'in as fair and just a light as I could'. Scholarship was becoming more exact, and the scholar more accountable. Goodwin recognized this, and wished his readers to be aware of it, too.

Granted that he was a friend of Thomas Rymer (d.1713), at the time engaged on the task of transcribing documents for his *Foedera* (published 1704–13), this is hardly surprising. It was probably through Rymer that Goodwin gained access to the manuscripts of state, particularly those of the chancery, held in the Tower of London. Be that as it may, there is no doubt that Goodwin made full use of a whole range of formal royal records, including the patent and close rolls, along with the French, Norman and Gascon rolls. Less formal evidence was also called upon. Goodwin frequently cited documents in the great collection assembled by Sir Robert Cotton (d.1631), in these very years being transferred to the public domain. The order imposed by Cotton on the extensive material collected by him, recognized in the headings found in the catalogue compiled by Thomas Smith and printed as recently as 1696, will have helped Goodwin in his search for evidence.[16] In the end he appears to have cited at least thirteen separate manuscripts from the Cotton collection. The text of what we know as the *Gesta Henrici Quinti*[17] clearly lies behind a passage on page 61, taken from MS Julius E IV, which also included a text of the *Liber Metricus*.[18] Documents on the relations between England and France were to be found assembled in MS Tiberius B VI (cited more frequently than any other Cottonian manuscript), in MS Tiberius B XII (material collected by Bishop Thomas Bekynton), and in MS Caligula D V. All three of these suffered in the fire at Ashburnham House on 23 October 1731, MS Caligula D V being particularly badly damaged, a fact that may endow Goodwin's work with an element of added value for the modern reader.

Although France, and French affairs, formed the hub of Goodwin's narrative from Book II to Book VII, it was a sign of how far things had changed that the victory won at Agincourt was not allowed, in itself, to dominate the flow

15   See, for example, Goodwin, *History*, pp. 13, 106, 160, 260 and elsewhere.
16   *Catalogus librorum manuscriptorum Bibliothecae Cottonianae … scriptore Thoma Smitho* (Oxford, 1696).
17   *Henrici Quinti … Gesta*, ed. Williams, p. 10; *GHQ*, p. 17.
18   'Elmhami Liber Metricus de Henrico Quinto', *Memorials of Henry the Fifth, King of England*, ed. C. A. Cole, Rolls Series 38 (London, 1858), pp. 77–165.

of events. As the eighteenth-century reader will have understood, winning wars involved more than simply fighting. Rather, the outcome was presented as the preliminary which encouraged Henry to develop a planned policy of war and diplomacy against the French, leading to a further invasion which began in the summer of 1417, and the formation of a network of diplomatic understandings with other rulers aimed at weakening the position of France in Europe. Lord Cutts would have appreciated that there were similarities between English policies towards France pursued by Henry V and those favoured by his own political masters.

In planning his book in this way, however, Goodwin was also reflecting the influences of the sources available to him. His narrative structure was largely founded on a sizeable group of chronicles, French, English and Burgundian, rather as such a narrative might be based today. Bringing these together, and supplementing them with information found in a variety of records, both official and private, Goodwin created a narrative which he enhanced by adding information regarding the contribution of named individuals, an approach which placed such persons within a structure describing what was nothing less than a national effort to bring the king's policy to a successful conclusion. The names of active individuals (some scarcely known to early readers of the book but better known today) found in, for instance, the Norman rolls and in documents from the Cotton collection, added a significant dimension to the work.

The 'second Incursion' into France, which began in the summer of 1417 and would ultimately lead to the conquest of Normandy and, later still, to the political settlement enshrined in the treaty of Troyes, was described in Books IV to VII. Once again, the reader will have been impressed by the range of sources used and the themes to which the author drew attention. The nature of the conflict in France, fought by the English against an enemy at war with itself, could only lead to one result, especially when the French showed themselves to be as divided as the English were united behind their king. While the outcome of the military campaign may have been presented as an almost foregone conclusion, the language used to describe the events of these years lacked the sense of moral superiority which Goodwin had not been entirely successful in hiding earlier on in his reconstruction of the battle of Agincourt. Perhaps it was the less dramatic nature of the war, in which Normandy and the surrounding areas were gradually brought under English control (the only outstanding events being the sieges of Caen and Rouen) and the lack of any unforeseen outcome, which made for a more matter-of-fact approach to the narrative. The text, indeed, even drew attention to, and showed some sympathy for, those Frenchmen who strove to thwart English designs upon their country.[19]

---

[19] See, for example, Goodwin, *History*, pp. 179–80.

An important and interesting aspect of the *History* is the attention given by Goodwin to ecclesiastical and religious matters, and the role which these played in England's history during Henry's reign. Perhaps, it may be claimed, this was to be expected in a book describing events written by a clergyman, in particular one who could write that the 'Affairs of the Church belong to History, as well as those of the State.'[20] In the event, the reader is left in no doubt that the reign took place at a time when both the Church and, in particular, the papacy, were being confronted by a widespread demand for reform, not least in England. Thus the challenges to ecclesiastical authority voiced by Sir John Oldcastle and the Lollards, as successors of John Wyclif, were given their due place in the wider context of European opposition to the papacy, led by John Hus and Jerome of Prague, with whose views Goodwin clearly sympathized.[21] Even more important, and probably a reason why Goodwin appeared to favour and admire Henry V so much, was the support which the king gave to the demands that the papacy should limit its claims to appoint to high ecclesiastical offices within the Church in England.[22] The opposition to papal pretensions in this and other fields, already expressed in earlier English legislation, was an essential factor linking the reformers of English society to those on continental Europe. Furthermore, Goodwin was able to give prominence to events at the Council of Constance, and in particular to the part played there by English envoys and ecclesiastics, as is shown by his use of both Walsingham's chronicle and correspondence and other diplomatic papers in Cotton MS Cleopatra F VII.[23] Once again the reader was being asked to appreciate England's active participation in the affairs of Christendom and Europe. Goodwin was treading the difficult path of underlining the 'protestant' achievement of 'dissenters' in both English and European society, while emphasizing that the Catholic Church made England part of the wider spiritual community which embraced the whole of Christendom, in whose affairs England had a role to play.

One of the strengths of Goodwin's work was the way the author managed to maintain momentum by changing the pace of his narrative. Writing in a prose style characteristic of his time, he was able to introduce a variety of source materials into the creation of a readable and interesting text. The achievement of this involved quoting at length from printed records and, sometimes to greater effect, from manuscript sources, many found in the Cotton collection, others 'in archivis regiis'.[24] These gave the reader the benefit of being able to read the *ipsissima verba* of particular individuals, which enliv-

---

20 Ibid., p. 118.
21 Both Hus and Oldcastle, Goodwin thought, suffered 'Martyrdom' (ibid., p. 163).
22 Ibid., pp. 301–2.
23 Ibid., pp. 120–49.
24 See examples in ibid., pp. 11, 15, 33, 109.

ened the text by adding a certain immediacy to the situation discussed, while also bringing the reader closer to characters as they spoke. It would no longer do to rely on the traditional chronicle sources alone. So we see Goodwin encouraging advances in historical studies, in particular in the critical use made of the greatly extended choice of sources now becoming available to the scholar. In their turn these complemented one another to increase the historical value of what each contained. Of course, the emphasis placed in the past on military matters was not forgotten; the current war with France helped to emphasize the importance and immediacy of that fought by Henry, and of its effects upon English society. Most notably, the king was still seen in some sort of heroic vein, as the defender of national interests against the French. Yet what is surely more significant is that the material now available to Goodwin enabled him to paint a picture of the man and his rule which not only went beyond anything so far attempted, particularly in the shades of colouring which he was able to create, but emphasized the complexities of the reign and its events with greater subtlety than any previous attempt had sought or managed to do. Not without good reason was Goodwin's work entitled *The History of the Reign of Henry the Fifth*.

What gives the modern reader confidence in Goodwin is enhanced by two further factors. One was his critical approach to the sources which, as he admitted several times, did not always agree with one another, something which occasionally forced him to advise the reader that he should decide how the evidence was to be interpreted.[25] The other was his willingness to analyse a complex political, military or diplomatic situation; on more than one occasion he broke off his narrative to discuss the way forward for Henry. Goodwin was also capable of appreciating a particular situation from the French side whose divisions, he thought, made it difficult for them to pursue a single policy towards their English enemies. In so doing he also accounted for Henry's difficulty in dealing with the French. Who really spoke for them? It was a dilemma which the king never fully resolved.

Goodwin was clearly attracted to the personality of the man whose career as king he had made it his task to describe. He recognized the parallels between his own time and those of the Lancastrian king. As he reminded Lord Cutts, France was still the enemy whose ambitions to dominate must be curtailed in the name of liberty.[26] In Henry's day another power, the papacy, was striving to reassert its influence, even its control, over the Church and its institutions in many countries. Goodwin clearly enjoyed praising Henry for standing up to papal pretensions in the important matter of clerical appointments and promotions within the Church in England, and for wishing 'to reform those corrupt Practices which in *England*, as well as other Parts of

---

[25] 'the Reader may judg[e] as he pleases'; and 'let the Reader judg[e] ...' (ibid., pp. 32, 168).
[26] See the 'Dedication' (ibid., pp. iii–iv).

Europe, had vitiated the Purity of the Christian Religion'.[27] At the same time, however, he described the foundation of a number of monastic institutions by the king with evident approval.[28] He was sensitive, too, in not openly criticizing the theological beliefs of the Catholic Church, and in particular, those of the king, although he was in clear sympathy with Sir John Oldcastle (whose personal defence of his beliefs he quoted from manuscript sources, as well as from the work of John Bale) when he was brought to account for himself before the ecclesiastical authorities. Although he drew a detailed picture of Oldcastle, 'the Great Lord Cobham', defiant to the last, and showed admiration for John Hus and Jerome of Prague, both burned for heresy at the Council of Constance, Goodwin did not allow this potentially divisive subject to spoil his otherwise favourable portrait of the king. Blame for hunting down Oldcastle was to be levelled against the leaders of the Church, not against the king.

In order to emphasize the 'quality' of Henry's kingship Goodwin used the simple expedient of contrasting the fortunes of his kingdom (England) with those of the other (France) in these years. France, a divided society lacking effective leadership, was at war both with external enemies and with itself. Thanks to his personal qualities, Henry could provide England with what France did not have. His virtues were praised because they enabled him to do what was expected of a king, to govern for the common good, peace and unity of his country and people. So Henry was shown providing firm rule and pursuing his military and religious aims abroad with determination; while at home he supported the rule of law, brought order through the exercise of both mercy[29] and justice, and enabled internal rivalries to be ended through reconciliation between parties caught up in old enmities.[30] The bond linking Henry to his subjects is emphasized by Goodwin's use of the rolls of parliament to place before the reader 'official' evidence that the king not only consulted his subjects over policy, and asked for their financial support as he tried to carry it out, but that he reacted to their petitions by approving legislation in cases when they sought it. This was part of Goodwin's intention to show the king to have been a benevolent ruler concerned with more than his own reputation.[31] The portrait of Henry thus created was of a man who understood the effects that war might have upon his country, and who realized that the demands made upon the nation's finances and manpower could cause him difficulty in securing the support needed to fulfil his military ambitions. Yet this was to be no whitewash. Goodwin criticized some of the king's actions, while his hint that, in the last year or two of the reign, support

---

27 Ibid., p. 230.
28 Ibid., p. 303.
29 Ibid., p. 324.
30 Ibid., pp. 2–4, 38, 47, 96.
31 Ibid., pp. 98, 170–1, 304–5.

for the war with France may have been waning would probably accord with modern assessments of the reign.[32]

It is fairer to judge Goodwin's work not by today's standards and criteria but, rather, by what his predecessors had written about Henry. In this respect, the advance made by the *History* can be judged to have been spectacular. Many factors contributed to this development. The provision of a 'Catalogue' of the works he had consulted enabled Goodwin to do several things. It underlined the need to broaden not only the number but the variety and range of sources upon which the study of an English king's reign should be based, a step which allowed Goodwin to 'flesh out' the king himself, and (for example when discussing a policy memoranda) to get into his mind and thus 'humanize' him in a way that had not been attempted before. But that was not all. As already observed, Goodwin sought to involve his readers. In his view, it was the historian's task to present, not to dispute; he should leave his readers to judge for themselves. However, this made sense only in an intellectual and social climate in which those readers were both sufficiently well informed and willing to rise to such a challenge. It was a conclusion reached, years ago, by David Douglas[33] that, carrying on what the late Elizabethans, such as William Camden, had begun, there had developed in the late Stuart age an important revival in the study of medieval antiquities which had helped to create and develop a new intellectual society based upon three complementary factors: first, the active research and scholarship provided by a body of clergy, both Anglican and non-conformist, men such as Edmund Gibson, who re-edited Camden's *Britannia* in 1695, and (although not named) Thomas Goodwin himself; secondly, the support given to these efforts by members of the aristocracy who collected documents and gave scholars access to their collections (in which development Sir Robert Harley continued to play the role encouraged by Sir Robert Cotton a century or so earlier); and, thirdly, the growth of interest in history, in particular English medieval history, among the aristocracy and country gentry,[34] a development which would manifest itself in the second half of the eighteenth century in the antiquarian interests and (re-) creative genius of Horace Walpole, whose defence of Richard III would make use of historical evidence, as Sir George Buck had done before him, to exonerate Richard III of the crimes attributed to him.[35]

---

[32] Ibid., p. 302.

[33] D. C. Douglas, *English Scholars* (London, 1939), chapter 1, concerns the background to this development.

[34] See the list of subscribers ('fautores') to *Titi Livii Foro-Juliensis, Vita Henrici Quinti, Regis Angliae*, ed. T. Hearne (Oxford, 1716), pp. xxvii–xxxi, and *Thomae de Elmham, Vita & Gesta Henrici Quinti, Anglorum Regis*, ed. T. Hearne (Oxford, 1727), pp. xxxvii–xliv.

[35] *Historic Doubts on the Life and Reign of Richard III* (London and Dublin, 1768).

Several characteristic aspects of Goodwin's approach to the writing of history are emphasized by the seven appendices added to his book. That he hoped to place Henry's reign in its wider European (and, particularly, Anglo-French) setting is underlined by the inclusion of a list of 'Kings and Princes in *Europe* Contemporary with *Henry* V', along with two lists of French royalty and officers of state. His readers would doubtless have welcomed the names of 'the Knights of the Garter elected in his Reign', English 'Ministers of State, and Commanders in the Navy and Army', together with a list of 'Learned Men in England during K. *Henry*'s Reign, with a catalogue of their Writings'.[36] Besides providing information of interest to readers, such 'lists' (which can be regarded as inspired by the antiquarian tradition) constituted clear evidence of the way the author hoped to extend the study of Henry's reign beyond the traditional limits of the conflict with France. Hardly surprisingly for a man who had lived and travelled in continental Europe (Goodwin had been on an extended tour in 1683–4) the history of England was to be seen in a broader context to which the life of the spirit should also be regarded as making its own contribution.

Goodwin was far from being alone among his contemporaries in having an interest in Henry V. Among the manuscripts preserved at the British Library is that of a study of the reign written by Robert Sanderson (d.1741), archivist at the Rolls Chapel, assistant to Thomas Rymer from whom he would inherit the editorship of the *Foedera*. His *History of the Reign of Henry V* is a detailed narrative, originally in nine folio volumes of which only six, covering the period 1416–22, have survived.[37] Given Sanderson's background, it is not surprising that he, too, should have used both printed and manuscript sources as the basis of his work.[38] The year 1706 saw the publication of *A Complete History of England, with their Lives of all the Kings and Queens thereof*, partly edited, partly written by White Kennett, bishop of Ely (d.1728). For Henry V, the author appears to have relied on a small number of acknowledged sources, which included Monstrelet and Holinshed, although on half a dozen or so occasions he also cited Goodwin's recent work as his authority.[39] Perhaps following Goodwin, too, Kennett added a list of some eminent intellectuals and public figures of the reign.[40] The works of the two writers bear certain similarities of presentation, but there is no doubt that Goodwin's is the superior work, in particular when it came to using manuscript materials in building up his text. Within a generation of both Goodwin and others publishing their books on Henry V, the Oxford antiquarian, Thomas Hearne, would contribute to

---

[36] Goodwin, *History*, pp. 345–62.
[37] BL MSS Additional 19979–84.
[38] N. Ramsay, 'Sanderson, Robert (1663?–1741)', *ODNB*.
[39] W. Kennett, *A Complete History of England ...* (London, 1706), pp. 315, 316, 321, 324, 327, 338.
[40] Ibid. pp. 340–1.

the publication of important material still in manuscript form with editions of Titus Livius's *Vita* and Thomas Elmham's *Vita et Gesta*, editions consulted, used and valued to this day.

With these editions, so typical of an age returning to the sources of history and making them available to a wider readership, we can see how the historiography regarding Henry V was making great strides in the early years of the eighteenth century. The intellectual milieu supported such initiatives. In 1707, only three years after Goodwin's book had come off the press, a group of men interested in England's history and antiquities came together to found the Society of Antiquaries of London, to whose fellowship Robert Sanderson was elected very early on, an organization which flourishes to this day. Douglas may have failed to mention Goodwin by name, but his book describes the creation and development of an intellectual movement into which Goodwin's *History* may be placed, its author's aims and methods better understood and its success in promoting interest in one of England's most famous kings accounted for. The work was both the product of pioneering research and significant evidence of a changing attitude to the writing of history occurring in the early eighteenth century.

*

Goodwin's *History* was written by a man who, son of a father with evident literary talent, was better qualified than many of his day to write on the subject of his choice. His upbringing was probably important in forming his view of the world, patriotic but neither narrowly English nor religiously bigoted, ready to see the past in a broader, more European context. Relying on editions of chronicles, histories and collections of documents going back to 1521 (and further, if one includes a 1480 edition of Caxton's *Chronicle of England*) Goodwin made excellent use of the opportunities thus presented to him. Where he read these works, we do not know. It would be interesting to learn whether he owned copies of them (picked up, perhaps, on his travels?) or whether he owed access to them to others. The importance to Goodwin of these printed sources, however, cannot be in doubt. He had friends and contacts among the English scholarly community, a 'net-working' which clearly brought him practical benefits. Thomas Rymer, 'that known Judg[e] in all parts of Learning',[41] was not the only like-minded scholar to whom he admitted indebtedness.

Reading a variety of sources in print must have made Goodwin realize that an account of Henry's reign based simply on the chronicle literature would prove too restricting. By using manuscript sources he could extend and give greater life to his narrative. These sources would add balance to the story

---

[41] Goodwin, *History*, p. vi. For more on Rymer, see Douglas, *English Scholars*, chapter 11; and A. Sherbo, 'Rymer, Thomas (1642/3–1713)', *ODNB*.

which could be developed on a canvas broader than the traditional one which had concentrated on military affairs. This was not simply adding detail for its own sake. The effects of the scientific revival of the late seventeenth century had influenced other branches of knowledge. Not least was the encouragement given to the critical use and consideration of evidence which, when drawn from manuscripts, could offer information that would give much-needed oxygen to a new narrative of the reign. In effect, Goodwin was laying open to scrutiny aspects of Henry's rule, administration and reputation and, not least, the part played by men hitherto unknown or unsuspected in aspects of that rule which had, so far, remained beyond the spotlight.

Goodwin's *History* marked a milestone in the study of the reign of Henry V. We have seen something of the changes of both attitude and practice which it encouraged. The case for the use of manuscript sources had been made ... and understood. The publication, in 1827, of Sir Harris Nicolas's *History of the Battle of Agincourt* did more than draw attention yet again to the English victory at the battle (although its publication may have been nicely timed, since the defeat of Napoleonic France was still fresh in the public memory). Its main contribution lay in the documentation, including the so-called 'Agincourt roll', which it contained. Nicolas (d.1848) was more of an antiquarian than he was a historian, and this would not be his only foray which constituted, in effect, an invitation to those writing the history of England to use its many and varied sources to produce a new kind of history of which Goodwin's was an early and an important example.

Did Goodwin, in the course of writing, create any pointers towards today's understanding of the reign of Henry V? Are there insights in his work which link him to an appreciation of the king's achievements, and of the world in which he lived, to which we today may usefully draw attention? Although the 'recovery' of France through the use of arms remained the dominant theme of Goodwin's story, the context in which the military process was considered was greatly extended. A study of the reign must imply consideration of aspects of kingship other than the ability to lead in, and win, battles. Waging war successfully in the fifteenth century increasingly involved the search for allies, a process which gave due place to foreign relations and diplomacy. This, in turn, led to greater emphasis being placed upon the wider European milieu in which Henry worked, a broader canvas than had ever been used before. The text of the *Gesta Henrici Quinti* had been written to give those attending the Council of Constance an English version of events.[42] This supports Goodwin's view that the perspective which Henry realized must be given to English achievements was one which went beyond the borders of England, into Europe itself. In Gerald Harriss's view, 'in five short years

---

[42] See *GHQ*, pp. xxiv–xxviii.

from 1417 to 1422 Henry set himself to educate the English in a new European role'.[43]

The affairs of the Church, of Christendom as a whole, brought England further into that wider European scene. Goodwin proposed this as part of Henry's contribution to 'reform'; so, consequently, the English role in ending the Schism at the Council of Constance, the resistance to papal pretensions in England and the encouragement of religious renewal were all viewed as aspects of a broader process of 'reform'.[44] Furthermore, the problems arising from the activities of Sir John Oldcastle were associated with the wider reforming movement within the Church (as Oldcastle saw it) which John Hus and Jerome of Prague would defend to the death at Constance. In England, the execution ('Martyrdom') of Oldcastle and other Lollards was presented by Goodwin as the penalty to be paid for two 'crimes'. They were condemned to 'be burned for Heresy and hang'd for Treason', the form of execution underlining the nature of the offences of which they had been convicted. That is pretty well how the matter is seen today.[45]

Goodwin's treatment of the re-conquered lands in northern France 'subdu'd to the Crown of *England*, two hundred and fifteen Years after the Conquest of it by *Philip* King of France',[46] was described in terms not incompatible with the results of modern historical research. Once the military process was completed, Henry tried to come to terms with those whom he now regarded as his people. His rule in Normandy, it was claimed, contrasted with the tyranny exercised there by the French crown.[47] The Church was restored to its due place in society: economic life was encouraged; weights and measures were regulated; the coinage was reformed; the soldiery was disciplined and controlled, and a measure of order was achieved. The 'discovery' (largely in the records) and, then, the use of such information added a whole new dimension to the effects of the English re-conquest. It is in Goodwin's *History* that we find first references, taken from record evidence, of the grants of lands made to Englishmen willing to settle in Normandy, part of a 'land settlement' which, years later, would play a role in the expulsion of the English from the duchy in the reign of Henry V's son and successor.[48]

The chief contrast between Goodwin's work and that of earlier writers on Henry V lies in the broader picture he drew of what kingship was about and, consequently, by what criteria a king might be judged. Although Henry

---

[43] G. L. Harriss, 'Conclusion', in *Henry V*, ed. Harriss, p. 209.
[44] For other aspects of 'reform' encouraged by the king, see Goodwin, *History*, pp. 230, 232.
[45] Ibid., p. 163; M. Aston, 'Lollardy and Sedition, 1381–1431', *Past and Present* 17 (1960), 1–44.
[46] Goodwin, *History*, p. 209.
[47] Ibid., pp. 177, 293–4, 313.
[48] See C. T. Allmand, *Lancastrian Normandy: The History of a Medieval Occupation* (Oxford, 1983).

was a man 'renown'd for Military Vertue', and though military affairs occupied a substantial part of Goodwin's book, Henry was not to be judged
solely, or even mainly, on his record as a soldier: there were other boxes to
be ticked. While Goodwin's approach was to present a patriotic king, he also
gave readers much to think about as various aspects of Henry's 'wise care'
of his people's 'Welfare and Prosperity' were described or referred to. With
responsibility to 'promote the publick Good', the king was shown doing
justice, fighting abuses, making good laws, all of them aspects of 'the Arts of
peaceful Government'. For this purpose, he regularly consulted parliament,
'the General Council of the Nation', 'concerning the State and Safety of the
Nation'.[49] Directly or indirectly, since he was writing the history of a reign
as well as that of a man, much of the book had to do with the everyday
affairs of government, the making of policy, the organization of the army
for war, the administration of justice, as well as with trying to answer the
needs of his people expressed in their petitions to parliament. The work is not
only about a king. It is also about kingship, about the relationship of a ruler
with his people and how he regarded his obligations towards their welfare.
Henry would be judged by how he led the people of England (in time of
both peace and war); how he reacted to papal pretensions to defend both his
and other interests; how he tried, in due time, to promote the material good
of his French subjects once they had become his to govern and defend. All
this could not be done by one man, single-handedly. The fulfilment of such
obligations, well understood in the early eighteenth century, could only be
achieved through the establishment of good government based on the mutual
confidence which king and subjects had in one another. The need for the
historian to describe aspects of that government involved the introduction,
into the story, of men who might otherwise never have appeared. The history
of a reign, as understood and presented by Goodwin, went far beyond the
language of the 'deeds' (*Acta* or *Gesta*) of a single man. It was the history of
a national enterprise, guided and led by the king. Although historians may
differ today over interpretations regarding this question or that, this success
or that failure, and in particular over their understanding of the king's character, that is still, in essence, how we see his reign today.

---

[49] Goodwin, *History*, pp. v, 2–3, 7–8, 5.

INDEX

Abbeville (France)   250, 255, 262
Aberystwyth (Wales)   105
Abraham, John   118 n.97
Acton, Sir Roger   115
Adlington (Ches.)   175
Agincourt, battle of   1, 6, 8, 48, 50, 51,
    56, 94, 95, 103, 134, 136, 141, 143, 149,
    150, 152, 153, 154, 155, 156, 157–70,
    171, 175, 176, 178, 179, 184, 188, 207,
    215, 222, 223, 227, 228, 229, 230, 231,
    233, 234, 235, 236, 237, 238 n.126, 244,
    246, 275, 278–9
Alderton, Robert   132 n.8
Aldgate see London
Alençon (France)   226
    duke of   235
Alexander the Great   218, 224, 227, 231,
    232, 243
Aljubarrota (Portugal)   236
Allart, William   268 n.97
Allerdale (Cumb.)   90
Allerton, Robert   132 n.5, 135 n.31
Allerton wapentake (Yorks.)   24 n.70
Allington, William   134
Almeley (Here.)   104, 122, 124
Alnwick (Northum.)   91, 97
Alyngton, William see Allington, William
Amersham (Bucks.)   111 n.54
Amiens (France)   242, 250, 260, 262–3,
    266, 270
Anglesey, isle of (Wales)   22, 133 n.17
Aoust, Richard   258 n.41
Appleton, Richard   61
Aquitaine (France)   23, 24, 44, 53
Araines (France)   266
Arden, Geoffrey   51 n.89
Ardres (France)   163
Argentan (France)   252, 256, 264 n.77
Aristotle   243
Armagnac party   261, 262
Arques (France)   237
Arras (France)   260
Arthur   218, 224
Artois (France)   266

Arundel (Sussex)   141
Arundel, earl of see FitzAlan, Thomas
Arundel, John   137
Arundel, Thomas, archbishop of
    Canterbury   41, 54, 105, 106–7, 109,
    117, 126, 148, 196
Asborough (Corn.)   29 n. 101
Ashburnham House see Westminster
atte Well, Beatrix   121
atte Well, William   121
Aubert, Guiot   255 n.29
Audelay, John   219, 224
Audlem (Ches.)   179, 181
Avignon (France)   267
Avranches (France)   267

Babthorp, Robert   167, 169, 170
Bache, Simon   14, 28
Badby, John   105
Baddington (Ches.)   176
Baddisley Clinton (Warks.)   122, 123
Bagot, Sir William   22
Baguley (Ches.)   178
Baker, Richard see Gurmyn alias Baker,
    Richard
Bale, John   152, 277, 282
Balne, William   134
Bamburgh castle (Northum.)   92, 97
Bangor (Wales), diocese of   133
    bishop of see Nicolls, Benedict
Bardolf, Sir William   52
Barenbon, John   202
Barentyn, Christina   167
Barentyn, Drew   167
Bargier, William   270 n.109
Barnaby, John   123
Barre, Sir Thomas   50 n.80
Barrow (Ches.)   179
Barthomley (Ches.)   182 n.52
Barton, John   108
Barton under Needwood (Staffs.)   123
Basin, Thomas, bishop of Lisieux
    252 n.12, 254
Baskerville, John   51 n.89

289

God's Words, Women's Voices: The Discernment of Spirits in the Writing of Late-Medieval Women Visionaries, Rosalyn Voaden (1999)

Pilgrimage Explored, ed. J. Stopford (1999)

Piety, Fraternity and Power: Religious Gilds in Late Medieval Yorkshire 1389–1547, David J. F. Crouch (2000)

Courts and Regions in Medieval Europe, ed. Sarah Rees Jones, Richard Marks and A. J. Minnis (2000)

Treasure in the Medieval West, ed. Elizabeth M. Tyler (2000)

Nunneries, Learning and Spirituality in Late Medieval English Society: The Dominican Priory of Dartford, Paul Lee (2000)

Prophecy and Public Affairs in Later Medieval England, Lesley A. Coote (2000)

The Problem of Labour in Fourteenth-Century England, ed. James Bothwell, P. J. P. Goldberg and W. M. Ormrod (2000)

New Directions in later Medieval Manuscript Studies: Essays from the 1998 Harvard Conference, ed. Derek Pearsall (2000)

Cistercians, Heresy and Crusadse in Occitania, 1145–1229: Preaching in the Lord's Vineyard, Beverly Mayne Kienzle (2001)

Guilds and the Parish Community in Late Medieval East Anglia, c. 1470–1550, Ken Farnhill (2001)

The Age of Edward III, ed. J. S. Bothwell (2001)

Time in the Medieval World, ed. Chris Humphrey and W. M. Ormrod (2001)

The Cross Goes North: Processes of Conversion in Northern Europe, AD 300–1300, ed. Martin Carver (2002)

Henry IV: The Establishment of the Regime, 1399–1406, ed. Gwilym Dodd and Douglas Biggs (2003)

Youth in the Middle Ages, ed. P. J. P. Goldberg and Felicity Riddy (2004)

The Idea of the Castle in Medieval England, Abigail Wheatley (2004)

Rites of Passage: Cultures of Transition in the Fourteenth Century, ed. Nicola F. McDonald and W. M. Ormrod (2004)

Creating the Monastic Past in Medieval Flanders, Karine Ugé (2005)

St William of York, Christopher Norton (2006)

Medieval Obscenities, ed. Nicola F. McDonald (2006)

The Reign of Edward II: New Perspectives, ed. Gwilym Dodd and Anthony Musson (2006)

York Studies in Medieval Theology

I   *Medieval Theology and the Natural Body*, ed. Peter Biller and A. J. Minnis (1997)

II *Handling Sin: Confession in the Middle Ages*, ed. Peter Biller and A. J. Minnis (1998)

III *Religion and Medicine in the Middle Ages*, ed. Peter Biller and Joseph Ziegler (2001)

IV *Texts and the Repression of Medieval Heresy*, ed. Caterina Bruschi and Peter Biller (2002)

York Manuscripts Conference

Manuscripts and Readers in Fifteenth-Century England: The Literary Implications of Manuscript Study, ed. Derek Pearsall (1983) [Proceedings of the 1981 York Manuscripts Conference]

Manuscripts and Texts: Editorial Problems in Later Middle English Literature, ed. Derek Pearsall (1987) [Proceedings of the 1985 York Manuscripts Conference]

Latin and Vernacular: Studies in Late-Medieval Texts and Manuscripts, ed. A. J. Minnis (1989) [Proceedings of the 1987 York Manuscripts Conference]

Regionalism in Late-Medieval Manuscripts and Texts: Essays celebrating the publication of 'A Linguistic Atlas of Late Mediaeval English', ed. Felicity Riddy (1991) [Proceedings of the 1989 York Manuscripts Conference]

Late-Medieval Religious Texts and their Transmission: Essays in Honour of A. I. Doyle, ed. A. J. Minnis (1994) [Proceedings of the 1991 York Manuscripts Conference]

Prestige, Authority and Power in Late Medieval Manuscripts and Texts, ed. Felicity Riddy (2000) [Proceedings of the 1994 York Manuscripts Conference]

Middle English Poetry: Texts and Traditions. Essays in Honour of Derek Pearsall, ed. A. J. Minnis (2001) [Proceedings of the 1996 York Manuscripts Conference]

Manuscript Culture in the British Isles

I   *Design and Distribution of Late Medieval Manuscripts in England*, ed. Margaret Connolly and Linne R. Mooney (2008)

II *Women and Writing, c.1340–c.1650: The Domestication of Print Culture*, ed. Anne Lawrence-Mathers and Phillipa Hardman (2010)

III *The Wollaton Medieval Manuscripts: Texts, Owners and Readers*, ed. Ralph Hanna and Thorlac Turville-Petre (2010)

IV *Scribes and the City: London Guildhall Clerks and the Dissemination of Middle English Literature, 1375–1425*, Linne R. Mooney and Estelle Stubbs (2013)

Heresy and Inquisition in the Middle Ages

Heresy and Heretics in the Thirteenth Century: The Textual Representations, L. J. Sackville (2011)

Heresy, Crusade and Inquisition in Medieval Quercy, Claire Taylor (2011)